THE ROYAL BALLET

Zoë Anderson is the dance critic of the *Independent*. As a freelance critic, she has written for the *Dancing Times*, *Independent on Sunday*, and *Daily Telegraph*. She has a doctorate in Renaissance literature from the University of York. She lives in London.

THE ROYAL BALLET

75 Years

ZOË ANDERSON

faber and faber
OCM 775410861

First published in 2006
by Faber and Faber Limited
3 Queen Square London WC1N 3AU
This paperback edition published in 2007

Typeset by Faber and Faber Limited
Printed and bound in Great Britain by
TJ International Ltd, Padstow, Cornwall

A CIP record for this book
is available from the British Library

ISBN 978-0-571-22796-9
ISBN 0-571-22796-1

2 4 6 8 10 9 7 5 3 1

For Mary Clarke and Alastair Macaulay

Contents

List of Illustrations

10 *Giselle* Johan Kobborg and Alina Cojocaru
11 *Requiem* Leanne Benjamin and Carlos Acosta
12 *Daphnis and Chloë* Federico Bonelli and Alina Cojocaru
13 *Les Noces* Zenaida Yanowsky
14 *La Sylphide* Ivan Putrov, Laura McCulloch and Yuhui Choe
15 *Manon* with Tamara Rojo, José Martín and Genesia Rosato

CHAPTER HEADINGS
Chapter 1
a) Ninette de Valois, founder of the Royal Ballet
b) The Academy of Choreographic Art, advertisement from *The Dancing Times*

Chapter 2
a) *Checkmate* June Brae and Harold Turner
b) *Les Rendezvous* Alicia Markova

Chapter 3
a) The Sadler's Wells Ballet in Brussels, January 1945. Left to right: Moira Shearer, Alexis Rassine, Margot Fonteyn, Douglas Stewart, Pamela May, Elizabeth Kennedy, Eric Hyrst.
b) *Dante Sonata* June Brae, Robert Helpmann, Michael Somes and the corps

Chapter 4
a) The reopening of Covent Garden, 20 February 1946
b) *Symphonic Variations*. Left to right: Margot Fonteyn, Henry Danton, Pamela May, Michael Somes, Moira Shearer, Brian Shaw.

Chapter 5
a) *The Firebird* Margot Fonteyn
b) *Birthday Offering* Svetlana Beriosova, Rowena Jackson, Elaine Fifield, Margot Fonteyn, Nadia Nerina, Violetta Elvin, Beryl Grey

Chapter 6
a) Georgina Parkinson, Antoinette Sibley, Monica Mason, Vyvyane Lorrayne, Ann Jenner, Deanne Bergsma, Jennifer Penney.
b) The corps de ballet in *La Bayadère*

Acknowledgements

I have received help and advice from many people in the writing of this book. Dancers, musicians, critics, historians, staff and friends were generous in answering my questions, making suggestions and passing on their memories.

My first thanks are to the people who worked in or with the Company: Lionel Alberts, John Bakewell, Monica Beck, Joan Benesh, Deborah Bull, Lesley Collier, Jonathan Cope, Anthony Dowell, David Drew, Julia Farron Rodrigues, Beryl Grey, Jeanetta Laurence, Brenda Last, Thomas Lynch, Donald MacLeary, Deborah MacMillan, Monica Mason, Pamela May, Merle Park, Georgina Parkinson, Vanessa Palmer, Helen and David Quennell, Genesia Rosato, Anthony Russell-Roberts, Lynn Seymour, Antoinette Sibley, John Tooley, David Wall and Peter Wright.

At the Royal Opera House, Janine Limberg was tireless in arranging and suggesting interviews. I would also like to thank Simon Magill, Anne Bulford, Katie Town and Georgie Perrott.

I would like to record my gratitude to the staff of the Royal Ballet Archives, particularly Francesca Franchi, Julia Creed, Rachel Hayes and Tom Tansey. I also wish to thank the librarians and archivists of the Theatre Museum, Laban and the Royal Academy of Dance. Jane Pritchard, of the Rambert Archives and the Theatre Museum, was exceptionally generous in giving me access to her own archive, and in reading and correcting some of the manuscript. Jon Gray, at the Theatre Museum and at *The Dancing Times*, advised on sources and photographs, correcting the final proof with great care and kindness. Clement Crisp made invaluable suggestions. Gail Monahan and Meredith Daneman read portions of the manuscript, making essential comments.

I would like to thank Gavin, Maggie and Leo Anderson, Patricia Daly, Sarah Frater, Robert Gottlieb, Robert Greskovic, Clare

Jackson, Laurie Lewis, Claire Lindsay, Barbara Newman, Jann Parry, Joan Seaman, David Vaughan and Sarah Woodcock for all their help and support.

I wish to thank my agent, Michael Alcock, and my editor, Belinda Matthews. At Faber and Faber, I would also like to thank Elizabeth Tyerman and Kate Ward.

Finally, I thank Mary Clarke and Alastair Macaulay, both critics, historians and friends. Mary Clarke, editor of *The Dancing Times* and author of the invaluable history of the Company's first twenty-five years, made vital introductions, suggestions and criticisms, and permitted me to consult and quote her correspondence. Alastair Macaulay, most generous and scrupulous of readers, took infinite care in reading, correcting and commenting on the manuscript. He also allowed me to consult the proceedings of the RAD Fonteyn conference ahead of publication, and lent me enough rare books and recordings to fill two taxis. This book is dedicated to both of them with gratitude and love.

ONE

Preparation

1926–31

"RHYTHM"

The Academy
of Choregraphic Art

LONDON.

6a, Roland Houses,
Roland Gardens,
S.W.7.

Principal: Ninette de Valois.
Chief Assistant: Ursula Moreton.
Theatre Art Class: James Whale.

DUBLIN.

Abbey Theatre: Vivienne Bennett.

Students can join by the year, or for a Three Months' Course. In either case the curriculum comprises Twelve Lessons per week.
Prospectus sent on application.

NOTE.

At the special request of William Butler Yeats, a Branch of this Academy has been opened in Dublin in connection with
THE ABBEY THEATRE.

ABOVE The Academy of Choreographic Art, advertisement from the *Dancing Times*: by courtesy of *Dancing Times*, January 1928
PREVIOUS PAGE Ninette de Valois, founder of The Royal Ballet, in 1949: © Gordon Anthony Collection, The Theatre Museum, V&A Images

The Royal Ballet's seventy-fifth anniversary falls on 5 May 2006. The Company hasn't always counted its birthdays correctly: its founder, Ninette de Valois, once held a coming-of-age celebration in the wrong year. What can't be miscounted is how much de Valois achieved, how quickly. She built a company from scratch, taking it to world-conquering fame in less than two decades. Her methods have shaped not just British ballet but companies across the world: directly, through the troupes founded or led by Royal Ballet dancers, and indirectly through the image of the Company.

From very early on, The Royal Ballet was a repertory ballet company. It took works from the past, from other traditions, while creating its own new choreography. De Valois's model helped to shape ballet in the twentieth century and beyond. She and her successors created a repertory that is one of the richest in the world, including classic stagings of ballets from the nineteenth century and the Diaghilev era. Frederick Ashton and Kenneth MacMillan were the Company's own defining choreographers, spending most of their creative lives with The Royal Ballet. Dancing these works, the Company developed its own distinctive accent, with clear musicality and a strong sense of drama.

Maintaining a tradition can be as hard as founding it. The Royal Ballet's toughest moments have come in the last twenty-five years. Its standards and identity have been threatened. This history concerns survival as well as growth, decline and recovery as well as influence. It was written at a time of optimism and excitement. Under Monica Mason, the Company has been rediscovering a neglected past; as I wrote, ballets I had been researching were brought back to the theatre. A new generation of dancers has responded to their challenges of technique, style and authority.

*

Ninette de Valois was a formidable, charming and contradictory woman: far-sighted, ruthless and selfless. She was a disciplinarian who adored rebels, an Irishwoman who founded a pillar of the British establishment. She built a highly organised system, and she loved upsetting apple carts. After visiting Russia, she came straight back to her own school and taught her teachers new steps and methods, re-examining her own basic principles. She was always ready to change her mind.

Her company and her school had several name changes before settling down as The Royal Ballet, but de Valois never put her own name above the title. 'It is the belief of the present Director,' she said sternly in 1932, 'that if the ballet at Sadler's Wells does not survive many a Director, then it will have failed utterly in the eyes of the first dancer to hold that post.'[1] Her planning was always long-term, always for the sake of the Company. For her eightieth birthday, the Friends of Covent Garden held a lunch in her honour. Many of her ballerinas were seated at the main table: Moira Shearer, Beryl Grey, Nadia Nerina, Svetlana Beriosova, Lynn Seymour, Antoinette Sibley and others. When de Valois thanked the Friends, she spoke in an Irish accent: the voice of her childhood came through in moments of emotion. Yet she didn't dwell on herself, or on the celebrations arranged for her. Within minutes, she was speaking of conditions at Covent Garden, of the Company's wants for the future: 'We need better dressing rooms!' Members of her audience found themselves in tears. Every ballerina was wiping her eyes. De Valois's unselfish care for her company was movingly practical.[2]

She was superbly pragmatic. John Tooley, who worked with her at Covent Garden from the 1950s, remembers how clearly she would set out her plans, all leading firmly in a chosen direction. 'Then something would happen which caused her to deviate. She would say, "I can't miss that opportunity. I know it's not quite in the direction we talked about, but it's taking us forward." She was so much like that.' Throughout her career, de Valois would turn her chances to account. 'Circumstances thrust a lot on you,' she wrote serenely, 'and when they arise you simply meet their demands.'[3]

At first, de Valois was the ballerina of her own company, but she regularly put herself second cast after visiting dancers. Having

4

started as chief choreographer, she gradually stepped aside in favour of Ashton and others. There was nothing she loved more than choreography, she said in a late radio interview, 'but it would have been quite wrong, because I hadn't all that talent. Nothing like the talent of an Ashton . . . I was more cut out to help in the English picture in the line I followed, so I say choreography *of the general scene*.'[4] In 1959, she planned one last ballet, *The Lady of Shalott*, to music by Arthur Bliss. It never happened. She decided that Kenneth MacMillan, already singled out as The Royal Ballet's next major choreographer, should do a new ballet that season, and handed over her own rehearsal time.

Plenty of dancers and teachers were terrified of her. Monica Mason remembers de Valois's visits to The Royal Ballet School in the late 1950s. 'The whole atmosphere was rather like nurses and matrons used to be when the surgeon was coming round – everybody was spruced up and on their best behaviour, on their mettle . . . People seemed scared to death.' In rehearsals, de Valois could be hasty, impatient, furious. Her rages were quick, and quickly over. 'She wouldn't let you gloat over it,' said Pamela May, who remembered the storms of her classes. During the war, de Valois was nicknamed 'Madam'; she cheerfully accepted the name, and would sign letters to members of the Company with it.

As teacher and director, de Valois had favourites. She loved extroverts, dancers who could stand up to her. The young Margot Fonteyn noticed that pupils fell into two categories for de Valois: nice children and little devils. It was the little devils who got on – though there were many kinds of devilishness, from Fonteyn's stubbornness to Wayne Sleep's mischief. Fonteyn was to be de Valois's greatest favourite, her first ballerina, cherished and carefully protected in a mixture of bias and pragmatism. De Valois saw what Fonteyn could give the Company and groomed her devotedly, helping her to become one of the greatest, most loved dancers of the twentieth century. Fonteyn led The Royal Ballet for thirty years, helping to fix its identity. Other careers certainly suffered: fewer performances, fewer ballets, almost no first nights. Dancers such as Beryl Grey and Moira Shearer were given little chance to challenge Fonteyn.

De Valois could be possessive and domineering about her company, yet she sought out gifted colleagues. When Frederick Ashton became the Company's main choreographer, he did a great deal to change its style. De Valois accepted it. She used Constant Lambert not just as a music director but as an adviser on every aspect of the ballet. 'You know,' she told the critic Clement Crisp, 'I used to pray at night: "Please God, don't let anything happen to Constant."'[5] If she was possessive, she was not selfish. When the Sadler's Wells Ballet returned from its first, triumphant American tour, the Covent Garden audience gave the dancers an ovation. After cheers for the dancers, there were repeated calls for de Valois, the Company's creator. When at last she appeared on stage, she was furious. 'Ladies and gentlemen,' she snapped before bringing down the curtain, 'it takes more than one to make a ballet company.'[6]

When de Valois started her career, there was no real British ballet tradition. For centuries, the British had felt that dancing was the business of the French, the Italians, the Russians. There had been dancing in the court and city masques of the sixteenth and seventeenth century and – as de Valois was to find out – plenty of dances in plays by Shakespeare and his contemporaries. Both traditions were broken by the English Civil War. While Louis XIV led the French court in grand ballets, the English had executed their king and closed public theatres. The theatres reopened with the restoration of the monarchy, but dance never regained its influence at court. It survived in the commercial theatre, which by the late eighteenth century was dominated by foreign guest stars.

At the start of the twentieth century, British ballet survived in pantomime, opera and especially in music hall – the larger halls maintained their own troupes. Most dancers had a low status within the theatre, and a poor reputation outside it. There was a touch of lewdness about music hall, with innuendo on stage and prostitutes picking up clients in the bars. 'Ballet girls', who worked in this louche environment, were not respectable. Great stars could escape such censure: the Danish Adeline Genée, much admired for her dancing and her porcelain beauty, was later made a Dame of the British Empire. The public was readier to accept foreign stars; many

British dancers took exotic stage names. It was a breakthrough when Phyllis Bedells became a star under her own name. Bedells and Genée were fine dancers, performing in spectacular but hardly ground-breaking ballets. Britain, like the rest of balletic Europe, was galvanised by Sergei Pavlovich Diaghilev.

Diaghilev transformed western ideas of ballet as an art, as a collaboration between the arts. In 1909, he presented his first season of ballet in Paris, using stars from the Imperial Theatres of St Petersburg and Moscow. The dancers Nijinsky, Pavlova and Karsavina were a revelation, but so were the new ballets: choreography by Fokine, designs by Benois, Roerich and Bakst. Design and music were not just background to the ballerina, but essential elements of a united production. Male dancers, starting with Nijinsky, could become as important as the women. In 1911, Diaghilev formed his own permanent company and made his first visit to London. Between 1909 and his death in 1929, he commissioned scores from Stravinsky, Ravel, Debussy, Satie, de Falla, Richard Strauss, Prokofiev and others. The designers he introduced to ballet included Picasso, Matisse, Derain, Goncharova, Laurencin and Coco Chanel. The company's influence extended through ballet to the rest of theatre, even to fashions in dress and interior decoration.

Diaghilev depended on fashionable audiences. He kept their interest by moving his company through waves of experimentation: always something new. The early years were dominated by Fokine – romantic works like *Les Sylphides*, opulent orientalism in *Schéhérazade*, the profoundly Russian *Petrushka*. Then Diaghilev encouraged Vaslav Nijinsky to try choreography, with the scandals of *L'Après-midi d'un faune* and *Le Sacre du printemps*. Diaghilev went on discovering and developing choreographers. Nijinsky was followed by Leonide Massine, Bronislava Nijinska (Nijinsky's sister) and finally the young George Balanchine.

The Russian ballet offered new opportunities to British dancers. Pavlova soon left Diaghilev, setting off on her own world tours, filling her corps de ballet with British girls – who were quick to learn, she said, and less temperamental than Russians. The ballerina's fame and grace helped to make dancing respectable. Plenty of middle-class mothers hoped their daughters might become second

Pavlovas. If her dancing was sublime, her programmes were often second-rate, but they showed off a glorious ballerina and she took them all over the world. In Lima, the young Frederick Ashton saw her and was dazzled: 'She injected me with her poison and from that evening I wanted to dance.'⁷ In Australia, she encouraged the teenaged would-be dancer Robert Helpmann. Both men helped to shape British ballet, and The Royal Ballet.

British dancers also joined Diaghilev. Until the Russian revolution, he had taken most of his dancers from the Imperial theatres. When, in 1917, his company was cut off from its roots, he found his next generation of dancers in Europe. Several came via London, where better training was becoming available. The teacher Edouard Espinosa had been fighting to raise standards; he was joined by important Russian teachers who had fled the revolution. Two of Diaghilev's 1920s stars came from the London studios of Princess Serafine Astafieva: Patrick Healy Kay, who became Anton Dolin, and Alicia Marks, Diaghilev's 'little English girl', who joined his company as Alicia Markova. Other British dancers in the company included Ursula Moreton and Ninette de Valois.

You can see the options open to British dancers in de Valois's own career. She was born Edris Stannus in 1898 at her parents' country estate near Dublin. Her family was Anglo-Irish; her father was an officer in the British Army. Her first dance was an authentic Irish jig, taught by a country woman on the stone floor of the farm kitchen.⁸ By 1905, the Stannus family could no longer afford to run their property, and left for England. In London, Edris's mother then decided to have her trained for the stage. She was sent to the Lila Field Academy for Children, a theatre school whose pupils had included Noël Coward. In 1913, taking the stage name Ninette de Valois, she went on tour with a group of the Academy's pupils. Billed as the Wonder Children, they performed a programme of dances and short plays in the old pier theatres of seaside resorts – de Valois remembered the 'springboard sensation' of running along the gas-lit pier deck. She had, she would later boast, danced the *Dying Swan* on every pier in England – 'dying twice nightly', because she was sure of an encore.⁹ She went on to dance at the Lyceum Theatre's Christmas pantomime. The 'Grand Ballet' would include one of the Lyceum's celebrated Transformation Scenes, achieved through elaborate gauzes and gorgeous lighting. The end of the scene, she remembered, 'always found one standing in a golden chariot, or reposing on a cloud, or lying in a seashell . . .'[10] She also danced in music hall, in opera, in West End musicals and revues.

Looking back at her dancing career, de Valois felt 'a renewed anxiety to leave English dancers some security and definite standards . . . England had no Sadler's Wells, no Arts Council, no big private schools, and no institution such as the Royal Academy of Dancing devoting its work to raising the standard of teaching and giving advice and guidance throughout the country.'[11] Her own serious schooling began after she started in pantomime. She went to Edouard Espinosa, who retrained her feet from scratch, taking her out of pointe shoes for four months. Her footwork became her greatest strength, one she was to pass on to the school she later founded. In 1919, she became one of Cecchetti's first London pupils; when he left the country, she took lessons with the Russian teacher Nicholas Legat. De Valois was proud of having French, Italian and Russian training, and of combining all three in the teaching of her own school.

At Cecchetti's classes, de Valois was also to meet Diaghilev's dancers. Her friendship with Lydia Lopokova began with consolation after one of the Maestro's criticisms: 'Never mind, my dear,' the Russian ballerina told her, 'you have nice legs . . .'[12] It was in London that Diaghilev staged his greatest and most influential flop. In 1921, this most avant-garde impresario decided on a return to classicism, to the full-length ballets of the nineteenth century. He revived Petipa's *Sleeping Beauty*, renamed *The Sleeping Princess* – arguing that not all of his Auroras were beauties. This was the first time one of Petipa's ballets had been performed, in full, outside Russia. It was staged by Nicholas Sergueyev, who had been a régisseur at Petipa's own theatre, the Maryinsky in St Petersburg. Aurora was danced by the ballerinas Trefilova, Lopokova, Egorova and the phenomenal Spessivtseva (whose name was shortened to Spessiva by Diaghilev). Bakst's designs were magnificent and vastly expensive. Inspired by the long runs of musicals like *Chu Chin Chow*, Diaghilev planned a season of three months. It was too much. The Ballets Russes public was used to six-week seasons of different ballets; they didn't fill the theatre for so many nights of the same work. The economist John Maynard Keynes, who was courting Lopokova, remembered going most evenings. He would sit in the stalls, he later claimed, 'with no one else in sight in any direction'.[13]

'It was fortunate for our future that England was the one country to have seen his version in its first full-length presentation,' wrote de Valois of Diaghilev's *Sleeping Princess*. 'This influence has had far-reaching effects on the English scene and the result has been commented on time and again outside the country.'[14] De Valois and others were exposed to the classical tradition at its grandest. Marie Rambert, who had trained in Dalcroze Eurhythmics and worked with Nijinsky on his radical *Sacre du printemps*, was converted to the beauty of Petipa's choreography. The young critic Arnold Haskell became convinced that classicism lay at the heart of ballet. Frederick Ashton, by then at school in England, saw the production. Fifty years later, he could still remember the impact of Spessivtseva's entrance for the Rose Adagio. 'I am fifteen years too early with this production,' said Diaghilev, when forced to close it down.[15] In 1939, de Valois prepared the second western production of the ballet.

After the failure of *The Sleeping Princess*, the Russian dancers were stranded in London. They formed a small company, led by Lopokova and the choreographer Léonide Massine. De Valois joined them, and loved it. She had never danced such good choreography, nor seen such a disciplined routine of class and rehearsals. When the other dancers returned to Diaghilev, they remembered and recommended de Valois. She joined the Ballets Russes in September 1923, staying for two years. She would later write that 'everything of value' that she had learned about 'the presentation of ballet, the study of choreography and the development of the artist . . . came from this apprenticeship in the most famous of companies'.[16]

When de Valois joined the Ballets Russes, Nijinska was its chief choreographer. De Valois danced in five new Nijinska ballets, including *Le Train bleu* (made to show off Dolin's athleticism), *Les Biches* and *Les Noces*. In *Les Biches*, Nijinska herself danced the role of the Hostess, using de Valois to work out the choreography. The role has the fast footwork associated with de Valois, together with powerful use of the torso and witty musical timing. The young Balanchine was the next choreographer at the Ballets Russes. A pas de trois, made for an opera ballet, 'left me swooning in the dressing room and solemnly assuring everyone that he was "a genius"'.[17] She also danced in *Zephyr et Flore*, by her old colleague Massine. She remembered grumbling with the other dancers about their costumes, designed by the Cubist painter Georges Braque. Diaghilev told them to

stop wondering whether the costumes suited us, but to consider instead whether we suited the costumes. He went on to tell us that the costumes had been designed to fit the ballet and the scene and not, as we had imagined, for each individual dancer. The next morning I went to the theatre to see the backcloth for the ballet. It was then that I understood. In this simple cloth lay the key to everything that one could not find an explanation for in the costumes. My mind could put them together there and then, and I stood as entranced as if the whole ballet had been paraded for my special benefit.[18]

Diaghilev ballets were famous for uniting the different arts in one production. De Valois was seeing how it was done.

In these years, Diaghilev was often accused of a craze for novelty, for short-lived fashionable ballets – though *Les Noces* and other 1920s works have proved to be enduring classics. In fact, de Valois wrote, the Ballets Russes was 'a repertory company running classical and modern ballet side by side – and what is more important – in many cases blended'.[19] In her two years, De Valois danced in older ballets by Fokine, Massine and Nijinsky, and in two nineteenth-century revivals, shortened versions of *Swan Lake* and *The Sleeping Beauty*. She learned, not just about the new Russian ballets, but about the nineteenth-century Russian school that lay behind them. De Valois, who had had to organise her own training, found herself with artists who had progressed through the same Imperial School, danced in the same ballets, learned the same style.

When de Valois founded her own company, the Ballets Russes was her most important model. She learned to make classical schooling the basis of her enterprise, and gained direct experience of a mixed repertory. The preparations of the Lopokova– Massine troupe had impressed her; now she was in a company with a home theatre in Monte Carlo, with the chance of careful rehearsal and development of ballets. Diaghilev shaped her ideas of what a ballet company should be, and she paid tribute to him to the end of her life. 'You came up against everything there,' she said in a radio interview, her voice rising with excitement:

the best music, the best décor. A man with a vision that I'd never in my life encountered before. It was nothing to meet Picasso in the morning coming in to watch a class . . . I saw the whole of the theatre in relation to the ballet. They had this heritage behind them, they'd all been trained at the Imperial Ballet, the classwork was impeccable, and then we had these ballets and these marvellous choreographers. I just had every-thing on a plate. What could I do but stand and sort it out like a jigsaw puzzle, and realise that we had absolutely *noth-ing* in England and all I wanted to do was to get back and start something.[20]

After two and a half years with Diaghilev, she did just that. It was an extraordinary step. Dancers would leave Diaghilev after quarrels or for better money, but rarely through sheer idealism. De Valois had been given good roles at the Ballets Russes; the critic Arnold Haskell was shocked that she should throw away such a promising career. Yet de Valois knew what she wanted – a company, an estab-lishment, a future for British ballet – and her early departure contributed to her success. Diaghilev died four years later, in 1929. His company drifted apart, then re-formed under different manage-ments. His dancers became available as guest stars. Plenty of ballet enterprises started up after 1929. By then, de Valois's enterprise was well under way. She could make the most of any Ballets Russes artists that came her way, and catch some of the Diaghilev audience, temporarily deprived of Russian ballet.

Back in London, de Valois started by setting up a school. Her stepfather financed the Academy of Choreographic Art, which opened in March 1926. The name advertised an ambition that went beyond dance teaching. Besides ballet, the Academy offered courses in production design, folk dance, Dalcroze Eurhythmics and mime. There was a theatre and a music reference library. Ursula Moreton, another Diaghilev dancer, was de Valois's assistant. Marie Rambert, who had opened her own studio in 1920, nearly lost her nerve when she read de Valois's prospectus, thinking of giving up teaching in the face of such competition. Frederick Ashton was one of de Valois's earliest occasional pupils. He was just becoming a choreographer; his first ballet was made in June 1926. Molly Lake, another of de Valois's assistants, remembered Ashton 'always arranging things, even then'.[21]

De Valois was only twenty-seven years old. She was at her fiercest in these years – eager to seek offence, wrote Haskell, remembering angry letters he had received. 'As serious as God and as touchy as Hell,' said another associate.[22] Norman Marshall, who worked with her in Cambridge, described her as 'rather like a young schoolmistress who made a point of dressing neatly and sensibly to set the girls a good example . . . the company nicknamed her "The Games Mistress"'.[23] Her attitude, and her early choreography, was earnest. The Academy pupils gave de Valois a handful of dancers to work with, but this little company would not get far on its own. She planned to take her students to an existing theatre, give them stage experience in dramatic productions and gradually build them up into a resident ballet company. De Valois would follow the Diaghilev model for artistic policy, but not for organisation. She wanted permanence, a company attached to a school and to a theatre – something like the state theatres of Russia, which could provide guaranteed employment for much of the year. Her dancers would have a living wage and the security they needed to develop their work over time.

Britain had no state theatre. Instead, de Valois turned to the repertory theatre movement. This had developed as an alternative to the commercial theatre, in which managers would assemble a company of actors for the run of a single play. The financial risks meant that they tended to concentrate on safe box-office material.

In the repertory system, the theatre would keep a company together to perform a range of works over the course of a season. These theatres could develop coherent artistic policies, showing classic and modern plays. De Valois described this outlook as 'a vision of practical idealism' and argued that theatre could be made 'as vital to the welfare of the community as the hospital'.[24] She hoped to persuade one of the repertory managers to take on her fledgling company. Her first choice was Barry Jackson, director of the Birmingham Repertory Theatre. He was sympathetic, but turned her down. She then tried Lilian Baylis of the Old Vic.

The Old Vic was repertory theatre at its most idealistic. Lilian Baylis had taken over as manager on the death of her aunt Emma Cons, a Victorian philanthropist. The Royal Victoria Hall was set amid Lambeth slums on the unfashionable south side of the river Thames. It had been one of London's rowdiest music halls, notorious for drunkenness; Cons was used to seeing Lambeth women with black eyes and bruises, inflicted by husbands who had spent Saturday night at the Old Vic. She took the theatre's lease, replaced its bars with coffee stalls, and set out to provide uplifting entertainment for the masses. 'My dear boy,' her niece told the young Laurence Olivier, 'if it hadn't been for drunken men beating their wives we would never have got this place.'[25] When she inherited the Old Vic, Baylis promoted opera and Shakespeare performances with astounding success. Productions were rough, ready and extremely cheap, yet performance standards were very high. West End stars like Edith Evans and John Gielgud came to the Old Vic for the chance to learn; in her first season, Evans remembered, she played eight big Shakespearean roles, had a single day off and lost seventeen pounds in weight. Admission prices were kept abnormally low. The audience, drawn at first from local people and then from all over London, was loyal and unusually attentive. At opera performances in the 1920s, there was sometimes such excitement that a singer couldn't finish an aria. 'The audience would finish it for him, then burst into applause.'[26] If an actor forgot his lines in Shakespeare, helpful voices could prompt him from the other side of the footlights.

In the summer of 1926, de Valois, wearing her best summer

clothes and a huge floppy hat, went to tell Miss Baylis about her
ambitions for British ballet. Baylis liked de Valois's face, her professional experience and her practical approach. For the moment,
though, she could do nothing for the ballet. The dilapidated Old Vic
already housed an opera and a theatre company; there was no space
for a third company. But she had acquired, and was already rebuilding, the Sadler's Wells Theatre in north London. Something might
be done in the future. Meanwhile, Baylis had a number of jobs for
a teacher and choreographer. She needed someone to arrange the
dances in her Shakespeare productions, to teach the drama students
how to move, to coach the office workers who performed (unpaid)
in the opera ballets. She wanted a short ballet to precede *Hansel and
Gretel*, the Christmas opera production – to be danced by some
good ballet school, for expenses only. She also wanted someone to
provide more angels for the opera itself. The pay was very low, but
there was the promise of the rebuilt Sadler's Wells, which Baylis
kept 'ever dangling in front of my eyes'.[27] Baylis inspected the
Academy of Choreographic Art, and de Valois was hired.

Baylis knew little about ballet, but she knew that hopes for a
British company were in the air. She would ask Philip Richardson,
the editor of *The Dancing Times*, 'When are we going to have a
British Ballet?'[28] She was not the only one asking the question.
British teaching standards were rising. The 'Association of Teachers
of Operating Dancing of Great Britain', now the Royal Academy of
Dance, had been established in 1920 with Richardson's encouragement. When Anton Dolin opened his school of dancing in 1925, he
said he hoped to establish a company. Marie Rambert's pupils had
started to arrange ballets for charity performances and revues. They
were becoming a company, soon called the Ballet Club and then
Ballet Rambert. Baylis, indeed, had discussed the Old Vic's dancing
needs with Rambert, who had been put off by the request to 'look
after my office girls'.[29] Baylis couldn't give de Valois much, but she
accepted her long-term aims at once. After that first half-hour interview, Baylis told her secretary, 'Ninette de Valois is going to form a
ballet company for us. When we open at the Wells, it will be on a
whole-time basis.'[30] She had recognised in de Valois a kindred spirit,
another single-minded and practical idealist. Lilian Baylis never

wavered in her support for the ballet. She had a powerful influence on the development and character of the Company.

De Valois was to complain about writers who, describing Lilian Baylis, succeeded 'only in stressing her as a quaint character.'[31] The trap is not easily avoided: Baylis's eccentricities were so legendary, so much a part of her work. She was a woman of immense dedication and remarkable flair, who saw art as a kind of social work and ran her theatre as if it were a church hall. Britain's National Theatre, Royal Ballet and English National Opera companies all started out under her wing. She was born in 1874 to a musical family. In her teens, she toured South Africa with a family concert group, billed as the Gypsy Revellers. She returned to London in her early twenties, ready to help with her aunt's missionary work at the Old Vic.

A dowdy woman with a twisted lip, Lilian Baylis was gruff, shy, strong-willed and deeply religious. The Old Vic, taken over for temperance purposes, had become a religious cause in itself. Its manager would pray for help when the Vic was in trouble, and was convinced that God's direct influence kept it from disaster. The most famous Baylis anecdote is of the actor who asked for a raise and was told, in all sincerity, 'Sorry, dear, God says No.' That, wrote de Valois, 'meant that Miss Baylis's conscience – aware of overdrafts, voluntary workers and others in the same financial plight – prompted her not to be persuaded by anyone; in such circumstances she would ask for guidance and be convinced she had received it.'[32] She would go down on her knees in her office to pray for more funds or better actors. Her manner of speech became famous, and she played up to her reputation. 'Look, you bounders,' she would tell audiences from the stage, 'we need better Monday nights.' This unexpected approach helped to build a sense of community at the Vic, fostering the famously warm audiences. She bullied and cared for 'her people' in the audience, treating them as she treated her staff. This was not the public of the music hall, of the opera house, of Diaghilev. It was a different theatre audience, one with a sense of community, ready to support the next Baylis venture.

Money was always short. The policy of affordable prices meant costs had to be kept impossibly low – and Baylis was easily carried away with creative parsimony. Some of her economies caused long-term expense; others were no help to her staff. Ashton said that 'when one was doing a new ballet, she always tried to palm off on one old costumes, ancient clothes, second-hand evening dresses, peers' robes and other oddments that people had given her.'[33] Vic-Wells staff were hired on tiny salaries, exploited, urged to work in appalling conditions and to do most of it for love. Baylis got away with it because she also fostered a sense of shared endeavour, of belief in the theatre's work. De Valois was to win that kind of dedication from her company. 'Ninette was wonderful to us,' remembers Monica Beck, who as Monica Ratcliffe was a student at the Academy. De Valois 'warned us that we would be badly paid, hopelessly overworked – but added that she had complete faith in us to make it all work – for her, for the theatre, for us, and for the future of British Ballet.'[34]

While Lilian Baylis gave de Valois a home for her company, the Old Vic organisation also offered other benefits. The theatre had an opera company, with an orchestra already available, so de Valois could plan a serious music policy from the start. In 1929, the composer Constant Lambert was brought in to orchestrate music and then to conduct. Lambert, already deeply involved with ballet in London, settled at the Vic-Wells company because it could give him most work. De Valois had only a corner of the Old Vic, but it meant she could work on a bigger scale than any of her rivals. It would be five years before her company's first full evening of ballet in the theatre, but that evening took place on a stage of reasonable size, in front of a regular public. The shared theatre encouraged de Valois's vision of ballet's role within British theatre, and gave her the chance to use artists from the other companies. The opera company's John Greenwood appeared in a range of mime roles for the ballet, including Carabosse in the first Vic-Wells production of *The Sleeping Princess*. Elsa Lanchester, one of the West End stars who came to act at the Vic, also danced the Arabian Dance in the Vic-Wells *Nutcracker*. The exchange went both ways. When Robert Helpmann joined the Company, he was able to take acting as well as dancing lessons. From the beginning, The Royal Ballet had a powerful sense of drama.

As Ashton's complaints suggest, design standards were much lower. The Old Vic had a tendency to dowdiness, and that went for ballet as well as opera and theatre. Where Rambert's Ballet Club produced glamour on a tiny budget, Old Vic productions could look poverty-stricken. Margot Fonteyn remembered a Sadler's Wells wardrobe mistress 'whose idea of correcting an ill-fitting dress was to say "It's you that's crooked, dear, I can't do anything about it."'[35] Ashton and Lambert made the Vic-Wells more stylish, but they had to work hard against the earnestness of their theatre. 'I quite realise that the schoolroom atmosphere must irritate you even more than it does me,' Lambert wrote to Ashton in 1937.

Baylis had given de Valois a place to start, but opportunities and money were small. She looked around for more work for herself and her dancers. Her first job came from her cousin Terence Gray, who was setting up an experimental theatre in Cambridge. Gray was an ardent theorist, eagerly opposed to naturalistic productions. Like Lilian Baylis, he wanted someone to teach his actors how to move; but he had much more ambitious ideas about that movement. He complained that the spoken word had come to dominate theatre, and planned to emphasise dance, lighting and design. De Valois became his resident choreographer, starting with the choruses in Greek plays. She later staged small ballets and dance dramas at the Festival Theatre, featuring her students.

The following year, the poet W. B. Yeats saw and admired her work in Cambridge, and invited her to produce and choreograph at the Abbey Theatre in Dublin. This was the first state-subsidised theatre in the English-speaking world, staging plays by Yeats, J. M. Synge, George Bernard Shaw and Sean O'Casey. The Abbey had great political as well as cultural impact. In 1926, two years before de Valois started work at the Abbey, audiences had rioted over O'Casey's depiction of the Easter Rising in *The Plough and the Stars*. ('You have disgraced yourselves again,' Yeats told the Abbey audience, remembering another riot over Synge's *Playboy of the Western World*.) De Valois was asked to set up a dance school, and would visit every three months to act in Yeats's own *Plays for Dancers*, stylised masked dramas. Yeats later dedicated *The King of the Great Clock Tower* to de Valois, 'asking pardon for covering her expressive face with a mask'. One of de Valois's Abbey dancers was Jill Gregory, who later joined the British company and went on to become its ballet mistress.

Through her theatre work, de Valois developed her sense of the stage, learning about production as well as choreography. At the same time, she started to make bigger ballets. *Rout*, first performed at the Festival Theatre in January 1927, was a modernist work to music by Arthur Bliss. *The Dancing Times* printed a respectful account of its London premiere, emphasising Lopokova's admiration for the work. In 1928, de Valois took the small Court Theatre (now the Royal Court) for three full performances. She lost money, but optimistic reviews spoke warmly of the company's promise. She also took on more work at the Old Vic. From 1928, the opera ballets were arranged by de Valois or her assistants. Monica Beck remembers playing 'Spanish dancers, gypsies, angels, priestesses, innocent rose-maidens and then wild corybants . . .' The first self-contained ballet, *Les Petits Riens*, was the promised curtain-raiser to *Hansel and Gretel*. De Valois danced the pastoral heroine, with Ursula Moreton as a slighted nymph. Stanley Judson and Hedley Briggs danced the male roles, with students from the Academy as the corps. Through this first Vic-Wells ballet, de Valois found her future music director. She asked Constant Lambert to orchestrate the Mozart music. 'A most efficient young man,' she told the dancer who had recommended him, 'he's going to conduct for us too!'[36]

De Valois spent much of these years travelling. After a Cambridge first night, she would leave for London by the milk train, sleeping stretched out in a third-class carriage, getting to her school in time for morning class. Apart from her work at the Abbey, the Festival, the Academy and the Old Vic, she went on dancing. She did an apache number with Anton Dolin in revue, and arranged dances for his music hall appearances. She gave more performances with the Ballets Russes – once rushing to Italy in answer to a telegram from Diaghilev that read 'Come at once dance *Les Biches* Turin'.

Diaghilev died in Venice in 1929. It was the end of an era: his company could not continue without him. His artists scattered. By the early thirties, many of them were drawn back together into successor 'Ballet Russe' companies. In the meantime, no company was presenting ballet in Britain on the scale achieved by Diaghilev. Philip Richardson and Arnold Haskell founded the Camargo Society to fill the gap in Britain. This society, named after the eighteenth-century ballerina who shortened her skirts to display her quick feet and pretty ankles, was what Haskell described as 'a management without a company'. De Valois called it a 'fairy godmother for English Ballet'.[37]

Richardson and Haskell and the music critic Edwin Evans gathered together influential dancers (Russian and British), choreographers, composers and designers for the committee of their society. The aim was to stage new and classic ballets, using the dancers available in Britain. A subscription audience supplied the money. There were performances several times a year, held on Sunday evenings and Monday afternoons to leave the dancers free for professional work. Lydia Lopokova, though always encouraging, had to be persuaded to join the Committee. She had never belonged to one before, and it was a serious step, 'like parting with one's virginity'.[38] Keynes, by now Lopokova's husband, became the society's treasurer the next year. Both proved especially keen to support de Valois and her dancers. 'I doubt if The Royal Ballet would be with us now if it were not for them,' said de Valois sixty years later.[39]

The first Camargo performances took place in October 1930. De Valois danced a pas de deux with Anton Dolin and contributed one of two new ballets. The hit of the evening, however, was Frederick Ashton's *Pomona*, with music by Constant Lambert. Over the next few years, the society commissioned a series of new ballets, including *Job*, *La Création du monde*, *Cephalus and Procris*, *The Lord of Burleigh*, *A Day in a Southern Port* (later renamed *Rio Grande*) and *Façade*. Camargo productions were on a scale that neither the Vic-Wells nor the Ballet Club could afford. Many were taken into the Vic-Wells repertory.

In 1932, the society took the Savoy Theatre for an ambitious four-week summer season. Spessivtseva was invited to dance *Giselle* and the second act of *Le Lac des cygnes*, as *Swan Lake* was then called. Critics and audiences were enthusiastic, but expenses were heavy. 'The Camargo,' Lambert wrote to a friend in April 1933, 'is at present following a policy of masterly inaction owing to the usual low funds.'[40] Shortly afterwards, Keynes found a way to wipe out the society's debts. An international conference of economists was held in London that summer, and Keynes suggested that the Camargo Society might give two gala performances in honour of the occasion. With the assistance of the Government Hospitality Fund, the galas took place on 27 and 29 June 1933, at the Royal Opera House, Covent Garden. Lydia Lopokova danced in the Vic-Wells production of *Coppélia*; Markova and Dolin danced the second act of *Le Lac des cygnes*, also a Vic-Wells production. The Queen attended the first performance, while the Prime Minister, with other members of the Cabinet, came to the second. The theatre was sold out, leaving the Camargo with a small profit. This was not the last time Keynes would encourage state recognition of British ballet.

Having cleared its debts, the Camargo Society gave no more performances. Most of its assets went to the Vic-Wells Ballet, starting with the profits from that gala. The Ballet Club took *Façade*, whose costumes had been paid for by Marie Rambert. Other productions went to the Vic-Wells, which had the facilities to perform them. Over the course of the 1930s, dancers, designers and choreographers were to join this drift to Sadler's Wells, many from Rambert's Ballet Club. Marie Rambert was a vital figure in the creation of British ballet. She started her company in 1926 with the performance of Ashton's first ballet *A Tragedy of Fashion*. She worked on a tiny scale, first at her studio and then at the little Mercury Theatre, but she discovered Ashton and Antony Tudor. Haskell would give Rambert the credit for breaking down British reserve and self-doubt: 'She stung her girls into becoming *solistes* and they showed countless others that it could be done.'[41] Her dancers did not hide behind foreign names; they presented themselves with confidence in classical roles. Ashton agreed: 'Lopokova used to call Ninette's little troupe "the ugly ducklings". They were all efficient, while Rambert's girls were beautiful.'

Rambert had remarkable flair, but no gift for long-term planning. Having done wonders on her tiny stage, she showed no ambition to find a larger one. Ashton 'begged Rambert to be more active in the professional theatre because I found the club constricting and I longed to get away. I wanted a wider field and a bigger stage. That was where Ninette was sensible. She got a proper theatre, instead of occasional performances with a piano. One wanted more than that.'[42] The traffic between the Ballet Club and Sadler's Wells was almost wholly one-way, though Vic-Wells dancers did perform at the Mercury on Sunday evenings, and de Valois even made a ballet for Rambert, the 1934 *Bar aux Folies-Bergère*. But the Wells offered the chance to develop steadily. After 1931, its dancers had regular salaries and opportunities on a scale greater than the small elegance of the Ballet Club.

Frederick Ashton and Constant Lambert, the other architects of The Royal Ballet, had both worked with Rambert and the Camargo Society. Ashton was born in Ecuador in 1904, the son of a minor diplomat. He was brought up in Lima, Peru, where he saw Pavlova and decided to become a dancer. Instead, he was sent to public school in England and then to a job in the City of London, where he spent more than half his salary on dancing lessons with Massine. At last his family agreed to support his dancing career – on the condition that he did not become a chorus boy. Massine, who was about to leave London, sent Ashton to Marie Rambert.

In 1926, Rambert pushed him into choreographing his first ballet, *A Tragedy of Fashion*. The production was designed by the artist Sophie Fedorovitch, who had met Ashton at Rambert's studio and who became his close friend and collaborator. Characteristically, Rambert had no immediate plans for a public performance. The ballet was taken up by the producer Nigel Playfair, and shown in his revue *Riverside Nights*. De Valois was much impressed, recognising Ashton as 'a real choreographer'.[43] Diaghilev saw the ballet twice, and asked the choreographer to audition for his company. Ashton went to the theatre and then, overcome with nerves, couldn't bring himself to go in. In 1928, he auditioned, as a dancer, for Ida Rubinstein's company in Paris. The appeal was not Rubinstein, a limited actress-dancer whose rich lover was paying the bills, but the choreographer Nijinska. The experience made Ashton a professional. He asked permission to watch all Nijinska's rehearsals, whether or not he was dancing in them, soaking up steps, methods, and Nijinska's distinctive use of the torso. In 1929, he returned to

London and to Rambert. His first job at the Vic-Wells ballet came that year, when he danced in de Valois's second Christmas ballet. From here on, however, his main work was as a choreographer – for Rambert, for the Camargo Society, for revue performances, including those by Alicia Markova. He made his first ballet for the Vic-Wells in 1931. Four years later, de Valois took him on as resident choreographer. He became one of the century's greatest classical choreographers, and he transformed the Company's dancing.

De Valois was training quick, strong dancers who were, as the dancer Julia Farron puts it, 'straight up and down'. She focused on footwork, on clean execution, on lower-body movement. Legs turned out clearly from steadily placed hips, but the torso stayed upright and relatively stiff: 'It was all so fast, you couldn't really bend.' Ashton wanted luxuriance from his dancers – the use of the torso he had seen in Nijinska's choreography, a readiness to bend and flow with the music. 'When he coached anything, it was all about huge movement,' says the dancer Georgina Parkinson, who danced for him in the 1960s. 'He didn't like anything prissy or underdone. He always wanted it out, big, sensuous, glamorous.' At her first Ashton rehearsal, Fonteyn was astounded:

> After listening to a few bars of music he would fling himself into some swoops and twists and dives, his movements just flowing out of the music, apparently spontaneously. Then he would stop and say, 'What did I do? Now you do it.' I was flabbergasted by these extraordinary inventions, which were only occasionally related to the common steps of our daily class . . . [We] tried to repeat what Ashton had shown us, but I could never manage without losing my balance and nearly toppling over.[44]

Later Ashton would draw steps from his dancers, asking them to suggest material and then refining it. He went on urging them to bend, and he encouraged a different kind of musicality. 'Madam was absolutely adamant about being on the beat,' remembers Merle Park, who joined the Company in the 1950s. 'Fred adored syncopation, loved you to be between the beats whenever you could.' He and de Valois both cared about footwork, about musicality, about classical line. Building on de Valois's clear foundations, Ashton gave the Company its three-dimensional richness.

At the same time, he demanded a different kind of theatricality from his dancers. As a choreographer, de Valois tended to be dramatic or expressionistic. She had a producer's approach; she didn't dwell on pure classicism. 'Technically the steps were not difficult,' wrote Annabel Farjeon, who loved dancing the de Valois ballets, 'but to get the style correct – that balance between restraint and display, that sense of period and character . . . '[45] Ashton used the dramatic qualities of de Valois's dancers, but he also loved personal glamour. He would describe the great ballerinas he had seen, giving imitations of Pavlova, Spessivtseva, Karsavina, Lopokova. He would show how a dancer had done a step, how she had created an effect, goading his own dancers into greater efforts. 'He used to talk in visions,' says Lynn Seymour, 'always trying to get you to live up to these images.'[46] When de Valois complained that Spessivtseva was unmusical, Ashton replied, 'All your girls are musical, and *none* of them is Spessivtseva.'[47]

Ashton wanted his ballerinas to be alluring, on stage and off. De Valois, still fighting the image of the disreputable ballet girl, urged her girls into twin-sets, tweeds, sensible shoes. The dancer Pamela May remembered Ashton complaining: 'You look nothing on earth! Look at your shoes! Terrible shoes! A dancer should wear wonderful shoes. Haven't you ever noticed what Markova wears?'[48] The contrast is characteristic. De Valois was empire-building, working on several levels at once – from cheap, hard-wearing clothes to the reputation of her company. Ashton was all for beauty.

Not surprisingly, they fought. 'They were jealous of each other,' says Julia Farron now, 'and they needed each other.' De Valois recognised Ashton's gifts; she paid generous tribute to him throughout her life. She needed help in building a British repertory. His ballets gave her company more depth and a richer classical style. Ashton, who could be waspish about de Valois, was also entirely practical when it came to developing his craft. He knew that she was giving him opportunities that he couldn't find elsewhere. The Company 'gave me security. It gave me a regular salary, which I hadn't had before, and I was immensely appreciative of the luxury of using proper dancers at last and having proper facilities. It was very stimulating working with Constant and Sophie Fedorovitch and having de Valois there and the whole thing growing and expanding and getting better.'[49] Ashton grew, too. At Sadler's Wells he met Margot Fonteyn, de Valois's discovery and his own greatest muse. After the elegant, witty ballets of his Rambert period, his work with Fonteyn showed a new depth, a tender classicism. 'Had I not been able to work with Margot I might never have developed the lyrical side of my work. As it was, it evolved into a personal idiom.'[50]

Despite clashes and differences in outlook, Ashton and de Valois came to rely on each other. They had a shared goal. 'They got away with it because they laughed,' said Pamela May. 'They would have these arguments, and we'd be sitting wondering how it would come out. But it always ended in laughter.'

Constant Lambert is the most elusive of the Sadler's Wells founders. He died too young, with too much of his promise unfulfilled. Lambert was a distinguished musician, hailed young as a gifted composer, and a brilliantly cultured man. Discussing music, he could move easily and persuasively to painting, literature and theatre. De Valois saw him as 'our only hope of an English Diaghilev'.[51] He put all that knowledge at the service of the ballet. As music director, he set superb standards in general policy and in day-to-day performance, conducting, composing, choosing and arranging music. During the war, he played at every performance in two-piano tours; afterwards, he trained an inexperienced orchestra in time for the reopening of the Royal Opera House. He inspired immediate loyalty in his musicians, and in his dancers.

First-class ballet conductors are hard to find. Charles Mackerras gave it up because, he found, 'the dancing comes first so the music gets distorted rhythmically'.[52] Lambert had a gift for serving his dancers and his composer. He would discuss tempi with choreographers (or, for classical revivals, with de Valois) and that was generally that. The music would not be warped to fit. At the same time, he knew his dancers. He was aware of individual technique, of tiny variations in timing steps. Pamela May remembered that Fonteyn liked a faster tempo for Odette's variation. Once, when

May was dancing the role, Lambert started at Fonteyn's tempo – and then corrected himself, slowing down to the speed that May preferred.

He knew how to urge his dancers on. 'When Constant makes a tempo change it doesn't worry us, he always makes you want to respond,' dancers told de Valois.[53] His recordings show sure and buoyant rhythm, a sense of the music's drama and of its larger architecture. Above all, Lambert could create thrilling theatrical effects. At the Company's triumphant New York opening in 1949, Lambert was 'the hero of the occasion', according to Lincoln Kirstein and to Balanchine:

> absolutely on the note in every variation; no boring bits; and he supports the dancers on the huge stage by giving them assurance with his authority. He whipped people up into applause, purely by sound; when nothing was really happening from a dancer he seduced everyone into imagining that she was divine.[54]

Lambert's early career was meteoric. In 1926, when he was twenty, he was invited to write a ballet for Diaghilev. The new *Romeo and Juliet* did not go well. Diaghilev kept altering the ballet, introducing new designs by the surrealists Max Ernst and Joan Miró and demanding changes to Nijinska's completed choreography. Lambert was appalled, and threatened to withdraw his music. Diaghilev, shocked by such insubordination, had the score removed to a strong room in case the composer tried to destroy it. Watching these solemn precautions, Lambert was caught between fury and laughter. In all this, Diaghilev hadn't changed a note of music. Lambert confronted the world's greatest impresario for the sake of his choreographer and designer. From the start of his career he showed a sense of theatre, a love for ballet and strong ideas about how its elements should fit together. The ballets that endure, he suggested in a later radio broadcast, 'are those in which no one collaborator can say, "This is my ballet." Nightly quarrels round the supper table are far more fruitful in the long run than polite letters from a distance.'[55]

Having fallen out with Diaghilev, Lambert kept up his interest in ballet. While he looked for conducting or composing work, he earned his living playing the piano for dancing schools. In 1928, he conducted *Leda and the Swan*, one of Ashton's earliest ballets. He was one of the accompanists at the Ballet Club, and soon worked with the Camargo Society. He had already started to conduct for de Valois – who had danced the Nurse in his *Romeo* in one of her guest appearances with Diaghilev.

Lambert's work with the Sadler's Wells Ballet was to be his greatest achievement. It suited his breadth of knowledge, his gift for collaboration, even his self-destructive streak. He was fascinated by things he couldn't grasp, by elusive beauty – and ballet is a fleeting art. He wrote less music, pouring his energies into the company. As with *Romeo*, he cared about every aspect of the ballet, and his taste and learning helped to shape the repertory. Most of his suggestions were made 'round the supper table', but a 1936 letter to Ashton shows just how strong an influence Lambert could be. He had an idea for a Liszt ballet, '1830 romanticism of the fruitiest type plus a leavening of surrealism'. His suggestions show an easy familiarity with Ashton's work, with the Sadler's Wells dancers – in fact, with all aspects of ballet production:

My dear Fred,

I was up in London last night and pursued you from theatre to theatre like a symbolist poet chasing a courtesan and equally in vain . . .

It will be a longish affair 3 big scenes with a prologue and epilogue. The prologue & epilogue a super-Gothic poets study, the 3 scenes respectively a ball room with a Polish accent, a snow clad plain and a brothel. I think it will suit very well the style you developed in *Valentine's Eve* and *Mephisto* (actually my favourite ballet of yours.)

For that reason I think Sophie [Fedorovitch, who had designed Ashton's *Mephisto Valse*] might be the best person for the décor if she can be juicy enough. The ball scene and brothel scene want to be as like Constantin Goys as possible – the rest should be a little more fantastic.

The man's part will suit Bobby [Helpmann] very well and the

woman's part will be ideal for either Spessiva or Fonteyn (whom to my great surprise you don't seem to appreciate at her true level. Though obviously immature at the moment she is to my mind the only post-Diaghilev dancer, with of course the exception of Toumanova, to have that indefinable quality of poetry in her work.)

You may of course not like the idea at all. But if you do I hope we will be able to spend some time on it going through the pieces again and again and really moulding the ballet into shape. All the Wells ballets suffer not only from being put on too quickly but from being too cut and dried. The best Diaghilev ballets were always the result of a long and close collaboration between the artists and boring though this may be I am sure it is necessary.[56]

Apparitions, as the ballet was called, turned out to be one of the company's greatest early successes. It was completed on the lines Lambert suggested, with Helpmann, Fonteyn and designs by Cecil Beaton.

Lambert made his own reputation early, from his work for Diaghilev but also from his own personality. His conversation alone made friends and colleagues trust in his genius. He was a dazzling companion, pouring out jokes, ideas, quotations, knowledge. It made for close collaboration with de Valois and Ashton, and it helped to educate the company's young dancers. Margot Fonteyn – with whom he had a long affair – and Robert Helpmann both turned to him for advice on books, music, art. He taught the young Beryl Grey how to read a score. And he paid attention to everything on stage. 'He was almost like a ballet master,' Grey remembers now. 'He'd come round in the interval and tell you off if the knot in your shoe ribbon was showing, if your tights were dirty. He was in love with ballet, he was in love with Margot . . . He was a great inspiration.'

By the end of the 1920s, de Valois was gathering her artistic team. Lambert was already at work. Ashton was recruited later, once the company was big enough to need more than one choreographer. For the moment, opportunities at the Old Vic were still limited to opera ballets, with a few short works as curtain-raisers for operas. *Les Petits Riens* had been made for Christmas 1928. Five months later, de Valois staged *The Picnic* (later renamed *The Faun*) to music by Vaughan Williams. Harold Turner, one of Rambert's dancers, had a leading role as a satyr. The next Christmas, Lilian Baylis agreed to stage a slightly larger ballet, again with *Hansel and Gretel*. De Valois's *Hommage aux belles viennoises*, danced to Schubert waltzes and mazurkas, proved very popular. The 1930 Christmas ballet was a *Suite of Dances* to Bach, starring Turner. It was another success with the Old Vic audience, encouraging Lilian Baylis to give more room to the ballet.

She was about to have more room at her disposal: the new Sadler's Wells Theatre was nearly ready. The appeal for money to buy and rebuild the theatre had been launched in 1925; Baylis had hoped to open in 1926. Inevitably, it took longer. The building had stood derelict for some years, and the scale of work and costs kept rising. All the money had to be found from private donors. There was no state subsidy for the arts, and no system of business sponsorship. The rebuilding committee were lucky to have an enthusiastic and generous builder, Frederick Minter, who allowed them to stop and restart work when money ran short. Even so, the theatre was to start out with debts of £15,000. At last, Sadler's Wells reopened on 6 January 1931, with a performance of *Twelfth Night* to suit the date. The opera and theatre companies would play alternate fortnights at each theatre, in a season running from September to May. There would now be a third company, the new Vic-Sadler's Wells Opera Ballet Company.

The opening of Sadler's Wells had given de Valois her chance. She produced the accounts for her well-run Academy of Choreographic Art, offering to hand over this successful business in exchange for the establishment of a ballet company and training school within the Sadler's Wells Theatre. Her scheme was brilliantly designed. The new company would be set up at no cost to the Vic. Better still, it was expected to be self-supporting. Profits from the School would help to pay the salaries of six dancers, who could also be used in the theatre and opera companies at both Vic and Wells. The ballet company would perform at both theatres, but the School would remain at Sadler's Wells. As before, the dance students would perform in operas and in larger ballets. (For years, this arrangement went on saving money for the Vic. In 1933, Pamela May was still paying school fees while dancing *Les Sylphides*.)

The Governors of the Old Vic accepted de Valois's proposal. She was engaged as '*prima ballerina*, director and principal choreographist'.[57] Ursula Moreton was the first of de Valois's six salaried dancers. The other five, all senior pupils at the Academy of Choreographic Art, were Freda Bamford, Sheila McCarthy, Joy Newton, Beatrice Appleyard and Nadina Newhouse. The Vic-Wells would start by performing opera ballets and, as curtain-raisers, their existing repertory of five ballets. (The fifth was *Danse sacrée et danse profane*, first produced by the Camargo Society.) Male dancers would be hired for individual performances. As the venture prospered, the company could be expanded and more ballets produced. De Valois and Baylis aimed in due course to present whole evenings of ballet, as often as once a week.

The Vic-Wells Ballet started with modest numbers, but it was organised with heroic ambition. Without any financial support, de Valois set up her company on the pattern of the great state theatres, a system of school, salaries and home theatre that was unprecedented in British ballet. The dancers of her young company would have nine months of guaranteed work each year. Salaries were not large, but their livelihoods were at last assured. They could devote themselves to dancing full-time – and to dancing ballet full-time, rather than taking commercial work to pay the bills. The Company would have the chance to work steadily and consistently, to grow, to develop its own repertory and style. The School would provide the next generation of dancers, trained to meet the Company's needs and standards. De Valois had created the conditions for a lasting British company.

In guaranteeing her dancers' livelihoods, de Valois risked her own. Once her School moved to Sadler's Wells, she no longer needed the studio in Kensington – but she had hired it for several years. She was still liable for rent, and she had given her business and its income to Sadler's Wells. She placed two advertisements in *The Dancing Times*. One proudly announced the opening of the new School at Sadler's Wells, 'A Theatre School organised to maintain an English Opera Ballet permanently in a London Theatre'. The second offered her old studio to let: 'Small premium. Moderate rent. Good lease.'[58] Her luck did not fail her, and she soon found a tenant. But the risk she took with the studio shows just how readily she would make personal sacrifices for her company. 'She was very proud of that,' remembers Beryl Grey. 'She didn't sell her School to Lilian Baylis, she *gave* it to Lilian Baylis. Ninette never wanted anything for herself. It was all for the Company.'

TWO
Building British ballet
1931–39

ABOVE Alicia Markova in *Les Rendezvous* by Frederick Ashton:
© Gordon Anthony Collection, The Theatre Museum, V&A Images
PREVIOUS PAGE *Checkmate* by Ninette de Valois, with June Brae as the
Black Queen and Harold Turner as the Red Knight: Studio Iris, Paris

Once established, the Company grew fast. De Valois hired dancers for performances until she could give them regular employment; she staged first drafts of ballets that could be expanded and redesigned. Throughout the 1930s she was working at the limit of her resources. This was most obvious in the older works she brought into the repertory. Some of these ballets were just beyond her company's numbers and budget, her dancers' levels of technique or sophistication. Yet they won audiences, and the Company grew into them. 'I would say, "Oh, no, Madam, I can't do that,"' remembers Pamela May. 'And she would tell you, yes, you could do it. And you did.' The Vic-Wells Ballet started with heavy use of guest artists. By the end of the decade, it was producing its own stars.

In these years, the Company developed a distinctive identity. Vic-Wells style came from Ashton and de Valois, but it also came from the nineteenth-century classics. Now that almost every ballet company has its own *Swan Lake*, it's hard to appreciate that de Valois was bold to stage the whole ballet. The dance historian Beth Genné points out that *Giselle*, *Coppélia*, *The Sleeping Beauty*, *The Nutcracker* and *Swan Lake* became the full-length 'classics' of the western ballet repertory largely because de Valois said so.[1] *Giselle* and the second act of *Swan Lake* were performed by several 1930s companies, often to show off a particular ballerina. The ballets themselves were not necessarily revered. Fokine had rebelled against the artificiality of nineteenth-century conventions; as late as 1949, P. W. Manchester could write that much of the choreography was 'dead wood which will rot at a touch'.[2] De Valois made them cornerstones of her repertory, using Petipa as well as Ashton to develop a native style of ballet. Her idea of balanced repertory was so influential that it no longer looks radical: it has become standard.

The new company started quietly. The Vic-Wells Ballet gave its debut performance just after Christmas 1930, with a visit to the Bournemouth Pavilion. Back in London, they started work on opera ballets. De Valois, her dancers and her students had replaced the volunteer opera ballet, and they were on in every performance, during the operas or in curtain-raisers. The dancers were also settling into Sadler's Wells. Compared to the Old Vic, the new theatre was luxurious. The auditorium had tip-up seats, even in the gallery. The electrical equipment was up to date. There were sinks in the dressing rooms – a change from the cold tap in the Old Vic prompt corner, where artists had been able to wash only 'when a noisy battle or chorus was in progress on the stage'.³ Even so, the new theatre turned out to be painfully cramped. Stage rehearsal time was limited to two hours a week, and even that depended on the opera schedule. There was little space for storage, for scene-painting, for rehearsal. Alicia Markova remembered working with Sergueyev in the theatre's little Board Room. The School and the ballet company shared the main Sadler's Wells room – but not in the evenings, when it was used as a coffee room for the audience. Worse, it had a concrete floor. Concrete has no give; for the dancers, the Wells Room floor meant sore feet, jarred landings and an increased risk of injury. Lilian Baylis refused to pay for a wooden floor. De Valois accepted this in silence, and found a patron who would donate the necessary money.

The Old Vic had always worked on a shoestring. Funds were even tighter once Lilian Baylis had taken on her second theatre. 1931 was, she wrote, 'a ghastly year, financially speaking'.⁴ Sadler's Wells opened during the Depression, at a time of high unemployment. The theatre itself was in debt from the beginning, and the three companies were soon clamouring for further alterations to the building. The number of opera performances had doubled: it took time for the box office to catch up. Prices were kept deliberately low. Under the terms of the Sadler's Wells Foundation, performances should be 'suited for the recreation and instruction of the poorer classes', and priced accordingly.⁵ The ideal of the popular audience was also behind the decision to have opera and theatre performances at both theatres. In theory the Vic and Sadler's Wells had entirely separate audiences, the people of Lambeth and of Islington. Lilian Baylis clung to this idea: these were the people she and Emma Cons had set out to improve.

In fact, there was a shared public for both theatres, and the planned alternation caused considerable confusion. People kept turning up at the wrong theatre. It became clear early on that ballet and opera did better at the Wells, Shakespeare at the Vic. The exchange was reorganised several times, with ballet and opera spending longer periods at Sadler's Wells. The interchange was not completely abandoned until the 1935–36 season. In the meantime, the dancers spent much of their time travelling between north and south London. Twice a month, the scenery was packed up and sent to the other theatre by horse and cart. Travelling expenses added to the theatre's financial troubles. Overall, Sadler's Wells made a heavy loss on its first short season.

The one exception was the ballet company. The School at Sadler's Wells gave the company a good basic income, while classes for office workers added to the funds. Moreover, the small ballets were proving so popular with audiences that Lilian Baylis decided to present a complete evening of ballet. The Royal Ballet dates its existence from 5 May 1931, when the first full programme was given at the Old Vic. Constant Lambert conducted. Anton Dolin, a huge star in ballet and in music hall, agreed to dance as a guest artist. De Valois, her dancers and students were joined by three more men: Stanley Judson, Ivor Beddoes and (from the theatre company) Leslie French. Many of the extra dancers were performing in other shows on the same evening. 'It was a nightmare of worry to arrange the programme so that everyone could make the appearances required of them at other theatres,' wrote de Valois.[6] Judson crossed Waterloo Bridge twice in the course of that first night.

The Company showed four of their most popular ballets and one new work, *The Jackdaw and the Pigeons* by de Valois. This bird fable had a specially composed score by Hugh Bradford. Its designs were by William Chappell, a Rambert student who went on to dance for the company. The ballet was slight and rather silly, though P. W. Manchester remembered de Valois's 'piquancy in her delightful Jackdaw costume'.[7] The Old Vic night was completely sold out, and two more performances were given at Sadler's Wells. Dolin, who was dancing in a West End musical, got leave to dance at the first Wells performance on 15 May. At her own request, Lydia Lopokova appeared at the second, six days later. She danced *Cephalus and Procris*, which de Valois had made for the Camargo Society in January, and refused her fee. She asked that the money be given to the young members of the ballet company – who at once returned it to Sadler's Wells.

The management was startled by the success of these performances. The Annual Report for the season found it 'astonishingly satisfactory to discover so large and enthusiastic a public waiting for the presentation of this difficult and eclectic form of art, which has not hitherto been treated seriously in London unless it hailed from a foreign country'.[8] The Report's authors were right: there was a ready-made ballet public. Audiences had been built up by Diaghilev and by Pavlova. Some balletomanes stayed loyal to *Russian* ballet, but by 1931 they had been deprived of that for two years. Since Diaghilev's death, there had been little ballet in Britain. Pavlova had given her last performances, other stars had given music-hall appearances and the Rubinstein company had come (let down, again, by Rubinstein's own dancing). The fledgling efforts of de Valois, Rambert and the Camargo Society all benefited from an initial lack of competition.

The first Vic-Wells evenings were a small beginning. The Company was still inexperienced; none of these ballets survived in repertory. Nevertheless, an audience of balletomanes and Old Vic regulars welcomed them. For the next season, Lilian Baylis decided, the ballet could give one performance every fortnight. The Company hired its first male dancers, Stanley Judson and Travis Kemp, while Constant Lambert was engaged as conductor and Musical Director. Over the summer, de Valois and her dancers were at work for the Camargo Society. *The Jackdaw and the Pigeons* was revived, but the major contribution was de Valois's new work, *Job*. This had a greater impact than any Camargo ballet to date, and established de Valois's reputation as a choreographer. It was a distinctly British work, with music by Ralph Vaughan Williams. As Lydia Lopokova wrote to Geoffrey Keynes, her brother-in-law, 'My chief pleasure was that it differed from the Russian ballet tradition, the most important merit of *Job*.'[9]

The idea for the ballet came from Geoffrey Keynes. He argued that Blake's *Illustrations of the Book of Job* provided settings and groupings that would work as a stage production. In 1927, he offered the ballet to Diaghilev, who turned it down – 'too English'.[10] When the Camargo Society was formed, Keynes approached de Valois. She accepted Vaughan Williams's requests that it should be called 'A Masque for Dancing' and that it should have no pointe-work, instead using grouping and gesture as she had used them in her Greek choruses. *Job* made its impact as a complete theatrical production more than through individual dances. Some critics even wondered if it was a ballet. 'Let those dance critics try to cast it with anything but really skilled dancers,' replied de Valois crisply.[11] In a production full of flowing mime, *Job* had one role for a star dancer. De Valois made the most of Anton Dolin's stage presence and athleticism. He was a superbly arrogant Satan in a role full of jumps and backbends.

When British ballet was struggling for recognition, *Job* had the advantage of ambitious, unmistakable seriousness. 'Ballets containing even one little idea have been rare in the last sixteen years,' wrote the *Daily Telegraph*'s Richard Capell in 1934. 'Many have had no idea at all. The idea of *Job* is grand, and it is carried out with daring and nobility.'[12] On loan from the Camargo Society, it opened the 1931–32 season. It was a great popular success – indeed, wrote de Valois, 'it was the English Ballet's only subsidy'.[13] It was the Vic-Wells Ballet's first substantial production, but it did put a strain on the Company's resources. Job's seven sons caused particular trouble. De Valois had only two men on the staff; as soon as one lot of guest artists had learned the ballet, they would get engagements elsewhere. The sons were rarely the same twice running, and at one performance there were only six of them. Dolin, too, was combining his work for the Vic-Wells with musical comedy work. On opening night, a taxi waited at the stage door to rush him back to the Hippodrome as soon as the curtain calls were over.

The first Vic-Wells performance of *Job* shared a bill with *Regatta*, Frederick Ashton's first ballet for the Company. It was a nautical romp with music by Gavin Gordon. De Valois played a glamorous Foreign Visitor, and a trio of Yachting Girls came down with sea-sickness. Two more productions, both choreographed by de Valois, were added before Christmas. De Valois's *Fête polonaise*, another Camargo production, was a suite of dances to Glinka. In December Ashton returned to dance the title role in her next ballet, *The Jew in the Bush*.

De Valois was working hard to keep the attention of her audience. Besides frequent new productions, she turned to guest stars. At Ashton's invitation, Alicia Markova had been appearing at Rambert's Ballet Club. At the end of 1931, de Valois went backstage and told Markova that 'it was about time' she appeared with the Vic-Wells Ballet.[14] The two women were old colleagues. When Markova joined the Ballets Russes, aged fourteen, de Valois had been asked to look after her. Markova had grown up to be a classical dancer of brilliant technique and ethereal quality, but Diaghilev's death had interrupted her career, depriving her of the chance to dance the great classical roles. When de Valois brought Markova to her company, everybody benefited. De Valois had a star who could draw the public and justify her decision to stage the classics.

This profitable association started in January 1932. At a special matinee, Markova danced *Cephalus and Procris* then appeared barefoot in de Valois's new *Narcissus and Echo*. This was thought to be 'a very "modern" piece,' Markova remembered, 'with its Arthur Bliss score, its black and white décor and costumes, danced in profile'.[15] Barefoot or on pointe, Markova was an immediate hit with the Vic-Wells audience, and the management quickly arranged a special season in March. Markova and Dolin would lead the company for eleven performances. The permanent Company was expanded, with ballets added to the repertory. Dolin staged *Le Spectre de la rose* and danced it with de Valois – hardly obvious casting for the dreamy heroine. This was the Company's first Fokine ballet. Markova staged the second, *Les Sylphides*, which was becoming a standard for most ballet companies. This first Vic-Wells version was gauntly designed and not particularly distinguished. In 1937, the Company was able to bring in the original Benois designs.

The other new works were an *Italian Suite* by Dolin and de Valois, Rupert Doone's *The Enchanted Grove* ('a ghastly bit of Rococo chinoiserie', wrote P. W. Manchester) and de Valois's *Nursery Suite*.[16] This was a series of dances for nursery-rhyme characters, set to an Elgar score that had been written for the Princesses Elizabeth and Margaret. Their mother, then the Duchess of York, came to see the first night, bringing the company a flurry of publicity.

The Camargo Society's most ambitious performances took place that summer, with dancers from the Ballet Club and the Vic-Wells. The Society took the Savoy Theatre for a month, giving de Valois's dancers the chance to perform an extensive repertory in the West End, with tickets sold to the general public rather than a subscription audience. Olga Spessivtseva came from Paris to dance *Giselle* and the second act of *Le Lac des cygnes*, as *Swan Lake* was then usually called. 'I hope that you have watched closely,' she said to Markova after a performance of *Giselle*. 'This is a ballet that will be good for you.'[17] De Valois acted as ballet mistress for both productions, and danced Giselle's mother at one performance. She had also been invited to take a group of British dancers to Copenhagen, where there was a British Trades and Arts Exhibition that summer. 'The British Ballet Company' featured Vic-Wells dancers with Phyllis Bedells, Markova and Dolin in leading roles. They took *Job*, *Les Sylphides* and other short ballets from the Vic-Wells and Camargo repertories, Adeline Genée appeared at the last performance and reviews were generally enthusiastic. 'It is a remarkable thing,' said one British journalist, 'that we have to come all the way to Copenhagen to have brought home to us that we have such good dancers in England.'[18]

Back in London, the 1932–33 season opened with Markova and Dolin in the second act of *Le Lac des cygnes*. The two stars carried the performance; the Company did not shine. The season continued with several new ballets. De Valois appeared in her own *Douanes* as a tightrope dancer flirting her way through Customs. Dolin danced a Man from Cook's, with Antony Tudor as the Passport Officer. Ashton's *The Lord of Burleigh*, made for the Camargo Society, concerned characters from several Tennyson poems. Hints of a plot turned into an appealing but long divertissement: 'Freddie, I loved the first three days!' Lopokova had told the choreographer after the first performance.[19]

The Origin of Design was another Camargo Society ballet. It had an attractive Handel score, but de Valois's choreography was thin. *The Scorpions of Ysit*, her next work, lasted a little longer. The effective designs were Sophie Fedorovitch's first work for the Vic-Wells, carried out with an economy that must have warmed Lilian Baylis's heart. Beatrice Appleyard, the Goddess Ysit, wore an imposing headdress made from curtain rings. The rest of the ballet was an awkward mixture of tragedy and comedy. Ysit revived a baby that her attendant scorpions had stung to death. De Valois had meant the scorpions to be funny, but the tone was so uncertain that audiences didn't know whether to laugh. Nevertheless, Ursula Moreton gave a moving performance as the mother. In December 1932, Dolin danced his new solo, *Boléro*. De Valois dismissed it as 'music hall', but the audience loved it and Lilian Baylis asked for two more performances. After the last performance she paid Dolin with one hand, then took the money back with the other. 'For the Endowment Fund, Anton.'[20]

Ashton's *Pomona*, set to a score by Lambert, had been made for the first Camargo Society programme. It didn't quite come off. The young Vic-Wells could not match the sophistication of the original cast, led by Anna Ludmila and Anton Dolin. Still, *Pomona* brought Ashton's own following to Sadler's Wells. Lambert's love for Purcell prompted *The Birthday of Oberon*. The Company's first choral ballet had music from *The Fairy Queen* and attractive choreography by de Valois. It was a large-scale production, with thirty dancers and a chorus of forty. Lambert wrote to a friend, 'People objected to the chorus being in masks but, as I said, had they seen them without? It had excellent notices but wasn't a success after the first night.'[21] In these years, ballet was often reviewed by music critics. Lambert was keeping the orchestra in good shape.

The next production, *Coppélia*, was even more ambitious. Lydia Lopokova suggested that Nicholas Sergueyev (who had staged the Diaghilev *Sleeping Princess* and the Camargo *Giselle*) should come to Sadler's Wells to produce *Coppélia*. She wrote to Sergueyev, who was teaching in Paris and thinking of forming his own company –

'an obviously impracticable project', wrote de Valois tartly.[22] De Valois, in fact, seems to have been eager to make sure of Sergueyev. She went to Paris herself, taking Evelyn Williams, then Lilian Baylis's secretary, to draw up a ten-year contract. Sergueyev arrived in London a few weeks later, bringing tin trunks full of notation books. These recorded, in Stepanov notation, many of the ballets that Sergueyev had rehearsed in St Petersburg. He had smuggled them out of Russia when he fled the revolution, and used them to stage a series of productions for the company.

Sergueyev and the notation were invaluable, but both needed interpreting. The Stepanov system was not a complete record of steps. The notes, which worked as a reminder for dancers or producers who already knew the ballets, left out upper-body details. Nor did they record the exact gestures and pacing of mime scenes. Markova remembers Sergueyev's care with mime: the mad scene from *Giselle* was 'set strictly to the music. This Sergueyev was very insistent upon, because of the timing and the fact that it was rather like an "orchestration" in that it involved not only Giselle, but also Albrecht, Bathilde, the Duke, Hilarion and Berthe.'[23] Sergueyev was not always so precise. In St Petersburg, according to the Maryinsky dancer Anatole Vilzak, Sergueyev would get his staff to demonstrate the choreography – 'Always somebody else to show, but not himself.'[24] When it came to staging whole ballets in London, he 'went haywire when he was producing things,' said de Valois. 'There were never two days done the same way!'[25] She also found him to be 'completely devoid of any real stage sense':

> The production side, concerning entrances and exits, or the evolutions of human beings in the form of crowd work, had always to be dealt with by me on the quiet. He was unmusical to a degree bordering on eccentricity; he always carried a blue pencil, and would carefully pencil out a bar of music, which, for some reason, wearied him . . . This would mean that I must 'phone Constant Lambert, who would come down in the lunch break and put the bars back. Sergueyev would return, and because, in his absence, I had extended some small choreographic movement to cover Mr Lambert's tracks,

he would be unaware that the position was musically where it had been before the onslaught of the blue pencil![26]

While Sergueyev staged the choreography, de Valois got on with production. Fonteyn, who learned *The Sleeping Beauty* in 1939, remembered 'confusion about fitting the steps to the music, accent up or accent down. De Valois had so little confidence in his ability to get everyone together in the same rhythm that she called "secret" rehearsals to "tidy it up".'[27]

Coppélia was the first of the Sergueyev stagings. The Company danced only the first two acts, dropping the third-act divertissement. Lopokova helped with rehearsals, translating words and steps, then danced an exuberant Swanilda at the first two performances. Ninette de Valois danced the role for the rest of the run, showing off her wit and celebrated footwork. Fonteyn, who saw her as Swanilda and in other roles, recalled '*brisés* which seemed faster than the speed of light, and faster than any conductor could catch'.[28] *Coppélia* made a good company ballet, with roles for rising dancers. A photograph taken a few years later shows the line of Swanilda's friends, all promising soloists: it includes May, Fonteyn, Elizabeth Miller and the future Ballet Mistress Jill Gregory.

During the March 1933 rehearsals, a young Australian dancer arrived with an introduction to Ninette de Valois. As she took his hand, Robert Helpmann recalled, she said, 'looking at me, "You know, something could be done with that face."'[29] Her tone was not flattering, but de Valois was already looking for her next leading man. Dolin, she said later, 'was flitting about all over the world. You couldn't rely on him.'[30] Helpmann was technically weak, and she put him in the corps de ballet while he worked on his academic schooling. He stood out at once. 'I like the boy, dear, who puts too much brilliantine on his hair,' said Lilian Baylis. 'Do stop him, his head's rather large anyway, and it makes one keep looking at him.' Perhaps, replied de Valois, 'that is what he means you to do.'[31] For the opening night of the next season, he was cast as Satan in *Job*, the most important male role in the repertory. Helpmann could not match Dolin's technique, or his Blakean muscles, but he had striking stage presence and attack.

Helpmann used his sense of theatre to compensate for limitations in his dancing. 'He could make you believe he'd done a thousand turns,' remembers Beryl Grey, 'when he'd probably only done one and a half.' His early training had been irregular, and he was never a strong classical dancer. Instead, he found a way of *acting* the classical princes. At a time when British ballet was desperately short of men, his performances carried conviction and won audiences. He became an outstanding partner to Markova, Fonteyn and other ballerinas. The critic Dale Harris claimed that Fonteyn's fish dives were more brilliant with Helpmann than with any of her other partners. A 1930s film suggests he was right. Dancing the duet from *The Sleeping Beauty*, Fonteyn plunges into Helpmann's arms, diving as if into deep water.

As the brilliantine – an extra-glossy mix of paraffin and Vaseline – suggests, Helpmann was keen to hold his public. 'He showed me so much in the way of stagecraft,' said Fonteyn, 'and in fact forced me, in self-defence, to learn how to claim one's own share of the stage. When I opened the door of Giselle's cottage and stepped out, it was to step into the *atmosphere* of Giselle. Bobby, on his first entrance with cloak and sword, had already made the audience sit up and participate.'[32] Helpmann could not set an example in classical dancing, but he was the first star to come from the Company's ranks.

British ballet had had several years without Russian competition. That summer, Russian Ballet returned to London. Les Ballets 1933 had Balanchine choreography and the 'baby ballerina' Tamara Toumanova. De Basil's company, billed as Les Ballets Russes de Monte Carlo, had two more babies, Irina Baronova and Tatiana Riabouchinska, plus the Diaghilev stars Massine and Danilova. The small Vic-Wells company could not match this level of glamour, but it survived the competition. It had its own public and, indeed, its own star: Alicia Markova had signed a contract for the whole of the 1933–34 season. For three months, the Vic-Wells also had the ex-Diaghilev dancer Stanislas Idzikowski as a guest artist. Idzikowski was a virtuoso, short and stocky, with a radiant smile and a powerful jump. On opening night, he danced *Le Spectre de la rose* and the Blue Bird pas de deux with Markova. This was the first dance from

The Sleeping Beauty to enter the Vic-Wells repertory. Markova also danced the Bride in de Valois's new ballet, *The Wise and Foolish Virgins*. The evening ended with Helpmann's debut in *Job*.

La Création du monde, to Milhaud's jazzy score, was the next ballet to enter the repertory. De Valois's ballet showed the Creation in the form of an African ceremony. At the Camargo Society and in this first Vic-Wells revival, the dancers wore black body paint. (Blacking up didn't cause offence in 1930s Britain, but the dancers did have some trouble getting it all off again.) The ballet was never a popular success, but it had enthusiastic admirers. The choreography was musically precise – 'very difficult,' remembered William Chappell, who played the first-created Man. Ursula Moreton, dancing the Woman, 'had to count ceaselessly to keep me on the off beat!'[33]

Milhaud's score had been commissioned by Les Ballets Suédois. In its first decade, the Vic-Wells Ballet often staged new versions of existing ballets. De Valois was to choreograph two more Suédois scores, *The Jar* and *The Wise and Foolish Virgins*. The later *Barabau* and *The Gods Go a'Begging* both used music written for Diaghilev. *Le Baiser de la fée* came from Rubinstein's company, *Le Roi nu* from Lifar's Paris Opéra. This was sometimes a matter of convenience: *Le Roi nu* was hastily choreographed when *The Sleeping Princess* had to be postponed. These ballets also followed models established by the Ballets Russes: character comedies, a Stravinsky fairy story. Diaghilev remained a strong influence on de Valois and her colleagues. The next Vic-Wells production was Fokine's *Carnaval*, first performed in 1910. The ballet was revived for Idzikowski, who was the only distinguished thing about it. Markova was miscast as Columbine, while the ballet's atmosphere eluded the company.

Les Rendezvous, which had its premiere in December, was Ashton's first important work for the Company. '*Les Rendezvous* has no serious portent at all,' he said, 'it is simply a vehicle for the exquisite dancing of Idzikowski and Markova.'[34] Dancers met, greeted each other, and danced to Lambert's arrangement of music by Auber. Chappell designed and kept redesigning *Les Rendezvous*. His first version, with roses and lilies of the valley on the women's dresses and in their hair, was by far the most admired. Ashton's steps were crisp and witty, with a conversational elegance in the flourishes of arms and wrists. This was Markova's best created role at Sadler's Wells. 'No one who saw her will ever forget her exit at the end of her brilliant solo,' wrote P. W. Manchester, 'head jauntily tilted, shoulders and arms delicately lifted, her narrow feet exquisitely placed.'[35] She always left the stage in a roar of applause. Ashton also made demands on the rest of the Company – not least its newly acquired men, who danced a pas de six. Just as British ballet again faced Russian competition, Ashton showed off the Vic-Wells as a company of dancers.

At the end of 1933, the Vic-Wells Ballet inherited most of the Camargo Society's assets. The Society announced that it would give up its rights to *Job*, and handed over the scenery and costumes for a number of ballets. Early in 1934, John Maynard Keynes announced that the Society would in future devote itself to helping the Vic-Wells Ballet. The 'management without a company', set up to encourage ballet in Britain, had become a support for just one company. Again, de Valois had overtaken any rivals by sheer professionalism: she had regular performances on a stage big enough to show the Camargo Society works. Keynes backed her wholeheartedly. In April 1934, he would give her company a different kind of support by bringing a whole congress of economists, eight hundred strong, to see the Vic-Wells Ballet.

On New Year's Day, 1934, Markova danced her first *Giselle*. There was a thick, choking fog that night. Many in the audience were delayed, arriving all through *Pomona*, the opening ballet. The fog had got into the theatre itself: 'Though it enhanced the mystery of the second act setting,' Markova remembered, 'it also caught at our lungs.'[36] Her dancing had an unearthly quality; she was weightlessly fragile, with delicate musical phrasing. She was at her most ethereal in *Giselle*, which became her supreme role. She was partnered by Dolin on the first night, with Hermione Darnborough dancing the Queen of the Wilis and Helpmann making the most of Hilarion. The new production was designed by Chappell.

Giselle was followed by Sergueyev's production of *The Nutcracker*, then called *Casse-Noisette*. Again, Lopokova was on hand during rehearsals, translating and demonstrating. Sergueyev caught sight of the actress Elsa Lanchester, then rehearsing for Ariel in the Old Vic production of *The Tempest*. He was entranced, and at once decided she should do the Arabian dance. Lanchester, already a star, brought *Casse-Noisette* publicity and took most of the notices. (The next year, she went to Hollywood as *The Bride of Frankenstein*.) Hedley Briggs designed storybook settings on a very small budget. Markova was a perfect crystalline Sugar Plum Fairy. By now de Valois could call on a cast of forty dancers. She brought in the Lord Mayor's Boy Players to play mice and toy soldiers.

De Valois's next ballet gave Helpmann a starring role. *The Haunted Ballroom*, which had its premiere in April 1934, was theatrically effective and immediately popular. Geoffrey Toye's music was vivid and tuneful. Helpmann, in tartan tights, was the doomed Master of Tregennis, danced to death by three ghosts. The theatre designers Motley created a cobwebbed ballroom that faded to a night sky, with costumes in grey, white and black with touches of crimson. Markova, Ursula Moreton and Beatrice Appleyard – the last sweeping a lavish backbend – were the ghosts. In an epilogue, the Young Tregennis realised that he would grow up to meet the same fate. This mime role, danced by Freda Bamford at the premiere, became a first opportunity for a series of young soloists. One was Margot Fontes, later Margot Fonteyn.

The Haunted Ballroom had a long life in repertory, and *Les Rendezvous* survives today. The ambitious 1933–34 season had been a success: the Company was beginning to establish its own repertory. It also had Markova, who could guarantee good audiences, and who agreed to return for the next season. Ruth French, a strong technician, was engaged to share roles with de Valois. She made her debut in *Fête Polonaise* on the first night of the new season. On the second, Helpmann danced Albrecht to Markova's Giselle. De Valois's next ballet had its premiere in October. *The Jar* was a comedy with music by Casella – like *La Création du monde*, the score had been commissioned by Les Ballets Suédois. Chappell's designs were bright and very pretty. Walter Gore played a china-mender who got stuck inside a cherished jar, but neither he nor anyone else had much dancing to do.

The great event of the season was the Company's first production of *Le Lac des cygnes* on 20 November 1934. This was the first full-length production to be seen outside Russia. De Valois had danced in Diaghilev's two-act version, which struck her then as old-fashioned and boring. Only Trefilova's Odette–Odile saved her 'from complete disillusionment: here I certainly sensed the greatness of the execution and the perfection of the central structure of the ballet.'[37] She set out to make her own production as authentic as possible. Once again, Sergueyev came from Paris to stage the ballet. He restored Odette's mime scene, dropped by Diaghilev and by later Russian companies. 'The scene is particularly lovely,' wrote de Valois, 'difficult to play, and an excellent test traditionally for the young dancers of this generation; it is, moreover, an important link between the ballet of today and yesterday, and that in itself is sufficient reason why it should be left to fulfil its mission.'[38] Odette's mime was to become important in the Vic-Wells tradition of the ballet. Sergueyev also offered Markova 'two versions of the Swan Queen's solo in the lakeside scene. One had been danced by Legnani, creator of the role, the other by Mathilde Kchessinskaya, first Russian interpreter of Odette. In the event I learned both, and combined elements from both in my performance.'[39]

Markova had a triumphant success. The ballet audience already knew her Odette; her Odile was poised and glittering. 'There was a touch of sinister in her,' wrote Jasper Howlett, 'and a dazzlingly brilliant hardness . . . With her flawless technique, her apparent contradictions of strength and fragility, Markova made herself bewildering, and intoxicating, if not inherently evil.'[40] Hugh Stevenson dressed her in a golden tutu with red sequins – Odile was not yet firmly identified as the *Black* Swan. Stevenson was working on a tight budget, so his designs were not lavish. The swans' bodices had feather patterns, rather like fish scales, and the wigs were terrible. As Prince Siegfried, Helpmann acted and partnered well, and jumped unexpectedly high in his third-act solo. Elizabeth Miller and Doris May (soon to be renamed Pamela) danced the pas de trois with Walter Gore. The production was well rehearsed and smoothly staged, but it was carried by Markova. As a company performance, this was a modest beginning.

Le Lac des cygnes was also the Company's first charity gala, given in aid of Queen Charlotte's Hospital. Money was still short at Sadler's Wells, but the gala was an investment. It gained goodwill for the Company, bringing publicity and a fashionable audience to Sadler's Wells. The Islington theatre could not quite match Covent Garden for glamour, however: the *Daily Telegraph* noted that various society ladies had left their tiaras at home.

When *The Lord of Burleigh* was revived early in the New Year, Ashton cast Margot Fonteyn in a duet with Markova. It was Fonteyn's first appearance as a soloist. Markova had to tell her, in a whisper, when to take her bow. In March, she was cast in Markova's old role in another Camargo Society ballet. *Rio Grande* was set to Constant Lambert's best-known score, with vivid designs by Edward Burra. Ashton's first title for the ballet had been 'A Day in a Southern Port' and Fonteyn, not yet sixteen, danced a Creole prostitute. Her 'technique has been strengthened', noted 'The Sitter Out' in *The Dancing Times*, 'and her stage personality has developed. She is able to grip her audience, and provided she continues in the way she has begun and does not grow too tall she should develop into a really great artiste.'[41] Like 'The Sitter Out', the Vic-Wells audience had been following Fonteyn's development. The Company had a balletomane public that eagerly watched dancers emerge from the corps de ballet. The dancer and critic Leo Kersley remembered watching from the gallery that season and singling out May and Fonteyn. With May, he noted her beauty in arabesque, in still poses; with Fonteyn, he noticed the flow of movement. Even when Fonteyn stood still, however, 'you still kept her eyes on her. So she got a nickname in the gallery, she was the "glow-worm"!'[42]

Margot Fonteyn was born in 1919, under the name Margaret (Peggy) Hookham. Her father was English, her mother half-Brazilian, half-Irish, and she had spent some of her childhood in China. In 1933, her mother brought her back to Britain to find out if she had the talent for a professional career. She took lessons from Princess Serafine Astafieva, who had taught Markova, before starting at the Vic-Wells School. De Valois noticed her at once. Echoing Espinosa's response to her own patchy training, de Valois said, 'We are just in time to save her feet.'[43] In Fonteyn's case, the rescued feet did not become her greatest strength – though Ashton was to make intensely demanding steps for them. Ashton, de Valois and Lambert all worked to shape the young Fonteyn. In turn, she helped to shape their company. 'It is one of my greatest pieces of good fortune that I was exactly of the right age to be able to develop coincidentally with the Vic-Wells Ballet,' she wrote. 'I was like a surfer riding a particularly long wave, and it was Markova's departure that launched me.'[44]

In February, Markova had said she hoped to stay for another season. In fact, she left that year. Vivian Van Damm, the manager of the Windmill Theatre, offered to set her up with her own company. (He already knew her family: Markova's sister Doris was appearing at his theatre.) Laura Henderson, the Windmill's owner, would pay for a London season and a regional tour. Markova signed a contract for a year. The Vic-Wells had lost its ballerina.

It also risked losing her regular partner. The new Vivian Van Damm Productions Ltd tried to engage Helpmann, but he had already agreed to appear in a West End revue over the summer break. Dolin was signed up instead. The next question was Markova's company. After discussions with Lilian Baylis, Henderson agreed to use the whole Vic-Wells company. 'You will do much good for British ballet – but you will lose a fortune,' Baylis told her.[45] She was right: Henderson lost £30,000, much of it for the benefit of the Vic-Wells Ballet. Markova's commercial backers had been outmanoeuvred. The company appeared under its own name, not as the Markova Ballet. Henderson also paid for a refurbishment of *Giselle* and for a new ballet, *The Rake's Progress*; the Vic-Wells kept both productions. There was another, more important benefit. The prospect of a rival Markova company prompted de Valois to put Frederick Ashton under contract. He would be paid £10 a week, with no royalties, to make at least three ballets a year.

Having made one tour through Van Damm and Henderson, de Valois arranged others. The Company visited the regions every year until the war. By 1937, the Company could make a small profit on touring, despite the expense of a full orchestra. 'Sorry, dear,' Lilian Baylis told de Valois when agreeing the tours, 'we can't afford to send out a house manager with you. Go and see the theatre manager, look at the contracts, pay the orchestra, pay the theatre staff.'[46] De Valois, characteristically, was glad of the experience.

Baylis had carried out most of the Van Damm negotiations. De Valois was ill; she had a hysterectomy that spring. She went on working from her hospital bed, but her next ballet had to be postponed from April until May. *The Rake's Progress* therefore had its premiere during the special season at Sadler's Wells. Gavin Gordon, the composer for *Regatta* and *The Scorpions of Ysit*, had written music for a ballet based on the series of paintings by Hogarth. Constant Lambert had suggested the score to Ashton, who wasn't keen. The project suited de Valois much better. It was a character ballet with a period setting and, as with *Job*, she could take paintings as her source. Her *Rake's Progress* was forceful, concise, and theatrically vivid. It became a key work in the repertory, a distinctively British ballet.

Following Hogarth, the ballet charts the Rake's decline, from an orgy to prison and the madhouse. Gordon's score was fast-paced and vigorous, always moving the action forwards. Rex Whistler's designs were atmospheric and beautifully drawn. De Valois had planned to cast Helpmann as the Rake, but he was still appearing in revue. The role was taken by Walter Gore – the choreographer's favourite Rake, but one who made little impression when the ballet was new. As the Betrayed Girl, Markova looked out of place, a ballerina detached from the robust world of the ballet. Harold Turner earned an ovation as both the Dancing Master and, in the Bedlam scene, the Man with a Rope. The Company's women led a splendidly rowdy orgy. Gordon's score used a nursery instrument, the 'nightingale', to suggest the voice of Joy Newton's unkempt Ballad Singer. The rest of their dancers would chorus, under their breaths, words invented by Constant Lambert: 'Oh dearie me, I do want to pee, and I don't much care if the audience see. Oh dearie me, I do want to pee, and I'll do it on the stage!'[47]

On her last night at Sadler's Wells, Markova danced *Le Lac des cygnes*. The audience was excited to the point of hysteria. For the first time, the ballerina made a speech from the stage – 'Thank you all from the bottom of my heart.'[48] She had led the Company for two years, but she had always been a guest star. Whenever she danced, there were queues for standing room. On other nights, the theatre was half-empty. Now some of her admirers wondered if they would have any reason to come back to Sadler's Wells. The Australian Helpmann feared that 'I had travelled many thousands of miles to take part in a funeral. I remember thinking, well that's the end of ballet.'[49] Markova's departure marked a new phase for the company. It had to learn to survive by itself.

Markova's departure was one great change. The other was the arrival of Frederick Ashton. His ballets were already among the most important and popular in the repertory. From 1935, he produced a series of works that raised the Company's prestige and developed its dancers. Between them, Ashton and the nineteenth-century classics transformed the Vic-Wells Ballet. De Valois's own ballets tended to be dance-dramas, dominated by plot and by mime. She was much weaker when it came to dances for their own sake. Ashton made ballets full of dancing. Even in narrative ballets, he told stories in danced images, conveying emotion through footwork and glowing line.

And Ashton loved classical dancing. He had seen and adored older ballerinas; he learned his craftsmanship from Nijinska and from Petipa. 'I always return to Petipa over everything,' he said in a 1971 interview; 'people sometimes find me at a matinee of *The Sleeping Beauty*, which I have seen literally hundreds of times. And they ask me what I'm doing and I say "having a private lesson".'[50] His style was individual and characteristic, but its classical temper meant that qualities learned in Ashton's ballets could be carried over into Petipa's. Dancing these ballets side by side, the Company could develop a consistent style. Each ballet might need a different approach, but there was a clear foundation for the dancing. At the same time, the Company kept its dramatic attack, its concern for characterisation. From the mid-1930s, Ashton and de Valois both coached classical roles. 'She was very good at palming off certain rehearsals on to Fred,' said Pamela May. 'She knew he'd do some variations, some scenes, better than she could. But she hated to admit it!'

Ashton was ready to throw in his lot with the Vic-Wells, but he was worried about its future. 'How *can* we come back to London next season when we have no prima ballerina?' he asked de Valois. 'We've got a perfectly good ballerina,' she replied. 'We've got Margot.'[51] This was not a good enough answer for Ashton, who didn't yet share de Valois's admiration for her favourite. Markova was a fully fledged ballerina, and it took several dancers to fill her roles. From within the Company, de Valois promoted Fonteyn, May and Elizabeth Miller. She also brought in dancers from outside. Pearl Argyle, a dancer of astonishing beauty, had worked with Ashton at the Ballet Club. Mary Honer, a brilliant technician, had danced mostly in musical comedy. Working on a West End production, de Valois had spotted the young dancer June Bear – who, as it happened, had been friends with Fonteyn in Shanghai. The name was promptly changed to Brae. 'I can't have performing bears in the Company,' declared de Valois, who had already changed Doris May into Pamela.[52] She went on changing her dancers' names: in the 1990s, she was still wishing she had done something about Deborah Bull.

As de Valois signed up one choreographer, she let another go. When Antony Tudor started dancing with the Vic-Wells, in 1932, he had already made successful ballets for Rambert. He repeatedly asked for the chance to choreograph. De Valois gave him two opera ballets, *Faust* and *Carmen*, but nothing for the ballet evenings. In 1935, he got tired of waiting. He moved to the Ballet Club, where he made important works such as *Jardin aux lilas* and *Dark Elegies*. In 1938, he founded the London Ballet, then went to American Ballet Theatre during the war. By then, he was recognised as one of the important choreographers of his generation. He was not asked to make a ballet for the Company until 1967, when Ashton had taken over as Director. Tudor remained bitter about de Valois's treatment of him. She was often reproached for letting this talent escape her.

De Valois, who remained prickly about Tudor, argued that she had room for just two choreographers. Ashton had had more experience, and provided a much greater contrast with her own work. Tudor's ballets were dramatic, steps timed with the impact of gesture. 'Had de Valois had the courage and foresight to resign her own choreographic ambitions, concentrating exclusively on directing the company,' argued the critic Clive Barnes, 'she might have made use of both Ashton and Tudor, with possibly far-reaching results . . . The only real question seems now to have been who was to assist Ashton in the building up of the native repertory.'[53]

De Valois certainly disapproved of Tudor's spending the war in America. She had also cold-shouldered him in the 1930s. In 1974, she told the critic Clement Crisp that she had doubted Tudor's professionalism:

> You know the truth about Tudor? He was a dancer with us – a very bad one – and at the time [1934–35] I could only have four boys and I needed another good classical soloist to set against Helpmann. Tudor was hopeless as a dancer and he wanted to be a choreographer. So I told him he ought to go to de Basil for a couple of years to work and get experience. He needed that sort of professionalism. But he said to me 'How do I know you'll want me again in two years time?' And I told him, 'If I don't, you can come and tell me I have broken my word!'[54]

Tudor did not test her word.

There were changes at the theatres, too. The interchange of companies was gradually being abandoned. From this point on, most of the ballet performances would be at Sadler's Wells. The theatre's finances were in better shape. For the first time in four years, an overall profit had been made. The two theatres had also been given an exemption from Entertainment Tax. Lilian Baylis claimed to have achieved this by approaching the Chancellor of the Exchequer directly: 'Look here. If you don't take it [the tax] off me within a fortnight, I'll have to close both my theatres. Then I shall spend the rest of my life on a lecture tour of the United States, telling them what a philistine you are to kill Shakespeare and opera in your own country.'[55] She didn't mention ballet, but once again it had outsold the opera. In this happier financial climate, the orchestra was expanded. Ballet performances would now be given twice a week.

'The Company has improved almost beyond recognition,' P. W. Manchester wrote after the first night of the 1935–36 season.[56] Touring, with daily performances, had given the dancers greater unity. They were eager to prove themselves, no longer overshadowed by a single great star. The evening clashed with a premiere by the Woizikowsky Ballet, and the theatre was not quite full. There was a good audience, however, and a sense of excitement over several debuts. De Valois had set out the Company's new and growing talent, her new choreographer and the dancers who would have to replace Markova.

Fonteyn danced *Les Rendezvous*, partnered by Harold Turner. In this role, Chappell remembered, Markova had been 'sharp, and quick as a wasp'.[57] The sixteen-year-old Fonteyn could not match her in speed or precision, but she already showed an individual grace. Arnold Haskell, who had tended to sniff at the Vic-Wells as a support for Markova, hailed Fonteyn as a future ballerina. *The Rake's Progress* was danced by Helpmann and Elizabeth Miller, who made more of the ballet than the original cast. The evening ended with *Carnaval*, now with settings after Bakst. Pearl Argyle danced Columbine, with Mary Honer as Papillon.

There are fragmentary film records of the Vic-Wells Ballet, home movies now held in the Rambert archive. The clips of *Les Rendezvous*, from 1936 or later, record both Fonteyn and Elizabeth Miller in the lead. Fonteyn uses her head more, her line and presence already striking. Miller is quicker, neater, with real sparkle in the Markova exit. The Company's dancing is remarkably fresh and vivid. This ballet shows an elegant world. There's gossip and fashion in the kissed greetings, in the curls of wrists and hands. Yet these dancers don't have the hardness of sophistication. They look young and soft and eager, with a bloom on their dancing. When the women jump, they don't get very far from the ground – but every girl lets an expansive ripple flow upwards through her torso before she lands. They're in the air long enough to enjoy it.

In October 1935, Ashton brought *Façade* into the repertory. This comic divertissement, made for the Camargo Society in 1931, was an immediate hit with the Sadler's Wells audience. The ballet is a series of social dance and music-hall numbers, set to William Walton's lively suite. Ashton himself danced the Dago, valiantly partnering Molly Brown's half-witted Débutante through a tango. In the Polka, originally made for Markova, Fonteyn came on, took off her skirt and danced a jaunty solo in her underwear. Turner and Chappell, deadpan in striped blazers and straw hats, danced the Popular Song – bored and blasé music-hall dancers doing their soft-shoe routine for the hundredth time. Over the years, Ashton added and dropped dances. For the first Vic-Wells revival, he made a short-lived new Country Dance in which Helpmann, a Squire in a deerstalker, seduced Pearl Argyle's village maiden.

Ashton loved *Le Baiser de la fée*, Stravinsky's Tchaikovsky-based score. He had danced in the premiere, Nijinska's production for the Rubinstein company, and in November 1935 he staged his own version. Pearl Argyle was the Fairy, in dances that showed off her beautiful line. Harold Turner danced the young man claimed by her kiss, Fonteyn the Bride he left behind. Their duet was a classical pas de deux, Ashton's first use of the formal Petipa structure of adagio, variations and coda. It was also the first of many lyrical adagios he was to make for Fonteyn. Like many other choreographers, Ashton had trouble with the score's awkward structure: the long village scene was a disappointment. Sophie Fedorovitch dressed the ballet with grand simplicity. Her opening storm scene had a backcloth of darkening red semicircles, 'like an angry rainbow'.[58]

Ashton had resisted Fonteyn until now, finding her uninspiring after Markova. During rehearsals, he 'went on and on' at her, trying to make her more precise. She seemed obstinate, but at last burst into tears and flung her arms around his neck. 'From that moment, we were never at real loggerheads again.' He became 'aware of her innate musicality and her wonderful physical proportions. In addition to these gifts she had, even as a young girl, a considerable sense of line. In fact, with her particular proportions, it was very difficult for her to make an unpleasing shape. It was her line that I concentrated upon most; that, and her very beautiful arm movements.'[59] Fonteyn's next challenge came just before Christmas, when she danced Odette in *Swan Lake*. She did not yet have the technique for Odile, so Ruth French danced the third act. At sixteen, Fonteyn was not a finished ballerina – though an excited Arnold Haskell hailed her as one. She already showed qualities of lyricism, rhythm and tenderness. There was clearly more to come.

In January 1936, de Valois staged *The Gods go a'Begging* with

Pearl Argyle and William Chappell as the disguised gods. Hugh Stevenson's designs were an enchanting pastiche of Watteau paintings. De Valois, wrote P. W. Manchester, 'has invested the role of the Serving Maid with some special magic, for every dancer of this part has been completely irresistible'.[60] The ballet was quietly popular, and survived until well after the war. *Apparitions*, the Liszt ballet planned by Ashton and Lambert, had its premiere in February. Helpmann was the Poet, pursuing Fonteyn's Woman in Ball Dress through visions and nightmares. Cecil Beaton, already established as a West End designer, agreed to design the ballet for £50, the flat fee offered by Lilian Baylis. His sets were wonderfully evocative: elaborate scenery for the prologue, brilliant use of gauze and shadows in the central scenes. Distrusting the Sadler's Wells wardrobe department, Beaton turned to the great costumier Karinska, who had realised designs by Derain and Chagall, and who would later design costumes for Balanchine. He gave her his £50 to make the dresses for the ballroom scene. On the first night, the costumes were still arriving by taxi as the opening ballet was being performed. They were ravishing. *Apparitions* established Fonteyn as Ashton's muse. They had shared a taxi after the disastrous dress rehearsal. Ashton 'started to tell me everything that was missing from my interpretation of the woman in *Apparitions* . . . The next night, by some alchemy of despair, I had matured just enough to meet the demands of the ballet.'[61]

Ashton's ballroom was the ballet's finest scene. The Poet pursued the Woman through diagonal lines of dancers, swept up by the feverish music. He seemed to fall deeper into his dream as the corps held lovely frozen poses or plunged into frantic dances. The Woman eluded or taunted him, yet in one encounter she appeared as his loving muse. Later scenes were slighter, but still theatrically effective. Helpmann was compelling. Fonteyn showed a new glamour, without losing her youthful tenderness. 'Ashton has made it live,' wrote Haskell. 'He has conceived it as a romantic and not as a modern looking back upon a quaint period.'[62]

Barabau was the last new ballet of the season. The characters included peasants and, unexpectedly, Fascist soldiers, but de Valois's burlesque comedy made no political points. Edward Burra's bold décor seems to have been the best thing about it. De Valois also made the first new ballet of the 1936–37 season. *Prometheus*, set to Beethoven's only ballet score, was another heavy comedy. June Brae made an impression as the hero's Other Woman. She also danced the Rich Girl in Ashton's next ballet. *Nocturne* was set to Delius's *Paris – the Song of a Great City*. Fonteyn danced a poor flower-seller who fell in love with Helpmann's rich man. When his rich fiancée returned, he abandoned the flower-seller, leaving her heart-broken. Ashton played a compassionate stranger who watches the action. Sophie Fedorovitch's set suggested the city with a balustrade and pillars pasted with advertisements for a ball. Her costumes were in rich, muted colours. It was an atmospheric ballet, beauti-fully judged, and immediately popular.

In 1936, the Vic-Wells Ballet made its first television appearance, dancing excerpts from *Job*. Television was still in its early days, and the screenings were not very effective. Nevertheless, the Company returned to make other programmes a few months later. Lilian Baylis was disappointed by the size of the screen. '*That's* no good,' she said. '*Much* too small. Those girls will never get married like that.'[63]

Fonteyn danced her first *Giselle* in January 1937. Like her Odette, it made an immediate impression: even her immaturity was touching. Her early performances had a particular directness and innocence. Audiences responded to the performance that was already there, and waited eagerly for what would come. Helpmann was a sympathetic partner. Pamela May danced Myrtha, the Queen of the Wilis, with cool and beautiful line.

Lambert, always keen to investigate unfashionable composers, had rediscovered the skating ballet from Meyerbeer's opera *Le Prophète*. He made an irresistibly buoyant arrangement of Meyerbeer numbers and offered it to de Valois. Ashton heard him playing it – 'and I kept saying "That's not for her, that's not for her."'[64] As with *The Rake's Progress*, they swapped.

Les Patineurs was a triumph, technically dazzling and always endearing. Chappell's pretty set framed a skating rink with arches and Chinese lanterns. Ashton used classical steps to create the illu-sion of skating. His dancers slid along in chassés and hopping steps, showed off, teetered or fell. Harold Turner danced the virtuoso Blue Skater, leaping and spinning with terrific panache. Mary Honer turned superb fouettés, 'and you'd think "What could top that?" and then on came Elizabeth Miller, turning with such *speed*, and power. And brio,' remembered the dancer Leslie Edwards.[65] June Brae and Pamela May danced the delightfully unsteady Red Girls. The pace varied with a lyrical duet for Fonteyn and Helpmann. Throughout, Ashton showed off the Company's now considerable technical strength. There were demanding steps for the corps de ballet, including some bounding jumps for the young Michael Somes.

After the sweetness of *Les Patineurs*, Ashton's next work was witty and dry. *A Wedding Bouquet*, which had its premiere in April 1937, was a choral ballet. The composer Lord Berners set words by Gertrude Stein, mostly from her play *They Must. Be Wedded. To Their Wife*. Berners also designed the ballet, dressing dancers and chorus in stylised Edwardian costumes. His faintly sinister frontcloth showed a vast bouquet and the doll-like figures of Bride and Groom. Stein's words introduce characters, explain events or plunge into surreal comment. At Constant Lambert's suggestion, the character descriptions were printed in the programme. Stein loved the ballet. 'English dancers when they dance, dance with freshness and agility and they know what drama is, it all went so very well.'[66]

The wedding party is a series of social disasters. Mary Honer's Bride was blissfully silly, always facing the wrong way in her wedding dance. Fonteyn's lovelorn, dishevelled Julia clung to Helpmann's Bridegroom. Helpmann, who had become associated with romantic roles, established himself as a brilliant comedian. Ashton made a teasing role for de Valois, casting her as Webster, the bossy maid. June Brae was the tipsy Josephine. Julia Farron, the smallest girl in the company, played Pépé the dog. When *A Wedding Bouquet* was new, Fonteyn brought her role too close to tragedy. Later, she found a streak of morbid comedy in the role. At one matinee in 1937, she played two forlorn, demented girls: Julia followed by Giselle.

Checkmate, de Valois's next ballet, had its premiere in June, 1937, Paris, where the British Council had invited the Company to perform there for the Paris International Exhibition. There was hardly any advance publicity, so the theatre was less than half-full. Reviews were good, and attendances picked up a little as the week went on. In London, *Checkmate* had been eagerly awaited. The ballet showed a battle between Love and Death, played out on a chessboard to a commissioned score by Arthur Bliss. Sets and costumes were by E. McKnight Kauffer, best known for the boldly modernist posters he designed for the London Underground. De Valois's production was impressive, strongly characterised, with some bold dancing. It suffered from poor pacing – climaxes were delayed, solos overlong. June Brae made a cruelly seductive Black Queen, disarming and destroying Turner's Red Knight. Helpmann was a pitiful, terrified Red King. May, already known for the beauty of her dancing, showed a new dramatic depth as the tender Red Queen. To de Valois's delight, the great conductor Toscanini named *Checkmate* as his favourite ballet.

On 25 November 1937, Lilian Baylis died. Her death was unexpected, though her health had been battered by years of overwork. She had run two theatres and overseen the creation of national theatre, opera and ballet companies. A Fund for the completion of her theatres was launched in her memory. The aim was to raise £40,000 to clear existing debt and make changes to Sadler's Wells, with subscriptions requested in Baylis's memory. Builders were able to start work on Sadler's Wells by the end of the 1937–38 season.

Sergueyev joined the Company as ballet master this season. His classes were exhausting, and not much liked. 'He would do the worst things for one's leg muscles,' complained Moira Shearer.[67] Pamela May, who enjoyed his teaching, remembers that he would make them dance enchaînements from the classical repertory – such as the petits ronds de jambe from the opening of Odette's variation. '*Three* ronds de jambe, each a little larger and higher,' she recalls. 'Now, that's something you don't see now. We had them drummed into us in class, by the hour.'[68]

In the winter of 1937, Helpmann went to the Old Vic to act Oberon in *A Midsummer Night's Dream*. Tyrone Guthrie's Victorian-style production was influential and exquisite. Vivien Leigh played Titania, Oliver Messel designed sets and costumes and Ninette de

Valois arranged the dances. Helpmann would return to acting; he went on, uniquely, to play leading roles in Stratford and at Covent Garden in the same season.

Horoscope was another ballet conceived by Constant Lambert, who wrote the music and libretto. The ballet, choreographed by Ashton, showed a pair of lovers influenced by the signs of the zodiac. The signs of Leo and Virgo struggled to keep them apart; they were at last united by the Moon and the Gemini. The score was dedicated to Fonteyn, whose affair with Lambert was then at its height. Ashton too was in love, with the young Michael Somes, who had his first leading role in this production. Margaret Dale, who had recently joined the Company, felt that emotion shone through the ballet. 'You've got to understand that Fred and Constant were both in love,' she said.[69] Somes, a handsome and strikingly musical dancer, was a source of pride for the Company and its audiences. He was the first leading man trained at the Vic-Wells School. Ashton gave him a fiery opening dance and a lyrical duet with Fonteyn. As the Moon, Pamela May danced with ideal purity of line. Alan Carter and Richard Ellis danced the Gemini. Most of Sophie Fedorovitch's costumes were in shades of moonlit grey. Her atmospheric drop-curtain showed the zodiac against a clouded sky.

Audiences and critics welcomed *Horoscope* as an important ballet. Within two years, it was lost, abandoned as the Company fled from the Nazi invasion of Holland. Some of the choreography found its way into later ballets. When May and Ellis watched the 1965 ballet *Monotones*, they recognised steps they had danced. 'As I first watched *Monotones*, I knew what was going to happen next,' Ellis told the critic and historian Alastair Macaulay.[70] Perhaps, wrote Mary Clarke, 'the gods loved *Horoscope*: it never suffered from indifferent casting or too frequent performance, and it lives in the memory in the full beauty of its youth.'[71]

The Company staged two short-lived works before the theatre closed for building work. De Valois's *Le Roi nu* was a version of *The Emperor's New Clothes*. *The Judgement of Paris*, by Ashton, was made for a Royal Gala in aid of the Lilian Baylis Memorial Extension. It used a score by the young British composer Lennox Berkeley, but was quickly forgotten. De Valois had hoped also to stage *The Sleeping Beauty* in 1938, but conditions at Sadler's Wells had made this impossible. More space was needed for scenery, for the storage of so many costumes, and on the stage itself. Over the summer, the new scene dock, wardrobe room and ballet rehearsal room were built at Sadler's Wells. The stage was extended, adding fourteen feet in depth.

The threat of war was growing. Work stopped in August due to the Munich crisis, and in September the theatre was still not ready. The 1938–39 season opened with performances in the London sub-urbs Streatham Hill and Golders Green. Back at Sadler's Wells, Ashton staged a revised version of *Harlequin in the Street*, a ballet he had made as a curtain-raiser for a production of *Le Misanthrope* starring Lydia Lopokova. Keynes donated the ballet's sets and cos-tumes, both by Derain, to the Vic-Wells Ballet. Gordon Jacob made a fizzing arrangement of music by Couperin. Alan Carter, a lively and brilliant technician, danced Harlequin. The ballet remained in repertory until 1941, when Carter was conscripted into the armed forces. Derain's delightful sets were then painted over due to the wartime shortage of canvas.

The great event of the season was the new production of *The Sleeping Princess* – as de Valois, following Diaghilev, still called it. Constant Lambert prepared the music, working from the only com-plete score of the ballet then in London. As with *Le Lac des cygnes*, de Valois aimed to go back to the original production – in which Sergueyev had danced as a child. Pamela May remembered:

> None of those Russians were musical – the musicality of those classical ballets we worked out with Ninette, with Constant, and with Fred – but Sergueyev gave you the style. When he staged *The Sleeping Princess* for us in 1939, I used to sit and watch him coach June Brae in the Lilac Fairy solo; he really showed her how to make the charm emerge *through* the steps.[72]

Brae's Lilac Fairy had a magical impact. Mary Clarke remembers how she bowed to the wicked fairy Carabosse, and smiled. That smile staggered John Greenwood's Carabosse: Brae was radiantly sure that things would end happily.

The production was let down by Nadia Benois's dreary designs. De Valois believed that Bakst's sumptuous décor had overwhelmed the Diaghilev production. She decided on an austere staging, without frills or sequins, which would also suit her very limited budget. The dancers were horrified. Fonteyn, who was to dance Aurora, nearly cried when she told her mother about the costumes. 'I could not believe that the scintillating princess described by all who had ever seen the ballet was going to burst onto the stage in such stark, ugly dresses.'[73] At least Fonteyn's costumes were plain. Julia Farron danced the 'finger' variation, misnamed 'The Breadcrumb Fairy' in this production. She wore a headdress with odd brown ears sticking out, like slices of bread so the role was promptly nicknamed 'the Hovis Fairy'.[74] Corps costumes were depressingly dowdy. Wigs, not a Vic-Wells strong point, were particularly dreadful.

The Sleeping Princess was an immediate success with audiences, even though, technically, the Company was not quite ready for it. Cyril Beaumont complained that the production as a whole lacked 'brilliance, grandeur, and style . . . while youth and beauty have a charm of their own, they are not a complete substitute for experience, faultless technique and the ability to achieve appropriate style-atmosphere.'[75] As with *Le Lac des cygnes*, the Company was to grow into the ballet. Several dancers were already impressive. Elizabeth Miller was a delightful Fairy of the Song Birds, Pamela May a purely classical Diamond Fairy. Farron and Brae were admired, and Turner and Honer gave virtuoso performances in the Bluebird pas de deux.

Fonteyn, of course, was Aurora. She had now built up the stamina for full-evening roles, starting with the complete *Lac des cygnes* three months before. Her Aurora, *The Times* reported, was 'probably the best performance of her career'.[76] In 1942, P. W. Manchester wrote that Fonteyn's first entrance was 'like a burst of sunshine. When she comes on for the adagio in the last act there is always a gasp from those members of the audience who are seeing it for the first time . . . and she carries round her an aura of radiance that makes her a real enchanted princess.'[77] As with Odette–Odile and Giselle, Fonteyn took time to grow into her role. Beaumont's complaints about the Company did not exclude its ballerina; some observers felt that she did not wake up in the role until after the war. Her Aurora was to become a defining performance – for her, for The Royal Ballet, and for *The Sleeping Beauty* in the twentieth century. For Fonteyn and for the company, the 1939 production was a first sketch.

After this great effort, the season ended with a flop. Ashton's new *Cupid and Psyche*, to a score by Berners, had its premiere in April. The gods were caricatures with a burlesque Venus and a Fascist, goose-stepping Jupiter – an inept joke for 1939. It was booed by the gallery. Julia Farron and Frank Staff had their first leading roles in this ballet, and its failure may have set back their careers. *Cupid and Psyche* was most notable for Ashton's first use of skimming lifts, the woman held just off the ground, walking on air.

By now, the Vic-Wells Ballet was fully established. It had a distinctive style, a homegrown ballerina and an impressive repertory of new and classical ballets. Its reputation was growing. In March, the company was invited to appear at a Command Performance at Covent Garden, a gala in honour of the French President. They danced two acts of *The Sleeping Princess* – although, as the critic James Monahan admitted, the 'make-believe splendour on the stage could not, in fact, begin to compete with the display on this side of the footlights'.[78] The *Sketch* had reported in February that negotiations had started for a New York visit, to coincide with the 1940 World's Fair. A year earlier, de Valois had considered visits to Australia and South Africa. In the meantime, a new production of *Coppélia* was planned for the next season.

By autumn, all plans had to be cancelled. In August, the Company set out on its usual summer tour. News was bleak: the invasion of Poland was imminent. The British Government had already issued emergency regulations and evacuation plans. On Sunday 3 September, the Company travelled to Leeds. Their train stopped at Crewe, where a public announcement was being broadcast. War had been declared.

THREE

Ballet under the bombs

1939–45

ABOVE Ashton's *Dante Sonata*: 'a seething obscene mass, piled one on the other' with dancers including June Brae (top), Robert Helpmann (centre) and Michael Somes (kneeling foreground): © Gordon Anthony Collection, The Theatre Museum, V&A Images

PREVIOUS PAGE Moira Shearer, Alexis Rassine, Margot Fonteyn, Douglas Steuart, Pamela May, Elizabeth Kennedy and Eric Hryst, ENSA tour to Brussels

At the start of the war, the Vic-Wells Ballet was still a fledgling company. By 1945, it had become a beloved national institution. The company grew in these years, despite severely limited resources. Most of the men, including the Company's chief choreographer, were conscripted into the armed forces. The dancers survived air raids and just escaped the invasion of Holland. They toured to garrison towns and London parks, reaching a wider audience than ever before. They would dance as often as nine times a week. The Company kept going on grit and conviction, as the country kept going in the face of disaster. Those wartime performances were an ideal reflection of national mood.

There was a clamour for the arts in these years, as solace and as an expression of faith in something beyond the war. The pianist Myra Hess arranged concerts in the National Gallery, held in rooms whose pictures had been removed to safety. Kathleen Ferrier also sang there, as well as in factories around the country. Both women became national heroines, as did Fonteyn. In a ballet like *Dante Sonata*, the company expressed the horror of the time. In *Le Lac des cygnes*, they could transcend it. The ballet fan Joan Seaman, later Membership Secretary of the Ballet Association, recalls Fonteyn and Helpmann dancing the Black Swan pas de deux as a V1 flying bomb, nicknamed 'doodle-bug' for its buzzing engine, droned overhead. When the engine cut out, the bomb would fall and explode. As Helpmann guided Fonteyn to her final pose, the engine stopped. 'Not for a second did anybody in that theatre relax . . . The climax of music, dance and explosion coincided perfectly. Fonteyn turned her head to the audience, and gave her special radiant smile.'[1] They had come through: they would survive.

*

69

After hearing the declaration of war, the dancers travelled on to Leeds. Their performances were cancelled: all theatres and cinemas had been closed, by order of the Home Office. The Company was disbanded. Later that month, de Valois opened the School as usual. London theatres remained closed, and the ballet season had to be abandoned. It was Ashton who arranged the first wartime perform-ances, finding backing from Kenneth Clark and Alice von Hofmannsthal for a tour of the regions. Constant Lambert and Hilda Gaunt, the rehearsal pianist, accompanied performances on two pianos. The dancers worked on a co-operative basis: £3 a week plus a share of any profits. The tour was an immediate success. 'It was like a little concert party,' de Valois said later. 'I let them do it on their own, there was no point in me going.' Ashton complained later that she 'absolutely abandoned us . . . When Ninette saw it was going to work she came back and took the whole thing into her hands again.'[2]

The declaration of war was not immediately followed by heavy fighting. There were no attacks on British cities. London theatres started to reopen. The Company returned to Sadler's Wells on 26 December 1939, with a full orchestra. On 23 January, they danced *Dante Sonata*. Ashton had chosen the *Inferno* as a theme. Lambert suggested Liszt's *D'après une lecture de Dante*, and played it for rehearsals. When he came to orchestrate the music, he had Ashton's choreography in mind. The ballet, explained the programme note, 'represents the warring attitudes of two different groups of equally tortured spirits'.[3] In these two groups, the Children of Light and the Children of Darkness, the ballet set good against evil. Neither side won; both were overcome with shame and horror. The choreography was barefoot, expressionist, despairing. The women wore their hair loose. Sophie Fedorovitch's backdrop, based on John Flaxman illustrations of the *Inferno*, suggested earth and clouds in a few flowing lines. She dressed the Children of Light in white. The Children of Darkness had black strips writhing around their bodies. The ballet diarist Lionel Bradley described them 'left in a seething obscene mass, piled one on the other, with Helpmann crawling on the top'.[4] Pamela May danced an anguished solo, rocking back and forth in frustration and grief. The ballet was an overwhelming emotional experience for audiences. At the start of the Vic-Wells season, there had been empty seats in stalls and circle, though the loyal gallery was packed. After *Dante Sonata*, the house sold out.

The Company's men were already being called up. *The Sleeping Princess*, with its large cast, suffered; once Helpmann appeared as the fourth prince in the Rose Adagio before reappearing as the hero in the next act. The Company set out on a second regional tour, again with two pianos. In April, the new *Coppélia* was staged at Sadler's Wells. It had been postponed by only six months. Sergueyev staged the second production – all three acts this time. Mary Honer was a lively Swanilda, dancing with sparkling virtuosity. Helpmann danced Franz, with Claude Newman as Dr Coppélius and Pamela May was outstanding in the last-act divertissement. Chappell's designs were cheerfully bright.

Coppélia was followed by Ashton's next ballet, *The Wise Virgins*. Like *Dante Sonata*, it had piled-up groupings and no pointe-work, but this time Ashton created a mood of serene beauty. William Walton orchestrated music from Bach cantatas, including 'Sheep may safely graze'. Rex Whistler's décor showed a doorway flanked by muscular baroque angels. Fonteyn, with bare feet and gauzy draperies, danced a slow, rapt solo. Mary Honer led the foolish virgins. It became very popular, though some critics complained about the use of Bach. 'This ballet, too, we performed with intense fervour,' wrote Fonteyn, 'though there was a lot of mirth when we saw it advertised on a billboard as "*The Wise Virgins* (subject to alteration)".'[5]

In May 1940, the British Council and the Foreign Office sent the company to Holland, Belgium and France. This was a propaganda tour; a German ballet had just made a similar visit to Holland. The call-up of male dancers was specially deferred to allow the tour to take place. De Valois remembered the shock of arriving in a neutral country: no blackout, no rationing, an audience in full evening dress with kid gloves and tiaras. 'Standing at the corner of the foyer I suddenly find myself very near tears: I have been long enough in the country to recognise the outward signs of courage everywhere.'[6] A German invasion was expected at any moment. The audience was demonstrative, showering the dancers with tulip petals.

The dancers returned to The Hague after each visit to another city. Driving to Hengelo, only five miles from the border, they passed blockades, troops, barbed wire. When they reached the town, German sympathisers spat at the dancers, jeering at the women for wearing make-up. The orchestra wouldn't play all the music for *Façade*; Constant Lambert kept the performance going by singing. The Company were supposed to stay overnight in Hengelo – even though all trains had been commandeered by the government. De Valois wanted to leave after the performance, and compromised on a very early start. On the way to Arnhem, they passed crowds of refugees leaving the city. The Company danced *Dante Sonata* that evening, and received a standing ovation. That night, the Nazi army invaded. Four hours after the Company's departure, Arnhem was occupied.

Air battles started that night, just after the Company had arrived at The Hague. Leaflets were dropped informing 'peace-loving citizens' that the German army was there to protect them. 'However, the German troops will punish every deed of violence committed by the population with a death sentence.'[7] The Company were dragged out of bed; Fonteyn was discovered with Constant Lambert. Most of the dancers rushed to the roof to see the first parachutists landing outside the city. After a burst of gunfire they took refuge in the cellars. Helpmann, the Company's jester, launched into an imitation of a fanatical balletomane: 'Those *poor* girls. Simply surrounded by Germans . . . *Poor* Margot. And such a promising little dancer . . .'[8]

In the morning, de Valois and Lambert set off for the British Embassy, where staff were feeding bonfires with documents. After four days' wait, the Company were evacuated. Personal belongings had to be left behind; scenery, costumes, and music were abandoned. The dancers put on as many clothes as they could. De Valois wore Ashton's new dinner jacket. The journey to the coast was terrifying. The buses kept stopping and changing direction to avoid new groups of parachutists. One girl, who could speak Dutch, understood what the soldiers were saying. 'She was very good,' recalls Julia Farron. 'She didn't tell us.' They travelled back to Britain in the dark, crowded hold of a cargo boat. Farron remembers a government cocktail party for the dancers, held shortly after their return. An official told them that the invasion had been expected. 'If they'd stopped us going, that would have shown that they knew it was coming. So they thought they had to send us.'

The Company had been lucky. No one was killed or injured in the invasion. The sets, costumes and music for *Dante Sonata*, *The Rake's Progress*, *Façade*, *Les Patineurs* and *Horoscope* had all been left behind. Johanna Beek, the impresario for the Holland trip, hid some scores and properties in her own home, returning them at the end of the war. By then, *Horoscope* had fallen from the repertory. *Dante Sonata* was revived at once, in June 1940. Fedorovitch's simple designs were easily recreated, but Lambert's orchestration took longer to prepare. At first, the ballet was danced to a recording he had made with Louis Kentner. The Company stayed at Sadler's Wells throughout the summer of 1940, as fighting in Europe intensified. Audiences were affected by bad news from the front, dwindling during the fall of Norway, the retreat from Dunkirk, the fall of France.

De Valois's next ballet had its premiere in July 1940. *The Prospect Before Us* showed the rivalry of two eighteenth-century theatre managers, both trying to hire the most celebrated dancers of the day. The plot was wildly complicated, but characterisations were sharp and lively. Roger Furse designed the ballet in the style of Rowlandson's cartoons, including a drop-curtain showing 'The Burning of the King's Theatre'. Lambert arranged music by William Boyce. Helpmann clowned magnificently as Mr O'Reilly, one of the managers. His final drunk dance was the ballet's highlight. May was haughtily elegant as the ballerina Mlle Théodore. Another comedy followed. *Façade* was revived, with an extra number for the Dago and a delightful new Foxtrot, bubbling over with steps from 1920s dances like the Charleston and the Black Bottom. Critics disapproved of John Armstrong's new designs, replacing those lost in Holland, and of the Company's broader comic playing. Audiences still adored the ballet.

The season ended on 6 September 1940. The next day, the London Blitz began: fifty-eight consecutive days of bombing, with frequent heavy raids for months afterwards. The Sadler's Wells Theatre was commandeered for the newly homeless. Sergueyev and his wife were among them, arriving with their belongings neatly and sensibly arranged. They were, they explained, 'used to being refugees'.[9] The School continued at Sadler's Wells for most of the war, but the ballet management was moved to Lancashire. The Company itself set out on a tour of garrison theatres and regional towns. Conditions were makeshift, and most of the audiences had never seen ballet. Some were unconvinced; Fonteyn described the bang of seats when people walked out. Many more were converted. Tyrone Guthrie, who became Administrator of the Vic-Wells organisation after Baylis's death, remembered his own misgivings about the garrison tour:

> Nervously we decided that it was our patriotic duty . . . to expose the company to the jeers and whoops and wolf-whistling of uncouth creatures called troops. Little did we know. *Les Sylphides*, with a young gentleman whirling around in white tights among white muslin coryphées to waltzes and mazurkas of Chopin, proved exactly the stuff to give the troops. Indeed, what everybody wanted almost as much as food or drink during those years was to see youthful and beautiful creatures beautifully moving through ordered evolutions to a predestined and satisfactory close.[10]

Wartime touring made ballet popular – 'a sell-out always and everywhere', said Guthrie – throughout the country, across a broad public. By 1945, the Sadler's Wells Ballet, as it was called from 1941, had become in practice the national company of Britain.

In January 1941, they came back to London. Despite the bombing, the city was trying to carry on as usual. Audiences were returning to theatres. The manager Bronson Albery offered his New Theatre (now the Albery) to the three Vic-Wells companies. Guthrie hoped to 'make the comparatively easy success of the Ballet finance and further the aims of its sister company, the Opera' – that is, to spend the growing ballet profits to cover opera losses. De Valois refused. She suggested that Albery should take over the management of the ballet company, which, wrote Guthrie, 'for all practical purposes, ceased to be part of the organisation which Miss Baylis had built up'.[11] Yet the ballet's success remained an example to the theatre company: when Laurence Olivier and Ralph Richardson came out of the armed forces in 1944, the success of de Valois's organisation was one model for their revived Old Vic company.

At the New Theatre, performances were given during the day, giving the audience time to get home before darkness, the blackout and night bombing. The productions were adjusted for the theatre's tiny stage. The *Wedding Bouquet* chorus was abandoned, and Constant Lambert declaimed the words from a box – dry, witty and with occasional devastating interpolations. Ashton's next ballet, *The Wanderer*, was performed at the end of January. He and Lambert had chosen Schubert's *Fantasia in C*; Lambert explained that the central character, played by Helpmann, was 'a mental and emotional traveller' reacting to love, success, doubt and despair. In this, Ashton came close to the symbolism of Massine's recent symphonic ballets. Fonteyn was cast against type, representing worldly success in an acrobatic pas de deux. May and Somes danced a lyrically erotic pas de deux, lovers 'tenderly intertwined, absorbed in mutual delight'.[12] The ballet was criticised for this explicit depiction of sex, and for its designs. In these years, the Company had a striking design policy, with successful ballets by Fedorovitch, Furse, Whistler. *The Wanderer* was the painter Graham Sutherland's only stage work. His two backcloths were enlarged paintings; there were, wrote Beryl de Zoete, 'moments when the dance groups actually seem to take mobile form from within the canvas'.[13] Sutherland's costumes were ugly, though: several men were put into khaki shorts, like Boy Scouts, while Fonteyn's tights and feathers suggested an equestrienne.

The Company returned to London in May 1941, after another tour. By late spring, days were long enough to allow early-evening performances, and attendances rose. The next new production was de Valois's *Orpheus and Eurydice*. She had planned to stage Gluck's opera at Sadler's Wells, using both opera and ballet companies. Now the two were touring independently, and she settled for a ballet, keeping some recitatives and arias. The result was poorly paced, but Pamela May was a moving Eurydice.

That summer, de Valois and Lambert took the risk of bringing back the orchestra. 'I can still hear and see his brisk attack on a rather veteran orchestra,' she wrote. 'There is nothing more heart-ening or more exhilarating than a true professional demanding *his* money or your life.' As one of the players told Lambert, 'Tchaikovsky comes up nice and fresh, don't he, Sir?'[14] The orchestra was a triumphant success, improving ticket sales at once. With the orchestra, de Valois brought the classics back into the repertory. It was another risk. The New Theatre stage was small, and the Company was not at full strength. But the full-length ballets were popular, they were good training for the dancers, and they required few male soloists.

Most had by now been called up. Of the pre-war men, only the Australian Helpmann and the young John Hart remained. Dancers would come back to perform when they got the chance. Michael Somes, given forty-eight hours' leave, once danced the Blue Bird and his first Carabosse in a single performance of *The Sleeping Princess*. George Bernard Shaw, Haskell and Osbert Sitwell all argued that male dancers should be exempt. De Valois refused to join this campaign, patriotically accepting the call-up. She promoted boys from the School when the older generation left. Before he was called up, at the age of twenty-one, Hart had danced the lead in all five classical ballets. Inevitably, the standard of male dancing fell.

Helpmann held the Company together. That season, he danced Carabosse as well as the Prince in *The Sleeping Princess*. In *Coppélia*, he moved from Franz to Dr Coppélius. He played the role with comic gusto, influencing generations of British dancers. Helpmann was a star, but he was no virtuoso. His success and prestige, together with the shortage of adult men, encouraged an emphasis on characterisation over technique. That tendency increased after Ashton was called up in summer 1941. His sense of ballet as dancing had prevented Ashton, wrote de Zoete, 'from allowing miming to encroach on dancing. It is in this direction that the Sadler's Wells Ballet is now tending . . . it is to counteract this trend that his presence would above all be valuable.'[15]

There were other shortages. Sophie Fedorovitch, with her gift for simplicity, cut rationed fabric without wasting a scrap. Tarlatan, timber and electrics were in short supply; a lack of gelatines made it difficult to light ballets correctly. Ballet shoes were exempted from rationing, but they were still hard to find. Food rationing was severe. The dancers were doing exhausting physical work on inadequate diets. Devoted fans would save their coupons for favourite performers.

At the same time, the workload increased. In the summer season of 1941, the Company gave early-evening performances six days a week, a matinee on Thursdays and three performances on Saturdays. On the first of these Saturdays, Fonteyn danced *Giselle* and *Les Patineurs*, rested during *Coppélia*, then appeared in *Les Sylphides*, *The Wise Virgins* and *Façade* in the evening. Helpmann danced in all six ballets that day. The Saturday schedule was abandoned, Fonteyn wrote, after 'one or two girls had fainted on stage'.[16]

In October, Pamela May was injured while dancing the Lilac Fairy. Mary Honer, dancing the Blue Bird duet at that performance, stepped forward and finished the scene for her; Julia Farron then danced the Lilac Fairy in the apotheosis. The substitutions were managed with perfect aplomb, but it was more than a year before May danced again. She and June Brae both married early in the war. Both had children, and spent time away from the Company.

There was also the strain of regular touring. 'We would sleep in the trains,' recalls Grey. 'I've slept in the rack where the cases go, and sometimes we'd put the cases down the middle and sleep criss-cross.' Helpmann kept the Company entertained on long journeys, acting out roles – a touring prima donna, a North Country mother, a wanton Edwardian maid – with Lambert as his supporting cast. The Company was caught up in air raids outside London. When the dancers arrived in Bath after one attack, they found their hotel destroyed, and camped out in the theatre. There were more bombs that night. The dancer Jean Bedells got up when she heard crackling, 'and there was the back of the theatre . . . scene dock blazing away.'[17] Helpmann and Lambert were already fighting the fire. The theatre was saved. The Company's scenery was still at the railway station, but it was hardly safe. A time-bomb had been discovered close by.

The loss of Ashton was the worst blow. He left for the RAF in August 1941. The Company needed new ballets to draw audiences and De Valois could not handle the modern repertory alone. She chose Helpmann as the Company's next choreographer. He had almost no choreographic experience, but he had a strong sense of drama, knowledge of theatre production and a loyal public. Lambert, always a good source of ideas for ballets, suggested arranging a Purcell score for a ballet on Milton's masque *Comus*. The ballet had its premiere in January 1942. Helpmann spoke two of Milton's speeches, and arranged the action in mime. Fonteyn played the chaste Lady. The ballet was gorgeously designed by Oliver Messel. Helpmann's dances were thin, but this was a handsome, professional production. The general popularity of *Comus*, and of the Company, is suggested by a passing line in an Agatha Christie thriller. The heroine mentions seeing '*Comus* at Sadler's Wells and it was lovely and Margot Fonteyn danced like a kind of frozen angel.'[18] By that stage, neither the Sadler's Wells Ballet nor Fonteyn needed any introduction.

Ballet was becoming spectacularly popular. The wartime performances won audiences who stayed loyal to the Company: the New Theatre public became the regulars of Covent Garden. Seat prices were modest, but the Company began to make substantial profits. There were good advance sales for Helpmann's next ballet, *Hamlet*, which opened in May 1942. It had been rehearsed during the spring tour. Helpmann chose *Hamlet*, he claimed later, 'to convince Tyrone Guthrie that I could play the play!'[19] Working with the theatre director Michael Benthall, Helpmann showed the play's events rushing through the mind of the dying hero. There was a Freudian strain to the ballet, with Hamlet confusing the images of Ophelia and his mother. The ballet, staged to Tchaikovsky's Fantasy Overture, was concise, fast-moving and well acted. It had superb designs by Leslie Hurry, a young artist whose work Helpmann had seen in a West End gallery. Hurry's sets had architectural weight and dream-like, distorted perspective, with an avenging figure looming overhead. In the little New Theatre, the effect was overwhelming. Supporting roles were strongly played, but Helpmann's Hamlet dominated the production. Two years later, he 'played the play' at the Old Vic, and acted the role again at Stratford in 1948.

In August 1942, the Company gave a week of open-air performances in Victoria Park, Bethnal Green. They were seen by thousands: 2,200 at one performance. The autumn tour was the most successful yet. Back in London, Helpmann produced *The Birds*, designed to show off the Company's younger dancers. Chiang Yee designed a delicately pretty Chinese garden and some slightly clumsy bird costumes. The choreography was flimsy, but Moyra Fraser made the most of her role, a Hen trying to be a Nightingale. There was a classical pas de deux for Beryl Grey and Alexis Rassine. Grey had danced her first Odette–Odile five months earlier, on her fifteenth birthday. She was a tall, long-limbed dancer, with an exceptionally strong technique and an easy, expansive style. Her fouettés were effortless – she could turn them to the left or the right – and Haskell remembered her rushing to the dressing rooms, 'asking the older girls how to be wicked as Odile'.[20]

Rassine, a South African dancer, had made his name with the Anglo-Polish Ballet. On the next tour, he partnered Fonteyn in her first performance as Swanilda. Mary Honer had left the ballet for pantomime, and Fonteyn shared the role with Peggy van Praagh. Helpmann continued to dance Dr Coppélius. 'I am guilty of encouraging Helpmann's interpretation of Dr Coppélius up the height of its utmost humour,' wrote de Valois. 'Great clowns are rare and Helpmann clowned Dr Coppélius with genius.'[21]

By 1943, seats at the New Theatre had to be rationed when the Sadler's Wells Ballet was appearing: no more than four tickets per patron for any one performance. *The Quest* was the first new production of the year. Ashton, given special leave from the RAF, made a patriotic affair based on the first book of Spenser's *Faerie Queene*. It was the third literary ballet in little more than a year. William Walton was commissioned to write the score, following Ashton's detailed scenario. He wrote slowly; the music reached Ashton a page or two at a time. The ballet was choreographed on tour; they spent a week in Coventry, Grey remembers, waiting for more music. 'And it *didn't* come, for the whole of that week. He choreographed the whole last scene without the music. He had told Walton what he wanted, so it was sort of there, but lacking the inspiration that music always gives dancers.' And choreographers: *The Quest* was a weak ballet. Helpmann and Fonteyn played the leads, and two younger dancers attracted notice. Grey played the wicked Duessa, 'with stuffed breasts' to make her more womanly. Ashton cast Moira Shearer as Pride. Like Grey, Shearer had started to dance solo roles that year. She was already known for her beautiful colouring, red hair and very white skin. She danced with crisp elegance and growing self-possession. John Piper designed attractive sets, with one scene based on a masque design by Inigo Jones.

Le Lac des cygnes was refurbished in August. Leslie Hurry designed new sets and costumes. Like his *Hamlet* designs, they had a swirling theatrical intensity; painted swans loomed out of his scenery for lake and court. Hurry revised the production several times, making it simpler and clearer. From the beginning, he gave the ballet a new richness and grandeur, in spite of the shortage of materials. This was the most expensive production yet staged by the company. Fonteyn and Helpmann danced the first night. Later performances were led by Grey with David Paltenghi.

Hurry's designs, with their sense of fantasy, underlined the drama in the Sadler's Wells approach to the classics. De Valois and her team insisted on clean dancing, on purity of line, but the dancing itself was dramatic. Almost fifty years later, Fonteyn coached a group of young Royal Ballet dancers in Odette's second-act mime scene. 'She taught wonderfully well,' remembers dancer and répétiteur Donald MacLeary. 'She said, "Odette gets verbal diarrhoea. At last, she's got somebody to talk to." She's frightened, then once she starts talking, she can't stop.' The music for this scene is quick and urgent: 'She gets very excited. "But wait a minute!" And the prince keeps interrupting. Suddenly she realises she's said too much, and retreats again.' This sense of drama, the story lived moment by moment, continued through the ballet. Throughout the second act, Odette turns to the prince and retreats from him. Her fear and her need are built into the dancing, into the steps and floor patterns.

The first performance was a benefit for Sergueyev, who was retiring as ballet master. He was replaced by Vera Volkova. Fonteyn had already taken lessons at Volkova's London studio, and was to work closely with her on classical roles. 'Vera was marvellously Russian – but without the carry-on: absolutely pure,' said Julia Farron. 'The best teacher Margot ever had, without any doubt at all.'[22] After the war, de Valois offered Volkova a permanent position with Sadler's Wells – on condition that she close her own studio. Volkova refused; the Sadler's Wells dancers were forbidden to attend her classes. 'Ninette was very possessive,' remembers Grey:

> It was all right if a teacher was in the company, but someone outside – she wasn't keen. Probably because she had had a lot of press opposition. People didn't believe there could be a British company, they thought the British didn't have the temperament. She didn't have an easy time building up the company, and I think she wanted to prove that she could do it all on her own.

Volkova, let slip by de Valois, went to teach in Copenhagen. Under Kenneth MacMillan, the Company tried to entice her back, without success.

De Valois's next ballet, *Promenade*, had its premiere in Edinburgh in October 1943. It was a slight, pretty work to a lively arrangement of Haydn. Like *The Birds*, it showed off the younger dancers. There was a wistful pas de deux for Grey and Paltenghi, and an eager, speedy solo for Pauline Clayden. Moira Shearer was deft and very appealing in a pas de trois with Rassine and Ray Powell. Gordon Hamilton, who had given de Valois the nickname 'Madam', played an aged butterfly-hunter, chasing insects as dances went on around him. For the finale, de Valois used Breton folk steps that she had learned from Lieutenant de Cadenet of the Fighting French Air Force.

Back in London, Pamela May rejoined the Company, giving an overwhelming performance in *Dante Sonata*. The number of new productions had dropped, but there were several revivals over the winter. *Job* returned in December. As in early Vic-Wells days, the cast had to be reduced; this time the cuts affected the Children of God and the Sons of the Morning. *Le Spectre de la rose* was revived for Fonteyn and Rassine in February 1944. The woman's role had been made for Tamara Karsavina, who coached this revival. The ballet was swamped by Rex Whistler's elaborate new designs.

The next new ballet came in June 1944. The year before, de

Valois had engaged Andrée Howard, who had made ballets for Rambert, as choreographer for the School. *Le Festin de l'araignée* (later called *The Spider's Banquet*) set to Roussel's score, was Howard's first work for the adult dancers. The painter Michael Ayrton, a friend of Lambert's, designed a sinister, oversized garden set. Celia Franca prowled venomously as the Spider while Shearer and Clayden played fluttering insects. It was a slight, disappointing ballet.

The first flying bomb attacks came that month. During one performance, a bomb landed a few hundred yards from the theatre. The blast from the explosion blew open the doors at the back of the Dress Circle, but the performance continued. Given this new danger, de Valois decided to close the School early for the holidays. It remained closed for three months – the only interruption to teaching in the whole of the war. 'When it's yourself, you feel, "I know I'll be all right,"' remembers Anne Heaton, who started training during wartime. 'But when I look back at my parents, having to let me go up to London, just praying that it would be all right . . .'[23] In June, the Allied armies landed in France. Paris was liberated on 24 August 1944.

In September, after a short holiday and another tour, the Company opened at the Princes Theatre, now the Shaftesbury. This was larger than the New Theatre, with a steeply raked stage. Helpmann's new ballet, *Miracle in the Gorbals*, had its premiere in October. It was a modern morality play, set in a Glasgow slum, with sharply realistic designs by Edward Burra and a short, emphatic new score by Arthur Bliss. Helpmann played the Stranger, a Christ figure who brings a Suicide to life, is denounced by the authorities and killed by a mob. He 'allowed himself little variety as the Stranger,' wrote Mary Clarke, 'being content to walk through the ballet with an air of sanctity that might well have antagonised any hard-boiled community.'[24] There was little dancing, but the company gave vivid dramatic performances. Haskell admired the ballet so much that he wrote a book about it; several other critics dismissed it as melodrama. It was sensationally popular.

Nocturne was revived at the end of the season. Ashton, on leave, took the final rehearsals and played his old mime role, the Spectator.

He was welcomed back with a standing ovation, and made a speech from the stage. 'I want to thank you for the affection with which you have remembered my ballet,' he said, 'and to tell you how pleased I am to discover that, after three and a half years' absence, I can still raise my arms.'[25]

With the end of the war in sight, the Company toured further afield. In January 1945, they returned to Europe. The visit to Brussels and Paris was organised by the British Council and ENSA – the Entertainment's National Service Association, fondly nick-named 'Every Night Something Awful'. The dancers were issued with heavy khaki uniforms, and needed them. Brussels lay under heavy snow, and for the first four days there was no hot water, no heating, no electric light during the day. But there was no shortage of tinned American food, or of champagne cocktails. Performances sold out within hours, and the Company was warmly received. In Paris, the British Council had to arrange extra performances. The Company spent a month in the city, taking classes with the Russian teachers based there and meeting French dancers, design-ers and musicians.

In April, the Sadler's Wells Ballet returned to the New Theatre for a ten-week season. Michael Somes and Harold Turner were the first male dancers to return from the Forces. Ashton was released shortly afterwards. *Le Lac des cygnes* and *Coppélia* were both revived. Pamela May danced her first Swanilda. The role is associated with soubrette dancers, but the purely classical May was irresistible in it. 'She always made dancing so exciting and such fun that I longed to be up there on the stage with her,' remembered Peter Wright.[26] The Company danced *Coppélia* on VE night. Helpmann, clowning extravagantly, hung Coppélia's balcony with Union Jack flags. The last wartime season took place at the reopened Sadler's Wells. It was a success, but it was clear that the Company had outgrown its old home. Change was in the air. The Company had been invited to move to the Royal Opera House, Covent Garden.

Throughout the war, the Royal Opera House had been run as a dance hall by Mecca Enterprises. It now became available as a lyric theatre after careful negotiations by Maynard Keynes and the Council for the Encouragement of Music and the Arts. David

Webster, a businessman who had managed the Liverpool Philharmonic Society during the war, was appointed General Administrator at Covent Garden. The new theatre would have resident companies, opera and ballet. The opera company would be built up from scratch. Massine had written offering his services for a new ballet company. Instead, Keynes turned to Sadler's Wells.

Here was recognition of the fact that the Sadler's Wells Ballet was a national company in all but name. Uncharacteristically, de Valois hesitated. Her company was already overstretched, depleted by constant touring. 'I visualised the possibility of a sudden weakening – a position akin to that of an army, its lines stretched to a point where a break through could be effected almost anywhere,' she wrote. Yet de Valois had been campaigning for something like this. In April 1943, Eveleigh Leith – the honorary secretary to the Vic-Wells Ballet Fund, and the Company's acting press representative – had argued in *The Dancing Times* that the Company should become the National Ballet. Once the war was over, the School should be enlarged, the Company should be seen 'in the heart of London', and a second company established at Sadler's Wells.[27] De Valois's opportunity had come, but she had doubts. The Royal Opera House had shown Russian ballet only in summer seasons. She and her dancers would be

> setting out on the adventure of making this building extend
> its hospitality to us throughout the year, challenging it, at the
> beginning, with nothing more than a bedraggled, war-weary
> company. It could be likened to a crazy nightmare, wherein I
> might be given Buckingham Palace, a few dusters, and told to
> get on with the spring cleaning . . .[28]

Ashton had no such qualms. 'If you won't,' he is said to have told de Valois, 'I will.'[29] She was persuaded.

When the ballet moved to Covent Garden, the Sadler's Wells Theatre lost the most profitable branch of its organisation. The theatre was given some compensation by the new Arts Council of Great Britain, the peacetime successor to CEMA. The ballet used some of its wartime profits to pay off half the theatre's building loan. Much of the rest was spent on new buildings for the enlarged ballet school. De Valois was still obliged to provide dancers for the Sadler's Wells Opera. As the 1943 plan had proposed, she set up a second company at the old theatre. This was a disappointment for Marie Rambert, who had hoped to move into Sadler's Wells. De Valois wrote to Rambert, explaining why she needed a second company. It would be more than an opera ballet; as early as 1940, de Valois had been planning 'a nursery where young choreographers would be given a chance'.[30] Cautiously, she wanted to keep a link with Sadler's Wells, in case the Covent Garden scheme failed.

Once again, de Valois was planning for the future. The younger company would use senior students from the School, led by established artists such as June Brae and Leo Kersley, with Peggy van Praagh as Ballet Mistress. The second company quickly established itself as the touring branch of the Sadler's Wells organisation. The choreographers John Cranko and Kenneth MacMillan, among others, were given early chances here. The Sadler's Wells Theatre Ballet relationship with the Covent Garden branch was complicated. At times, it acted as a nursery, a place for experiments; at others, it developed into a larger and much more independent troupe. From the 1970s, under Peter Wright, it took the independent course, developing into the present Birmingham Royal Ballet.*

The School and companies were strengthened at once by a generation of dancers from the Commonwealth. New Zealand, South Africa, Australia and Canada had teachers but few professional opportunities. The Sadler's Wells Ballet already had Australian and South African dancers, including Helpmann and Rassine. As soon as the war was over, many more headed for Britain, for the already famous Sadler's Wells Ballet. These dancers were often better fed and healthier than their British counterparts, who had suffered air raids and rationing. Alexander Grant put his early toughness and stamina down to good New Zealand food. The Irish de Valois, following the fashion of her class and generation, persisted in describing her company as English – once writing in two sentences that Helpmann, 'arrived from Australia', had become a 'leading English dancer'.[31]

* For a full history of the touring company, see Sarah C. Woodcock, *The Sadler's Wells Royal Ballet, now the Birmingham Royal Ballet*, Sinclair-Stevenson, 1991.

The Sadler's Wells Ballet was now formally accepted as the national company of Great Britain. On 20 February 1946, they would reopen Covent Garden with a new production of *The Sleeping Beauty*.

FOUR

Covent Garden, and the world

1946–49

ABOVE *Symphonic Variations*. Left to right: Margot Fonteyn, Henry Danton, Pamela May, Michael Somes, Moira Shearer, Brian Shaw: © Getty Images
PREVIOUS PAGE The reopening of Covent Garden, 20 February 1946

The move to Covent Garden began with a period of frantic work. The Company had six weeks to rehearse the new production. All around them, the building itself was being restored. The dance floor, once laid over the whole of the stalls, had gone, but decorators were at work in the auditorium. Covent Garden firemen chased rats through the building. Dancers rehearsed on one side of the stage while carpenters hammered and sawed on the other. Lambert was busy training a full-size orchestra – seventy players at last. Male dancers were still returning from military service, sometimes coming in for class before they received their discharge papers. 'Project! Project!' de Valois kept saying in rehearsals. 'English people don't *project* – you've got to get to the back of the gallery.'[1]

The bustle was a good introduction to the new theatre. Great avenues lead up to the Paris Opéra; the London opera house was tucked in beside a vegetable market. 'The great thrill of approaching the theatre from the front', wrote Arlene Croce in 1979, 'was the sudden sight of its pediment and white columns jutting from the ramble of streets and shops – as surprising as finding a four-poster in an upper berth.'[2] David Webster, who had run a department store in Liverpool, fostered a sense of community across the building. Stage-door keepers knew every name; ushers clubbed together to buy flowers for performers. Covent Garden was not ideal for dancing. The nineteenth-century auditorium is horseshoe-shaped; sightlines are often poor. But it is a welcoming space, with a surprising sense of intimacy for such a large theatre. In 1946, Covent Garden had no large rehearsal room. The Company had to work in nearby halls or studios, or in the foyers of the theatre itself. (There were other suggestions. Kenneth Clark, director of the National Gallery but also a member of the Covent Garden Board, once tried to make the Gallery available as rehearsal space.) The theatre was still associated with the triumphant seasons of Russian ballet. By dancing there, the Sadler's Wells Ballet claimed new status. The Company also moved away from the Baylis ideal of a people's theatre. From the beginning, Covent Garden prices were higher than those at Sadler's Wells or the New Theatre. Even so, there were all-night queues for tickets.

In 1946, there was a new idealism at Covent Garden. The restoration of the theatre was an extraordinary gesture for a bombed, almost bankrupt nation. Setting up the Arts Council of Great Britain was one of the last acts of the wartime coalition government, continuing the wartime recognition of the importance of art. *The Sleeping Beauty*, as the ballet was now called, would symbolise a new awakening after long years of war. The production, designed by Oliver Messel, was a vision of splendour at a time of bitter austerity. Paint and canvas were scarce, rationing was still in force, coupons had to be found for fabrics, gloves and boots. The Queen's train was made from somebody's velvet curtains. Messel was still working on the costumes as the curtain went up for the first night; Beryl Grey sewed more sprigs of lilac onto her tutu between entrances. Messel's sets combined airy architectural fantasy with a sense of place. The soft colours set the dancers off, surrounding them with light and space. Not all the costumes were satisfactory, but the range of colour was beautiful: groupings looked marvellous. The production followed Sergueyev's text, with a few new additions. Ashton choreographed a Garland dance for the first act, and reworked the Jewel Fairies' dance as a pas de trois for 'Florestan and his two sisters'. Following Nijinska, de Valois made a short Russian number, 'The Three Ivans', to follow the grand pas de deux.

The first-night gala 'smelt bravely of mothballs', wrote de Valois. 'I donned the evening dress that I had not left in Holland, and I presume Frederick Ashton was resplendent in the dinner jacket that I slept in on the straw of the cargo boat'.[3] The production was a triumph from the first, but the Company were still adjusting to the new theatre. Fonteyn danced with new strength and grace; but, wrote Mary Clarke, 'she had yet to take the measure of the great auditorium.'[4] Helpmann, dancing Carabosse and the Prince, had no such trouble. Beryl Grey danced the Lilac Fairy with grand ease and warmth. Pamela May, Moira Shearer, Margaret Dale and Alexis Rassine were all impressive in solo roles. Julia Farron was a gracious Queen, with Leslie Edwards as Catalabutte, the master of ceremonies. How 'beautifully Constant Lambert conducted', wrote Philip Hope-Wallace: 'there is no ballet conductor more appreciative of the enormous importance of his role; with him choreography and score always seem to flow together as if mutually inspiring one another.'[5] On the second night, May danced a purely classical Aurora, with great beauty of line. That evening, the Bolshoi-trained Violetta Prokhorova (later Elvin) danced the Blue Bird pas de deux. She had a strong, supple back and beautifully expansive movement. Early in March, Shearer made her debut as Aurora. She showed immediate stage presence and fluid style, though she too had difficulty reaching the whole auditorium. Grey, who danced the role at the end of the season, was a favourite with the gallery: her dancing had a scale and warmth that filled the house.

Ashton knew that Fonteyn's performance was not projecting. In later performances, he remembered:

> I went all over the house . . . and I said, 'You're *still* not registering. I don't know what's the matter. I've been upstairs, I've been downstairs,' and then one day she held a pose a fraction longer and I went back and I said, 'I've got it. You've been used to a small theatre. You've got to *hold* everything much more, so as to register . . . You mustn't go rushing too quickly. Show everything clearly.'[6]

The Company grew into *The Sleeping Beauty*, and into their theatre. The classics were easily translated to a grander scale. Not all the ballets transferred so well. On 18 March, the company danced a triple bill of *The Rake's Progress*, *Nocturne* and *Miracle in the Gorbals* – one by each of the Company's choreographers. *The Rake's Progress* was given in the settings made for the New Theatre, framed by a false proscenium. Dancers and ballet looked diminished. Sophie Fedorovitch was unhappy with the look of *Nocturne* on the larger stage. Ashton's new ballet, *Symphonic Variations*, had been scheduled for 20 March, but was postponed when Michael

Somes was injured. It was replaced by *Dante Sonata*, which lost most of its impact in peacetime.

With the postponement of *Symphonic Variations*, Helpmann's *Adam Zero* became the first new ballet at Covent Garden. It was designed to show off the capabilities of the new theatre. *Adam Zero* was bursting with technical wizardry: lifting and falling platforms, changes in lighting, costume changes and use of a moving cyclorama. Michael Benthall's allegorical scenario showed the life of man in terms of a ballet company staging a new work. Because Benthall and Helpmann were concerned with life cycles, most dancers played roles with several aspects. June Brae played the Choreographer (Creator and Destroyer) and Ballerina (first love, wife, mistress). Between symbolism and stage effects, there was no room for dancing, though Brae – who had led the first performance of the new touring company just two days before – was admired. *Adam Zero* was soon dropped from the repertory.

Ashton's new work had its premiere a fortnight later. After all the recent literary ballets, *Symphonic Variations* presented classical dancing on a bare stage. Ashton had started with an elaborate theme of the seasons, moving from winter to fertility, then pared it away until only dancing remained. There are stylised trees in one of Sophie Fedorovitch's sketches for a backdrop; the final version showed sweeping lines on a ground of fresh green. The ballet opens with an image of cool repose, the six dancers standing still. The three women start to move to César Franck's insistent piano line, and return to stillness. A man joins them and the dancing quickens, the women circling him and holding poses. Dances flower in *Symphonic Variations*, solos flowing out of a group dance and then returning to it. Ashton choreographed fast allegro steps, a duet with skimming lifts, radiantly simple linking passages where the dancers took hands and ran into place. Feeling in this ballet is sublimated; when Fonteyn curved one arm around Somes's head, a caress became a sculptural line. The ballet grows in warmth and freshness, but it keeps its sense of serenity. The open space of the Covent Garden stage was part of Ashton's ballet. The dancing was no longer too small for the theatre.

The original dancers were Fonteyn, May, Shearer, Somes, Brian

Shaw and Henry Danton. They were perfectly matched. The balance of his cast was important to Ashton. Having spent so long away from the Company, he consulted Fonteyn and May about the third woman. He was interested in Shearer – 'but I don't know her work,' he told May. 'I'd have Beryl Grey, but she's too big.'[7] He also considered Gillian Lynne, who had danced in the last revival of *The Wanderer*. At last he returned to Shearer. All three women had danced Aurora that season. Apart from their pure classicism and even height, there was a new harmony in the women's colouring. 'Margot is dark, Moira is red, and you are – mouse,' Fedorovitch told Pamela May, persuading her to dye her hair blonde for the opening night.[8] It is hard to believe, looking at Ashton's choreography for Somes, Danton and Shaw, just how much British male dancing had been depleted by the war. He asked for double tours en l'air, off-balance turns, considerable strength in partnering.

The state of the Company's men was under discussion that month. The first foreign ballet companies were beginning to visit Britain. Roland Petit's Ballets des Champs-Elysées arrived early in April, starring the astounding Jean Babilée. American Ballet Theatre had a Covent Garden season that summer, bringing a strong male corps. British male dancers had been weakened by interrupted careers, by poor food, by too much work too young. Visiting companies showed how far standards had slipped. 'De Valois was adamant in her refusal to invite as guest artists any of the new young dancers from abroad who, not having lost a slice of their careers, were then more inspiring to watch,' wrote Fonteyn. 'Said de Valois emphatically, "I will not do it. If I take any of these foreign boys it will discourage our own dancers and we will never develop a tradition for male dancers."'[9]

Giselle was revived in June, with new designs by James Bailey. They were suitably romantic, but some critics found them too elaborate; Bailey later revised his designs. Fonteyn was partnered by Alexis Rassine with Beryl Grey as an impressive Myrtha, and fine dancing from Shearer and Lynne as Moyna and Zulma. By now, Fonteyn was learning to project to the whole theatre, but her Giselle seemed less moving than before. In her decades of dancing the role, she was admired for the beauty of her dancing, her musical phrasing, her pathos. Yet her Giselle seems never to have had the authority of her Aurora or her Odette–Odile. She reconceived the role several times – not just deepening her interpretation, but changing it. In a 1960s film of the second act, she dances with grave simplicity, her long-breathed phrases filling the musical line, without distortion or exaggeration. Yet that *Giselle* is less affecting than a shaky, silent film from the 1930s, where a teenaged Fonteyn dances the village scenes with springy rhythm and wonderful, vulnerable happiness.

The first Covent Garden season had been a triumph. The second began patchily. *Coppélia* was revived, with exaggerated new designs by Chappell. *Les Sirènes*, Ashton's second ballet at the Royal Opera House, was an elaborate flop. Working with Cecil Beaton and Lord Berners, Ashton assembled various characters on an Edwardian beach: a Spanish dancer, a tenor, an Eastern potentate. There was little dancing, and the comedy fell self-indulgently flat. The next new production was arranged by Constant Lambert. He had long loved Purcell's semi-opera *The Fairy Queen*. At last, Covent Garden gave him the resources to stage it, using both ballet and opera companies with actors from the Old Vic. He cut the text, edited the score and worked closely with Ashton, the designer Michael Ayrton and the stage director Malcolm Baker-Smith. Then the Company discovered that David Webster, the General Administrator of Covent Garden, had asked Karl Rankl, the Music Director of the Opera, to conduct the work. The performers, outraged, refused to go on unless Lambert conducted. Even with Lambert in the pit, *The Fairy Queen* was not a success. Drama, dance and opera proved hard to reconcile; audiences who liked one aspect were bored by the others.

Lambert was not settling in to Covent Garden. He and Webster disliked and resented each other. Lambert's affair with Fonteyn had finished, and he married again in October 1947. By then, he had resigned from his post as Music Director of the Company. His health was poor: he had undiagnosed diabetes, made worse by heavy drinking. He suffered falls and blackouts. In one crisis, towards the end of the war, he was spitting blood. His skill as a conductor remained, however. According to Margaret Dale, he might set slower tempi if he had been drinking, but his pacing was still sure. Even so, as his wife admitted, 'he could not be relied upon to give *consistently* good performances.'[10] 'You couldn't rely on him,' said de Valois later. 'We knew what was coming and there was nothing to be done about it, and we knew that he didn't want anything to be done about it. All his friends knew this, but one hung on for ever because he was such a wonderful man.'[11] Under pressure from Webster, Lambert resigned in July. Robert Irving was appointed conductor to the Company at the start of the next year. Helpmann, too, was detaching himself from Covent Garden. He played Oberon, an acting role, in Lambert's *Fairy Queen*. Early in 1947, he took leave from the Sadler's Wells Ballet to act. He turned increasingly to theatre and film work, and left the Company altogether in 1951.

During the war, de Valois had made plans to bring in guest choreographers:

> a) those who are not established . . . b) Those who are already famous, and must eventually visit us *for a period of time* in which they should be given free scope – and 2 or 3 consecutive productions at least afforded to them. In the first category I place for the moment Tudor &, in smaller degree, Howard. In the second such artists as Nijinska, Massine & possibly Jooss. The war makes the second type of producer, at present, rather out of the question.[12]

In 1947, she offered Massine his 'period of time' with the Company. He started by reviving *The Three-Cornered Hat*, one of the successes of his Diaghilev years. The old Ballets Russes public, still dubious about British ballet, rushed back to Covent Garden. Massine himself, at fifty-one, danced the Miller with taut authority. At its first sight of him, the audience burst out cheering. 'It must take many performances for the unfamiliar style to be fully assimilated,' wrote Haskell of the Company, 'but the spirit was there.'[13] Fonteyn danced the Miller's Wife with energy and ardour, though Massine's character style did not suit her. Later, Violetta Elvin had an irresistible glamour in the role. Alexander Grant, who had moved to Covent Garden from the touring company, stood out as the Dandy. Massine lent the Company the original Picasso décor, its colours faded but the lines as bold as ever. Lambert conducted an exhilarating account of the de Falla score. After that, *La Boutique fantasque* came as a disappointment. Massine no longer had the suppleness for the celebrated Can-Can. His partner was Shearer, lively but miscast. She was to work with Massine again that summer, making the film *The Red Shoes*. The third Massine revival came early in the 1947–48 season. *Mam'zelle Angot* had been made in 1943 for American Ballet Theatre, where it had not lasted long. The Sadler's Wells production was substantially revised, with delightful new designs by Derain. The Barber was Grant's first leading role. His buoyant, appealing performance was an immediate success. Fonteyn soon withdrew from the title role. She was out of her element in Massine, though her performance had admirers. She was replaced by the vivid Julia Farron. Massine's light, bubbly ballet was revived regularly for the next twelve years.

The Massine works left no rehearsal time for a new Ashton ballet. In 1947, he directed two operas – one for the growing Covent Garden company – and made *Valses nobles et sentimentales* for the young dancers of the touring company. *Scènes de ballet*, his next work for Covent Garden, came in February 1948. Ashton heard Stravinsky's score when listening to the radio in his bath, and was fascinated by the complex, broken rhythms. He discussed the ballet with the critic Richard Buckle, who suggested a complex metaphysical scenario. Ashton rejected it, turning to pure dance and to geometry. Though he had hated it at school, he became fascinated with geometrical theorems. He came to rehearsals with a volume of Euclid, sending the corps de ballet through complex patterns. Movements are passed from one group to another, echoed and returned, often in different spiky rhythms. The corps women nod their heads crisply, turn their backs, bend double, yet these idiosyncrasies are part of their classical elegance. The ballerina role has echoes of the Rose Adagio from *The Sleeping Beauty*, the woman partnered by several men. After a brilliant first entrance, her second solo is full of crisp pointe-work, one foot tapping the floor as her arms wind and curve like drifting smoke. André Beaurepaire dressed the women in geometric tutus with hats and pearl chokers, a now dated chic. Again, Ashton challenged the Company's men. The ballet opened with Michael Somes, framed by four male soloists. As the music started, Somes did repeated entrechats six. The choreography was full of jumps and beaten steps, needing fast and brilliant execution.

Ashton was responding to his dancers. In 1947, Fonteyn had taken leave of absence to study in Paris, where she had started an affair with the choreographer Roland Petit. She returned newly glamorous, dressed by Dior. At first, however, she found it hard to respond to the ballet's sophistication. Moira Shearer, at the second performance, seemed better suited to its stylish precision. Ashton was also promoting Somes as Fonteyn's new partner. He was handsome, musical, a better technician than Helpmann, but he took time to develop as a partner. He became a self-effacing cavalier, presenting her beautifully, never challenging her for the limelight.

Helpmann returned to the role of Satan in a new production of de Valois's *Job*, first given at a gala in aid of the Company's own Benevolent Fund. John Piper's new designs were a freer interpretation of Blake than Raverat's first version. There was superb new lighting by Michael Benthall. 'When Satan is on God's throne,' wrote Buckle, 'Benthall makes it shine like a poisonous amethyst, and his sunset glow matches the serenity of the final music.'[14] Sir Adrian Boult conducted. That season, Markova and Dolin returned as guest artists. Markova had lost some of her steely technique, but she was still exquisitely ethereal in *Giselle* and in *Les Sylphides*. Dolin danced Satan again, and triumphed. The two made distinguished debuts in the full-length *Sleeping Beauty*. Guest artists were an example to the Company, and Markova's return acted as a particular spur to Fonteyn. Shortly after the premiere of *Scènes de ballet*, she had returned to Paris to dance a new ballet by Roland Petit. Challenged by a new style, and put on her mettle by Markova, she started to dance with greater assurance and warmth. From 1948, wrote the critic Edwin Denby, Fonteyn led a 'revolution' against the 'thinness and meagreness of temperament' in British and American ballet.[15]

Massine now made his first new work for the Company. *The Clock Symphony* turned out to be a fussy, trivial ballet. Moira Shearer and Alexander Grant did their best in leading roles; the rest of the Company had little to do. Shearer danced her first, acclaimed, Giselle at the end of the 1947–48 season, making waves within the Company. Finding the Covent Garden production stereotyped, she had gone to Karsavina for private coaching. When de Valois saw Shearer's performance, with its changed details, she was furious. As soon as the first act was over, she rushed backstage to berate her. Shearer told her: '"Anything that you find unacceptable, I got from Madame Karsavina." . . . That stopped her absolutely cold. She didn't say another word; she marched out of my room. And the next thing I knew, Karsavina had been invited for special rehearsals with Margot.'16 That coaching was for Fonteyn alone. Rehearsals were closed, with the Company's other Giselles firmly excluded. Fonteyn had earned her pre-eminence, but she was also protected by de Valois. Other dancers were held back from challenging her – even though, as her response to Markova demonstrated, Fonteyn thrived on competition. De Valois was prepared to sacrifice other careers for the sake of her first ballerina.

In 1948, Fonteyn had no closer rival than Shearer. Days after that first *Giselle*, *The Red Shoes* was released. The film, with Shearer, Helpmann and Massine in leading roles, introduced millions to ballet. Shearer was both ballerina and film star, and she had important roles in Ashton's next ballets. *Don Juan*, which opened the 1948–49 season, was set to Richard Strauss's tone-poem. Helpmann, in his last romantic Ashton role, dallied with Shearer's Young Wife before succumbing to the fatal kiss of La Morte Amoureuse, danced by Fonteyn. Strauss's tone-poem is short, and the ballet was compressed almost into abstraction. Helpmann's role was such a blank that even he could not make his presence felt. The ballet failed. On the first night, Fonteyn tore a ligament, which kept her off stage for three months. Ashton had already cast Fonteyn in the title role of *Cinderella*. Shearer danced the first night.

Cinderella, which opened on 23 December 1948, was the Company's first new three-act ballet. Ashton used Prokofiev's music, written during the war. Prokofiev's ballet is a fairy story, but it doesn't unfold with the majestic pace of *The Sleeping Beauty*. The score is tuneful and lively, with bold characterisation and urgent dance rhythms. Ashton made classical dances of strange, expressive force.

The Waltz of Stars has an explosive sparkle: the corps spring from pose to pose, fingers pointing, torsos bending. Ashton's Season Variations were beautifully crafted, showing off the first cast but long outlasting it. Spring, made for Nadia Nerina, had flicked wrists and quick, buoyant jumps. Summer made the most of Elvin's sensuous breadth of movement, with languorous, curling arms. Autumn – choreographed on May, but danced by Pauline Clayden – went skittering through sharp, off-balance turns, as if kicking up leaves. Winter was Beryl Grey, sweeping grandly from one frozen arabesque to the next.

Cinderella's arrival at the ball is the ballet's most dreamlike moment. She descends a staircase, on pointe – supported by the prince, but without looking at him. It has the effect of a classical vision scene: is she really there? Only when the ballroom music breaks in does this radiant, remote heroine see her prince and fall in love. In their pas de deux, Ashton again used low, skimming lifts. As her prince lifts her, Cinderella sweeps her legs together in a scissoring movement, a trembling beat, like a shiver of feeling. Ashton cut Prokofiev's third-act divertissement, in which the Prince visits different countries in search of Cinderella. 'I didn't like any of the places he went to, nor the music for them.'[17] The ballet rushes to its conclusion, with the hero and heroine are in danger of being overshadowed by the Ugly Sisters, danced at the first performance by Ashton and Helpmann.

Their roles had elements of self-caricature. Helpmann was bossy, extrovert, set on the limelight. Ashton was forgetful and insecure: 'the shyest, the happiest, most innocent of monsters,' wrote Edwin Denby. 'At the Prince's she is terrified to be making an entrance; a few moments later, poor monster, in the intoxication of being at a party she loses her heart and imagines she can dance fascinatingly ... Ashton does it reticently, with the perfect timing, the apparently tentative gesture, the absorption and the sweetness of nature of a great clown.'[18] Shearer danced Cinderella with brilliant lightness and grace. Violetta Elvin, at the second performance, was softer and more tender. When Fonteyn at last danced the ballet, she gave Cinderella new warmth and vulnerability, with a heartfelt response to her prince and in her farewell to the sisters. The ballet needs a dancer who, like Fonteyn, can draw it together, uniting its different sides. The designs, by Jean-Denis Malclès, were appealing and stylish. *Cinderella* was an immediate hit, selling out for the whole run. In its first season, it was seen by sixty thousand people.

If anything, the Company had become more popular since the war. When booking for the new season opened that February, there were more overnight queues at the box office. This was a loyal public. Constant Lambert returned that season, newly appointed as one of the company's Artistic Directors. When he appeared in the pit to conduct *Apparitions*, he was greeted with an ovation – more applause than there was for the ballet itself, which had lost its intimacy and its force on the Covent Garden stage. Fonteyn and Helpmann, now mature artists, had lost the pathos of their early performances.

Alexandra Danilova visited the Company that spring, partnered by Frederic Franklin. Danilova was recovering from injury, but her attack and energy were striking. Her last performance of *La Boutique fantasque* had glorious vitality. In May 1949, the company made a successful visit to Florence. They had made several European tours since the war – Germany in 1945, Vienna in 1946, Oslo and Eastern Europe in 1947, an emotional return to Holland in 1948. Now they prepared for their most ambitious trip abroad. In autumn 1949, the American impresario Sol Hurok presented the Sadler's Wells Ballet in a four-week season at the Metropolitan Opera House, New York. The Met season was followed by a tour of the United States and Canada.

Hurok had seen and loved the Messel *Sleeping Beauty* in its first season. (He told de Valois that her company had 'a queer sort of idealism about it'.[19]) He offered then to present the Company in New York, led by a guest star like Markova or Danilova. De Valois refused. In 1949, he offered again. This time, he wanted the world-famous Moira Shearer for opening night. 'Moira is the star of *The Red Shoes*, and a most beautiful dancer,' de Valois told him, 'but Margot is our ballerina, and she has to open, and Sol, if you don't like it, we'll go to Coventry – we've been offered an Arts Council tour.'[20] Hurok gave in.

The announcement of an American tour caused great excitement in Britain. The United States had already emerged as the post-war superpower. It was also the creditor for most of Britain's massive war debt. Winning American approval had become vital. British fashion houses rushed to dress the Company's women in clothes that would be shown off in New York. The dancers were looking forward to unrationed American food. De Valois issued them with dollars and urged them to buy steaks and eggs rather than fattening pastries. There was excitement in New York, too. Hurok put tickets on sale four months before the opening, and was rewarded with brisk sales. Photographers met the Company at the airport. The first night was completely sold out.

They opened on 9 October 1949, with *The Sleeping Beauty*. De Valois had wanted a mixed bill of British ballets – but Hurok knew that, while America had its own dramatic and pure-dance works, it had nothing like the Sadler's Wells Ballet's full-length classics. De Valois said, 'I want all my ballerinas in the first night.' In the Prologue, beside Grey as the Lilac Fairy, both Elvin and May danced as fairy godmothers – May reverting to the role she had learnt in 1939. 'Madam said, "You were good in it then and you'll be good in it again,"' recalled May. She also danced in the Florestan pas de trois in Act 3, beside Nadia Nerina and the young Kenneth MacMillan. Shearer danced the Bluebird pas de deux, one of the ballet's famous set-pieces. Helpmann played the Prince, with Ashton as Carabosse. De Valois's greatest and wisest risk was her choice of conductor. She had worried about Lambert's sobriety, but, as she recalled, he '*made* that first night'. 'He stepped into the pit and started and everyone was electrified,' agreed Ashton.[21] The dancers – lifted by the occasion, by the music and by warm New York applause – outdid themselves. This was the most exciting, and the grandest *Sleeping Beauty* they had ever given. By the end of the Prologue, with its brilliant variations, the Company was already a smash hit. Grey was cheered as soon as she walked on; Avril Navarre took three calls after her solo. The Mayor of New York leaned from his box to tell de Valois, 'You're in, lady.' She had to ask if that was good or bad.[22]

Tchaikovsky's score builds up to Aurora's first-act entrance, a pulsing heartbeat before she appears. Lambert made it so exciting that the audience began to applaud before Fonteyn was even on stage. In the Messel production, Aurora runs right across the back of the stage, pausing for a moment in arabesque. The audience glimpses her, she vanishes into the wings, then reappears at top speed, dancing full out. At its first sight of Fonteyn, the Met went wild with delight. In the Rose Adagio that follows, Aurora holds a series of balances, partnered by four princes in turn. The last prince, John Hart, 'stood smiling at the side of the stage, with folded arms,' remembered Pamela May, 'waiting for Margot to come off balance. After what seemed to be an eternity he offered her his hand . . . the applause was unbelievable. The Company members standing in the wings all had tears rolling down their cheeks with excitement – I was one of them and will never forget it.'[23] The Company's reception 'surpassed anything that the Metropolitan has ever experienced', reported *Dance News*, 'and there have been ovations at the opera house before Sadler's Wells arrived here.' De Valois stepped forward to give a speech: 'We were *terrified* of you,' she said.[24] Mayor O'Dwyer gave a party for the Company at his official residence. The dancers were driven there with a police escort and wailing sirens, something usually reserved for the President or foreign rulers. The first-night reviews arrived soon after midnight. They were ecstatic.

By the second week, Hurok had given up advertising the Company: no more tickets to sell. It was soon clear that the full-length classics were the hit of the season. 'In a way it was a disappointment to see the British guests come down to our level of ballet presentation,' wrote Anatole Chujoy about the mixed programmes. 'We should have preferred them to stay on the height of large and lavish production, unapproachable to us, at least for the time being.'[25] *Façade*, brought at Hurok's insistence, was a hit. *Symphonic Variations* was seen as watered-down Balanchine. *Miracle in the Gorbals* and *Hamlet* had a mixed reception. If anything, *Le Lac des cygnes* outdid *The Sleeping Beauty*. 'Margot Fonteyn is, and I am happy to be unequivocal about this, the greatest Swan Queen I have ever seen,' wrote Walter Terry in the *Herald Tribune*. The critic Robert Gottlieb remembers Fonteyn's Odile as alluring and uniquely evil: 'Her Odile was like a vicious caricature of Odette – she was diminishing and slandering her "rival". Her beauty, her splendour were directed not only at seducing Siegfried but at making horrible fun of Odette.'

Throughout the season, the Company's authority and unity of style came as a revelation. 'It is doubtful if we have ever before seen in this country a company whose productions have been so meticulously prepared, so thoughtfully assembled, so beautifully rehearsed,' wrote John Martin in the *New York Times*. 'Behind the performances themselves lies a school in which the greater part of the personnel has actually received its training and in which it still is trained from day to day. The unity of technical style, which makes the ensemble really an ensemble, is no accident.' Grey, Shearer, May and Elvin were all admired. There was some criticism of the Company's men, though their bearing and style was praised. De Valois was particularly proud of a comment from Vera Nemchinova, one of Diaghilev's ballerinas. 'Diaghilev gave us all something,' she told de Valois after *The Sleeping Beauty*, 'but you took something from him.'[26]

From the beginning, the Company's success was seen as a British triumph. Martin admitted that American national pride had been given 'a terrific wallop'. The Sadler's Wells Ballet was also an inspiration: if a young British company had achieved so much, couldn't Americans aim as high? Maria Tallchief, ballerina at the New York City Ballet, saw Fonteyn's example as something to aspire to – 'a vision of our potential', as the American critic Doris Hering put it.[27] 'I feel like writing my Congressman to increase aid to the British today,' exclaimed one radio commentator. 'There has never been anything to make you admire the British and grow fond of them more than this.'[28] 'In four weeks,' reported *Time* magazine, 'Margot Fonteyn and Sadler's Wells had restored as much glitter to Britain's tarnished tiara as any mission the English had sent abroad since the war.' *Time* and *Newsweek* put Fonteyn on the front cover – like that police escort, something usually reserved for political leaders. Back in London, the government was delighted. Sir Stafford Cripps, the Minister for Economic Affairs, proclaimed his pleasure that the ballet should have, 'among all its other excellent qualities, that of a first-class dollar earner. You have no idea what pride that has aroused in the fastnesses of Treasury Chambers.'[29] The Company had grossed $256,000 (close to $3 million in today's money) in New York alone. *Variety* reported in a front-page banner headline

– the first it had ever given to ballet. After New York, the Company set off on tour in a special train – six baggage cars for the scenery and costumes. The tour ended in Montreal on 11 December 1949.

Transatlantic success changed the rhythm of Company life. During New York curtain calls, the audience had shouted to the dancers to come back. They did, making long American tours every other year for the next decade, with regular visits thereafter. In 1979, Arlene Croce remembered the American feeling that 'owing to its many US tours, the Royal belonged partly to us'. There was a sense of family loyalty to the Company in New York as well as London.[30] Croce believed that touring gave The Royal Ballet 'dimension', a greater breadth of outlook. It had another, more immediate impact on the repertory. There was suddenly less time to prepare and rehearse new works. De Valois did not change her artistic policy, her care for classical schooling and balanced repertory. But she had to work harder to maintain them, and to maintain them under much greater scrutiny. Her company had a new authority, a new reputation to keep up. In New York, the Sadler's Wells Ballet became an international success, one of the glories of world ballet.

FIVE

International company

1950–59

ABOVE The seven ballerinas of *Birthday Offering*: Svetlana Beriosova, Rowena Jackson, Elaine Fifield, Margot Fonteyn, Nadia Nerina, Violetta Elvin, Beryl Grey: © Alpha Photo Press Agency Ltd
PREVIOUS PAGE *The Firebird*, Margot Fonteyn: © Getty Images

'Women are good for the pioneer work,' Ninette de Valois liked to say, 'but when it has developed to a certain point the men must take it over.'[1] She stayed in charge of the Company until 1963, but by 1950 its pioneering days were decidedly over. The Sadler's Wells Ballet had settled in to Covent Garden; now it had to adjust to world fame. There was greater recognition at home, too. During the 1950s, the Company was granted a Royal Charter, with a final change of name, and there were honours for individual members of the Company. De Valois and Fonteyn would both become Dames during the course of the decade, and Ashton was given a CBE.

There was still work to be done, however. Although de Valois was especially proud of improvements in male dancing in these years, a remarkable generation of ballerinas also grew up during this period. Ashton's *Birthday Offering*, made to celebrate the Company's Silver Jubilee, showed off seven women in dazzling variations. The 1950s were packed with celebration evenings: for the Festival of Britain, the Coronation, anniversaries for the Company and its theatres. As a national company, the Sadler's Wells Ballet had to face new expectations, not least an expectation of dignity. At the same time, any hint of complacency was observed and fiercely criticised. From now on, the Company had to live up to its own past.

Pioneering continued with the touring company. The Sadler's Wells Theatre Ballet was developing quickly under the direction of Peggy van Praagh. It kept the smaller Sadler's Wells works in active repertory, and acted as a training ground for young choreographers, starting with the young John Cranko. By 1950, he had made several successful works. In 1951 he had a huge hit with *Pineapple Poll*, a nautical comedy set to Charles Mackerras's arrangement of music from Gilbert and Sullivan operettas. In 1954, it was voted the best post-war work in a poll organised by the *Ballet Annual*. Kenneth

MacMillan emerged as a choreographer, making a series of works for the Sadler's Wells Theatre Ballet. Leading dancers were often transferred from the touring company to Covent Garden. Nadia Nerina had already moved; Elaine Fifield, Svetlana Beriosova, David Blair and others would follow.

Before the Covent Garden company's first North American tour was over, de Valois was back in London planning new ballets for the repertory. *Don Quixote*, her own first, and last, ballet for Covent Garden, had its premiere in February 1950. It was dry, subdued and episodic, received with respect but little enthusiasm. Edward Burra's striking sets showed a barren Spanish landscape. Roberto Gerhard's score, praised for its subtlety, lacked sweep and melody. De Valois relied heavily on gestures, and even those were broken off. In the title role, Helpmann tried to hold the ballet together on very limited choreography. The famous windmills were pairs of dancers, dressed in drab grey with five-inch platform shoes, swinging their arms as sails. Fonteyn's peasant Aldonza had some crisp de Valois footwork, which she danced with eager mischief. As the idealised Dulcinea, she had characterless classical steps. Alexander Grant was a touching Sancho Panza.

In 1950, there was an exchange of ballets between Sadler's Wells and Balanchine's New York City Ballet. Ashton went to New York in February to create *Illuminations*. In return, Balanchine came to London to stage *Ballet Imperial*, his 1941 setting of Tchaikovsky's second piano concerto. The ballet's imperial qualities are in the dancing – in the courtly way the corps acknowledge the principals and each other, in the grandeur of these brilliant, demanding steps. Eugene Berman's designs framed the dancing with ermine-draped pillars, with an Imperial eagle on the backcloth. The dancers wore silver-grey wigs, with velvet bodices to the women's tutus. They had to adjust to Balanchine technique – to carrying their weight much further forward – but they learned the ballet in three weeks and danced it full out. 'This phenomenal speed was also doubtless a comment on our keenness to dance this work,' wrote the dancer Franklin White.[2] Fonteyn did not suit the dashing brilliance of the ballerina role, one of the most demanding in the Balanchine repertory. She told the critic Robert Gottlieb: 'I used to wait in the wings during that long introduction, thinking, "If I can only get through the opening passage successfully, I'll be fine." But I never could.' She also avoided the bold, off-balance quality of Balanchine's steps. When Shearer took over the role, she gave a quick, daring performance. At his own request, Balanchine coached her, encouraging her in the risky changes of weight. Violetta Elvin, the third-cast ballerina, had scale but lacked speed. Beryl Grey, dancing the second lead, walked off with the notices. She moved with ease and grandeur, joyful and assured in the most difficult jumps and beats.

There was a second exchange later that year, this time between New York City Ballet and the touring company. That autumn, John Cranko went to New York to make *The Witch*. Balanchine's *Trumpet Concerto*, set to Haydn, had its premiere in Manchester in September 1950. It had a military air, with saluting, marching on pointe and drum-majorette costumes by Vivienne Kernot. It did not suit the Company, and the speedy leading role did not suit Svetlana Beriosova. It was to be the only work Balanchine made for either of the Sadler's Wells companies.

Not all British critics had admired *Ballet Imperial*, with its clear focus on dancing over theatrical display. (They had similar doubts when the New York City Ballet visited Covent Garden that summer.) The next new work at Covent Garden was almost all theatre. Having made a ballet for Fonteyn in Paris, Roland Petit came to London to create *Ballabile* for the Sadler's Wells Ballet. Constant Lambert made a delightful arrangement of music by Chabrier. The ballet was a light series of incidents – dancers on bicycles, Alexander Grant fishing, Margaret Dale as an equestrienne. There were good roles for Violetta Elvin and Anne Negus, and stylish designs by Antoni Clavé, but the choreography was very slight.

Ballabile had its premiere on 5 May 1950, nineteen years after the first full evening of ballet at the Old Vic. On 15 May, the anniversary of the first Sadler's Wells performance, the Company held a coming-of-age celebration – two years early for a twenty-first birthday, but nobody noticed until too late.[3] A gala was held at Sadler's Wells, with a programme of 1930s works. It was a family party, with dancers returning to their early roles. Most of the women dancing the orgy from *The Rake's Progress* were retired with children. 'Well,' said de Valois when the curtain came down, 'I shall *always* have that danced by married women in future.'[4] In *The Haunted Ballroom*, Fonteyn played her early mime role, the Young Tregennis. De Valois, fifty-two years old, danced Webster in *A Wedding Bouquet*. It was a giggly performance: when a pirouette was called for, she walked straight forward twirling her finger instead. She received a tremendous ovation from the audience, and another, louder and longer, from her dancers after the curtain fell.

The Company was already preparing for its second visit to North America. The first New York season had been followed by five weeks on the road. This time, the Sadler's Wells Ballet would tour for nineteen weeks, visiting thirty-two cities. Determined to show all sides of her company, de Valois chose a programme of three full-length and seven short ballets. As the London season ended, the stage staff were frantically marking and packing scenery to be shipped across the Atlantic. The work went on during performances. As one Sleeping Beauty was kissed awake, the stage carpenters, just out of sight, pasted travel labels on the back of her bed. Once again, the dancers were dressed by British shops and fashion houses. De Valois cheerfully advised the manufacturers to take a good last look at their products: they were unlikely to survive the wear and tear of travel.

The tour started at the Met on 10 September 1950. The opening ballet was *Le Lac des cygnes*. Compared to *The Sleeping Beauty*, it has fewer opportunities for applause. Emotion built up throughout the ballet. When Fonteyn and Somes finished the Black Swan pas de deux, the audience let rip. An 'ovation such as I have never heard yet in the theatre broke around us like a thunderclap', wrote White. 'I did not know that one single audience could make such a noise.'[5] The Company were no longer a novelty, and critics were more ready to find fault. *Giselle* was already familiar to American audiences. There were a few criticisms of the production and of Fonteyn's performances, though Shearer was praised in the ballet. *Don Quixote* was roundly disliked, while *Dante Sonata* now looked dated.

After three weeks in New York, the Company travelled south as far as New Orleans, then crossed to the West Coast. Sol Hurok's

publicity campaigns made the most of the Los Angeles performance, arranging a spectacular opening at the Shrine auditorium,
with an audience full of film stars. The Shrine holds nearly seven
thousand people; the Company played to full houses for two weeks.
The strains of touring were beginning to show in a series of injuries.
Pamela May and Gerd Larsen had to return to Britain for medical
treatment. There were other troubles, too. In San Francisco,
Helpmann gave his last performance as a member of the Company,
partnering Fonteyn in the pas de deux from *The Sleeping Beauty*.
Then he walked out. 'Bobby has resigned after much monkeying
with his contract,' de Valois wrote to Joy Newton, '. . . a dirty trick
or two and the removal of any "character" from yours very truly.'[6]

The next five weeks were the hardest of the tour: they covered fifteen cities and four thousand miles. Many performances were
one-night stands. The Company travelled on its own train, the Ballet
Special, taking orchestra and scenery with them. Most of the travelling was done overnight. The dancers tried to sleep through the
noise and shaking of the train; when there was a derailment one
night, hardly anyone noticed the difference. A night in a hotel
became a luxury. In Denver, high above sea level, they suffered from
altitude sickness. During *Les Patineurs*, the corps dancers became
giddy; oxygen cylinders had to be kept in the wings. On all the
American tours, the dancers were seen as unofficial ambassadors.
They had to behave, and dress, accordingly. Monica Mason, who
joined the Company in 1958, remembers 'clambering out of a bunk
on a train at eight o'clock in the morning, having got onto the train
the previous night, all trying to stand together in a little changing
room, and pulling ourselves into these corset things that we wore,
with suspenders attached – getting into stockings, high heels,
straight skirts, and climbing off the train with our hands in gloves
. . . in the middle of nowhere in America, because that's how everybody dressed.'[7] On the 1950–51 tour, the Company spent Christmas
in Chicago. They stayed for two weeks, opening with *The Sleeping
Beauty*. The tour ended with a month in Canada, where thousands
were turned away from the box office in every city. Performances
had been sold out for most of the tour; the dancers would call it a
poor house if there were three empty seats. They had taken two

million dollars at the box office (more than $21 million in today's money), bringing home half a million (or some 5.3 million) dollars in profit. While the Company was in America, de Valois was made a Dame in the New Year's Honours List.

The dancers came back to a heavy workload, with a busy London season starting three weeks after their return. Productions looked battered and travel-stained: one of the pillars in *The Sleeping Beauty* snapped off at the bottom, and was not repaired for months. The dancers, still exhausted, succumbed to injury and illness. Moira Shearer collapsed after a single performance; Beryl Grey was diagnosed with anaemia, and ordered to rest for five months; Pamela May was off until the autumn. Influenza went through the Company. With so many ballerinas ill, Nadia Nerina danced both Cinderella and Odette that spring. Nerina, a lively dancer with superb technique and a high, springy jump, had been associated with soubrette roles. She was starting to broaden her range.

Ashton's *Daphnis and Chloë* had its premiere on 5 April 1951. Ravel's score had been written for the Ballets Russes. Fokine, who had choreographed the first production, was by this point falling out with Diaghilev. His ballet was neglected and soon dropped from the repertory. Ashton moved the pastoral story from ancient Greece to the modern Mediterranean, 'as though it could still happen today'.[8] John Craxton designed a landscape of baked dusty browns and lush greens. Cubist rocks and trees stood out against a dark sea. The dancers wore stylised modern clothes: flowing skirts and pointe shoes for the women, shirts and trousers for the men. Ashton's corps wind through chain dances, kneel, stop as friezes for the principals. One pose, with a foot crossed over the other, recalls both Greek statuary and *Symphonic Variations*. In the rich simplicity of these dances, Ashton created a sense of divine nature. His dancers are spiritually, sensuously at home in their landscape. Chloë, abducted by pirates, 'confronts her captors with the unspeakableness of their crime against her. From Fonteyn,' wrote Arlene Croce in 1970, 'I had the impression that the crime was as much or more against nature, and that she couldn't understand how it could be happening'.[9]

Chloë was one of Fonteyn's most personal roles. The flowing choreography showed off her beauty of line, the rhythmic subtleties of her dancing. On stage, she could suggest inviolate purity with no denial of sexuality. *Daphnis*, wrote David Vaughan, was the first in a series of Ashton ballets 'about love . . . that recognise the fact that sexuality and innocence are not mutually exclusive'.[10] Daphnis is seduced by the married woman Lykanion in a duet that is both classical and explicit. As he lifts her, she swings one leg around him, forward and back, in a danced orgasm that ends with a shiver through her whole body. Daphnis was a lyrically passive role for Michael Somes, with a limpid and very difficult solo in the opening scene. Violetta Elvin danced the seductive Lykanion, with Alexander Grant as the pirate chief. At first, *Daphnis and Chloë* was poorly received. Most reviews were grudging, though the dancers were praised.

There was worse to come. After a holiday, the dancers returned to work on *Tiresias*. This ballet, which had its premiere at a royal gala on 9 July 1951, had been commissioned by the Arts Council. It was the Company's contribution to the Festival of Britain, the 1951 celebration of arts and culture meant to mark an end of post-war austerity. The score and scenario were by Constant Lambert. The choreography was by Ashton, who found 'the subject very difficult to cope with. How do you explain in a ballet who enjoys sex more?'[11] The male Tiresias, danced by Somes, was turned into a woman when he killed one of two copulating snakes. Fonteyn, the female Tiresias, danced a long duet with John Field before being turned back into a man. The gods Zeus and Hera ask Tiresias to settle their quarrel: do men or women take most pleasure in sex? When Lambert suggested *Tiresias* to the Camargo Society, twenty years before, he had planned something lightly satirical. As he worked on the ballet, it became longer and heavier – almost an hour of dryly percussive music. Ashton loyally made dances to it, but found inspiration only in the second scene. Lambert, who did not bother to show the male Tiresias experiencing sex, wrote a long pas de deux for his ex-lover Fonteyn. Ashton made an acrobatic duet, with floating lifts and poses derived from Cretan sculpture.

Fonteyn danced with particular intensity: 'there is an excitement and an "edge" to her work that I've never seen before,' one admirer wrote to Ashton.[12] The pas de deux was framed by long, dull scenes: a display of gymnastic dances, warriors clashing spears. The gods conducted their quarrel in incomprehensible gestures.

The gala audience was markedly unenthusiastic – partly from boredom, partly from disapproval. Fonteyn covered her filmy costume with a cardigan before being presented in the Royal Box, but the Princess Elizabeth pointedly averted her gaze. Reviews were generally poor. Richard Buckle, attacking the ballet in the *Observer*, questioned the Company's artistic direction. His headline was 'Blind Mice':

> Did you ever see such a thing in your life? Sadler's Wells has three artistic directors. See how they run. Ninette de Valois is too busy to supervise every detail of production; Frederick Ashton is too easily reconciled to compromise; Constant Lambert, one imagines, looks in occasionally with a musical suggestion. Lambert cannot take all the blame for the idiotic and boring *Tiresias*, which was given its first production on Monday . . . Ashton must have undertaken the choreography of such a work with reluctance and out of duty to his colleague, but de Valois should have forbidden it. Experimental risks must be taken even with the taxpayer's money – and this ballet must have cost five thousand pounds – but certain enterprises are clearly doomed to failure from the start . . . [13]

In a later article, Buckle suggested that some sort of artistic adviser be appointed over de Valois, Ashton and Lambert – something de Valois saw as an attempted takeover by Buckle himself. The dancers, who deeply resented the attacks on Lambert, closed ranks.

Two years after the first American triumph, the Sadler's Wells Ballet was facing the harshest criticism it had ever received. By its own standards, the Company was certainly off form. Standards of production, and of dancing, had slipped in the wake of the American tour. Though depleted, the Company still had real reserves of strength. Shearer, Grey and May were missing, but Fonteyn and Elvin remained, with Nerina growing into ballerina roles. *Daphnis and Chloë* was proof enough of the Company's vitality, though it had been undervalued and dismissed. That August, the

Apparitions (1936) The ball room scene, with Robert Helpmann as the Poet and Margot Fonteyn as the Woman in Ball Dress. The scenario was by Constant Lambert, the choreography by Frederick Ashton, the designs by Cecil Beaton.
The Sleeping Princess (1939) Margot Fonteyn as Aurora: © J. W. Debenham, The Theatre Museum, V&A Images

Constant Lambert with Margot Fonteyn, backstage before a performance of *Façade*, 1935:
© Getty Images
Ninette de Valois in class with Beryl Grey: © Getty Images

Hamlet (1942) Robert Helpmann's Freudian interpretation of the play. Fonteyn as Ophelia, Helpmann as Hamlet: © Getty Images

Le Lac des cygnes (1943) Fonteyn's Odette pleads with the huntsmen, with Helpmann as Prince Siegfried. De Valois's production preserved the traditional mime. The swirling designs, with swan motifs, are by Leslie Hurry: © Getty Images

The Sleeping Beauty (1946) The Prologue fairies and their cavaliers, with designs by Oliver Messel: The Frank Sharman Collection at Royal Opera House Collections
Ashton's *La Fille mal gardée* (1960) Nadia Nerina, with the corps in the finale: © Zoë Dominic

Marguerite and Armand, Margot Fonteyn and Rudolf Nureyev: © Zoë Dominic
Frederick Ashton coaching Lesley Collier: © Zoë Dominic

Nicholas Georgiadis, Kenneth MacMillan and Lynn Seymour
The rape scene from *The Invitation* (1960) with Desmond Doyle and Lynn Seymour:
© Houston Rogers, The Theatre Museum, V&A Images

Ashton's *The Dream* (1964) Antoinette Sibley as Titiania, Anthony Dowell as Oberon and Alexander Grant as Bottom: © Houston Rogers, The Theatre Museum, V&A Images
MacMillan's *Song of the Earth* (1966) Donald MacLeary, Anthony Dowell as the Messenger of Death, Monica Mason: © Leslie E. Spatt

Cinderella, Svetlana Beriosova: © Zoë Dominic

Sadler's Wells Ballet appeared at the Edinburgh Festival. While there, they received the news of Lambert's death, two days before his forty-sixth birthday.

His illness, his drinking and his disagreements with the opera house management had driven a wedge between Lambert and the Company he helped to found. He was still loved and desperately missed. In Edinburgh, the dancers gave a fervent performance of *Tiresias*. Fonteyn danced with extraordinary passion. Shortly afterwards, she injured her foot, and was off stage for five months. *Tiresias* was unpopular, but the Company kept it stubbornly in repertory. They tried to keep the ballet alive, wrote Mary Clarke, 'almost by the will-power exerted in its performance'.[14] This devotion lasted until Fonteyn became involved with Tito de Arias, her future husband. The ballet made him so jealous that Fonteyn gave up her role. There were just two more performances, with Elvin as the female Tiresias. De Valois went on paying tribute to Lambert. *Tiresias*, she insisted in 1957, 'shows a powerful intellect at work that not even illness could overthrow'.[15] Her last word on the ballet looked back to Buckle's 'Blind Mice': 'When I am struck blind again,' she declared, 'may it be in such equally worthy company.'[16]

The Sadler's Wells Ballet took a long time to recover from the strains of the American tour, the unhappy spring season and the loss of Lambert. In September 1951, the Company returned to Covent Garden, still in low spirits. There were several important debuts. Pauline Clayden danced Chloë with ease and authority. Nerina made her debut as Swanilda, and Elvin danced her first Giselle. The production had been carefully refurbished and much improved. James Bailey revised his designs, creating a softer and more romantic atmosphere. Beryl Grey, back with the Company after her long illness, danced Myrtha. On opening night, Shearer gave a superb performance as Giselle. This was her last season as a member of the Company. In 1952, she resigned to concentrate on acting.

Donald of the Burthens, given its premiere in December 1951, was Massine's second new work for the Company. He tried to repeat the success of *The Three-Cornered Hat*: another character ballet with a strong national flavour, with music and designs commissioned from the artists of that country. This time, the setting was Scotland. The choreography used traditional folk steps, while Ian Whyte's music brought bagpipes to the Royal Opera House orchestra for the first time. Alexander Grant played a woodcutter who made a pact with Death, danced by Grey in scarlet body tights. Designs were by Robert MacBryde and Robert Colquhoun. Massine was experimenting with a new method of choreography, trying to create steps with notation and then set them to music. He spent nine months in preparation – 'enough time to make a baby,' sighs Julia Farron, who played the mother of a sick child. His system did not work, and neither did the ballet. The Company danced well, but it was a gloomy end to a difficult year.

De Valois spent the winter working on the repertory, taking rehearsals and preparing a revival of *The Sleeping Beauty*. Messel's sets and costumes were carefully restored, and a beautiful new solo was created for Aurora in the second-act Vision. In this scene, Petipa had made a variation for Aurora to music that Tchaikovsky had composed for one of the third-act Jewel Fairies. This was the version that British Auroras had learnt from Sergueyev. The new dance, made by Ashton 'after Petipa', used the music Tchaikovsky wrote for Aurora. After a nervous Rose Adagio, Grey danced with spacious ease. Elvin, Nerina and the modest, musical Rosemary Lindsay also danced Aurora that season. Nerina was strong and vivacious, with an exultant jump.

Fonteyn returned in February 1952, dancing *Daphnis and Chloë*. The Company's spirits were lifting, though the next new ballets were thin. Andrée Howard's *A Mirror for Witches* showed a witch-hunt in a Puritan community. Howard and Norman Adams dressed the dancers in restricting period costume, limiting movement. After a successful visit to Portugal, the Company staged *Bonne-Bouche*, John Cranko's first ballet for the Covent Garden company. It was a 1920s comedy, with Pauline Clayden as a social climber and Pamela May as her diamond-mad mother. Osbert Lancaster designed a Kensington square and a Rousseau-influenced jungle with lurking perils for visiting missionaries; one was swallowed by a snake. Performances were lively, but *Bonne-Bouche* was garrulous and short-lived.

The 1952–53 season opened with *Sylvia*, Ashton's second three-act ballet. It was a lavish, confident spectacle. Ashton treated the pretty Delibes score with affection, accepting the conventions of French nineteenth-century ballet. Robin and Christopher Ironside designed elaborate painted sets, with forest glades, vistas, temples and a transformation scene. The ballet has almost the same plot as *Daphnis and Chloë*: an abducted heroine who is rescued, not by the hero, but by a passing god. Compared to *Daphnis*, *Sylvia* is superficial. It's a luscious pastiche, justified by the charm of the production and the opportunities it gives its ballerina. Fonteyn was dancing with new glamour and technical command, and Ashton made a virtuoso role for her. 'It gives us Fonteyn triumphant, Fonteyn bewildered, Fonteyn exotic, Fonteyn pathetic, Fonteyn in excelsis,' wrote Clive Barnes. 'The range of her dancing is unequalled, the heart-splitting significance she can give to a simple movement unsurpassed. The whole ballet is like a garland presented to the ballerina by her choreographer.'[17] Ashton also made the most of her musical timing. In 1949, Lambert had described a bravura quality in her musicality. 'Sometimes I catch a glimpse of her on the other side of the stage,' he told *Time* magazine, 'and I think for God's sake she can't possibly get back to the centre in half a bar – but she always does.'[18] *Sylvia* showed off that sense of excitement, especially in the phrasing of the famous pizzicato solo. Fonteyn would bet her conductors a bottle of champagne that they couldn't finish before she did.[19]

Ashton made considerable demands on the rest of the Company. The corps de ballet were given intricate academic steps. The set-piece dances included a sugary number for a pair of ceremonial goats. Like the snakes in *Tiresias*, these were danced by Pauline Clayden and Brian Shaw. (Clayden later went to Ashton with the list of her menagerie of roles, asking for the chance to play a human.) Michael Somes had just spent time in Paris, studying with Alexander Volinin. His solo displayed his improved technique, and he partnered Fonteyn with devoted care. Grey, Nerina and Elvin were all successful Sylvias, with Svetlana Beriosova impressive in the next revival. *Sylvia* remained associated with Fonteyn, and the ballet's success in repertory depended on her. After she withdrew from the role, Ashton revised it as a one-act ballet, but this lasted just two seasons. The full-length *Sylvia* was successfully revived in 2004.

In the autumn of 1952, Svetlana Beriosova moved to Covent Garden from the touring company. Lithuanian-born, trained by her father and by several distinguished Russian teachers, Beriosova was a long-limbed dancer with a lovely face and a spacious breadth of movement. In September 1952, she danced her first Covent Garden *Coppélia*. Like Pamela May, she was a purely classical ballerina who sparkled as Swanilda, dancing with mischief and glittering technique. The following spring, Beriosova danced the second act of *Le Lac des cygnes*, giving a performance of moonlit beauty.

On tour in autumn 1952, Margot Fonteyn contracted diphtheria. The symptoms can include paralysis; Fonteyn lost feeling in her legs, feet and mouth. Her recovery took five months. In December, she watched the new *Lac des cygnes* from the audience, looking frighteningly pale and tired. In this production, Leslie Hurry revised and rethought his 1943 designs, smoothing away wilder details without losing the sense of fantasy. He 'has gone from the grand manner complex to the grand manner simple,' wrote Haskell.[20] Ashton added a pas de six in the first act and a jubilant Neapolitan duet in the third; danced by Julia Farron and Alexander Grant, it brought the house down. Grey, partnered by John Field, danced Odette–Odile with clear, grand line and superb timing. She was followed by Nerina and the New Zealand-born Rowena Jackson. Jackson was already known for the brilliance of her fouettés, having rushed to replace an injured Margaret Dale in the middle of *Les Patineurs*. In her first full-length role, she gave a stylish, confident performance.

In January 1953, the ballet and opera companies joined forces on an English-language production of Gluck's *Orpheus*, directed by Ashton, with Beriosova dancing the role of the Blest Spirit. The designs were by Sophie Fedorovitch, who had worked with Ashton on his first ballet. The day before the first performance, Fedorovitch was found dead in her London studio. She had been killed by gas leaking from a faulty central-heating system. In her death, wrote Ashton, 'I lost not only my dearest friend but my greatest artistic collaborator and adviser.'[21] Orpheus was sung by Kathleen Ferrier, who was suffering from cancer; on the second night, she nearly collapsed on stage. The remaining performances were cancelled. Ferrier died later that year.

By the start of 1953, tensions were growing between de Valois and the administration of the Royal Opera House. Before the war, she had run her own company within the Old Vic organisation, consulting Lilian Baylis on larger policy matters. At Covent Garden, de Valois was answerable to the Board of Directors, but excluded from their discussions. With the ballet already up and running, the Board gave most of its attention to the fledgling opera company. John Maynard Keynes, who had brought the Sadler's Wells Ballet to Covent Garden, had favoured ballet over opera. After his death in 1946, the bias went the other way. When the Opera House reopened with *The Sleeping Beauty*, for example, the Directors had congratulated themselves that 'the success of the Ballet would have the effect of making the whole original £25,000 granted from the Arts Council available for Opera production'.[22] De Valois, meanwhile, could not argue her company's case directly. On 20 February 1953, she offered her resignation to Lord Waverley, the Chairman of the Board. 'I am left with no other course to take,' she wrote:

> In view of my exacting work and position of trust I feel that it is only natural that I should be in attendance on all ballet discussions that come under the survey of the full Board of Directors . . . major issues concerning the Ballet cannot be adequately presented, discussed or planned at second hand. The result is completely unsatisfactory for anyone with my responsibilities towards the Board. Under these circumstances nothing can be seen in its proper perspective or dealt with promptly.[23]

Threatened with the loss of Madam, Lord Waverley backed down. De Valois arrived in majesty at the May Board meeting. She argued that Covent Garden should do more to support her School. Like the touring company, the School was the responsibility of the Sadler's Wells Theatre. Covent Garden, which relied on dancers trained at the School, made a token contribution to its upkeep, while Sadler's Wells had exhausted its reserves in supporting it. De

Valois reminded the Board that American entertainment tax had been remitted largely on educational grounds: its association with the School had preserved the Company's profits. By September 1953, Covent Garden had agreed to make a further contribution towards the School's capital expenses. De Valois's next complaint concerned the American tour. She was determined to prevent any repeat of the draining 1950–51 tour. Other overseas opportunities were turned down when the Company needed to rest or to build up the repertory.

De Valois had won her point, but the imbalance at Covent Garden remained. Just as the first Arts Council grant was earmarked for the opera, the ballet company's profits were used to balance the books at Covent Garden. Costs were rising, and the theatre required upkeep. More divisively, opera costs were rising. The opera company had started to bring in distinguished but expensive guest singers and conductors. Until the 1970s, the Board would respond to financial crises by asking the dancers to go to America. In 1960, the Directors admitted that long foreign tours laid a heavy burden on the dancers; the Ballet Sub-Committee plaintively asked that, when discussing finances with the Treasury and the Arts Council, 'the Board might wish to insist that arrangements should be made to balance the budget without this kind of enterprise.'[24] In public, the Royal Opera House tried to deny that the ballet paid the opera's debts. The first Covent Garden Report was carefully rewritten to remove the suggestion that one company subsidised the other. De Valois, who had resisted Tyrone Guthrie's attempt to spend her profits, remained loyal to her theatre. She resented the opera's encroachments on her company's rehearsal and performance time, but she liked Covent Garden. She loved being part of a broader theatrical tradition. 'I don't think opera and ballet should ever be divided,' she declared in a late interview. 'They haven't been over three hundred years. Why should they now?'[25] Even so, she realised that her companies needed greater security. She started to plan a new constitution for the whole Sadler's Wells Ballet organisation.

De Valois also made plans to encourage new choreographers, suggesting small-scale workshop performances. The Sadler's Wells Choreographic Group was organised by the dancer David Poole.

Characteristically, de Valois decided not to divert funds from either of her companies: she raised the money by appearing in a cigarette advertisement. The hit of the Choreographic Group's first performance was Kenneth MacMillan's *Somnambulism*, a moody piece to a jazz score by Stan Kenton. MacMillan's first ballet was astonishingly assured, with distinctive steps and a sense of atmosphere. It caused immediate excitement. Fonteyn came backstage to congratulate MacMillan; Covent Garden Directors urged each other to see the ballet. *Somnambulism* was filmed for television in 1954.

For the Covent Garden company, the first months of 1953 were overshadowed by death and illness. The whole company mourned Sophie Fedorovitch, and Fonteyn's return was postponed. She started rehearsals for *Apparitions*, one of her least strenuous roles, but was quickly exhausted. That spring, Moira Shearer returned as a guest artist, dancing *Symphonic Variations*, *Giselle*, *The Sleeping Beauty* and *Le Lac des cygnes* with new warmth and expression. These were her last performances with the Company. Markova was the other guest that spring. In March, Cranko made his second ballet for Covent Garden. *The Shadow* was set to folksy music by Dohnányi, with designs by John Piper. Philip Chatfield was driven away from Svetlana Beriosova's gracefully shy heroine by a menacing figure. When at last he confronted the Shadow, it collapsed and vanished – the cloak and hat were whisked out of sight, leaving empty air. The ballet was light, romantic and very popular.

Fonteyn returned to the stage on 18 March 1953, dancing *Apparitions*. She was welcomed back with an ovation, an outpouring of joy and relief at her recovery. Dancers and theatre staff crowded into the auditorium to join the applause. There were shouts of 'Margot!' and the flowers laid at Fonteyn's feet stretched from one side of the stage to the other. David Webster, the General Administrator of Covent Garden, was one of many who wept. When asked, 'What on earth is the matter?' he replied, 'If you don't understand you certainly don't deserve to be told.'[26]

Andrée Howard's *Veneziana*, which had its premiere in April, was a gentle divertissement. The music was an arrangement of Donizetti by Denis ApIvor. The Venetian settings had been completed by Sophie Fedorovitch not long before her death. Violetta

Elvin, in the leading role, danced with soft poise. She had recently made guest appearances at La Scala, and was showing new authority in the nineteenth-century ballets. In these months, Fonteyn carefully returned to her old repertory. At first she appeared only in one-act ballets. *Tiresias*, with its long duet, was her first real challenge. In May, she danced her first full-length *Lac des cygnes* in two years. 'Fonteyn's performances this season . . . will be talked of for generations to come,' wrote Haskell. 'Those who have seen her will irritate their juniors as much as I have done when discussing Pavlova and, insomuch as we are seeing Fonteyn in greater and more testing works and in a finer ensemble, Fonteyn stands higher.'[27] Her Odette had a tragic purity of line. One photograph shows her with head flung back, abandoned to emotion – all within the stretched clarity of a classical pose. Feeling was held and amplified by dancing of lucid simplicity.

The next new ballet was staged to celebrate the coronation of Elizabeth II. *Homage to the Queen* was performed on Coronation Night, 2 June 1953. Ashton's ballet was carefully designed to show off the whole company. There were movements for Air, Fire, Earth and Water, each with its own Queen and soloists, all doing homage. The score was commissioned from Malcolm Arnold. Nerina, cast against type, danced the Queen of the Earth. Elvin led the Water section, full of sensuous flowing lines. Grey was the Queen of Fire. The ballet ended with Fonteyn, the Queen of Air, partnered by Somes in a pas de deux full of soaring, elaborate lifts. The formal entrances suggested a seventeenth-century court masque. Oliver Messel's designs, influenced by Inigo Jones, heightened the effect. In a patriotic apotheosis, the Company saluted two Queen Elizabeths. The first handed her orb and sceptre to the new queen – 'which unfortunately you can never see,' admitted Ashton, 'but still, that's what she's supposed to be doing . . . the lighting always goes wrong at that moment.'[28] It turned *Homage to the Queen* into an occasion piece. The ballet was enthusiastically received, but did not last long in the repertory. The Air section, the only surviving choreography, will be revived in 2006, with new Earth, Water and Fire sections by David Bintley, Michael Corder and Christopher Wheeldon.

The Sadler's Wells Ballet's third visit to America started at the

Met in September 1953, in the middle of a heatwave. This New York season was a personal triumph for Ashton. For the first time, the Company's modern works were received as warmly as the classical productions. *Daphnis and Chloë* was hailed as a masterpiece, while *Sylvia* was praised much more warmly in New York than in London. An all-Ashton night sold out at once. Nerina had particular success in *The Sleeping Beauty*. 'She is pretty as a picture, has great charm, and can dance like a million dollars,' enthused John Martin in the *New York Times*. 'When Miss Nerina has developed a musical phrase to equal her command of the physical medium, we shall all be fighting to drink champagne out of her slippers.'[29]

The New York season was followed by a nineteen-week tour of the United States and Canada. In Toronto, the Sadler's Wells Ballet danced at the Maple Leaf Gardens, to an audience of more than nine thousand people. In Vancouver, Violetta Elvin strained a ligament, and had to limp off stage during *Homage to the Queen*. Backstage, Svetlana Beriosova got ready to replace her. All that was missing was the headdress – which the shaken Elvin was still wearing. 'Margot took command,' remembered Pauline Clayden. She gently unpinned the headdress, 'talking quietly and sympathetically all the time to Violetta . . . With a broad grin, she handed it to Svetlana – the show must go on . . .' In the meantime, Avril Navarre had been filling in on stage – though she didn't know the ballet. She made up the solo as she went along, whispering 'Tell me when to stop!' when she was near the wings.[30]

This tour had been carefully managed. Elvin's was the only serious injury, and the other dancers returned to London in good shape, opening the Covent Garden season at the end of February 1954. In March, de Valois staged the one new production of the season, a revised *Coppélia*. Osbert Lancaster's very bright designs lacked sunshine, but it was a cheerful and immediately popular production. As Swanilda, Nerina danced with strong technique and bounding vitality. She was partnered by David Blair, a vigorous young dancer who had transferred from the touring company the previous summer. Ashton was a gently sympathetic Dr Coppélius. De Valois was determined not to overwork her dancers with too many productions at once. She kept fewer works in repertory this season, with more changes of cast. This *Coppélia* had five fine Swanildas: Nerina, Beriosova, Avril Navarre, Rosemary Lindsay and Margaret Dale. Towards the end of the season, Beriosova made a superb debut in *The Sleeping Beauty*.

That summer, the Edinburgh Festival staged a Homage to Diaghilev, marking the twenty-fifth anniversary of his death. The Company staged *The Firebird*, which had its premiere in Edinburgh in August. Fokine's 1910 ballet was rehearsed by Serge Grigoriev and Lubov Tchernicheva, who had been régisseur and ballet mistress with the Diaghilev company. The designs, by Natalia Goncharova, were from Diaghilev's 1926 revival, with the ballerina in a red tutu rather than Bakst's elaborate costume of trousers and pearls. Most of the Sadler's Wells Fokine productions had been dutiful; *The Firebird* was magnificently alive, from the enchanted forest to the grandeur of the closing scene. The first performances were conducted by Ernest Ansermet, one of Diaghilev's most celebrated conductors. Fonteyn was rehearsed by Karsavina, who had created the role of the Firebird. 'Forget your graces,' Fokine had told her. 'The Firebird is powerful, hard to manage, rebellious.' Karsavina added, 'Here is no human emotion.'[31] In this role, the lyrical Fonteyn became feral, imperious, wild. She danced with teeth bared. The Firebird must soar; Fonteyn had never had much elevation. Instead, she achieved a darting quickness in the air, a flashing brilliance that lent scale and grandeur to her low jump. Somes made Ivan Tsarevitch a folk rather than a fairy-tale hero, rugged and shrewd. Beriosova was a gentle Tsarevna. Ashton appeared as the enchanter Kostchei. When the Firebird danced his creatures to sleep, Ashton's head trembled and his eyes remained open, trying to stay awake. Ansermet was once so gripped by the sight of Ashton falling asleep that he lost his own place in the score.

In September 1954, an exchange between the Paris Opéra and Sadler's Wells ballet companies was arranged. This was a source of great pride to de Valois: her company, founded less than a quarter-century earlier, was placed on equal footing with a 275-year-old state ballet. In the event, the exchange was disappointing. Paris and London had very different tastes, and neither company was an outright success. Parisian audiences looked down on British scene-painting – even Messel's – and wanted more signs of temperament from the dancers. Fonteyn, however, was much admired, and Elvin took five bows after her second-act adagio in *Le Lac des cygnes*. The Company went on from Paris to a hearteningly successful tour of Italy. Back in London, Beryl Grey returned from maternity leave to dance *Le Lac des cygnes* with bold line and clear musicality. A welcoming banner was hung from the gallery, and Grey was given a thunderous ovation.

Ashton dedicated his next two ballets to the memory of Sophie Fedorovitch. Both were designed to show off the Company's younger dancers, and they were performed together on 6 January 1955. In *Rinaldo and Armida*, Beriosova was an enchantress who drew lovers to her garden, but died when she herself fell in love. Armida's lovers were danced by Somes and Ronald Hynd. Peter Rice designed a wintry garden in shades of black, white and grey – more modish than romantic. The new Malcolm Arnold score was disappointingly thin, reminding most critics of film music. The second ballet, set to Britten's *Variations on a Theme of Purcell*, was all fuss. Ashton made fiddly leading roles for Nerina, Rowena Jackson and Elaine Fifield, who had recently moved from the touring company. They danced 'millions of steps', remembered Nerina; 'they nearly drove the three of us demented – "knitting, tatting and crocheting" was what we called them.'[32]

A few weeks later, Fifield danced her first Covent Garden *Coppélia*. She was strong, speedy and musical, with strikingly arched feet. Her Swanilda was confident and delightfully lively. Beriosova, who had danced her first full-length *Lac des cygnes* as a guest with the Yugoslav State Ballet, gave her first Covent Garden performance in February 1955. There was a dreamlike quality to Beriosova's dancing. The poise of her head and neck gave her an air of mystery, and her arms opened eloquently from a strong, supple back. Despite nerves, this first performance showed her beauty of line, her warmth, her sensitive musical phrasing. She became one of the Company's best-loved dancers, the supreme Odette–Odile of her generation.

That month, the announcement of Fonteyn's marriage made headlines around the world. The day before her wedding, she danced the Firebird at the matinee and Chloë in the evening: her fiercest and her most loving roles. In the finale of *Daphnis*, the corps came on with their scarves full of confetti and streamers, and showers of rose petals fell on the stage. Fonteyn returned after just two weeks, again dancing *The Firebird*, more popular than ever before. Her performances were guaranteed to sell out – so much so that they were specially marked in the box office accounts.

Fifield starred in Ashton's next ballet. *Madame Chrysanthème* was based on a novel by Pierre Loti, the source for Puccini's *Madama Butterfly*. Alexander Grant was the sailor who finds a 'temporary' Japanese wife. Unlike Butterfly, Chrysanthème is not a tragic figure: when the sailor returns for a last farewell, he finds her quietly counting the silver dollars he had paid for her. Ashton highlighted Fifield's delicacy, her neatness and her beautiful feet. Isabel Lambert designed a soft Japanese landscape, framed by lanterns and paper screens. The melodic, unsentimental score, commissioned from Alan Rawsthorne, began and ended with a woman singing wordlessly. The ballet had its premiere during a newspaper strike, and received little publicity. It had enthusiastic admirers, but did not last long in repertory.

The Lady and the Fool was the last new production of the season. John Cranko had made the ballet for the touring company in 1954. In June 1955, he revived it for Covent Garden, dropping several characters and reworking some of the choreography. The heroine refuses several suitors before falling love with a clown. Charles Mackerras arranged a delightful selection of music from several neglected Verdi operas. Philip Chatfield danced the tall, romantic clown – a role made for Kenneth MacMillan – with Ray Powell as his shorter, sadder friend. Cranko had hoped to cast Fonteyn as his heroine; de Valois urged him to use Beryl Grey. Her height meant more changes to the choreography, and she danced her new role with warmth and great technical command. That month, Robert Irving stepped down as Musical Director, becoming Musical Adviser to the Company instead. Irving was much admired on the Company's American tours, and in 1958, he moved to the New York City Ballet. At Covent Garden, he was replaced by Hugo Rignold.

That summer, there were two great changes to de Valois's organisation. The Sadler's Wells School acquired White Lodge, an eighteenth-century royal hunting lodge in Richmond Park. It became a residential junior school, leaving the London premises free for the seniors and for company rehearsals. The second change affected the touring company. Repertory seasons of ballet and opera had become too expensive for the Sadler's Wells Theatre. Instead, the ballet would have short London seasons and long regional tours. A few months after this change in policy, Peggy van Praagh resigned as Director of the Sadler's Wells Theatre Ballet, to be replaced by John Field. 'Do something about the classics,' de Valois told him.[33] Field built up the company until it could dance the nineteenth-century repertory, then rarely seen outside London. Since their American success, the Covent Garden Company had made fewer visits to the provinces. De Valois insisted that her main company should still be seen in Britain as a whole, but that now meant occasional visits to cities with larger theatres. The touring company stepped up to fill the gap; by 1957, it had achieved enough status for Clive Barnes to call it 'the national ballet of the Provinces'.[34]

The Covent Garden Company toured America again that year, opening at the Met in September 1955. *Madame Chrysanthème* and even *Tiresias* were received much more warmly in New York than in London. *The Firebird* was admired and eagerly compared with Balanchine's 1949 production. Grey was popular in both *Lady and the Fool* and *Le Lac des cygnes*; Beriosova was praised as a new Aurora. This tour concentrated on larger cities, with no one-night stands and a much easier schedule for the dancers. After three nights at the Maple Leaf Gardens, they returned to New York to film *The Sleeping Beauty* for NBC Television. The ballet was cut to fit a ninety-minute slot, with some awkward filming, but this studio recording gives some sense of the Company's clarity and authority. *Variety* called it 'a stunning success', and it was seen by thirty million people.[35]

The Company's Silver Jubilee season began at Covent Garden on New Year's Eve, 1955, with an oddly unfestive triple bill. Grey danced *Les Sylphides* – one of her best roles, but all around her the corps had adopted a new and deathly make-up. Fonteyn was radiant in *Daphnis and Chloë*, but the final *Homage to the Queen* was given a routine performance. The next morning, it was announced that Fonteyn had been created Dame of the British Empire. Five days later, she and Somes danced the second-act duet from *Le Lac des cygnes* at the gala for the twenty-fifth anniversary of the reopened Sadler's Wells. At this same gala, the touring company performed *Danses concertantes*, MacMillan's triumphant first work as a professional choreographer.

MacMillan had made his darting, distinctive setting of Stravinsky's score in January 1955. The steps are spiky, with pointed fingers, legs crossed and uncrossed, pirouettes suddenly twisted. Arms reach onstage from the wings; the ballerina peers through hands held like spectacles. MacMillan added jazz steps and off-balance moves, accenting rhythms with sharp-edged pointe-work. De Valois had suggested that MacMillan look for a designer at the Slade School of Fine Art, and she took him to Gower Street to see the students' work. After wandering the corridors for some minutes, MacMillan said, 'Madam, there seem to be an awful lot of nurses about the place.' They had taken the wrong entrance, ending up in University College Hospital.[36] Next door at the Slade, MacMillan chose Nicholas Georgiadis, who was to work closely with him for nearly forty years. MacMillan was to show a gift for finding designers, often choosing students at the start of their careers. 'Georgiadis uses lots of colours splashed about in great variety,' said MacMillan, 'like the variety of rhythms I look for in a score.'[37] For *Danses concertantes*, he designed a glowing blue-green set with inky curlicues and winged sphinxes. The bright costumes were patterned with arrows. The ballet was confident, incisive and bold, and de Valois at once appointed MacMillan resident choreographer to the Sadler's Wells Theatre Ballet. He earned less than he had as a dancer: his salary was cut from £14 to £13 a week. MacMillan danced no more classical roles, but in January 1956 he returned as the Helpmann Sister in *Cinderella* at Covent Garden.

In 1931, Ashton had choreographed *La Péri* for the Ballet Club, casting Markova and himself in the leading roles; its composer, Paul Dukas, was then still alive. Now, twenty-five years later, he made a new version for Fonteyn and Somes as his next ballet for the Company. To Ashton's disgust, Dukas's publishers insisted that he stick to the composer's original instructions, and limit the male role to mime and partnering. Ashton had to cut the choreography he had made for Somes, who was left with almost no role. Ashton side-stepped a demand that he use the original Bakst designs by producing a photograph of one, saying, 'You don't think Fonteyn will dance in *that*, do you?'[38] Even so, *La Péri*, which had its pre-miere in February 1956, dwindled into a gala number.

It was now ten years since the move to Covent Garden. The Company marked the anniversary with a week of *The Sleeping Beauty*: six Auroras, starting with Fonteyn and ending with Fifield's jubilant debut. Elvin, Grey, Nerina and Beriosova were individual and admirable Auroras. The entire company gave a superb display of strength. In 1946, it had still been growing into the ballet. A decade on, it was radiantly secure. 'Balletomanes notoriously sigh for the snows of yesteryear, and murmur in their beards that ballet isn't what it was when they were what they were,' wrote Mary Clarke. 'Yet on this occasion the unanimous verdict was that the per-formance was better than it had ever been.'[39] The Lilac Fairy's attendants and Aurora's 'little friends' won particular praise. In these dances, bright rhythm and beautifully stretched feet were to be a hallmark of the Company's classicism for the next twenty-five years.

In 1956, as in 1946, Leslie Edwards played Catalabutte, the mas-ter of ceremonies. His performance was already a company tradition: dignified, amusingly unctuous, always a courtier. In March 1956, he also played the central role in a macabre story of a hypnotist who turns his powers on his audience. The setting was a seedy back-street theatre, the onstage audience perched in boxes by the wings. Nerina danced a Faded Beauty whose charm returned under hypnosis. This was *Noctambules*, Kenneth MacMillan's first work for the Covent Garden company, and the designs were again by Georgiadis. Humphrey Searle's commissioned score was freneti-cally theatrical, piling up crashes and climaxes, but MacMillan stepped confidently up to the larger scale of the Opera House: his ballet was never dwarfed by the bigger stage.

Later that month, David Blair danced the full-length *Lac des cygnes*. It was an occasion for pride: for the first time, de Valois invited critics to see the debut of a *male* dancer in a classical role.

Blair gave a handsome performance, strong and assured. An athletic, extrovert dancer, he brought a competitive edge which had a tonic effect on the men of the Company. He even started a club for male dancers, 'to which the entrance fee was the ability to execute eight pirouettes, later increased to twelve.'[40] This new vigour was put on display that spring, at the Company's Silver Jubilee.

The celebration performance took place at Covent Garden on 5 May 1956 – grander than the twenty-first birthday party, but with something of the same family feeling. Helpmann returned for *The Rake's Progress* and *Façade*, dancing a sensational Tango with Fonteyn. The nineteen-year-old Merle Park danced the Milkmaid with carefree aplomb. And Ashton made *Birthday Offering*, set to Robert Irving's selection of Glazunov, as a tribute to de Valois and to the Company. Ashton showed off seven ballerinas in individual variations: precise footwork for Fifield, brilliant turns for Rowena Jackson, Beriosova's eloquent grace, Nerina's soaring jump, Elvin's languor. Grey's solo showed off her strength and control; Ashton chose that music because, he claimed, he could hear her laugh in the melody. Fonteyn's solo was full of quick beaten steps – 'they're all going to have to look at Margot's feet,' said Ashton wickedly.[41] The seven men were displayed in a mazurka filled with demanding steps. This ended with Somes dancing tours en l'air, flanked by Blair and Desmond Doyle turning pirouettes, while Brian Shaw, Bryan Ashbridge, Philip Chatfield and Alexander Grant span beside them. *Birthday Offering*, made for a special occasion, lasted well beyond it. The dancers promptly nicknamed it 'Seven Brides for Seven Brothers'. The evening ended with a speech from de Valois. 'Twenty-five years old – that means we can take two paths,' she declared. 'We can sit back and just remember what we have achieved or we can sit up and remember what we still have got to do. Now I am going to ask you to use your imagination and guess which is the path we are going to take next season.'[42]

Before the London season ended, Fifield made a stunning debut in *Le Lac des cygnes*. She had a vivid flow of movement, with pure line and bold attack. The audience went on cheering her long after the house lights came up. She had another leading role in the Company's next new work.

Alfred Rodrigues had made four ballets for the touring company, including the intense *Blood Wedding*, in which Fifield had played the Bride. For the Edinburgh Festival in August 1956, Rodrigues cast her as the prostitute in a new production of Bartók's *The Miraculous Mandarin*. Luring Somes's miscast Mandarin, Fifield was both fearful and ruthless. The ballet's sex and violence caused a lively scandal, but it did not last in repertory. Back at Covent Garden, Nerina danced her first Firebird. The role showed off her soaring jump, her boldness, her aplomb. Nerina could get caught up in her own magnificent technique, losing the shape of her role or her music. In *The Firebird*, she recovered the verve she had shown at the start of her career.

The Bolshoi Ballet, who visited Covent Garden as part of a planned exchange with the Sadler's Wells Ballet, dominated the autumn of 1956. In September, the visit was almost called off when a Russian athlete was arrested and charged with shoplifting in Oxford Street. The Cold War was then at its height; most of the Bolshoi artists, including the prima ballerina Galina Ulanova, wrote to the Moscow newspaper *Isvestia* declaring that they feared similar 'provocation' in London.[43] The incident was at last smoothed over. These performances – the West's first chance to view the immense resources of Soviet Russian ballet since the revolution of 1917 – caused a sensation. The first night brought the huge, weighty realism of Leonid Lavrovsky's production of *Romeo and Juliet*: Ulanova, the most revered dancer in Russia, danced the heroine. 'Every dancer presented a complete, full-blooded character,' wrote Fonteyn, 'but we were stunned by the revelation that was Ulanova.'[44] The Bolshoi had an impact in London comparable to that of the Sadler's Wells Ballet in New York: rapturous acclaim, followed by a thoughtful look at native ballet companies. The Sadler's Wells Ballet looked, too. When Fonteyn danced Sylvia later that year, Clive Barnes noticed a new identification with her role, the involvement she had seen in Ulanova. Ashton added some Bolshoi-like steps to his ballet, including Sylvia's near-acrobatic dive into Aminta's arms.

While the Bolshoi danced at Covent Garden, the Sadler's Wells Ballet danced in Croydon, Coventry and Oxford, preparing for their own trip to Moscow. They were to open on 14 November with *The Lady and the Fool*, *Birthday Offering* and *Daphnis and Chloë*. Then, in late October, Hungary rebelled against Soviet rule. On 4 November, Soviet troops moved into Budapest. Three days later, David Webster sent a cable to Moscow: 'In view of public opinion in this country which strongly condemns the renewed suppression by Soviet forces of Hungarian liberty and independence . . . it has been unanimously agreed that in present circumstances the projected visit of the Sadler's Wells Ballet to Moscow cannot take place.'[45] The Company returned to Covent Garden for a hastily improvised season. None of the Moscow repertory could be used: the productions had already been sent to Russia. *Cinderella* was revived, to grudging reviews from Bolshoi-smitten critics. The season looked up with a revival of *Sylvia* and, after the return of the scenery, *The Sleeping Beauty*.

That autumn, the Company received its Royal Charter. It was granted on 31 October, just before the cancellation of the Moscow visit, and was announced publicly on 16 January 1957. The Sadler's Wells Ballet, Sadler's Wells Theatre Ballet and Sadler's Wells School were brought together under the title of The Royal Ballet, with the Queen as Patron and Princess Margaret as President. The Charter was the result of de Valois's new constitution for her organisation. As early as 1952, the Royal Opera House Directors had suggested renaming the Company 'The Covent Garden Ballet', acknowledging the change of address. De Valois saw the need, not just for a new name, but for a change of status. She had discovered that the Arts Council made grants to the Sadler's Wells Theatre and the Royal Opera House for the presentation of opera and ballet – not for any specific company. Legally, her companies did not exist. The Royal Charter established their independence. The Royal Ballet was still under Covent Garden management, but it had the right to withdraw if the need arose. 'The question of a name is but a first step in a plan that would enable our ballet to face its existence as an *entity*,' de Valois had written in a 1954 memorandum, 'and so ensure its continuity whatever conditions may prevail.'[46]

The next new production, *The Prince of the Pagodas*, was deliberately planned as a landmark. This was the first evening-length

British ballet to a commissioned score. In 1954, de Valois had asked John Cranko to submit a scenario. He devised a plot based on several fairy stories, then 'asked Britten if he had any ideas about composers, little dreaming that he would become excited enough with *Pagodas* to undertake it himself.'[47] After several delays, the ballet had its premiere on New Year's Day, 1957, with the composer conducting. Britten's music was gorgeously inventive, filled with fanfares and gamelan textures. It was closely tied to Cranko's rambling scenario, making an overactive, untidy ballet. The rather passive heroine kept getting sidetracked into divertissements. Cranko hung so many dances on his plot, wrote Alexander Bland, 'that it sags at times like an over-extended clothes line'.[48] The choreography included acrobatic tumblings and the high lifts recently shown by the Bolshoi. There were mechanical devices, dancing pagodas with opening paper fans, a flying carpet and a moving cloud. Effects tended to cancel each other out. John Piper's designs were bold and sometimes harsh, with aggressive use of blue and orange. Cranko made his best choreography for his heroine, and Beriosova danced with soft grandeur. There were demanding roles for the men, with strong performances from David Blair as the Salamander Prince and Gary Burne as the Prince of the South. Farron was commanding as the wicked sister.

After the success of *The Firebird*, de Valois decided to stage Fokine's *Petrushka*. The ballet was scrupulously revived. Grigoriev and Tchernicheva returned to rehearse the ballet, the Benois designs were carefully recreated, and Malcolm Sargent conducted the first performances. Alexander Grant gave an unsentimental performance as the puppet Petrushka, but could not bring the ballet to life. Fonteyn was tentative as the Doll. Critics complained that this was a dutiful reconstruction. The dancers looked too young and too classical in Fokine's shifting, naturalistic crowd scenes; the stamping coachmen were much too slender. In fact, Margaret Dale's television film of this production has more vigour than those reviews suggest: the weight may be missing, but there's plenty of juice in the crowd dances. Even so, The Royal Ballet were happier in a revival of *Ballet Imperial*. Nerina danced the ballerina role with triumphant virtuosity. In a second cast, Fifield had less bravura but sharper musical phrasing. Beryl Grey, outstanding as the second ballerina, resigned from the Company that spring. She gave her last performance as a member of the Company on 18 April 1957, dancing *Le Lac des cygnes*. She was to make regular guest appearances between 1959 and 1963.

Grey left in frustration. In recent months she had been given few performances, sometimes dancing only once in six weeks. Like Violetta Elvin, who had retired altogether the previous summer, she felt sidelined by Fonteyn's dominance. As the prima ballerina, as Ashton's muse, Fonteyn had more roles than any other dancer in the Company. She had not been obvious casting for *Petrushka*, any more than she had been for *The Three-Cornered Hat* or *Mam'zelle Angot*, yet she was automatically given the roles. She was a beloved star; she guaranteed a full house. In New York, she had not only opened every season, she had danced the first night of every classical production. That season, the Company lost a third ballerina. Fonteyn went to dance a guest season in Australia, taking three other Royal Ballet soloists chosen by de Valois. The Australian Elaine Fifield, an obvious choice for this tour, was desperately disappointed to find she was not one of them. She resigned. 'My child,' de Valois told her, 'you're going to regret this all your life. You've burned your boats.'[49] When Fifield asked if she could return to the Company, de Valois turned her down flat. At the same time, de Valois and the Royal Opera House did not know how long Fonteyn's career would last. She had married; she was now in her late thirties. She was making more guest appearances around the world. In 1956, the Covent Garden Board suggested that she was now essentially a guest artist. They wanted to make the most of Fonteyn while they still had her.

The future of the touring company was also in doubt. The Sadler's Wells Theatre had been running at a loss; in 1956, its Governors had warned the Arts Council that it might have to close altogether. It could no longer support the touring company. In May 1957, Covent Garden accepted responsibility for the touring company. Both branches would now be called 'The Royal Ballet', and their work would be co-ordinated. Repertories would be shared, with touring giving the Covent Garden dancers more opportunities.

De Valois's long-term aim was a single integrated company, sections of which could be sent on tour. This, in fact, was how the Bolshoi operated – while a hundred dancers had visited London, even more had remained to perform in Moscow. Fusion would, de Valois admitted, take time; until then, the companies would remain separate. In fact, true integration never took place. The relationship between the companies was repeatedly redefined, as The Royal Ballet tried to balance the duty and the expense of regional touring.

In September 1957, the Covent Garden Royal Ballet returned to America, starting with a four-week season at the Met. Box-office takings were higher than ever, although the new productions were not much liked. *The Prince of the Pagodas* did no better in New York than it had in London. MacMillan's *Noctambules* had a lukewarm reception, and his appealing *Solitaire* – taken over from the touring company – lost impact on the Met stage. *Birthday Offering* was the real success. The Met visit was followed by a tour of seventeen big cities in sixteen weeks, ending in Montreal in January 1958. The Company returned to Covent Garden in February with a lively performance of *Sylvia*. This was a quiet season, dominated by revivals. In March, weeks before his forty-ninth birthday, Helpmann returned as a guest artist in *The Rake's Progress*, *Miracle in the Gorbals* and *Hamlet*. His powers as a mime remained, though *Miracle in the Gorbals* now looked very melodramatic. Helpmann's Petrushka was a disappointment. Some critics had found Grant too forceful as Petrushka; Helpmann was too much Helpmann, his own personality distractingly visible. In June, Merle Park danced her first Swanilda, coached by de Valois. It was a confident, quick-witted performance. 'I loved Madam's coaching, it was so *logical*,' says Park now. '"No, dear, you wouldn't do it like that. *Think* about it. If you're shaking her dress, really *shake* it."' Park's dancing was crisp, daring and musical. She could zip through a step, switching directions without loss of clarity, and arrive in a pose with cut-glass precision.

The next new production, MacMillan's *Agon*, came in August. Stravinsky's score had been written for Balanchine and the New York City Ballet; that definitive production had had its premiere in December 1957. For MacMillan's version, Georgiadis designed a golden-orange backcloth, with silhouetted figures watching the action. The dancers had an air of cynical sophistication. Blair and Anya Linden, who had danced her first Aurora that spring, had leading roles. This *Agon*, never popular, was quickly dropped. Just after the premiere, the French ballerina Yvette Chauviré gave several guest performances with the Company, dancing Aurora with particular elegance.

Ondine, which had its premiere in October 1958, was Ashton's first work for the Company in more than two years. It was a three-act ballet, based on Friedrich de la Motte Fouqué's 1811 tale of a water nymph and her love for a mortal. Even more than *Sylvia*, *Ondine* was made to show off Fonteyn. She emerged from a fountain in darting, rippling steps, looking in wonder at the human world of earth and sky. The footwork of her entrance, stepping on pointe and dropping her heel with every step, had an effect of splashing water. She discovered and danced with her shadow – a device taken from Jules Perrot's nineteenth-century *Ondine* ballet, the famous pas de l'ombre made for the ballerina Cerrito. Ashton was following nineteenth-century models, with corps scenes and a big divertissement in the last act. He and his designer, Lila de Nobili, created old-fashioned stage wonders. The corps, like Fonteyn, materialised out of the scenery. In the second act, set on board ship, dancers swayed until the deck seemed to heave and pitch under their feet. De Nobili's misty Gothic sets were painted with delicate brushstrokes. Her costumes were variable: lovely draperies for Ondine, unflattering wigs and boots for the hunters who open the ballet. The music was commissioned from Hans Werner Henze, who gave up his modernist ideas for the ballet, trying to follow Ashton's romantic conception. Ashton and his first cast found the score hard to work with; dancers still do. Henze built washes of sound with tricky rhythms: sometimes striking, sometimes uninspired.

The dances for Fonteyn aside, *Ondine* was choreographically thin. Palemon, the hero, and Berta, his fiancée, were static and under-characterised. Ashton was more inventive in his dances for the sea lord Tirrenio – Alexander Grant in a dramatic silk cloak – and for the corps of ondines. Monica Mason, who had just joined the corps de ballet, was thrilled and fascinated by Ashton's coaching. He wanted soft lines, movement that would ebb and flow, and he urged his dancers 'to move our hands and arms as if we had water dripping off the ends of our fingers.'[50] He piled the corps up into a Busby Berkeley pyramid, a fountain with Ondine at its centre. The last-act divertissement was overlong and laboured. Ashton later made cuts, but the structure remained stodgy. In New York, two years later, Edwin Denby was 'surprised that so marvellous a creature as Ondine should pick her friends from among shoddy people and trivial immortals. The ballet is foolish and everyone noticed it.'[51] Yet de Valois adored *Ondine*: 'a noble and perfectly conceived work on a grand scale,' she wrote to Ashton, 'which is the only scale for you to concern yourself with from now on.'[52] She was eager for milestones, for works on a 'grand scale' that would prove her company's authority and status. As Ashton himself realised, this was not a scale that suited him. *Ondine* had lost vitality by being stretched to three acts, and its reproduction of nineteenth-century motifs seemed stale. British theatre was being transformed by plays such as Beckett's *Waiting for Godot* and Osborne's *Look Back in Anger*; *Ondine* and Pinter's *The Birthday Party* were both staged in 1958. The ballet's world of grottoes and hermits looked helplessly dated.

In September 1958, the touring company set out on a triumphant seven-month tour of Australia and New Zealand. Rowena Jackson and Philip Chatfield led the Company, and most of the Covent Garden principals appeared during the tour. Beriosova gave sensational performances in Sydney, and Helpmann – returning to his native country – was tremendously popular. He coached the younger dancers, particularly the Canadian Lynn Seymour and Donald MacLeary, her regular partner. 'He regaled us with amazing tales,' remembered Seymour. 'But it was his presence in rehearsals – suggestions, moments of stagecraft, try this, try that – he unlocked doors, gave us freedom to experiment.'[53] Seymour was a classical dancer of extraordinary individuality, musical and powerfully expressive. As a student, she had been singled out by de Valois and then Ashton; in the touring company, MacMillan gave her an important role in *The Burrow*, his first realistic dance-drama. In Melbourne, she made her debut as Odette–Odile. Her dancing had a melting, voluptuous quality: the softness of water, and its force.

Back in London, the Covent Garden section of The Royal Ballet staged a clutch of works that had been made for the touring company. In December 1958, *La Fête étrange* was revived for Beriosova. Andrée Howard's ballet had been made for the London Ballet in 1940 and revived for the touring company in 1947. A country boy, stumbling on an engagement party, falls in love with the heroine. It was a delicate, atmospheric ballet, with a wintry setting by Sophie Fedorovitch. The hero had been one of Pirmin Trecu's best roles at Sadler's Wells, and he returned to partner Beriosova. In March 1959, Cranko's 1951 ballet *Harlequin in April* was revived. This time, David Blair was the dancer returning to his original role. Cranko's Harlequin was a symbol of human aspiration, rising up from a mass of blind, plant-like figures and sinking into sleep with the end of the year. The ballet lost its impact on the larger Covent Garden stage, but Cranko gave Antoinette Sibley her first leading role as Columbine.

Five days after *Harlequin in April*, at a Benevolent Fund Gala on 10 March, The Royal Ballet danced Ashton's *La Valse*. When he was in Ida Rubinstein's company, Ashton had danced in Nijinska's first version of Ravel's score. He had made his own version for the ballet of La Scala, Milan in 1958. André Levasseur had designed a stylised ballroom set, around which a series of couples swoop and flow, with hints of drama. Men and women stand on opposite sides of the stage, eyes averted, reaching towards each other. In the couple dances, men lifted their partners, then let them sink slowly back to the floor. The next week, the Covent Garden company revived *Danses concertantes*. As before, Maryon Lane danced the ballerina role with speedy precision. From the beginning, MacMillan's ballet had been praised for its tart invention; it transferred boldly to the Covent Garden stage. Both *La Valse* and *Danses concertantes* remain in repertory.

Until this year, de Valois's students had never given school displays; in the early days, they had been dancing in the Company while still at school. The first public performance by The Royal Ballet School took place on 21 March, with an account of *Coppélia*. Antoinette Sibley and Graham Usher, young dancers who had recently joined the Company, played Swanilda and Franz. All other roles were danced by the students. Mary Clarke remembered, 'we were all bowled over by the fact, not that Sibley and Usher could do it, but that the School could . . . you would not have known if you'd walked off the street that it *was* the School. Madam wouldn't have risked it otherwise.'[54] There would be an annual School performance from 1959 on.

In June 1959, in a move they had been considering for some time, the Covent Garden Board of Directors agreed to raise prices for Fonteyn performances. Fonteyn was outraged: 'This is the sort of thing they do for guest artists,' she told David Webster, 'and I'm *not* a guest artist.'[55] Webster responded with a press release: on 10 July, it was reported that Fonteyn *had* been made a guest artist with The Royal Ballet. This was a financial decision, made to increase revenues. At the same time, the management was nervously aware of how much Fonteyn still dominated the Company. She had reached forty that year; it was assumed that she would soon retire. Troubled by a foot injury, she had stopped dancing *Le Lac des cygnes*. With Fonteyn as guest artist, the Company began to bill Nerina and Beriosova as its 'senior ballerinas'.

An exceptional younger generation was coming through. Seymour danced her first Covent Garden *Lac des cygnes* in May 1959. That summer, both sections of The Royal Ballet danced together at Covent Garden. The ideal of the integrated company was still being proclaimed, but it wasn't what happened on stage. For the most part, each group performed its own repertory, with few exchanges of dancers. MacLeary, a tall and lyrical dancer, was moved to Covent Garden to partner Beriosova. In August, Sibley danced the ballerina role in *Ballet Imperial*, giving a swift, proud account of Balanchine's exacting steps. She was a musical dancer with long, fluent arms, clear line and quick, expressive feet; like Seymour, she was being groomed for principal roles. She made her debut in *Le Lac des cygnes* that autumn, when the Covent Garden company toured to theatres in the London suburbs. In October, Nerina fell ill and Sibley replaced her as Odette–Odile at Covent Garden. Critics were hastily summoned, and reported a triumph. The glamour of overnight success was irresistible; Sibley had to fend off the photographers camped outside her flat.

Antigone, which had its premiere in October, was the last new production of the decade. Cranko and his composer, Mikis Theodorakis, aimed to show the modernity of Greek tragedy, framing the heroine with political plots and quarrels. Beriosova, in soft shoes, danced Antigone. The ballet's style was harshly dramatic, with brooding designs by the Mexican painter Rufino Tamayo. *Antigone* was never very popular, but stayed in repertory for several years. In December 1960, Cranko made the slight *Sweeney Todd* for the touring company. It was his last work for The Royal Ballet. With Ashton, guest choreographers and now MacMillan working for both companies, de Valois had given Cranko fewer opportunities. In 1961, he left to direct the Stuttgart Ballet. Links were maintained, however, between the Royal and Stuttgart companies: leading Stuttgart dancers Marcia Haydée and Richard Cragun had been trained at The Royal Ballet School, and several works made for Stuttgart were later staged at Covent Garden.

In this decade, The Royal Ballet had grown into its position as one of the world's pre-eminent companies. In 1960, this was the most influential company in the world. Neither Balanchine nor Russian companies could yet match the worldwide impact of The Royal Ballet, admired in Europe, America and throughout the Commonwealth. The 1950s had been a time of consolidation. De Valois needed to find a balance for her company – setting the need for new work against commercial demands, finding performances for a large number of established and promising dancers. Adjustment was sometimes bumpy. It had taken time to recover from the second American tour, and the criticism that followed it; *The Prince of the Pagodas* and *Ondine* both showed signs of forced ambition. But the Company's dancing standards were the wonder of these years. The Royal Ballet had astonishing strength in depth, from the seven ballerinas of *Birthday Offering* to the young generation led by Park, Seymour and Sibley. Male dancing had already been transformed by 1956, when the example of the Bolshoi spurred the Company on to new goals. The next decade would bring renewal and fresh excitement.

SIX

Beautiful people

1960–69

ABOVE The Shades scene from *La Bayadère*, showing the sensuous flow of
movement through the whole corps de ballet: © Zoë Dominic
PREVIOUS PAGE The Royal Ballet from Swinging London. 1960s publicity
shot with, left to right: Georgina Parkinson, Antoinette Sibley, Monica
Mason, Vyvyane Lorrayne, Ann Jenner, Deanne Bergsma, Jennifer Penney:
collection of Robert Greskovic

By the end of the 1950s, de Valois had achieved her dream of forming an establishment. Her company had its international reputation, its Royal Charter, its growing influence on young companies around the world. It had become a little stately. The next decade brought in fresh air, an openness that came from several sources. The most spectacular was Rudolf Nureyev, the first of the Soviet defectors, bringing a different schooling and his own extraordinary charisma. He overturned plenty of Royal Ballet assumptions, but the Company was already renewing itself from within. Frederick Ashton was turning away from the stifling 'grand scale', finding a fresh vein of lyricism. Kenneth MacMillan, The Royal Ballet's own Angry Young Man, established himself as its second defining choreographer. De Valois herself, always ready to change her mind, was bringing in guest artists and encouraging ideas from outside. The Company thrived. Performances gained a new stretch and expansiveness. This was to be a golden age for The Royal Ballet.

The change began with Ashton's first new work of the decade. *La Fille mal gardée* must have sounded like a successor to *Sylvia* or *Ondine*: another old ballet revisited. But *Fille* has no gods and no fairies. This is Ashton's story of everyday love, everyday beauties, and it is one of the best-loved ballets in the repertory. Ashton based his *Fille* on a 1789 ballet by Jean Dauberval, first presented in Bordeaux in the year of the French revolution. There had been several subsequent productions. Ashton consulted Karsavina about the version she had danced in St Petersburg, drawing on her memories of its ribbon and maypole dances. She also taught Ashton Lise's lovely mime scene, the heroine dreaming of marriage and children. The lively music was arranged by John Lanchbery from the scores of earlier productions, mainly the 1828 score by Hérold. The lightly comic designs were by Osbert Lancaster.

Ashton cast Nerina and Blair as the lovers, making glorious use of their technical strength: astonishingly quick footwork, buoyant jumps, high Bolshoi lifts. Blair was a virile, high-spirited Colas. Nerina blossomed as Lise, dancing with joyful exuberance and warmth. Love in Ashton's *Fille* is both lyrical and frank. The dances for the lovers have a fresh sensuality, a radiant combination of sexuality and innocence. When Colas kisses his way up Lise's arm, she rises on pointe, tremblingly responsive. As in *Daphnis and Chloë*, though in a different spirit, the lovers are part of an onstage world. Lise's friends hold the ribbons that flutter through the duet in the harvest scene, winding patterns around the couple. Ashton wove ribbon and folk dances all through *Fille*. His maypole dance was based on one of the national dances taught at The Royal Ballet School. Stanley Holden, who danced Lise's mother, the Widow Simone, had been a champion clog dancer in his teens. He provided Ashton with the traditional steps for the Widow's now celebrated clog dance. Holden's Simone was lovingly observed, with real affection for her wayward daughter. Ashton cast Grant as Alain, the comic suitor, with a series of clumsy-nimble dances.

Ashton expressed tenderness in dances of extraordinary bravura, country life in brilliantly intricate corps scenes. In *Ondine*, he had staged a storm with falling scenery, dancers miming the pitch of the ship, unseen hands waving billowing scarves. The storm in *Fille* is all in the dancing. Gusts of wind seem to drive the corps leaping and turning across the stage. There are flurries of rain in the quick footwork, little groups of dancers swinging knees and shoulders through eddying shifts of direction as their feet prance out the steps.

Fille, a work of perfect craftsmanship, was made in less than four weeks of rehearsal. Ashton had been planning the ballet for some time; he was prodded into action by de Valois. 'I know him,' she told John Tooley, 'we'll still be waiting here next year.' She promptly announced the ballet in the programme, 'so he's *got* to make it!' It was an instant, overwhelming success. 'So now I'm an Old Master,' Ashton said to Clive Barnes when he saw the reviews.[1] His response to Nerina and Blair was another breakthrough. In recent works, Ashton's success had seemed to depend in part on Fonteyn. *Ondine* or *Sylvia* worked less well without her; ballets for other dancers faded from the repertory. In *Fille*, choreographer and company had a triumph without their prima ballerina. Ashton was working with new dancers, finding new aspects of their gifts and his own. These roles were lovingly tailored for these dancers, but they survived later casts more readily than Ashton's recent parts for Fonteyn. Nerina's steps were so dazzling that observers wondered if any other dancer could get her feet around them – until Merle Park gave a lively performance of the first act at the Benevolent Fund gala that spring.

The Ashton–Fonteyn partnership had started with *Le Baiser de la fée*. In April, MacMillan staged a new version of the ballet, casting his own muse, Lynn Seymour, as the bride. He made melting, skimming steps that showed off her fluid movements and luscious feet. In this scene, wrote Edwin Denby, MacMillan 'showed his striking gift for poetry'.[2] Score and libretto remained problematic: the ballet lacked contrast and fell into anti-climax. Beriosova was a grandly fluent fairy, with Donald MacLeary as the young man. Seymour was adorably soft and spontaneous. Kenneth Rowell designed elaborate costumes with spiky plastic decoration – not at all a traditional fairy tale. His sets were half-abstract, strikingly lit; the village scene glowed like stained glass. They made this *Baiser* hard to stage – of sixty other works in the repertory, it could be programmed with only six.[3] Though admired, the ballet had few performances.

The great 1946 *Sleeping Beauty* was now fourteen years old. After 337 performances at Covent Garden, and many more across the world, the production was getting shabby. In the summer of 1960, Messel returned to revamp his designs, though his new colours and fabrics seemed harsher than the originals. There were some changes to the text: an extended Panorama, an expanded role for Carabosse. Other revisions would follow.

Ashton consulted Karsavina again for his new production of *Giselle*. She provided details of the ballet she had danced before the revolution, especially its mime. Cut passages were restored to the score, including the moment when Giselle is crowned Queen of the Vintage. Karsavina taught Gerd Larsen the scene in which Giselle's mother warns her daughter of the dangers of dancing and of the Wilis. Ashton covered any gaps with new choreography. He also made a new solo for the girl in the first-act 'Peasant' pas de deux. This *Giselle* used the ballet's original ending, with Albrecht and his fiancée reunited. This proved unpopular, and was later dropped.

The new *Giselle* had its premiere in New York in September, on the Company's sixth tour of America. For the first time, all three senior ballerinas had a premiere. Fonteyn danced *The Sleeping Beauty* and all the New York performances of *Giselle*, but she had given up Odette–Odile. Beriosova danced the first *Lac des cygnes*; Nerina had *Fille*. There were few performances left for younger dancers, but Annette Page, who had danced her first *Sleeping Beauty* in 1959, was hailed as an enchanting Aurora. De Valois brought Lynn Seymour to New York for *Le Baiser de la fée*. She made a great impression – not least on the modern-dance pioneer Martha Graham – though the ballet had mixed reviews. Cranko's *Antigone* was generally disliked. Outside New York, audiences complained about limited repertory; Hurok insisted that the Company stick to the classics on the road. Even so, P. W. Manchester recorded 'overwhelming admiration' for the Company itself. 'And it is not only admiration,' she added. 'There is something else more precious. It is love.'[4]

While the Covent Garden company continued their five-month tour, visiting twenty-six cities in the US and Canada, Seymour returned to London to work on MacMillan's next ballet. *The Invitation*, first performed in Oxford in November 1960, was MacMillan's second dance-drama. He was eager to give ballet its own new wave, to match recent developments in British theatre. Absurdist theatre, 'kitchen sink' drama – a deglamorised domestic realism – and the example of European companies were all in the air. MacMillan and his associates went to new movies, new plays. When he took Lynn Seymour to see Ionesco's absurdist drama *The Chairs* at the Royal Court, she was fascinated by the way the actress Joan Plowright used her body, her feet, and drew on it for *The Invitation*.

Ballet had had little connection with this explosion of expression. It's a surprise to find that Donald Albery had asked Fonteyn for her opinion when he considered staging *Waiting for Godot*. (She thought he should stage it.) The younger Sadler's Wells company did have a reputation for meaty dramas, but *The Invitation* still came as a shock. The setting is an Edwardian house party. Two young cousins, a boy and a girl, flirt shyly with each other. A married couple watch and intervene. The boy is seduced by the wife; the girl is raped by the husband. The rape, graphically choreographed, takes place on stage. MacMillan had the girl twisted into a knot around her attacker's hips. The Husband, with his back to the audience, visibly reaches sexual climax. The girl, still hooked around his body, slides down to the floor. Traumatised, she rejects her cousin, walking bleakly forwards as the ballet ends.

The Royal Ballet did have threatened rapes and onstage orgasms in its repertory, but *The Invitation* was unusually blunt and raw. When de Valois saw a late rehearsal, she asked if the rape could take place off stage, then agreed to show the ballet as choreographed. 'Kenneth was very pro giving quite ugly movements to people,' recalls Anya Linden, who danced the Wife in the Covent Garden revival. He 'loved that dissonance . . . like a Stravinsky dissonant piece of music.'[5] Seymour and MacMillan called the heroine's first entrance 'falling out of a tree', she remembered: 'there were all these vertiginous feelings he wanted reflected in this nearly-falling.'[6] The score was commissioned from the Hungarian composer Mátyás Seiber. Georgiadis's evocative sets were dappled and gauzy.

The Invitation received extensive and scandalised publicity. It was given an 'X' certificate, and left off matinee performances as 'unsuitable for children'.[7] All of which helped at the box office. Desmond Doyle and Anne Heaton showed the older couple's desperation as well as their callousness. Christopher Gable, who was becoming Seymour's regular partner, danced the gauche young cousin. Seymour gave an astounding performance. Her fluid movements were powerfully expressive. A rehearsal film shows her waltzing with the Husband: the gentle sway of her body looks instinctive and unguarded, a near-involuntary response to the dance, to his partnering. She is frantic in the rape, moving with the headlong force of panic.

MacMillan was to remain preoccupied with the themes raised in his early ballets. In *The Invitation*, he showed psychological damage, sexual violence, a society that repressed and failed to protect his characters. There was some untidy construction – and this, too, was to prove characteristic of MacMillan's work. The tension dropped in weaker passages showing house-party diversions and an allegorical cockfight. Even so, there was no doubt that he had arrived as The Royal Ballet's next defining choreographer, with Seymour as his muse.

Ashton made his next ballet for the touring company. *The Two Pigeons*, which had its premiere on 14 February 1961, was a Valentine's Day ballet. Messager's sweet score was written for the Paris Opéra in 1886, for a fable about love and infidelity. Ashton moved the story from ancient Greece to a Bohemian Paris; Jacques Dupont dressed the heroine and her friends in full-skirted dresses, like Degas ballet girls. The hero is a painter, trying to make his fidgeting girlfriend sit for a portrait. He is tempted away by gypsies, roughed up, and returns to be forgiven by the girl. Their final duet has a heartbroken tenderness. The lovers, danced by Seymour and Gable, were acutely characterised, funny and vulnerable. Ashton used real white doves to symbolise the lovers' separation and reconciliation, a touch of sentiment that works affectingly in the theatre. The gypsies were frankly stage gypsies: carefully ragged trousers for the men, gold earrings for everybody. Elizabeth Anderton was the heroine's rival, dancing virtuoso steps with sensuality and a light, springy jump.

That summer, the Covent Garden company at last visited Russia. De Valois and her dancers were elated and nervous. Their thirty-year-old company was descended from the Russian classical tradition; now they would dance *The Sleeping Beauty* in the Maryinsky Theatre, where the ballet had had its premiere. After bringing British ballet out of the shadow of Russian companies, de Valois and her dancers would be compared with the oldest and grandest Russian troupes. On 15 June 1961, The Royal Ballet opened in Leningrad with *Ondine*. De Valois was determined to show the full range of her company, its modern and its classical works. *Ondine* was her claim to the grand scale, the vehicle for her greatest ballerina. She must have hoped that Fonteyn would rival Ulanova's impact in the Bolshoi's *Romeo and Juliet* at Covent Garden. The premiere was warmly enough received, without matching the sensation of that

London occasion. Henze's music was unpopular; so was the last-act divertissement. Even so, the evening ended with shouts of 'Fonteyn' and twenty-one curtain calls. Khrushchev, the Russian premier, exclaimed 'Look at those girls, they might be Russians!' – a comment, luckily, that delighted de Valois.[8]

Ondine was overshadowed by *La Fille mal gardée*, the second ballet and the hit of the visit. 'It was a triumph,' Ashton wrote. 'They just wouldn't stop clapping & rushed to the front of the stage & threw flowers.'[9] David Blair long remembered the shock of those flowers, picked in the fields by Russian fans and wrapped in wet, heavy paper. They weren't supposed to bring them into the theatre, 'but somehow they do, and if they like you, they throw these flowers all through. It happened on the first night just after I had finished my first variation, and I wondered what on earth was going on – were they throwing cabbages? . . . From then on, it was a series of showers of flowers: the audience was enchanted.'[10] Ashton was applauded as he left the stage door. Nadia Nerina, already a favourite from guest appearances in Russia, was carried shoulder high to her hotel.

With *The Sleeping Beauty*, Russian and Royal Ballet dancers and audiences had a chance to compare their versions of Petipa's text: so similar, and so different. Fonteyn, nervous of the ancestral stage, later wrote that her first Leningrad performance was 'my worst ever'.[11] In Moscow, there were showers of flowers for all three Auroras: Fonteyn, Beriosova and Nerina. The short ballets, rare in Russia, were eagerly discussed. *The Lady and the Fool* was a great success for its romanticism, its clowning and for Beriosova's noble grace. *The Rake's Progress* – which had been brought only at Ashton's insistence – was very popular, as was *Les Patineurs*. The spiky *Danses concertantes* did not go down well: the critic and former dancer Mikhail Gabovich wondered if MacMillan hadn't done it for a bet. Blair remembered that Moscow audiences roared with delight in the final scene of *The Firebird*. Goncharova's backdrop of onion domes echoed the architecture of the Kremlin, a few minutes away from the theatre: the Russian audience was seeing its own history on stage. Ninette de Valois, triumphant, found that Russians 'could not understand how we could have done it all in the time', in the three decades of the Company's existence.[12]

The American and Russian tours had kept the Company abroad for six of the last ten months. De Valois now insisted that The Royal Ballet be given time to recover and to work on the repertory. The Covent Garden company made no overseas visits for the next eighteen months. There were two new ballets in September 1961. Rodrigues's slight *Jabez and the Devil* gave Antoinette Sibley her first created role. MacMillan's *Diversions* was a fluent pure-dance work, showing off Svetlana Beriosova and Donald MacLeary. Beriosova spoke as well as danced in Ashton's next ballet, *Perséphone*, which had its premiere in December. Stravinsky's score, commissioned by Rubinstein, included spoken sections for the heroine. Ashton took Beriosova to hear Stravinsky conduct a concert performance of the ballet. When they went backstage, the composer nodded approval of her beautiful voice. *Perséphone* was a personal success for Beriosova, but remained an awkward ballet. Supporting roles seemed typecast or exaggerated. The hybrid score made it a hard work to keep in repertory.

While The Royal Ballet were in Leningrad, a Kirov dancer had defected from the Soviet company's tour to Paris. On 17 June 1961, two days after the Russian premiere of *Ondine*, Rudolf Nureyev made his 'leap to freedom' at Le Bourget airport. He made news headlines around the world, and went on making them. That autumn, Fonteyn invited him to dance at her Gala for the Royal Academy of Dancing. Ashton made a solo for the occasion. Nureyev caused a sensation. Ninette de Valois, watching, was most moved by his curtain call. 'I saw an arm raised with a noble dignity, a hand expressively extended . . . I could see him suddenly and clearly in one role – Albrecht in *Giselle*. Then and there I decided that when he first danced for us it must be with Fonteyn in that ballet.'[13] When, writes de Valois, not if. Until recently, she had used guest artists sparingly, determined to prove the self-sufficiency of her School. Nureyev was another matter. She wanted him for The Royal Ballet, and even more for Fonteyn. The Company had ballerinas closer to Nureyev's age, but De Valois did not consider them.

Fans had started asking that Nureyev be invited to join The

Royal Ballet almost as soon as he defected. When three Fonteyn–Nureyev *Giselles* were announced for February 1962, the response was frenzied, with seventy thousand applications for tickets turned down. The performance lived up to the excitement. Fonteyn, who had revised her Giselle so often and so carefully, now seemed rekindled in the role. Nureyev's Albrecht was a radical portrayal. There were new virtuoso steps, with a dramatic series of entrechats in the last act. The velvety flow of his dancing was unexpected; a few critics found it almost feminine. Most, like the audience, were bowled over. At the curtain call, Nureyev sank to one knee and kissed Fonteyn's hand. It was a moment of real feeling and extraordinary theatricality. The most famous ballet partnership of the twentieth century had begun.

De Valois liked to point out that ballet produces only a handful of truly international stars – 'There are lots of great dancers, but international means every corner of the world . . . an international name that in two hundred years you will remember belonged to their time.'[14] In Fonteyn, her school had produced one of the greatest. Fonteyn and Nureyev together were to become something more than stellar. They were icons, a union of opposites. The allure of their partnership was so potent that – more than forty years later – people still wonder if they had an affair, eager to believe that such onstage chemistry must have continued off stage too.

They were physically well matched but vividly different. Fonteyn's proportions were famously harmonious: an oval face over a slender, balanced frame. Nureyev was all contrasts: broad shoulders over narrow waist, heavy-lidded eyes slanting down to sharp cheekbones. Temperamentally, his fieriness was set against her lyricism. More than that, he was determined to push himself forwards, to make the prince the ballerina's equal. Fonteyn had always risen to a challenge, responding to Helpmann or to the example of other ballerinas. Nureyev was new and magnificent competition.

Competition for The Royal Ballet, too. Nureyev never joined the Company, but he became its most regular guest, a semi-permanent colleague. As the 1960s began, The Royal Ballet was already opening out, stretching in new directions. Nureyev became part of that process. His impact on men's dancing was immediate. As David Blair's 'club' for pirouettes shows, British male dancers had come a long way since the dark days of the war, but Nureyev's virtuosity was something else. Blair, and others of his generation, found themselves overshadowed. For the younger men, Nureyev was a stimulus. Asked about his own authority on stage, his easy turn-out, David Wall replied, 'Oh, that came from Rudolf.'

From Fonteyn down, Nureyev had an impact on technique, over-turning de Valois's protective attitude to her dancers' schooling. He had started his own training late, and worked feverishly to make up for lost time. He was always ready to try outside teachers, taking Royal Ballet dancers with him. De Valois, who adored rebels, accepted Nureyev's revolutions without a murmur. 'Discipline practically went out of the window,' remembers the dancer Georgina Parkinson. Nureyev, she says, 'had to struggle to dance well. He had animal magnetism and charisma and charm, he had a beautiful jump, but there were lots of other things that could be improved in his work.' When he saw other dancers making the same effort, he was eager to help. The urge to refine their technique was a great bond between Fonteyn and Nureyev; between Nureyev and The Royal Ballet, too. 'He appreciated our dedication, our intensity, our lust for knowledge,' says Parkinson. 'He loved that, we did that together. He was very, very generous.'

Even so, Nureyev was never a Company man. The Royal Ballet was a superb choreographer's instrument. Its dancers had grown up with new work, expecting to be redefined by new roles. Nureyev was eager to dance new ballets, but reluctant to submit himself fully to any other style. Of Ashton, he said later, 'I was . . . trying, let's say, to keep my style undiluted . . . I was not willing. I was willing in my head, but my heart just wouldn't do it.'[15] No great ballets would be made for Nureyev, at The Royal Ballet or anywhere else. Though he could be intensely involved in a performance, in a role, he did little to vary his persona. Fonteyn's Ondine and Firebird were different creatures; Nureyev was always Nureyev, his personality firmly in the foreground. (He was reluctant to dance *Fille*, asking: 'What happens to me in the second act?'[16]) That was true of his partnering, too. Where Somes had provided perfect support,

Nureyev was not above neglecting or upstaging his ballerinas. Women had to learn, as Fonteyn had learned with Helpmann, how to hold the audience against an overwhelming partner. 'Performing with Rudolf was always one of the most alive moments, one of the most . . . scary,' says Monica Mason. 'He took you to the edge of the cliff, and then you leaned out into the wind.'[17]

In May 1962, the Danish *danseur noble* Erik Bruhn offered a different kind of male virtuosity. At a gala in May, he danced two divertissements by the nineteenth-century Danish choreographer Bournonville, *Napoli* and *Flower Festival at Genzano*. Bournonville's clean, buoyant style, with its quick footwork, suited Royal Ballet dancers. The young Anthony Dowell, perhaps the finest male dancer The Royal Ballet ever produced, was first noticed in a later performance of *Napoli*. At the same gala, MacMillan's *Rite of Spring* had its premiere. In 1959, MacMillan had suggested a ballet to Mahler's *Das Lied von der Erde*. The Covent Garden Board vetoed the project, worried about the expense of hiring the solo singers required by the score and feeling that 'the idea of a ballet to this work was objectionable in principle'.[18] Instead, they suggested Stravinsky's ballet – then rarely performed. The Australian artist Sidney Nolan dressed the dancers in red and orange body tights, marked with handprints, suggesting the ceremonial body paint of Aborigines. MacMillan used a huge corps of men and women, giving them odd suggestions of jazz dance, with splayed fingers and flexed feet. He chose Monica Mason, a young South African just out of the corps de ballet, as his Chosen Maiden. Tall and strong, with huge eyes and great stamina, Mason danced with extraordinary intensity. A fragment of film shows the scale and power of her dancing, Stravinsky's rhythms seething through her body. Standing still, she gives off a fierce concentration. The performance made her name.

It was a starry season, with more guest appearances from Beryl Grey, Bruhn, Nureyev, Yvette Chauviré and Sonia Arova. That summer, Ashton received his knighthood. In July 1962, Massine returned to revive another of his Diaghilev ballets. *The Good-Humoured Ladies*, made in 1917, shows a Venetian intrigue. The dancers, sumptuously dressed by Bakst, move with jerky marionette steps. Lydia Sokolova, who had danced in this ballet when it was new, came to The Royal Ballet to dance the vain old Marchesa. Seymour, Sibley and Linden were delightful Ladies, with Grant brilliant as the waiter. Another character role was to have been danced by Harold Turner, by then a teacher at the School. Leaving a stage rehearsal, Turner collapsed and died. The production had enthusiastic reviews, but it never became popular. When it was revived in the autumn, it had lost much of its character, and quickly fell from the repertory.

Lynn Seymour and Christopher Gable had moved to Covent Garden, where they danced *The Two Pigeons* and *The Invitation* that autumn. In *Pigeons*, Seymour was followed by Sibley, Park and Doreen Wells. Georgina Parkinson and Monica Mason were both vivid gypsies. In November, Nureyev staged the duet from *Le Corsaire* and danced it with Fonteyn. He was at his most exotic, she at her most elegant. It was an outrageous success: the applause lasted longer than the dancing. Fonteyn had returned to *Le Lac des cygnes*, by now called *Swan Lake*, dancing with Blair early in 1962. In February 1963, she danced the ballet with Nureyev. He added a moody solo for the Prince in Act 1, and Fonteyn dropped the traditional mime scenes. Both stars danced with fervent attack. Another new MacMillan ballet followed in February 1963: *Symphony*, set to Shostakovich's Symphony No. 1, with bold designs by Yolanda Sonnabend. It was planned as pure dance, but – responding to the drama of Seymour's dancing – MacMillan gave his dancers implied relationships. With Seymour ill, Sibley gave an assured performance on the first night.

Marguerite and Armand, Ashton's ballet for the Fonteyn–Nureyev partnership, had its premiere in March 1963. Publicity was feverish, and the ballet was a predictable smash-hit. For decades, no one other than Fonteyn and Nureyev danced *Marguerite and Armand*. (In 2000, after their and Ashton's deaths, it was revived for Sylvie Guillem.) The plot, from Dumas *fils*'s *La Dame aux camélias* (and also used in Verdi's *La traviata*) concerns the doomed love of a young man and a dying courtesan. As with *Apparitions*, made almost thirty years earlier, the music was Liszt, the designs by Cecil Beaton. The ballet was built around the chemistry of its stars. As Ashton pointed out, 'There's nothing wrong with a vehicle provided it goes.'[19] The choreography is thin, but Fonteyn and Nureyev loved and suffered with passionate frenzy. The strongest dance moment came with Fonteyn's exit from the party scene, Marguerite broken by Armand's insults. As she stumbled to the wings, sobs shook her whole body, running from her bowed shoulders to her trembling feet.

The Company showed a second vehicle that month, this time for Nadia Nerina. Robert Helpmann's *Elektra* was short-lived but lurid. 'Nadia had no nerves, she was fearless,' remembers Mason, who danced Klytemnestra. The choreography featured terrifying throws, Nerina hurled from one group of men to another. At one New York performance, a woman in the audience screamed and fainted at the sight. Helpmann had hoped to use designs by Francis Bacon for his *Elektra*. The Covent Garden Board admitted that these 'had a certain distinction', but found them oversized and impracticable.[20] Helpmann turned to the Australian painter and sculptor Arthur Boyd, who gave the ballet a blood-red floorcloth and a backdrop of looming, grappling figures. Malcolm Arnold's score was thumpingly emphatic.

The seventh American tour began in April 1963. The Company opened in New York with four weeks at the Met, ending in Los Angeles nearly three months later with a week at the vast Hollywood Bowl. *Le Corsaire* and *Marguerite and Armand* were great popular hits. *Time* and *Newsweek* ran cover stories on Nureyev – as they had on Fonteyn in 1949. At first, this frenzy detracted from the Company as a whole. Unusually for The Royal Ballet in New York, there were empty seats when the star couple were not performing. As the season progressed, audiences responded warmly to other dancers. There were cheers and rave reviews for Beriosova and the corps in *Giselle*. Lynn Seymour had a tremendous success in *The Invitation*: after one performance at the Met, the ballet had thirty curtain calls. *The Rite of Spring* and *The Two Pigeons* were less popular. Sol Hurok had warned Ashton that New Yorkers would be wary of his ballet: 'I can't sell it. You know what pigeons do to our park benches?'[21]

1962–63 was Ninette de Valois's last season as Director of The

Royal Ballet. She had announced her resignation three days after the premiere of *Marguerite and Armand*. The news came as a surprise. Ashton, appointed as Assistant Director in 1952, had not expected to take over for another two years. 'I feel rather like James I succeeding Queen Elizabeth,' he remarked.[22] He turned down an offer to choreograph the film *My Fair Lady* to concentrate on the Royal. De Valois became Supervisor of the School, where – in a characteristic volte-face – she started to teach senior students new steps and methods she had seen in her visits to Russia.

There was an easy handover from de Valois to Ashton. She had founded the Company, but he was one of its architects. Royal Ballet style was Ashton style: the Company's staff had grown up with his ballets, and they taught accordingly. Gail Thomas Monahan remembers John Field coaching the corps for *Swan Lake*. In the swans' first entry, he urged them to bend their heads and torsos down before opening up in their temps levé jumps. 'It was much harder work, but he was right: after I stopped dancing, I remember watching it and realising how beautiful and thrilling it was.' It's an Ashtonian quality: going down to go up. Until 1960, Fonteyn had had most of Ashton's attention. She had been extended and refined by the ballets he made for her. From *La Fille mal gardée* onwards, however, Ashton's leading roles were much more widely distributed. A new generation was being stretched in his ballets; these young dancers brought out new qualities in him.

De Valois had run the whole company, from top to bottom. Ashton was much readier to delegate, concentrating on coaching and choice of repertory. Before retiring, de Valois had appointed a trio of Assistant Directors to support him. John Field continued in charge of the touring company. At Covent Garden, John Hart took over the administrative side of the Company. Rehearsals, meanwhile, were dominated by Michael Somes. He would sit beside Ashton as he choreographed, suggesting cuts or changes and doing what Mason called the 'housework' of tidying up ensembles. He was later to do the same for MacMillan.[23]

When choreographing, Ashton didn't count out musical phrases. Somes, a highly musical performer who had never needed counts, could break the music down for other dancers. The dancer Antony

Dowson has said that, with Somes, 'you could exactly visualise what you were doing on each count'.[24] He would 'make sure you were on the beat – almost too much so', says Merle Park. He had a gift for uniting the corps de ballet, but he was a rigorous coach throughout the repertory. Looking through pictures of *Symphonic Variations* in the 1970s, Antoinette Sibley saw the exact placing of the dancers as 'the result of Michael Somes's insistence on perfection. He will help anyone at any time; he's devoted to The Royal Ballet.'[25]

That devotion could be angrily pedantic. His rehearsals were famously strict, with endless punishing repetitions. Dancers would be urged to do roles just as he or Fonteyn had danced them. Ashton and MacMillan, says MacLeary, 'would adapt to the person they were working with. They wouldn't change the steps, but change the way of doing it . . . It wasn't like a machine, they didn't come out all the same.' Somes's rages were notorious. 'When it was full moon, we all knew we were in for it,' says Park matter-of-factly. 'You wouldn't be able to do that today, the way he treated people.' He had a reputation both for making dancers, helping and developing them, and for ripping them down. 'The very good ones took it and got through,' says MacLeary now, 'but the people who needed confidence . . . He used to wreck people.'

Somes helped to fix The Royal Ballet's repertory and style, pinning the ballets down for the next generation. 'People don't recognise what we owe him,' de Valois told the dance historian Sarah Woodcock. 'A lot of it was maddening, very tiresome, because he was so conservative and so prejudiced, but it was a loyalty in the conservatism that was terribly necessary to the Company. Somebody had to have it or we wouldn't have a tradition.'[26]

Ashton began his Directorship with a work that would become a new Royal Ballet tradition. The year of Nureyev's defection, the Kirov Ballet had brought the Shades scene from *La Bayadère* to London. Now Ashton asked Nureyev to stage it for The Royal Ballet. It was an inspired decision. Nureyev was young, untried and temperamental, but he had an extraordinary gift for coaching. He taught *La Bayadère* 'in the most immaculate detail,' says Mason. 'He recognised that he could train the corps de ballet exactly the way that he wanted to, that we were very disciplined . . . I think he probably thought that he'd died and gone to heaven.' He chose young women for the three solo variations, showing off Seymour's highly arched feet, Park's speed, Mason's strength and attack.

'The Kingdom of the Shades' is a whole act of pure classical dancing. The Shades' first entrance is the most famous test of a corps de ballet in the repertory. The women enter down a ramp, one by one, repeating the same arabesque, the same port de bras. The repetitions are hypnotic: a hall of mirrors, a vision of eternity. Over the 1960s, the Royal corps had become stronger and more poetic, regularly hailed as the best in the world. *La Bayadère* became their ultimate showpiece. It allowed them to show what Mason calls 'a very classical, Russian classical side of ourselves'. This kind of dancing was new to The Royal Ballet, but they did not deliver a carbon copy of the Kirov production. They kept their own British arabesques, their Ashtonian épaulement and sensuous ports de bras. Photographs of this production show dancing of lunar serenity, Petipa grandeur with a Royal Ballet accent.

That accent was still epitomised by Fonteyn. Nureyev didn't just give her an Indian summer, he gave her a series of ballerina roles: *Le Corsaire*, Nikiya in *Bayadère*, *Raymonda*. She had gone on refining her dancing, making aspects of her technique stronger than ever before. As Nikiya, she had her old concern for line, for musicality, for the theatrical juice of steps. She acquired a new kind of majesty. The critic Edwin Denby wrote that a ballerina should be 'the central dynamo' of a company, its exemplar of style.[27] In the classics, Fonteyn was still The Royal Ballet's ballerina. From this point on, she was no longer at the heart of the Ashton repertory. She danced her last *Symphonic Variations* in 1963. She danced Chloë again the next year, with Christopher Gable's ardent Daphnis, but was taken out of the ballet when Gable left the Company in 1966. She danced her last *Sylvia* in 1965, her last *Cinderella* in 1967.

Fonteyn opened the new production of *Swan Lake*, staged by Robert Helpmann in December 1963. His approach was dramatic rather than classical, inclined to emphasise the plot. A new prologue (choreographed by Ashton) showed Odette caught and turned into a swan – pre-empting the ballerina's great entrance in the second act. Besides the moody solo he had introduced in 1962, Nureyev arranged a first-act polonaise and a mazurka. Maria Fay choreographed a new czardas. There were several new Ashton dances: a first-act Waltz, a Spanish dance and a sparkling classical pas de quatre. He based the two women's solos on social dances: Merle Park's on the cha-cha, Antoinette Sibley's on the twist. He also made an entirely new fourth act. This worked less well than the traditional Ivanov choreography, though it had some beautiful, sorrowful dances for the swans.

The four-hundredth anniversary of the birth of Shakespeare fell in April 1964. The Royal Ballet marked the occasion with an all-Shakespeare programme. Helpmann's *Hamlet* was revived, with Nureyev and then Gable in the title role. Both danced with Lynn Seymour in the most successful episode of MacMillan's short-lived *Images of Love*. The ballet's scenes were based on individual lines from plays and sonnets. Peter Tranchell's commissioned music was unhelpful: MacMillan burst into tears the first time he heard the full orchestral score.

At the time, most attention was paid to *Hamlet* and *Images of Love*, which both featured Nureyev. *The Dream*, taken lightly in 1964, proved to be the lasting success of the programme. Ashton used Mendelssohn's music for *A Midsummer Night's Dream*, arranged by John Lanchbery. It was a very Victorian *Dream*, influenced by the Old Vic production of 1937, in which Helpmann had played Oberon and de Valois had arranged the dances. Henry Bardon designed a handsome forest set. David Walker dressed the fairies in Romantic tulle, and Ashton set them skimming and fluttering across the stage. Sibley and the twenty-one-year-old Anthony Dowell danced Titania and Oberon. They were perfectly matched, with equal beauty of line, smooth musicality, graceful proportions. Ashton displayed them in mirrored dances, the couple doing the same steps side by side. Sibley danced Titania with abandoned sensuality. Dowell showed long-breathed, endlessly fluid phrasing and astonishing speed in the scherzo. Ashton crowned his production, and this golden new partnership, with a reconciliation duet to Mendelssohn's Nocturne. Titania goes through mercurial shifts of direction, darting outwards in windblown lifts, then melting back towards Oberon. The mortal lovers were briskly comic. Alexander Grant danced Bottom, with pointe-work for the donkey scenes and a brief, touching mime scene for his return to human form.

The next month, the Company staged its formal farewell to de Valois. A gala held on 7 May ended with a grand défilé: the dancers of both companies and the students from the School, all on stage to applaud de Valois. Ashton took his place in the défilé, flanked by Hart, Somes, Field and MacMillan: his assistants and his successor. The gala was also the Company premiere of Balanchine's *Serenade* with Beriosova, Nerina, Annette Page, Blair and Donald MacLeary. Balanchine already admired Beriosova: he had cast her in his *Trumpet Concerto* for the touring company, and in 1961 he had hoped that she might spend a season with New York City Ballet. The Royal Ballet tended to be softer than Balanchine's own bold, free dancers; even so, this was a strongly danced production.

Building alterations took place during the summer of 1964, and the Company moved to Drury Lane theatre for a five-week season. This was a triumphant end to Ashton's first season. A solid run of performances gave chances to more dancers. The Royal Ballet was in superb form, but it was hard to find opportunities for so many fine soloists. The idea that the Company might permanently move out of Covent Garden into its own dance house began to be raised. Balancing opera and ballet at the Royal Opera House was increasingly difficult. In the early 1960s, the opera company introduced five-year planning, with singers and productions booked far ahead. Ballet could not be planned on these terms. Dancers emerge quickly, sometimes going from school to stardom in less than five years. From now on, The Royal Ballet had to fit its performances and rehearsals around the opera company's existing plans.

The Touring Company appeared at the Spoleto Festival that summer. They danced Nureyev's production of *Raymonda*, a full-length Petipa ballet with a meandering plot and a luscious Glazunov score. Fonteyn was to have danced the title role, but was called away by her husband's illness. Tito de Arias was standing for election in Panama; in June 1964 he was shot and paralysed in an assassination attempt. After operations in Panama, de Arias was moved to Stoke Mandeville hospital in England while Fonteyn went to

Spoleto. Just before the opening night, news came that de Arias had had a relapse, and Fonteyn rushed back to Britain.

She was replaced, for all but one performance, by Doreen Wells, a dancer of soft femininity and clear classical style. *Raymonda* proved to be an uneven ballet. The best of the dancing was in the third act, an irresistible Hungarian divertissement mixing character and pure classical dancing. In 1966, this act was revived with new designs by Barry Kay, in a magnificent white-and-gold Byzantine set. Wells again danced Raymonda. She was soon partnered by David Wall, a dancer of sure, warm style and virile stage presence. Under John Field, the touring company had built up a devoted following. Across Britain, audiences adored the Wells–Wall partnership.

The London Royal Ballet had essentially given up visiting the regions of Britain, though Covent Garden dancers sometimes appeared with the touring company. Despite plans for integration, the two sections had remained distinct. From 1964, The Royal Ballet had a small third company. This had grown out of a series of evening lectures on ballet by Peter Brinson. In the early 1960s, Brinson asked Barbara Fewster, senior teacher at The Royal Ballet School, if some of her pupils could take part in travelling lecture-demonstrations. In 1964, Brinson established a formal link with The Royal Ballet, under the new name 'Ballet for All'. The first programme, called 'Ashton and *La Fille mal gardée*', was given in Portsmouth in September 1964, with Brenda Last and Gary Sherwood as Lise and Colas. Brinson drew his dancers from the touring company: young dancers would spend two or three months with Ballet for All, dancing extracts from leading roles. They played in towns and villages the touring company could not reach, dancing on small stages in school and church halls. By 1970, the group's work had expanded to include lectures, a television series and a paperback guide to ballet repertory. In 1973, de Valois and Ashton choreographed a ballet, *The Wedding of Harlequin*, for one of the programmes.

In the winter of 1964, Nijinska came to Covent Garden to revive *Les Biches*. Her ballets had fallen out of the repertory everywhere; if Ashton had not asked her to stage them for The Royal Ballet, both *Biches* and *Les Noces* would almost certainly have been lost. Nijinska reminded him that, with the Rubinstein company in Paris, he had watched all her rehearsals. 'Tu es mon fils,' she told him.[28] 'It was like watching a young boy, when he was in her presence,' remembered Mason. 'The delight all over his face . . . the past meeting the present.'[29] Nijinska spoke no English, and used very limited upper-body movement to convey steps. Michael Somes was 'like a mother to her,' says Georgina Parkinson, 'the way a baby talks, and the mother tells you what it means'. In *Les Biches*, Parkinson danced the 'Garçonne', a girl in a page-boy's coat and gloves. The ballet, made in the 1920s, shows a house party with classical steps and contemporary costumes, with designs by Marie Laurencin. It is both delicate and demanding, needing strong technique and a sense of atmosphere. The corps, in pink with extravagant feather headdresses, chatter and giggle, then each one jumps neatly off a sofa with a crisp pas de chat. Beriosova was a stylish Hostess – the role originally worked out on de Valois. Deanne Bergsma, who had been a superbly tipsy Josephine in that season's revival of *A Wedding Bouquet*, soon took over.

Ashton had asked MacMillan what he wanted to do for his next ballet. 'And in fear and trepidation I said *Romeo and Juliet*,' MacMillan remembered. Ashton had already choreographed the Prokofiev score, in a production for the Royal Danish Ballet. 'I wonder why . . . he didn't bring his own version to The Royal Ballet. That remains a mystery to me.'[30] Ashton was generous in giving MacMillan this chance. He must also have been relieved. Ever since the success of Lavrovsky's Bolshoi production in 1956, the Covent Garden administration had been clamouring for its own *Romeo*. Ashton was frankly reluctant to restage his Danish version, a classical ballet on an intimate scale. After the widescreen verismo of the Bolshoi, wouldn't the Ashton *Romeo* look small? He turned down repeated invitations to bring it to Covent Garden, and in 1963 encouraged a plan for an exchange of productions with the Bolshoi – *Fille* for Lavrovsky's *Romeo*. When that fell through, in February 1964, he suggested John Cranko's 1962 Stuttgart production as an alternative. Two months later, MacMillan asked if he could do the ballet. Ashton championed him to a hesitant Board of Directors, reminding them that MacMillan 'needed a big opportunity of this kind'. He added that the new *Romeo* might suit Fonteyn, who wanted a new role for the next New York visit.[31]

In the event, Fonteyn was to dance the first night, even though the ballet had been made for Lynn Seymour. Sol Hurok insisted that Fonteyn and Nureyev should dance the ballet's London premiere too, guaranteeing publicity ahead of the American tour. The Royal Ballet, which had resisted his demands for Shearer's Aurora, caved in over Fonteyn's Juliet. This imposition of a star cast caused widespread and enduring resentment.

MacMillan's version, like Cranko's, shows the impact of the Lavrovsky staging: a massive set on several levels by Georgiadis, particular weight and richness of gesture. Anther influence was Zeffirelli's recent Old Vic production of the play, with Judi Dench and John Stride as rebelliously modern lovers – 'realistic,' remembers Seymour, 'not the romantic stilted way that people had been used to seeing Shakespeare'.[32] MacMillan's mime scenes were newly naturalistic and informal. Deciding to take the potion, his Juliet did not dance: she sat on her bed, staring into space, the music surging around her. In the tomb scene, Romeo danced with an apparently lifeless Juliet, desperately clutching her dead weight.

MacMillan was becoming famous for his pas de deux; he would build his ballets around them, making the duets first and then adding the rest of the work. He had already made his balcony scene, with Seymour and Gable, for Canadian television: solos and partnering run together in an ecstatic flow of dips, surges, giddy off-balance turns. MacMillan's dances for Romeo and his friends showed off the new strength in The Royal Ballet's men. Mercutio, first danced by David Blair, had fast, tripping footwork; Benvolio's mocking solo in the ballroom was full of sinuous, swaying lines. MacMillan did his best work for the central characters – the lovers, Romeo's friends. His crowd scenes were padded out to fill the long stretches of Prokofiev's score. MacMillan's has become the most successful of all *Romeo* productions, kept in repertory by companies around the world.

Seymour and Gable made ardent, adolescent lovers, passionate and unromanticised. More than a decade later, the opening of Seymour's balcony scene could still cause a ripple of shock: she would arch back over the balcony with urgent physical abandon. Fonteyn and Nureyev, who took forty-three curtain calls on opening night, gave their roles a more traditional romantic glow. David Blair was a lively Mercutio, with Anthony Dowell as a slender, sarcastic Benvolio. As Tybalt, Desmond Doyle was icily contained. Julia Farron returned to dance a regal Lady Capulet. Unusually, *Romeo and Juliet* had been cast as if it were a nineteenth-century classic: five leading couples were announced, though the second-cast Annette Page was injured before rehearsals began. It has been wrongly claimed that Seymour was demoted to fifth cast – she was scheduled for the third press night – and that the other Juliets modelled their interpretations on Fonteyn's. In fact, MacMillan gave all his casts considerable freedom: each Juliet had an individual approach to the role. Sibley and Dowell were a lyrical pair of lovers. Park, still associated with soubrette roles, moved into the dramatic repertory with *Romeo*, with MacLeary a devoted partner.

For the Benevolent Fund Gala in March 1965, Grigoriev and Tchernicheva staged Fokine's *Polovtsian Dances*, taken from the opera *Prince Igor*. The Tatar Nureyev danced the chief warrior, but Fokine's dances didn't suit The Royal Ballet. The same gala included Ashton's *Monotones*. Dowell, Vyvyan Lorrayne and Robert Mead danced a serene, closely patterned trio set to Satie's *Trois Gymnopédies*. The dancers, dressed in white, flow through limpidly classical steps, starting close together and opening out to ever wider stage patterns. 'Ashton displays three wonderful gifts to an extreme degree,' wrote Richard Buckle, 'the linking of poses by movement, the relating of dancers to the framing rectangle of the stage so that they trace clear though invisible patterns in the air, and the rendering of the sense of a piece of music rather than the notes.'[33] In April 1966, Ashton made a second pas de trois to Satie's *Trois Gnossiennes*, with Sibley, Parkinson and Brian Shaw, dressed in green. The two pas de trois, often performed together as *Monotones I and II*, were a statement of The Royal Ballet's beauty in adagio, as much a definition of its classicism as *Symphonic Variations* or *La Bayadère*.

In summer 1965, the Company spent almost a month at the Met, before visiting seventeen cities in the US and Canada. Fonteyn and Nureyev were a sensation in *Romeo and Juliet*, with the other three couples warmly acclaimed. *The Dream* had a much more enthusiastic reception in New York than it had in London. 'For many balletomanes here,' wrote the American critic Lilian Moore, 'this season will be remembered as the one in which they discovered Sibley and Dowell.'[34] They were immediately invited to dance the *Dream* pas de deux on the Ed Sullivan television show. The year before, *Time* magazine had proclaimed London 'the swinging city'. The Royal Ballet, with Fonteyn, Nureyev, Sibley and Dowell among its 'beautiful people', had caught the wave of the decade's chic. The new *Swan Lake*, which opened with Beriosova and MacLeary, was also more popular in America than in Britain. In the autumn, the Company visited Italy, dancing in Milan, Rome, Naples and Bologna.

After so much travelling, the autumn season was dominated by revivals. Annette Page, now recovered from injury, danced her first Juliet, partnered by Gable. Ashton's *Cinderella* returned with new designs by Henry Bardon and David Walker. They gave the ballet a French Second Empire setting, with high-waisted dresses for the season fairies – superbly cast at this revival, with Sibley, Vyvyan Lorrayne, Park and Deanne Bergsma on the first night. Fonteyn danced Cinderella, followed by the poetic Beriosova and the eager, lively Nerina. Ashton and Helpmann again danced the Ugly Sisters.

In February 1966, the Company presented two ballets by John Cranko. *Brandenburg Nos. 2 and 4*, a new work set to Bach, was a plotless but hectically busy ballet. *Card Game*, set to Stravinsky's *Jeu de cartes*, had been a success with Cranko's Stuttgart company. Christopher Gable was a lively Joker, changing identities and at one point appearing in a tutu. Page and Seymour, both good comediennes, had leading roles. It didn't last long at Covent Garden, but was successfully revived by the touring company.

One of the major events of Ashton's Directorship came in March 1966, when Nijinska returned to stage *Les Noces*. Nijinska's masterpiece, made for Diaghilev in 1923, had barely survived his company: there had been just one short-lived revival, staged by de Basil in 1936. Nijinska's depiction of a peasant wedding is uncompromisingly stark. Goncharova's first draft of the ballet's design had been colourful; her eventual realisation was austere, the dancers plainly dressed in white and dark brown. Stravinsky's overwhelming score sets four pianos, percussion and voices in complex, churning rhythms. Nijinska piles the corps into stylised groupings – a pyramid of tilted faces, lines of bent backs, a fan of torsos and squared arms – or sets them twisting and stamping through wedding dances. With its simple staging and fierce, relentless patterns, *Les Noces* is both primitive and modernist. The Company danced it with unstoppable force. Beriosova, with her beautiful Slavic face, danced the Bride. Robert Mead was the Bridegroom, with Parkinson and Dowell leading the corps dances. At the premiere, the four pianos were played by the composers Richard Rodney Bennett, John Gardner, Edmund Rubbra and Malcolm Williamson. At the end, Ashton led Nijinska forward, calling her 'one of the greatest choreographers of our day'.[35] This Royal Ballet production 're-established Nijinska's place in history', according to the American critic Arlene Croce, writing in 1989. By then, there had been more productions of *Les Noces* since Nijinska's death in 1972 than there were during her lifetime. None, argued Croce, matched the unique power of The Royal Ballet staging: 'What I chiefly recall, and indeed never will forget, is the combination of wildness and precision.'[36] The Company is still unmatched in *Les Noces*, a ballet it has danced with devotion for forty years.

In 1964, MacMillan had returned to the idea of a ballet to *Das Lied von der Erde*, which was again rejected by the Board. Instead, MacMillan made the ballet for Cranko's Stuttgart company, where it had its premiere in November 1965 to tremendous acclaim. Six months later, in May 1966, *Song of the Earth* was staged by The Royal Ballet. Mahler had set a German translation of Chinese poems on the beauty and transience of life. MacMillan took some of his images from the words. The third song describes a porcelain pavilion reflected in the waters of a pool; the choreography includes reflections, dancers taking upside-down poses, and hints of chinoiserie in the turns of wrists and ankles. MacMillan also added symbolic figures: a Man, a Woman and the Messenger of Death – a masked figure who is sometimes solicitous, sometimes menacing. The Woman is onstage throughout the final song, dancing with the Man and the Messenger. MacMillan's dances flow across the stage in broad, winding floor patterns. In her solo, the Woman dances a long line of bourrées, a zigzag path cutting through the empty space of the stage. Georgiadis dressed the ballet very simply, with practice clothes and a plain backdrop. Marcia Haydée, who had created the role of the Woman in Stuttgart, came to Covent Garden for the first performance. Seymour danced several performances, but Mason was the outstanding Covent Garden interpreter of the role, grand and heartfelt. Dowell was a quick, clear-edged Messenger, with MacLeary vigorous as the Man. The young Jennifer Penney was enchanting in the third song, 'Of Youth'. Ashton later said that Song of the Earth was his favourite MacMillan ballet; de Valois wrote a poem about it.

The critics who hailed Song of the Earth as a masterpiece also mourned MacMillan's departure. Early in 1966, he had been offered the directorship of the Berlin Ballet. Cranko had had a great success in Stuttgart; Berlin hoped that a second Royal Ballet choreographer would do as much for them. MacMillan consulted Ashton, 'hoping he would say, "Don't go."' Instead, Ashton encouraged him to take the job, pointing out that it was a marvellous opportunity. 'So I went.'[37] Lynn Seymour soon joined him. That summer, The Royal Ballet went on tour to Europe, appearing in several Eastern European countries for the first time. Fonteyn led the Company – without Nureyev, who could not venture behind the Iron Curtain. On this tour, Ann Jenner made her debut in La Fille mal gardée. She became one of the Company's best-loved Lises, with a soaring jump, natural gaiety and great tenderness. 'When she began the wedding pas de deux,' remembers Alastair Macaulay, who saw her in this ballet in the 1970s, 'she took it so seriously: this was the great event of her life, and it was for real.' At the end of the summer, Nadia Nerina resigned from The Royal Ballet. She had long been exasperated by Fonteyn's dominance, and the wealth of talent at Covent Garden reduced opportunities further. Nevertheless, when she criticised Ashton's Directorship in an article for The Queen, Covent Garden received hundreds of letters supporting him.

The 1966–67 season opened in November with Balanchine's Apollo, made for Diaghilev in 1928. Stravinsky's neoclassical score had been a turning-point for the twenty-four-year-old Balanchine.

'In its discipline and restraint . . . that score was a revelation. It seemed to tell me that I could dare not to use everything, that I, too, could eliminate . . . '[38] It was Balanchine's statement of classicism, radical and influential, and an important addition to the repertory. This was a strongly cast revival: MacLeary was an elegant Apollo, with Beriosova, Mason and Parkinson as his three muses. Balanchine came to London for the last rehearsals, but this was still *Apollo* with a Royal Ballet accent. 'The grace and polish of our English style have turned an archaic frieze into a Hellenistic one,' wrote Richard Buckle.[39]

Ashton also healed The Royal Ballet's breach with Antony Tudor. In January 1967, more than thirty years after he left the Vic-Wells Ballet, Tudor returned to create *Shadowplay*. He used music by the neglected composer Charles Koechlin, based on themes from Kipling's *Jungle Book*. Anthony Dowell was a Mowgli figure, the Boy With Matted Hair, who encountered and grappled with Derek Rencher's Terrestrial and Merle Park's Celestial figures. The ballet was confused but atmospheric. Tudor showed a new, enigmatic quality in Dowell, who responded with growing authority and stage presence.

Fonteyn and Nureyev were still regular guests at The Royal Ballet, and still eager for new ballets. Roland Petit's *Paradise Lost*, staged in February, was another vehicle for them. It was a Pop Art ballet, deliberately modish. Nureyev, as Adam, ended the first scene by diving through a pair of giant lips. He was killed by a flash of electricity, and supported in an upside-down pietà by Fonteyn's Eve. The ballet was included in the repertory for the next American tour, which opened in New York in April 1967. This was The Royal Ballet's first appearance at the new Metropolitan Opera House at the Lincoln Center. The Company looked glorious, projecting strongly from the huge new stage. They were enthusiastically received; Sibley and Deanne Bergsma both had striking successes. 'That was also the year the New York audience disgraced itself by its massive rejection of Nijinska's *Les Noces*,' wrote Arlene Croce, 'one of the most significant revivals of the decade.'[40] The New York season was beset with injuries and accidents. In the first-night performance of *Cinderella*, the coach swung round so quickly that

Beriosova was actually tipped out, almost into the orchestra pit. She was not seriously hurt, and was able to complete the performance.

After six weeks at the Met, the Company toured for another ten weeks. In San Francisco, by now the centre of flower power, Fonteyn and Nureyev went to a party that was raided by the police, and were briefly arrested on suspicion of smoking marijuana. American touring was becoming less profitable. The days of the 'Ballet Special' were over; the US railroad network was collapsing, and the Company now relied on air travel. Moving between cities took longer, with fewer performances and a loss of income. There was still money to be made, but routes had to be carefully and economically planned.

Back in London, the autumn season was dominated by *Swan Lake*, *Romeo and Juliet* and *La Fille mal gardée*. In December 1967, Ashton staged a new one-act version of *Sylvia*. Nerina, now a guest artist, returned to dance the premiere. During a later performance, Beriosova was taken ill. Mason replaced her, giving a vivid performance. This shortened *Sylvia* survived for two seasons, danced by three of the Company's tallest women: Beriosova, Mason and Bergsma.

Ashton had made fewer ballets since becoming Director. In 1967, he made a single ballet, *Sinfonietta*, for the touring company; he had made nothing at Covent Garden since *Monotones* in 1966. His next work, *Jazz Calendar*, was made to fill a gap in the schedule, caused by the postponement of the opera company's production of *Aïda*. To a jazz score by Richard Rodney Bennett, Ashton illustrated the nursery rhyme beginning 'Monday's child is fair of face'. Derek Jarman, a young painter who would later take to filmmaking, made bold, colourful sets. Ashton tried to match it with pop choreography: Sibley and Nureyev had a bump and grind duet; Park, Dowell and Robert Mead danced a parody of *Monotones*. It was a weak ballet, but starry and popular.

Nureyev's new production of *The Nutcracker* was also postponed, and had an unseasonal premiere in February 1968. The ballet had become the standby of Dolin's London Festival Ballet, which had danced it every Christmas since 1950. Indeed, the Board of Covent Garden, worried about professional discourtesy, made a point of warning Festival Ballet that there would soon be a competing version. Nureyev's *Nutcracker* had a Freudian edge. The heroine Clara grew up to become the Sugar Plum Fairy, while the magician Drosselmeyer became her handsome prince. The guests of the first-act party were transformed into nightmarish bats. Nureyev picked up on the unisex, mirrored dances of *The Dream*, giving Clara and the Prince matching steps – and plenty of them. His choreography was desperately busy, with so many steps crammed in that there was no room to shape a phrase. There were sumptuous and very expensive designs by Georgiadis; the production went badly over budget. It was immediately popular. Sibley and Dowell danced the first night, followed by Nureyev with Park, who was showing a new grandeur.

Ashton was now in his fifth season as Director. The Company was dancing magnificently, with a very high standard of new productions. Yet the Covent Garden management were already considering his retirement. 'It was bungled,' says John Tooley now. David Webster, the General Administrator, expected to retire in 1970, to be replaced by Tooley. In April 1968, Webster summoned Ashton to a meeting, and told him that he would be required to leave at the same time. When Tooley joined them, Ashton turned to him and said, 'I've been sacked.' Ashton, who had complained about the demands of administration and mentioned his own retirement, had expected to stay on for a few more years. 'I wanted everyone to *beg* me to do it,' he admitted to Julie Kavanagh.[41] Far from begging, Webster insisted that Ashton wanted to leave. 'I said to David, "Did you ask him if he actually wanted to go?"' remembers Tooley. '"Oh no," he said, "I made it absolutely clear, because he was always going. There was nothing to talk about."'

Trouble had been coming for some time. In 1966, Webster had flown to Berlin to see the opening night of Kenneth MacMillan's first season there. He told MacMillan that Ashton would definitely retire in three years' time, and offered him the Directorship of The Royal Ballet from that date. Webster had also encouraged John Field to think of the Directorship, suggesting in 1963 that he might be next in line. The 1968 crisis was prompted when Field was offered the directorship of London Festival Ballet. Webster urged him to turn it down, and went on to confront Ashton. Even so, it was not until just before Ashton's retirement that Tooley asked MacMillan if he would accept Field as co-Director.

De Valois had also influenced events, as Tooley recalls:

> She used to ring up sometimes and say, 'Fred's getting on, you know. Time the older man gave way to the younger genera- tion.' I said, 'What do you mean?' She said, 'I think Fred should stand down.' Now, how much influence Ninette had had on David, I don't know. Webster's remarks about Fred wanting to go when he went were quite independent of Madam.

Webster had already told Lord Drogheda, the Chairman of the Board, that Ashton would be leaving – but asked that the subject should not be discussed in minuted Board meetings. Webster's health was poor; he had moments of confusion in these years. He had worked devotedly for Covent Garden, and hated the thought of retirement. He died in 1971, less than a year after leaving. He seems to have found some comfort in the idea that Ashton would retire with him; he planned that Georg Solti should stand down as Director of the Royal Opera at the same time.

Inexplicably, Webster's decision was accepted. Ashton, stunned, told Hart and Somes that he was being forced to resign. He did not approach Lord Drogheda, the Chairman of the Board, who might have tried to stop it. Rumours spread. An announcement had to be made quickly. In April, the Covent Garden Company had returned to New York – the Bolshoi had cancelled a Met visit, and Hurok begged The Royal Ballet to replace them. A few days after the open- ing, the dancers were told that Ashton would be leaving. The dancers were in tears. Ashton's retirement, desperately mishandled, caused great bitterness. Much of the resentment settled on MacMillan, Ashton's successor. A rift had been created in the British dance world; a new note of anger appeared in criticism of the Company's next Director.

There was an elegiac quality to Ashton's next ballet. In *Enigma Variations*, which had its premiere in October 1968, Ashton matched Elgar's musical portraits of his friends with danced character studies. The designer Julia Trevelyan Oman had suggested the ballet in the early 1950s; Ashton now invited her to design it. Her set and costumes were full of naturalistic detail: an autumnal English garden with falling leaves, watch-chains for the men, long skirts for the women. She even insisted that the men's shoes should have authentic brogue markings. Ashton's dances are lyrical, comic, sharply characterised. At the heart of the ballet is the relationship between the composer, his wife and his friend Jaeger: their closeness, and the loneliness of the artist. To the 'Nimrod' variation, the three step forwards, reach out – and stop, feelings left unspoken. The ballet's image of Elgar's friends also stands as a portrait of Ashton's Royal Ballet. He had a cast of dance actors, distinctive personalities who could express subtle emotion through classical steps. Derek Rencher was Elgar, Beriosova his wife, with Desmond Doyle as Jaeger. Other solos were danced by Sibley, Dowell, Parkinson, Alexander Grant, Brian Shaw, Stanley Holden, Robert Mead, Vyvyan Lorrayne, Wayne Sleep, Leslie Edwards and Deanne Bergsma. *Enigma Variations* is a hard ballet to revive. Its atmosphere is difficult to pin down, easily lost under Oman's tweeds and elaborate frills. The work's tenderness is elusive, but can still be deeply affecting.

In Tudor's *Lilac Garden*, made for Rambert in 1936 and staged by The Royal Ballet in November 1968, emotions are repressed rather than understated. The music is Chausson's lush *Poème*, but the Edwardian characters – a woman on the brink of an arranged marriage, her lover and her fiancé's mistress – express their feelings in quick glances, gestures of sympathy. The Royal Ballet production was carefully staged, but missed Tudor's economy and intensity. At the first performance, Beriosova and MacLeary danced the heroine and her secret lover. While in Britain for the revival, Tudor also made *Knight Errant* for the touring company. The ballet, based on an episode from Laclos's novel, *Les Liaisons dangereuses*, was slight, but showed off the young David Wall.

In December 1968, the Company staged a new *Sleeping Beauty*. Peter Wright's new staging was a deliberate change of approach from the beloved 1946 production. For the first time, Fonteyn was not the first-cast Aurora: Sibley and MacLeary opened the production. The designs, by Bardon and de Nobili, set the ballet in a medieval, pre-Raphaelite world. It went against Tchaikovsky's evocation of Louis XIV and Versailles, and the dancers hated the floppy line of de Nobili's full-skirted tutus. Wright invented a striking entrance for the fairies, who descended down a shaft of sunlight. There was some new Ashton choreography: solos for the Prince and for an extra prologue fairy, a new Garland dance, a Gold and Silver pas de trois. In New York, Edwin Denby noticed that the prologue variations now covered more space, the dancers travelling boldly along diagonals.[42] Ashton also added a romantic 'Awakening' pas de deux. The production was generally disliked, but the Company danced superbly. That season, Sibley was followed as Aurora by Lorrayne, Park and Jennifer Penney. Fonteyn was the fifth Aurora.

This was a clear change in casting policy. 'In those days, if Margot and Rudi were billed together the house was packed out, so therefore I'd got to [cast them],' Ashton later said of the 1960s. 'But I used to beg them both, "Please go away and do things abroad. Let other people have a chance."'[43] The 1968–69 season made it clear that a new generation, led by Sibley and Dowell, was ready to take over. That winter, they opened revivals of both *Swan Lake* and *Romeo*, dancing with lucid grace. The next year, Ashton revived *Daphnis and Chloë* for them. Sibley needed persuading. Ashton told her to read Longus's novel: she was relieved to discover that the original Chloë was blonde, that she could find a way of dancing the role without copying Fonteyn. Dowell danced Daphnis with silken line and poetic musical phrasing.

In February 1969, the Company staged *Olympiad*, which MacMillan had made for his Berlin company. It was not a success: the gymnastic dances did not fit Stravinsky's *Symphony in Three Movements*. Nor did they suit The Royal Ballet's men. The next new ballet was a Fonteyn–Nureyev vehicle, Petit's turgid *Pelléas and Mélisande*. Finding ballets for the star partnership was becoming difficult. The previous year, Fonteyn had even expressed an interest in MacMillan's one-act *Anastasia*, made for Seymour in Berlin – presumably before she saw it; the fifty-year-old Fonteyn was anything but likely casting for MacMillan's expressionist heroine. She was more at home in the third act of *Raymonda*, which was staged at Covent Garden in March 1969. Beriosova and MacLeary danced the first night. Shortly afterwards, the Company set off on its eleventh American tour: six weeks at the Met, followed by three months of touring. Costs had risen further, and this was the last of the large-scale, coast-to-coast American tours. Watching *La Bayadère*, Edwin Denby pointed out 'the concentration of the dancers . . . Every single person on the stage is entirely concentrated, just as they are in a new production.'[44]

The Company returned to Covent Garden in October 1969 for a quiet winter season, with no new productions. On 7 January, the complete reorganisation of The Royal Ballet was announced, to take effect from September 1970. Once again, an attempt would be made to integrate the touring and Covent Garden companies, creating a single group of about 125 dancers. A group of about ninety would perform at Covent Garden for the usual winter and summer seasons. In spring, this larger Royal Ballet would tour the regions or make trips abroad. Throughout the year, a group of twenty-five dancers, 'each one independently interchangeable with the larger group', would perform a smaller-scale repertory on tour and in London.[45] The New Group, as it was called, would be able to develop new ballets; the management promised greater flexibility and a more experimental repertory.

This was presented as an artistic decision, but it was prompted by financial difficulties. Throughout the 1960s, the Royal Opera House had been losing money. Disbanding the touring company had been suggested as a way of reducing costs in 1966. The new scheme effectively put it into practice, reducing the number of dancers and making a projected saving of about £100,000 a year. The regional press, well aware that their touring company was being broken up, attacked the scheme at once. The old touring section gave its last performance in July 1970 in Wimbledon, led by Doreen Wells and Desmond Kelly.

At the same time, Ashton's retirement was confirmed. As Director, Ashton made one more ballet for Covent Garden. *Lament of the Waves* had its premiere in February 1970, at The Royal Ballet's Benevolent Fund gala. The title came from the music by

Gérard Masson, which featured a rippling pizzicato that passed from one side of the orchestra to the other. Ashton chose the young dancers Marilyn Trounson and Carl Myers – because if he used more established dancers, it would become a ballet 'about Sibley and Dowell drowning'.[46] It was affecting, but did not last in repertory. The last new production of Ashton's Directorship was a portentous Nureyev vehicle, *The Ropes of Time* by Rudi van Dantzig. Nureyev was the Traveller, writhing to Jan Boerman's crashing electronic soundtrack, with Mason and Diana Vere as Death and Life.

In April 1970, the Company again appeared in New York. The highlight of the season was a gala for Ashton on his retirement. At his request, it opened with *La Bayadère* as a tribute to the corps. The evening included a superb *Symphonic Variations*, danced by Sibley, Dowell, Ann Jenner, Penney, Michael Coleman and Gary Sherwood. Back in London, the summer season was full of Ashton ballets, including *Fille* and *Scènes de ballet*. On 24 July, the Company gave a farewell gala for their Director, devised and produced by Hart and Somes with assistance from Leslie Edwards. It was a retrospective of Ashton's career with the Company. Excerpts from 'lost' ballets were reconstructed: Mason danced Pamela May's solo from *Dante Sonata*, Lorrayne the Moon from *Horoscope*, Grant danced a solo from *Rio Grande*, Penney a scene from Ashton's *Baiser de la fée*. Fonteyn returned to five of her old roles – including, amazingly, an excerpt of *Daphnis* with Michael Somes. She danced *Apparitions* with Nureyev ('My interpretation was *quite* different,' Helpmann told the audience).[47] At last the whole company joined the Waltz from *A Wedding Bouquet*, and Ashton was brought on to acknowledge the audience's cheers. It was an evening of nostalgia, and of love: the end of an era.

ABOVE *Mayerling*. Gerd Larsen as Baroness Hélène Vetsera, plotting her
daughter's future with Countess Marie Larisch, danced by Merle Park:
© Anthony Crickmay, The Theatre Museum, V&A Images

PREVIOUS PAGE *Dances at a Gathering*. Back row: Lynn Seymour, Michael
Coleman, the choreographer Jerome Robbins, David Wall, Monica Mason.
Centre: Laura Connor and Rudolf Nureyev. Front row: Ann Jenner, Anthony
Dowell, Antoinette Sibley: © Leslie E. Spatt

For The Royal Ballet, the 1970s started with radical change. The Company was completely reorganised, just as its familiar leaders retired or stepped down. The transition from Ashton to MacMillan was anything but easy. After thirty-five years as its defining choreographer, Ashton withdrew from the Company; hopes that he would make a ballet a year, as announced, soon faded. The Royal Ballet was also affected by changes in economic climate, in Britain and the rest of the world. Since the move to Covent Garden and international success, the Company had run smoothly and very profitably. By the early 1970s, the days of dollar-earning tours were over. And all these developments took place at once. MacMillan returned to a company that would have to change gears fast.

It was a company of outstanding dancers, with an abundance of strong principals and soloists. Royal Ballet style was clearly defined: lucid, musical and sensitive to dramatic nuance. Feet were strong, quick and flexible, lines unfolded with fluent, sculptural beauty. As Director, MacMillan maintained and broadened the repertory. In Berlin, he had shown his faith in the de Valois model, staging *The Sleeping Beauty*, *Ballet Imperial* and *Scènes de ballet* alongside the modern dramatic ballets already popular in Germany. At The Royal Ballet, he worked on productions of the classics and kept the Ashton ballets in regular performance. He brought in choreographers from outside, including Balanchine and Jerome Robbins, and experimented with modern dance.

Where de Valois and Ashton had both been extroverts, MacMillan was introverted, enigmatic, sometimes shy. 'Kenneth was more scary than Fred,' remembers the dancer Genesia Rosato. 'He would have dark glasses on, you wouldn't know *what* he was looking at. He was always looking around the sides. He was fascinated by people, a magnificent people-watcher, he wanted to see deep inside. Look at the characters he creates! They're amazing to do, to portray.' He inspired loyalty from his dancers. 'You trusted him,' says David Wall. 'In his rehearsals, you felt you could try anything.' He encouraged them to find movements and feelings, to do research, sometimes to work against the grain. 'It would always be a huge mistake, when Kenneth was choreographing, to do a step that you found hard,' smiles Rosato. 'Because he would, for sure, say, "Yes! I want that!" Always to the limit, Kenneth.'

Despite the demands of administration, it was a productive time for MacMillan as a choreographer. In seven years, he would make eight one-act ballets and two evening-length works for The Royal Ballet. The most significant development was his growing interest in longer works. Tooley remembers a conversation from 1969, just before the Bolshoi Ballet made another visit to London. MacMillan predicted that *Spartacus*, Grigorovich's new three-act ballet, would be the hit of the season. He was right. The public mood was changing. The classics had always done well at the box office; in the next decades, the evening-length ballet would become so popular that mixed bills were in danger of being squeezed out altogether. MacMillan's greatest gift was his ability to put character and complex feeling into movement. His expressive dramas often focused on a small group of principals, imagined in depth. Transferring them to the large canvas of a three-act ballet, he left thin patches. At the time, he was fiercely criticised. But there was real ambition in MacMillan's portraits of individuals and societies. In creating them, he made roles that dancers are still eager to dance.

The new regime had a difficult start. Feeling still ran high over Ashton's enforced retirement. The issue had been forced because Webster feared losing John Field; now The Royal Ballet had two designated Directors. John Hart resigned; Somes remained as Senior Répétiteur, with special responsibility for the Ashton repertory. That still left confusion over the Directorship itself. MacMillan had accepted Field as Administrative Director, expecting something like the association of Ashton, Hart and Somes. Field, who had expected a more equal partnership, resigned after three months. Peter Wright was made Associate to the Director, supporting MacMillan and taking over the administration of the Companies.

Or rather, the Company. The reorganisation had created one large Company, which was to divide into The Royal Ballet at Covent Garden and The Royal Ballet New Group. However this was presented, it meant that the touring company was cut from sixty-five dancers to twenty. Union negotiations had imposed restrictions on how the cuts could be made. 'We couldn't use it to cut out dead wood,' says Wright. 'In the end, we had to lose a lot of the younger dancers.' It left a top-heavy company, and some soloists had to be demoted. Somes, pointedly disdainful of the touring company dancers, did more to lower spirits. Then there was the administrative nightmare of deciding which dancer should join which group. MacMillan had invited Jerome Robbins and Glen Tetley to stage ballets for his first season, and was determined to give them a free hand in casting. Until they had chosen their dancers, it was impossible to decide who should be in which company – and Robbins was notorious for considering alternative casts until the very last minute.

MacMillan had inherited a great company and a terrible situation. He faced hostility over Ashton's departure, over the reorganisation, over sackings, demotions and the uncertainties of the new structure. Many of the dancers did not know their new Director; he had been in Berlin for four years. Moreover, the forty-one-year-old MacMillan was recovering from serious illness. He had collapsed in Germany, his health affected by overwork and heavy drinking. He had recovered, and given up alcohol, but was, Wright remembers, 'still physically pretty weak; he was nervous, very lonely, avoided communicating with the press and was unable to speak to the Company *en masse*'.[1] Morale was understandably low.

It was lifted at once by *Dances at a Gathering*, the first new production of the 1970–71 season. This had been Robbins' first work on his return to New York City Ballet in 1969, a critical and popular smash-hit. At The Royal Ballet, too, it made an exultant new beginning. Robbins' ballet is a series of dances, an hour long, to Chopin piano pieces. Dancers strolled into their variations: the steps were demanding, yet they looked almost improvised. There were touches of folk dance, a moment when a man touches the stage floor as if it were earth. The dancers changed moods, changed partners, responded to the music's rhythms and to each other – flirtation, affection, playfulness. The Royal Ballet gave it greater dramatic emphasis than the transparent New York City Ballet performance; they danced gloriously, and both Robbins and the audiences were delighted. In the opening mazurka, Nureyev walked, tilted his head in thought, sketched a step and launched into dance. Mason and David Wall waltzed together, constantly changing momentum. Seymour was whimsical and flirtatious as she tried to join first Jonathan Kelly, then Wall, then Michael Coleman. The first-night cast also included Sibley, Dowell, Ann Jenner and Laura Connor. *Dances at a Gathering*, a splendid addition to the repertory, also showed off the depth of talent in The Royal Ballet. This programme had opened with *Enigma Variations* – completely different in mood, but another ballet filled with solo dancing. The Company had a wealth of gifted dancers.

There were more stars when the New Group made its debut in Nottingham, but not so much euphoria. Tetley's *Field Figures* was at the heart of the programme: The Royal Ballet's first piece by a modern-dance choreographer, set to Stockhausen's electronic score. Nadine Baylis designed a spare setting of vertical metal rods. The dancers grappled through knotted movements: Deanne Bergsma hooked her legs around the crouching Desmond Kelly's knees and stayed there, leaning away from him in a precarious balance. The ballet was respectfully received. It was framed by performances of *Apollo*, rather under-rehearsed, and *Symphonic Variations* led by Sibley and Dowell. This was proof of MacMillan's determination to take Covent Garden stars to the regions, but it was an odd choice. The ballet has a small cast and a simple setting, making it cheap to tour, but Ashton's spacious choreography needs a large stage.

A few weeks later, the New Group danced MacMillan's first ballet since becoming Director. *Checkpoint*, danced to a score by Roberto Gerhard, had a theme taken from George Orwell's novel, *1984*. Elisabeth Dalton designed a set dominated by TV screens, video cameras and film projections. To escape surveillance, the ballet's lovers danced a precarious duet halfway up a wall, supported by invisible hands behind the set. The first night was a disaster. The reel of film was dropped and had to be hastily rewound, while the audience waited and complained. During the performance, projections failed altogether. Beriosova and MacLeary were fearless in their vertiginous pas de deux, but MacMillan's choreography was elaborate and awkward. *Checkpoint* was both difficult and expensive to stage, hardly suitable for touring.

Over its first seasons, it became clear that the New Group was unworkable. It was too difficult to keep switching dancers between companies; gradually the group settled down as a touring company. Meanwhile, attendances had dropped. The Royal Ballet's touring company had a loyal following, but it had always been easier to sell full-length classics than triple bills. The new touring group – with a change of name and a repertory of untried short works – did not appeal to regional audiences. Its numbers were increased, and old touring favourites like *Pineapple Poll* and *Les Patineurs* were brought back. Peter Wright – who had returned to The Royal Ballet expecting to lead the touring company – devoted as much time as possible to the New Group, gradually increasing its numbers. *Giselle* was revived in 1974, *Coppélia* in 1975. The New Group returned to the old model of a smaller classical company, with an admirable emphasis on new work.

At Covent Garden, the 1970–71 season continued with a work made for the original old-style touring company. *The Trial of Prometheus* had been Ashton's last work as Director, made for the Beethoven bicentenary celebrations. Beethoven's only ballet score has defeated many choreographers; Ashton's, wrote David Vaughan, 'somehow . . . did not look like an Ashton ballet at all . . . The dancers, too, seemed uncertain whether to play it straight or for laughs.'[2]

MacMillan's *Concerto*, made for his Berlin company in 1966 and set to Shostakovich's Piano Concerto No. 2, was much more successful. MacMillan had taken the central image for the pas de deux from the sight of Seymour warming up at the barre. During a rehearsal, he had been distracted by the beauty of her movements. Those warm-up poses became part of the duet, with her partner acting as the barre.

That year, there was no full-length ballet for the Christmas season.

MacMillan had hoped to revive *Cinderella* or *Fille*, but Ashton was working on his film *The Tales of Beatrix Potter*, with dancers from The Royal Ballet as Potter's animal characters. For the first half of this season, MacMillan had refused to programme the nineteenth-century classics. His corps de ballet, drawn from two sources, was not yet united; they needed more time before tackling *Swan Lake* or *La Bayadère*.

There was also casting to be considered. In their first meeting with the Covent Garden management, MacMillan and Field had raised the question of Fonteyn and Nureyev. In her fifties, Fonteyn was an artist of unique glamour and necessarily waning technique. Her partnership with Nureyev guaranteed full houses, with higher prices charged for their performances. As a result, Field and MacMillan told the Board, the other dancers 'had not been brought on as they should have been, and there would be a vacuum which no one could fill when Fonteyn ceased to dance. It was now almost impossible to arrange an overseas visit without Fonteyn and Nureyev.'[3] At the last New York visit, they had danced six out of eight *Romeo* performances. Sibley and Dowell were adored by dance fans, but Fonteyn and Nureyev still got the headlines.

MacMillan was determined to promote his younger dancers. The Covent Garden management, thinking of lost revenue, was reluctant, but Fonteyn performances were gradually cut back. Nureyev remained a frequent guest with The Royal Ballet until the late 1970s – not just in the classics or special vehicles, but in regular repertory. In this decade, he would also dance *Fille*, *Manon*, *The Dream*, *Field Figures* and *Afternoon of a Faun*, partnering most of the Company's ballerinas. He danced his first Covent Garden *Apollo* in 1971; he was never obvious casting in Balanchine, but his very personal approach to the role had fervent admirers.

After six months without a nineteenth-century classic, MacMillan brought back *Swan Lake* in February 1971. He had pressed for a new production, but funds were not available. Rather than the Helpmann–Ashton *Swan Lake*, the Company danced a revised version that combined aspects from the Covent Garden and touring company productions: the Hurry scenery and costumes, with some of the new Ashton choreography. The Prologue was dropped, but Ashton's fourth act was retained. No producer was credited. Though dancing by the principals was impressive, the overall standards were criticised. The effects of reorganisation were still being felt.

A revival of *Giselle*, replacing MacMillan's postponed *Anastasia*, was more secure. This was the touring production by Peter Wright, with designs by Peter Farmer. Sibley and Dowell danced the first night, with Bergsma a commanding Queen of the Wilis. Her bourrées were exceptionally quick and smooth: Ashton, she remembered, said he would love to 'get on my back when I was Queen of the Wilis and see what it was like to travel like that'.[4] In April, the Covent Garden Company made its first tour of the regions for fifteen years, dancing a programme of classics. It did not go well. Only Fonteyn nights sold out. The resident Company had got out of the habit of touring; it had a shaky sense of how to appeal to audiences outside London.

Back at Covent Garden, *Anastasia* at last had its premiere in July 1971. In Berlin, MacMillan had become fascinated with the story of Anna Anderson, the woman who claimed to be Anastasia, the youngest daughter of the last Tsar. In 1967, he made a one-act *Anastasia*, set to Martinu's sixth symphony. It showed Seymour's Anna as a patient in a clinic, tormented by memories of her past, losing and recovering her identity. The ballet began with film images, historical footage of the court and revolution. MacMillan's choreography here was jagged and expressionist, Seymour's limbs starkly splayed as she fought memory and confusion. Expanding the work for The Royal Ballet, MacMillan added two acts of classical choreography, set to Tchaikovsky's First and Third Symphonies. The first showed court life before the revolution, with Rencher's diffident Tsar dependent on Beriosova's gracious Tsarina. Seymour's Anastasia was a tomboy among her elegant sisters. Her entrance on roller-skates – MacMillan had seen skating in film of the Russian Imperial family – made a happy sensation. In the second act, revolutionaries broke into a grand court ball. Barry Kay's designs were ravishing. A swirling vortex hung overhead, a stylised beech forest that became the screen for the third-act film clips.

The Tchaikovsky symphonies established a grandly Russian

atmosphere, but couldn't support MacMillan's storyline. Both the new acts ended weakly – the first with an endless review of troops, created to fill Tchaikovsky's fugue, the second with a hurried attack by revolutionaries. The lively virtuoso Wayne Sleep was seriously miscast as the leader of a violent mob. Determined to provide roles for his company, MacMillan padded out the action with too many dance scenes. Despite these flaws, *Anastasia* creates an onstage world. Relationships within the Imperial family were vividly imagined, conveyed in quick details. As the Tsar hesitated over the telegram announcing war, his Tsarina gave him an affectionate little push, making him open it. The ballet was magnificently danced. Seymour went from childhood through searing adult terror to final resolve. Praising the ballet's 'steely bravura' in 1974, Arlene Croce called it MacMillan's best three-act work so far, 'not so much because of what it achieves as because of what it attempts . . . he produced a personal fantasy about a global cataclysm entirely from nothing.'[5] The first reviews of *Anastasia* were generally hostile. Critics complained about the weak structure, the use of Tchaikovsky, the contrast between the new material and the last act. The reception came as a great shock to MacMillan – and to the dancers, who were proud of the ballet.

Anastasia returned at the start of the 1971–72 season. The young Lesley Collier, already admired as a classical soloist, made a vulnerable heroine in the second cast. A second Robbins work, the atmospheric *Afternoon of a Faun*, was added to the repertory at the Benevolent Fund gala in December. In this ballet, made for New York City Ballet in 1953, Robbins rethought the Debussy–Nijinsky *L'Après-midi d'un faune*, moving it from pastoral Greece to a modern ballet studio. Jean Rosenthal's set, made of transluscent gauze, shows a barre, windows and skylight; gazing out at the audience, the two dancers look into an imaginary mirror. Sibley and Dowell, fluently musical, danced the gala performance. They appeared again in a pas de deux Ashton had made earlier that year, set to the swooning 'Meditation' from Massenet's opera *Thaïs*. Sibley was a veiled oriental vision, floating weightlessly in Dowell's arms. Ashton showed off their effortlessly fluid line in perfumed choreography. *Checkmate* was revived the same evening, with Helpmann returning as an incomparable Red King. Mason was a commanding Black Queen, while Nureyev made a spirited debut as the Red Knight.

MacMillan's next ballet, *Triad*, had its premiere in January 1972. Dowell and Wayne Eagling, an athletic young Canadian dancer, were brothers whose closeness is broken by the arrival of Sibley. MacMillan made winding choreography to Prokofiev's Violin Concerto No. 1. In one duet, the two men went on thinking of the absent woman, moving as if lifting her, partnering empty space. Peter Unsworth's designs were gauzily abstract, with the dancers dressed in delicately patterned leotards. In February, Fonteyn returned in *Poème de l'Extase*, a ballet Cranko had made for her in Stuttgart. She danced an older diva, contemplating an affair and carried away – literally – by memories of former lovers. Even Fonteyn could not make it a success. This season was affected by a fuel crisis in Britain, with power cuts delaying rehearsals. There were fears that *Poème de l'Extase* would be cancelled; orchestral calls for *Serenade* and *The Rite of Spring* had to be abandoned. A revival of *The Sleeping Beauty*, now refurbished, showed off the Company's strength. Reviewing the Prologue fairy variations, Buckle wrote: 'To see Seymour with her Cleopatra arms in the first, Collier shining in the second, Vere in the third mostly backwards one, Parkinson with her sudden changes of direction and elegant wrists in Ashton's inserted fourth, Jenner in the fluttering fifth and Mason in the pointing sixth, is to see stars.'[6]

In April, the Company returned to New York. They had visited the Met every year from 1967 to 1970; this was the first visit in two years, the first of MacMillan's Directorship. MacMillan, who was finishing a ballet for the touring company, was not there for the opening, a poorly planned mixed bill. The classics and the dancers were as popular as ever; Park, Mason and Wall were welcomed with delight. The recent works, however, were coolly received, with *Anastasia* and *Field Figures* – the latter included at Nureyev's insistence – generally disliked. Even more than in Britain, MacMillan's position as Ashton's successor was resented. Aggrieved fans stood at the stage door to shout, 'Ashton, Ashton, Ashton' when MacMillan came out; they screamed and spat and made vomiting noises. Back in London, there was press criticism of MacMillan's regime.

In the summer season, the ex-Kirov ballerina Natalia Makarova made her first guest appearances with The Royal Ballet. In June she danced *Giselle* with Dowell, followed by *Swan Lake* with MacLeary. It was the start of a close association with The Royal Ballet: like Nureyev, she danced a wide repertory with the Company. Makarova's dancing was grand and magnificently Russian. Her performances were utterly individual, passionately admired and often controversial: audiences used to Royal Ballet musicality were shocked by her high-handed approach to phrasing. In July, Tetley made a new ballet for the Company, in the same tangling style as *Field Figures*. *Laborintus* used Berio's score as chic accompaniment, ignoring the words declaimed by Cathy Berberian. The ballet was not popular, and was the last modern-dance experiment for some time.

That summer, the Company gave its first Proms performances, sponsored by Midland Bank. Prices were reduced, and the stalls seating was removed, so that a larger, mostly younger and very enthusiastic audience could sit on the floor. The question of reaching broader audiences was becoming important. Before the war, the Company had made profits on regional tours, but cinema and television had transformed the economics of live performance. The old touring circuits had gone, and many of the theatres had been closed or converted into cinemas. Outside London, there were now fewer opportunities for theatre-going, and audiences became more conservative. All these changes increased the expense of regional touring. In September 1972, the Arts Council warned The Royal Ballet that subsidies could be maintained only if the Company gave more performances in the regions. The Company was supported by taxpayers' money; it should be seen by the people who helped to pay for it. This was just, but financially difficult: with rising expenses, touring costs would be greater than the increased Arts Council subsidy. Despite repeated efforts to solve it, this dilemma remained.

Stravinsky had died in 1971. In tribute to him, the 1972–73 season opened with a programme of *The Firebird*, *The Rite of Spring* and *Les Noces*. That season, Ann Jenner made her debut as the Firebird, dancing with crisp energy and a tireless jump. Further revisions to *Swan Lake* showed that MacMillan had paid attention to criticism of the last revival. He now took responsibility for the production, which reverted almost entirely to the old Sergueyev text. Ashton's fourth act was replaced by the traditional Ivanov choreography. MacMillan kept Ashton's brilliant pas de quatre, but moved it to the ballroom scene, where it looked much more at home.

At the Benevolent Fund gala in November, the Company staged Robbins' *Requiem Canticles*, made for the 1972 Stravinsky Festival at New York City Ballet. A large cast danced a long series of mourning dances. The ballet was never popular, though it was revived the next season. For the same gala, Ashton made a new short piece, *The Walk to the Paradise Garden*. Park and Wall were the lovers claimed by Rencher's figure of death, who enveloped them in his pale cloak. Makarova danced *Les Sylphides*, taken at an extremely slow tempo, and *Birthday Offering* was revived with Fonteyn, Beriosova and Blair in their original roles. The other variations were danced by Sibley, Park, Penney, Jenner and Parkinson, a new galaxy of ballerinas. This was to be Fonteyn's last performance of the ballet: the demands of the choreography were now too much. There was another gala in January 1973, a 'Fanfare for Europe' arranged to mark Britain's entry into the Common Market. For Sibley and Dowell, MacMillan made a duet to Fauré's *Pavane*.

In 1973, the Company staged an all-Balanchine programme of *The Four Temperaments*, *Prodigal Son* and *Agon*. In one evening, MacMillan doubled the number of Balanchine works in the repertory; he had tried, without success, to persuade Balanchine to make a new ballet for the Company. All three works were very warmly reviewed. Balanchine style was still a stretch for the dancers, who had to prepare three works in a short rehearsal period, but they responded eagerly. In *The Four Temperaments*, made in 1946 to a score by Hindemith, Balanchine builds complex structures from simple steps, ideas echoed and transformed, with bold line and brilliant rhythmic variety. The cast included Desmond Kelly, Jenner and Dowell, Eagling and Bergsma. *Prodigal Son*, made for Diaghilev in 1929, sets the Biblical parable to a Prokofiev score. Bergsma was an icy Siren, seducing Nureyev's Prodigal in the cruelly erotic pas de deux. *Agon* was the hardest of these ballets to bring off. Here, Balanchine's classicism stretches back to court ballet and forwards to New York jazz, with thrusting limbs and complex rhythm. The Royal Ballet smoothed out some of Balanchine's dynamics. *The Four Temperaments* and *Prodigal Son* were later danced by the touring company, where Desmond Kelly was an outstanding Prodigal.

At Covent Garden, there were plenty of debuts that spring. The elegant Dowell had an unexpected success as Colas in *Fille*, showing a new extrovert quality. Park danced her first, characteristically musical, Odette–Odile. Collier and Eagling made their debuts in *Romeo and Juliet*. There was a new *Sleeping Beauty* in March 1973. Hopes were high: MacMillan's Berlin production had been admired. His new version, unfortunately, was a crashing disappointment. Though the American Friends of Covent Garden had paid for it, it was never taken to New York. Peter Farmer, brought in as designer at the last minute, used blocks of limited but sometimes clashing colour: Aurora, still in traditional pink, was surrounded by courtiers in lime and turquoise. MacMillan made a Garland waltz and a new Vision solo for Aurora. The Florestan pas de trois became a set of variations for Jewel Fairies. MacMillan added two solos in the last act, one for Bergsma's Lilac Fairy and one, for the fairytale character 'Hop o' my thumb', for Wayne Sleep. Sleep, an extrovert and very popular virtuoso, had made his name in a School performance of *Les Patineurs* in 1966. He was too short for most of the traditional repertory, but had several roles made to show him off. The Company danced strongly in the new *Beauty*, with Sibley and Dowell as the opening couple. Michael Coleman was a soaring Blue Bird, with Alfreda Thorogood a stylish Princess Florine.

The new *Beauty* was taken on a successful month-long tour of Brazil, where Fonteyn danced her last-ever Aurora. After dates in four cities, the tour ended with a performance at the 19,000-seat stadium in Brasilia. Excitement was so extreme that the dancers thought a revolution was starting. Outside, crowds trying to get into the overbooked auditorium were driven away by riot police. During *La Bayadère*, the orchestra was drowned out by the noise;

Sibley and Dowell, dancing the leads at that performance, sang the music for the other dancers. For the terrified corps de ballet, the famous, disciplined entrance became an ordeal. 'One by one, as they turned the corner, having made it down the ramp, we, in the wings, could see tears rolling down their cheeks,' remembered the dancer Ian Owen. 'Margot stood in the wings encouraging and talking to them, saying that the shouting (from the audience) was out of encouragement – that they were shouting out of enthusiasm and that the dancers should just keep going and not be afraid.'[7]

On their return to London, the Company gave a month-long season at the London Coliseum, while the opera company played at Covent Garden. The all-ballet season allowed MacMillan to show off a broad repertory of short and full-length ballets, with the full range of principals and soloists. In June, the Company returned to the Royal Opera House, where Makarova and Nureyev danced together for the first time in *The Sleeping Beauty*. Rehearsal time had been limited, as the set had only just arrived from South America. Both dancers showed signs of strain. They were better matched in *Romeo and Juliet*, Makarova's first appearance in British choreography, which she danced with feverish intensity and attack. That month, David Blair gave his last performance with the Company, dancing Colas in *Fille*.

In July 1973, Desmond Kelly made his debut as the Prince in *The Sleeping Beauty*, partnering Ann Jenner. At the end of the first act, Jenner was taken ill with appendicitis. Brenda Last, who had come backstage in the interval to visit Kelly, promptly took over. She had danced the role twice with the touring company, six years before; she did not know the production, and she was herself recovering from an operation. She was promptly dressed 'in Makarova's tutu and somebody's headdress', before sailing onstage to give a jubilant performance.

In 1961, MacMillan had made a version of Kurt Weill's *Seven Deadly Sins* for Western Theatre Ballet. This hybrid work, first choreographed by Balanchine for Les Ballets 1933, has a dual leading role: two versions of Anna, one danced, one sung – originally by Lotte Lenya. In July 1973, MacMillan revised his production with Jennifer Penney and the smoky-voiced singer Georgia Brown. The

Canadian Penney had ideally lovely proportions, natural turnout and a high, clear arabesque. Her Anna was both innocent and impulsive. Ian Spurling revised his colourful art deco designs for Covent Garden. It was uneven, but made for a light, slick ballet. The season ended with a revival of *Ballet Imperial*, now without Berman's Tsarist eagles and tutus. At Balanchine's request, the ballet was re-dressed in soft, drab costumes and renamed *Piano Concerto No. 2*.

The autumn season opened with Robbins' *In the Night*, made for New York City Ballet in 1970. Like *Dances at a Gathering*, it was danced to Chopin piano music; in Britain, as in New York, it was seen as a kind of sequel. This time, the dancers were definitely in couples, the relationships more adult, the mood more romantic. Danced by Sibley and Dowell, Mason and MacLeary, Park and Wall, it was instantly popular, although, like *Dances at a Gathering*, it fell out of the repertory with the end of MacMillan's Directorship.

Manon, MacMillan's third full-length ballet, had its premiere in March 1974. He took a literary subject, the Abbé Prévost's eighteenth-century tale of a woman tempted by love and money. Manon Lescaut falls for the young student Des Grieux, but her attention span is too short for fidelity. Lured by furs and diamonds, she slips readily into prostitution and is eventually transported, dying in a Louisiana swamp with Des Grieux in faithful attendance. Georgiadis designed a glittering, squalid world for the ballet: sumptuous costumes and a backcloth of rags. MacMillan was again working on a picture of a society, but in *Manon* the picture is romantically sweetened. The pretty music was a patchwork, arranged by Leighton Lucas, of existing material by Massenet, drawn from almost everything except his opera *Manon*. MacMillan built his ballet around four swooning duets for the lovers. Manon, said Dowell, the first Des Grieux, hardly touches the floor in these pas de deux.[8] She can become a passive victim – especially in the last act, where she is raped by the Gaoler before succumbing to hallucinations and death. Yet MacMillan plays with that passivity in two scenes: a decadent pas de trois, where Manon's brother Lescaut sells her to the rich Monsieur G.M., and in the brothel scene, where she is passed from hand to hand, unresisting yet in control.

The ballet's popularity lies in its big roles, and the dramatic opportunities they give to dancers: *Manon* is now danced by more than a dozen companies around the world. In 1974, critics complained about the ballet's structural weakness and, especially, the Massenet score, but the dancers were universally praised. In the first cast, Sibley greedily chased jewels and love, pulling the story onwards with dancing of etched clarity. She had fallen ill during rehearsals, and some of the role was choreographed on Penney, who gave a more innocent interpretation. As Des Grieux, Dowell was shy and then impassioned, dancing with effortless fluency of line. Wall was a superb Lescaut: casually amoral, relaxed and attractive as he cheated, lied and charmed his way through the ballet. MacMillan invented a Mistress for him, showing off Mason's clarity in two solos; the way she taps one foot in a semi-circle, legs crisp and bold, is one of the ballet's best dance images. She and Wall were show-stopping in the brothel scene, the Mistress welcoming signs of affection as he slides into drunkenness. In 1976, Dowell and Wall swapped roles when Seymour played Manon. She made a rapacious heroine, almost incestuously in league with Dowell's predatory Lescaut. Wall's Des Grieux went from serious divinity student to the frantic anger and despair of the last act. Again, MacMillan padded his ballet with dance scenes, but supporting roles were vividly taken: Rencher was all calculating lust as Monsieur G.M. Georgiadis and MacMillan dressed one of the whores, originally played by Jennifer Jackson, in boy's clothes, with trousers and a plumed hat. Since she had been given steps on pointe, often with the other prostitutes, she thought there must be some mistake. MacMillan took her aside to explain: '*You're* more expensive.'[9]

In April, the Company visited Bristol, where there was a bomb scare on opening night. Reviews were warm, but attendances, though better than for the last regional tour, were still poor. In May, the Company set off for New York and Washington. Once again, it was welcomed by American audiences – Sibley and Dowell were given a ticker-tape reception – but this tour was different in several ways. Sol Hurok had died earlier that year, and Fonteyn, for the first time, did not appear with the Company. The tour was supported by private sponsorship, as profits could no longer be expected from overseas visits. The revised *Swan Lake* was admired, but *Manon* was harshly reviewed by New York critics. Worried by reviews, the Covent Garden management considered replacing *Manon* with more *Swan Lake*s. 'If you take *Manon* off,' MacMillan told them, 'I'll put the Company on a plane and we'll fly home.'[10] The performances went ahead as scheduled, to full and enthusiastic houses.

The Company returned to a summer season at Covent Garden, with Nureyev and Makarova as guest artists. It also made its first use of the Big Top, a circus tent originally built for Cinerama film showings. Tooley had been looking for a new way of presenting the Company outside London. Covent Garden productions were often too big for regional theatres, and the tent was an ingenious solution. The first two-week season, held at the Plymouth Argyle football ground, was an immediate success. The Company avoided full-length works, but single acts of *Swan Lake* and *The Sleeping Beauty* were included. Tent seasons caught on; by the 1980s, other companies were appearing at the Big Top.

The autumn season opened at Covent Garden with MacMillan's extrovert new ballet, *Elite Syncopations*. This was set to ragtime numbers by Scott Joplin and others. (MacMillan was criticised for jumping on a bandwagon: after he started work on his ballet, the movie *The Sting*, with its ragtime soundtrack, was released.) The bare stage was set up as a dance hall. The band, led by pianist Philip Gammon, was on stage, and the dancers flopped down on chairs between numbers. MacMillan showed a marvellous cast in a series of comic numbers. The very tall Vergie Derman danced with the tiny Wayne Sleep; Mason had a solo with sexy bottom wiggles. Park, at her wittiest, strutted with a cane before unfurling her legs in a duet with Donald MacLeary. Penney and Wall were wistfully shy together. Ian Spurling dressed them in body tights covered in lurid spots, stripes and stars, with jaunty hats. *Elite Syncopations* was a smash hit, immediately and intensely popular. It was danced by a series of starry casts: Collier, Makarova, Penney and Jenner followed Park in the leading role.

Makarova returned that autumn, dancing *Song of the Earth* and a marvellous *Manon*, capricious and alluring. 'Probably no other of my roles in the West means as much to me as Manon,' she wrote soon afterwards.[11] In January 1975, the Dutch choreographer Hans van Manen made *Four Schumann Pieces*, a showcase for Dowell's speed, his endlessly smooth line and legato phrasing. The ballet was bland, but Penney, Eagling and Collier shone in supporting roles. On the first night, it followed a magnificent performance of *La Bayadère*. De Valois came on stage to present the corps de ballet with the London *Evening Standard* award for the year's best achievement in dance. In the past, the award had always been given to an individual: here was recognition of The Royal Ballet corps as a single entity, of its shared style and ideal unity. 'The corps is now unrivalled,' said the critic Clement Crisp, one of the judges. 'They are a national treasure.' The award was also a tribute to Jill Gregory, the Ballet Mistress, who had joined the company in 1932.

The Concert was the highlight of the Benevolent Fund gala held in March 1975. This was Robbins' first Chopin ballet, made for New York City Ballet in 1956 and subsequently revised. The Royal Ballet production had two new front-cloths by the balletomane artist Edward Gorey. The ballet is subtitled 'The Perils of Everybody'. Dancers assemble, with folding chairs, to listen to a concert, and are sidetracked into fantasies. Georgina Parkinson, elegantly hilarious, bossed Coleman, who dreamed up murder and revenge to the prelude famous from *Les Sylphides*. Seymour, already an established comedienne, tried on a series of feathered hats. Graham Fletcher, who had already made an impression in *Elite Syncopations*, was very funny as a timid young man. To the 'Raindrop' prelude, the dancers opened umbrellas or held out their hands to see if it was raining.

The next night, *The Concert* shared a programme with MacMillan's new ballet, *The Four Seasons*, danced to music from Verdi operas. MacMillan, eager to show off the Company's depth and strength, started with corps dances and went on to a bright set of classical variations. MacLeary partnered Vergie Derman and Marguerite Porter in a Winter pas de trois. Lesley Collier danced Spring, inventively partnered by Eagling, Coleman and David Ashmole. The most admired variation was Summer, a yawning, languorous duet for Wall and Mason. Autumn was a virtuoso display piece for Penney with Dowell and Sleep. Peter Rice's costumes suggested military or peasant dress. His fussy backdrop showed an alpine inn; since the women were inside the building, the men outside, several critics took it for a brothel. *The Four Seasons* had an unlucky design history: neither Barry Kay's elaborate Paris production nor the later Royal Ballet redesign was successful.

In April 1975, the Covent Garden company made its first visit to Korea and Japan. They spent three days in Seoul before moving on to Tokyo and eight other cities. The dancing was highly praised, and Sleep was a sensation as Puck in *The Dream*. The most popular ballet was *La Fille mal gardée*, which needed a local pony for the carriage taking Lise and the Widow Simone to the picnic. In Kobe, the mare refused to leave her young foal, so Leslie Edwards led it onstage beside the carriage. The same thing happened at Covent Garden in the early 1980s, with a foal so young that one of the farmhands carried it on.

The Company was to have had another season at the Coliseum in June, but had to cancel after a last-minute pay dispute with the stage staff. Instead, the Big Top was pressed into service, with financial backing from the Midland Bank. Both Royal Ballet companies appeared under canvas in Battersea Park. The tent had its drawbacks: it was much smaller than the Coliseum, there was no scenery, and sightlines were often poor. But lower prices, and the appealing setting in the Park by the river, brought in a new and enthusiastic audience. The season opened, in a noisy downpour, with Makarova and Dowell in *Swan Lake*. *Elite Syncopations*, which looked terrific in a circus tent, was filmed for television. The season was followed by three weeks at the Royal Opera House. MacMillan's *Symphony* was revived, its Sonnabend designs now toned down.

The autumn season opened in Newcastle, with a fortnight of *Swan Lake* and *Romeo* in the Big Top. Back in London, Mikhail Baryshnikov danced both ballets, partnering Merle Park – his first appearances with The Royal Ballet. He had never danced Romeo in Russia; he proved to be an eager, impetuous hero, ardently young. Around him, the Company was in dazzling form. Sleep led the mandolin dance with showstopping virtuosity. Dowell danced Mercutio with glinting energy and attack. MacMillan was encouraging his dancers to try different roles within the same ballet. Wall, one of the Company's most spontaneous Romeos, made his debut as Mercutio that year – the same season in which he and Dowell swapped roles in *Manon*. 'It helps both of us,' said Wall. 'I just love to be onstage as part of somebody else's performance, as opposed to it being all sections, Mercutio's performance and Romeo's . . . They're part of a whole. One talks about an individual interpretation; in a way, one should really be talking about the interpretation of the Company.'[12] Across the repertory, Royal Ballet dancers had this sense of collective drama. In 1974, James Monahan had singled out Rencher as the Duke in *Giselle* – 'a bluff, distinctive personality'.[13] These were performances within a unified ensemble. MacMillan first spotted Genesia Rosato when she and another dancer played out an argument at the edge of a crowd scene in *Romeo*. 'I've been watching it for months, and it's wonderful,' MacMillan told her. 'But it's got so it's *all* I watch in that scene – you need to tone it down.'

Rituals, MacMillan's next ballet, had its premiere in December 1975. He had loved the trip to Japan; *Rituals* was a stylised impression of the traditional Japanese arts he had seen, set to Bartok's Sonata for Two Pianos and Percussion. Sonnabend designed an airy set, with gauzes and calligraphy on papyrus. The first movement showed a kung-fu contest between Eagling and Stephen Beagley, both strong, flexible dancers. In the second, Wall and Vergie Derman were gorgeously clad *bunraku* puppets, manipulated by puppeteers. The ballet ended with Seymour in childbirth, with Mason as the midwife. Mason had also shown MacMillan the walk used by actors in traditional Noh theatre. Sightseeing in Nara that summer, she had got chatting with a woman at a bus stop, who had invited a whole group of the dancers home to dinner. There they met her father, a celebrated Noh teacher, who taught Mason the traditional walk. MacMillan adored it, and put it into his ballet. *Rituals* received good reviews, but it was a remote work; it did not last long in repertory. It shared a bill with an outstanding revival of *Les Biches*. Makarova danced the Garçonne with sensational aplomb, handsomely partnered by Wall. Mason showed all her strength and style as the Hostess, sweeping on with torso arched back, footwork quick and cutting.

Since his retirement, Ashton had stepped back from The Royal Ballet, turning down repeated invitations to make a new ballet. That Christmas, there were signs of a thaw, when he and Helpmann returned, for the last time, as the Ugly Sisters in *Cinderella*. Park, Penney and Makarova danced the heroine; Makarova returned in February 1976 to dance *Serenade*. Early in the New Year, Fonteyn danced her last full-length performance with the Company, *Romeo and Juliet* with Nureyev.

In February 1976, after an interval of five years, Ashton made another ballet for the Company. *A Month in the Country* was hailed with delight by critics and audiences. Ashton compressed Turgenev's five-act play into forty minutes, setting it to a series of Chopin works for piano and orchestra. A young tutor innocently disrupts a Russian country house: Natalia Petrovna, the bored married woman, her ward Vera and even the maid Katya fall in love with him. Ashton cast Seymour as Natalia, Dowell as the tutor Beliaev. Her first dances show Natalia in charge of her household, managing her husband and family with practised charm. Her torso curves through supple changes of direction, enhanced by the creamy flow of Seymour's movements, her quick footwork gleaming and exact. When she and Beliaev dance together, she drifts forward in rippling bourrées, suddenly floating as he lifts her just off the ground: a woman carried away by love. Denise Nunn, still in the corps de ballet, was an eager, vulnerable Vera. Ashton cast Sleep as Natalia's young son, asking him to bounce a ball and fly a kite between virtuoso steps. Natalia's admirer Rakitin, a central figure in the play, became a supporting mime role, subtly played by Rencher. Julia Trevelyan Oman's designs weigh the ballet down with naturalistic detail, her set filled with chairs and occasional tables. The action is surrounded by frills – a gauzy curtain is drawn back as the ballet begins – and costumes are thick with lace and ribbons.

A fortnight later, The Royal Ballet had a two-week season at the Bristol Hippodrome before setting out on another American tour: five weeks in New York, three in Washington DC and one in Philadelphia. The Company was welcomed with enthusiasm. Dowell and Makarova opened the New York season with *Romeo and Juliet*. With Sibley away through injury and maternity leave, this was becoming a second regular partnership. Dowell, stimulated, was dancing with fresh attack, developing a newly assertive stage manner. The first week at the Met was quiet; by the second, wrote Arlene Croce, *Romeo* had 'the tautness of a first night'.[14] *A Month in the Country* was a hit in America, with Seymour given star treatment. At the end of the tour, Grant – who had had his last new role as Natalia's husband – left to direct the National Ballet of Canada. The 1976 tour would be The Royal Ballet's last visit to New York for five years. The Big Top had made touring in Britain easier; after three weeks at Covent Garden, the Company returned to Plymouth for another three weeks in July and August. Sibley, back after an injury, danced Juliet and the *Thaïs* pas de deux.

Glen Tetley's *Voluntaries*, the first new production of the 1976–77 season, had been created in memory of John Cranko. The ballet was first danced by Cranko's Stuttgart company in 1973, months after his death. It was set to Poulenc's dramatic Concerto for Organ, Strings and Percussion, and began and ended with the ballerina lifted in a crucifixion pose. The acrobatic choreography was more balletic than Tetley's earlier works, and more popular with The Royal Ballet's audiences. Seymour and Wall danced the first night. In the early days of his Directorship, MacMillan had emphasised American choreography, Robbins and Balanchine. In his last year, he turned to Europe, with less success. Van Manen's *Adagio Hammerklavier*, created for the Dutch National Ballet in 1973, had its Royal Ballet premiere at the Benevolent Fund gala in November. Three couples danced slow-moving duets to a movement from the Beethoven sonata. The ballet was dropped after just three performances. At the same gala, Lynn Seymour danced *Five Brahms Waltzes in the Manner of Isadora Duncan*, Ashton's evocation of the modern-dance pioneer's style and stage presence.

MacMillan's latest ballet had its premiere a few days later, with the Stuttgart ballet. In a replay of the trouble over *Song of the Earth*, the Board of Directors had rejected MacMillan's plan to choreograph Fauré's *Requiem*, and he had taken it to Stuttgart with considerable success. MacMillan's relationship with the Board had not been happy. In the mid-1970s, the Directors had doubted

MacMillan, sticking with him because of 'the impossibility of finding a replacement who would be better'.[15] In 1976, he found that
the Board had gone over his head to arrange a new production of
The Sleeping Beauty. 'I've just been told that we are doing a new
Sleeping Beauty, and that Madam will be directing it,' he told his
wife. 'I am no longer Director of The Royal Ballet.'[16] He sent in his
resignation. The announcement was not made until June 1977,
when a successor had been found. Then, and during his lifetime,
MacMillan gave the burden of administration as his reason.

Injury removed Sibley throughout the 1976–77 season and
Dowell for most of it. In a display of the Company's luxury casting,
Dowell was often replaced by Nureyev or Wall. This led to one of
the events of the year, the reunion of Makarova and Nureyev, in
Dances at a Gathering and then *Swan Lake*. They had not danced
together since a well-publicised row in Paris in 1973. In other *Swan
Lakes*, MacLeary, now Ballet Master with the Company, came out
of retirement to partner Makarova. Winter was dominated by full-
length ballets, with revivals of *Romeo and Juliet* and *La Fille mal
gardée*. Another evening-length work, Cranko's *Onegin*, was
planned for February 1977. The production had to be cancelled
when Jürgen Rose's sets failed to meet London fire-safety regulations. *The Taming of the Shrew*, staged by the Stuttgart dancers
Marcia Haydée and Richard Cragun, was an unhappy substitute.
The knockabout comedy did not suit The Royal Ballet, though the
ballet was strongly cast with Park and Wall, Seymour and Eagling
and Collier with Stephen Jefferies, a strikingly dramatic dancer
from the touring company. *The Taming the Shrew* looked a little
better with Haydée and Cragun as guest artists. During the
rehearsal period, they had danced the roles MacMillan made for
them in *Song of the Earth*. It was a starry season. That spring,
Baryshnikov returned to Covent Garden, dancing *Romeo* with
Seymour before making his debut in *Fille*. Partnering Jenner and
then Collier, he was a blissfully good Colas: dazzlingly quick in the
bravura steps, sunny and vital.

The Fourth Symphony, danced to Mahler, had its premiere at the
end of March. This was made for the Company by John Neumeier,
an American choreographer who had studied at The Royal Ballet

School before settling in Germany, where he was director of the Hamburg state ballet company. Once again, Sleep was cast as a child, dancing in scenes with his parents and older couples. It was generally disliked, and dropped after only four performances.

In April 1977, the touring company moved back to Sadler's Wells, becoming the Sadler's Wells Royal Ballet. Peter Wright had gradually cut his own ties with Covent Garden. There were still links between the two companies: Stephen Jefferies had moved between the two, and Covent Garden principals sometimes gave performances with the touring company. Wright was encouraging new choreography, and several of his discoveries would go on to work with the resident company at Covent Garden. Over the next decade, however, the two groups separated, with the touring company gaining new independence. The third company, Ballet for All, would soon leave altogether. Its programmes overlapped with the touring company's, and in 1978 the Arts Council decided to withdraw funding. The group was taken over by the Royal Academy of Dancing.

In July 1977, the Covent Garden company crossed the river for a season at the Big Top in Battersea, followed by a week at the Royal Opera House. There were no new productions that summer, but more performances for younger dancers: Jefferies, Laura Connor, Derek Deane, Marguerite Porter and Wendy Ellis. The season ended with *Manon*, danced by Seymour and Wall. The dancers stood back to let MacMillan, who rarely appeared on stage, take a curtain call; there was a shower of flowers. It was a quiet but affectionate end to MacMillan's Directorship. He said at the time that giving up administration would be 'a great relief'.[17]

Finding a replacement for him had been difficult. There was no obvious candidate within the Company, though Nureyev was seriously considered. The Royal Ballet was in a sense his home company; he was a superb coach and a huge star. The drawback was that, at thirty-nine, he was determined to keep dancing. 'If I interrupt my dancing career to become a director, make a hash of it, which I might, then I can't continue my dancing, because then I've lost it,' he told Tooley when they discussed the Directorship.[18] And Nureyev wanted to dance as much as possible; he had given forty guest performances with the Company in 1976, and was resentful that the number was so low. Tooley couldn't risk it. Nureyev went on to direct, and to revitalise, the Paris Opéra Ballet, which did allow him to dance. When The Royal Ballet went through a serious slump in the 1980s, comparisons were inevitably drawn. Yet Nureyev's Paris record shows another reason why he might not have suited The Royal Ballet. Though he brought in new choreographers, he also filled the Paris repertory with his own productions, his own hectic choreography. His finest work as a producer came early in his career; each time he staged *Raymonda*, it had more Nureyev and less Petipa. The Royal Ballet had one of the finest repertories in the world, including the most authentic texts of *Swan Lake* and *The Sleeping Beauty*. There is reason to wonder whether Nureyev, who so readily altered steps and costumes to suit himself, would have respected that repertory.

Norman Morrice, the next Director of The Royal Ballet, had very little history with the Company. He had trained with Rambert and joined her company as a dancer, moving into choreography in the late 1950s. In 1965, he made *The Tribute*, a modern-dress ballet about a fertility rite, for The Royal Ballet touring company. The next year, he was appointed assistant director of Ballet Rambert, overseeing its successful transformation from classical to modern-dance company. He had resigned to concentrate on choreography in 1974. Both Rambert and de Valois thought Morrice would be good for The Royal Ballet: a voice from outside, a change of approach. Morrice was diffident, affable, interested in the Company's history and identity. 'Norman was one of the most delightful individuals anyone could ever meet,' says Anthony Russell-Roberts, who became Administrative Director of The Royal Ballet in 1983. 'He had this incredible way of looking at life philosophically and analysing it philosophically – which I think very often made him over-cautious in making decisions, as he could always see the downside as well as the upside.' He faced distrust and resentment from The Royal Ballet staff, especially Michael Somes; fearing that consultation would lead to 'destructive wrangling', Tooley had presented them with a *fait accompli*. 'I remember people kept saying that he was "an outsider", worrying about "the bloodline",' says Anthony Dowell. 'He had a heavy cross to bear.' The Royal Ballet has an unusually strong sense of family. Morrice took charge at a point when two generations of the family were still around. After his resignation, MacMillan was appointed Principal Choreographer to the Company. Ashton still had a hand in revivals of his ballets; de Valois remained keenly interested in the state of the Company she had founded. Morrice trod carefully.

He made one immediate change in policy, however, announcing a temporary ban on guest artists. Morrice wanted the Company to renew itself from within. Since the 1960s, too many of its dancers had developed late, held back by the wealth of talent further up the ranks. MacMillan had started with a top-heavy company; he had given the extraordinary 1960s generation its day. Some of these dancers – Beriosova, Sibley, Bergsma – had left; those that remained were now in their thirties. The generation below, which had suffered most from the reorganisation, looked thinner. Moreover, the Company was drawing its dancers from a smaller pool. Until the 1960s, dancers from half the world had automatically looked to The Royal Ballet; this was no longer the case. No South Africans had joined since 1961, when the country became a Republic and withdrew from the Commonwealth. Australia and Canada now had their own ballet companies (both had been directed by Royal Ballet dancers). After Britain joined the European Common Market, the employment of Commonwealth dancers was restricted. The Royal Ballet, less lavishly funded than most European state troupes, could not match Continental salaries. In 1981, James Monahan was to complain that 'in the last few years it has been disappointingly obvious that [the Company] lacks potentially world-class ballerinas between the ages of about twenty-five and thirty-three.'[19]

The ban on guests was Morrice's solution: given more performances, the younger dancers would have the chance to grow. It was a shock for audiences, who were used to regular appearances by Nureyev and Makarova. In the summer before Morrice's first season, London was awash with starry competition. Nureyev danced with London Festival Ballet and with his own group, including Fonteyn; American Ballet Theatre visited, bringing Baryshnikov,

Makarova, Gelsey Kirkland, Fernando Bujones. After a fifteen-year association with The Royal Ballet, Nureyev was appalled to find himself exiled with other guest stars. He partnered Seymour in three performances of the new *Beauty*, his last appearances at Covent Garden until 1982. Tooley urged Morrice to relent in Nureyev's case, without success. In May 1977, Nureyev threatened to withdraw The Royal Ballet's right to perform his productions of *La Bayadère* and *Raymonda*.

Morrice's first season opened with the new *Sleeping Beauty*. Injured in an accident, the seventy-nine-year-old de Valois conducted rehearsals with her neck in an orthopaedic collar and one foot in plaster, as fiercely energetic as ever. After two disappointing *Beauty*s, she was determined to get the production right. She included many of the post-1946 additions, including Ashton's solos for the Prince and Aurora, his Awakening pas de deux, MacMillan's Hop o' my Thumb solo. Until 1981, she used the revised 'Finger' variation she had learnt from Nijinska. In another departure from tradition, she cast a female Carabosse. Seymour was balefully funny, Mason imposingly grand. De Valois asked Ashton to work on the production, coaching Lesley Collier in the role of Aurora. She was quick, vivacious and musically alert. Dowell, back from injury at last, danced with fluent grace and was welcomed with cheers. Subsequent casts included Penney and Wall, Jenner and Jefferies, Park and Eagling, Seymour and Nureyev. David Walker's designs harked back to Messel, with a tendency to prettiness: too many frilled sleeves on the costumes. Marvellous in the prologue and first act, the production had some uncertain pacing in later scenes. British critics, taking Royal standards in *Beauty* for granted, were grudging, tending to see it as a copy of the 1946 version. However, in 1978, the American critic Arlene Croce compared the production to American Ballet Theatre's version, which used the old Messel designs:

> Watching Ballet Theatre do *Beauty*, one begins to doubt the status of the old ballet. The dances seem thin, the story hopelessly artificial, the roles insufficiently demanding. Watching the Royal, one doesn't know where to look, there is so much

to see. Style attaches to every move: a unison port de bras can become an event of magnitude. When the fairy flock arranges itself along the footlights in one of its perfect tableaux (which aren't in the ABT version at all), we see a picture of eternal youth and beauty, and we see motion in its stillness like the pieces of a reflection which float together on the trembling surface of a pool. Not a static or separate image but a materialization, the picture emerges as the grand resolution of countless small strokes, gestures quick and slow, that had been going on since the rise of the curtain. The cohesion of these strokes and the perspective they create for the major happenings and climaxes of the ballet are part of what *The Sleeping Beauty* is all about. It's the grand manner, and it's no more of an unreachable fantasy than was Versailles, which is the implied setting of the ballet. To get perfection of detail, harmony of proportion, motion in stillness (and stillness in motion), you need a finely tuned ensemble, and you also need a good director. The new Royal *Beauty*, supervised by Ninette de Valois, has everything it needs.[20]

In the autumn of 1977, Ashton was awarded the Order of Merit – a reward for outstanding service in art, learning, literature or science, its numbers limited to twenty-four living recipients. The same evening, The Royal Ballet danced a programme of *Enigma Variations*, conducted by Adrian Boult, *Symphonic Variations* and *Les Noces*. Ashton received an ovation. That season, The Royal Ballet presented three excellent casts of *Symphonic Variations*. Ashton also coached Marguerite Porter, who had danced the maid in *A Month in the Country*, for her debut as Natalia, a sensitive performance with delicate upper-body detail. Graham Fletcher gave warmth and depth to the virtuoso role of Natalia's son. Porter at this time danced her first Aurora, with Julian Hosking. Morrice was promoting his younger dancers: Wendy Ellis and Derek Deane also made their debuts in the leading roles of *The Sleeping Beauty*.

Released from administration, MacMillan had spent months working on *Mayerling*, his finest and most ambitious picture of a society. Using a scenario by Gillian Freeman, and John Lanchbery's arrangement of Liszt, he showed events leading to the death of Crown Prince Rudolf, heir to the Austro-Hungarian empire, who committed suicide with his teenaged mistress in the hunting lodge at Mayerling. The deaths of Rudolf and Mary Vetsera had been romanticised in several movies. MacMillan's version was bleakly historical, showing Rudolf's unhappy marriage, his debauchery and drug addiction, his obsession with guns and death. Following his hero's decline, MacMillan made a wealth of supporting roles for the Company's women: Rudolf's mother the Empress Elisabeth, his wife Princess Stephanie, his ex-mistress Marie Larisch, the prostitute Mitzi Caspar, Mary Vetsera. Each act ends with a morbid, sexually explicit pas de deux. These, like the ballet's other duets, are psychologically acute. The first duet for Rudolf and Mary starts with a confrontation; at a change in the music, they are suddenly in tune, hypnotised by the possibilities of lust and death.

It's a sprawling, complex story, but MacMillan's focus remains remarkably sharp. Early on, we see a grand procession, the whole court following Rudolf and his bride. Georgiadis's designs have a majestic glitter, his costumes moving well, but with a sense of weight and restriction. Yet that opening march is unexpectedly brisk: this stately court sails along at a hectic, unhealthy pace. Undercurrents of social and political intrigue show even in the first court waltzes, some of MacMillan's loveliest corps dances. The ballet builds an image of a whole crumbling society from the way people dance, stand, watch each other. Waiting for her wedding night, the Princess Stephanie (Wendy Ellis at the first performance) sits nervously, a small figure in a big chair, as her women dance buoyantly about her. The web of relationships is boldly realised, the characters driven by urgent needs. Not all MacMillan's ideas translate into dance – it isn't clear that the Hungarian officers are urging Rudolf to support the cause of an independent Hungary, nor that the Emperor is worrying about the future of the state – but this society and its characters are powerfully realised.

The ballet was magnificently performed by the dance actors of The Royal Ballet. In a huge, demanding role, Wall showed bitter unhappiness as well as frenzy. Seymour was greedily voluptuous in her last MacMillan role. As Larisch, the most complex of these characters, Park was scheming, worldly, needy. Parkinson made an icily graceful Empress. Graham Fletcher gave a heartfelt performance as Rudolf's coachman. Genesia Rosato, in her first solo appearance in Royal repertory, made a striking impression as Stephanie's sister Louise. *Mayerling* received a standing ovation, and MacMillan's best reviews in years. The ballet had three strong casts. Eagling was a frail, nervous Rudolf; Jefferies was urgent, filled with self-disgust. Collier was a headstrong Mary, followed by the morbid, sensitive Thorogood. *Mayerling*'s many female parts have given Royal Ballet women a chance to prove their dramatic diversity: Mason, Park, Penney, Rosato and Collier are among those who have danced two or three of its roles.

In April 1978, the Company danced a musically weighty double bill of *Song of the Earth* and *The Firebird*. Mason – who insisted on being coached by Fonteyn, to revelatory effect – was a magnificent Firebird, imperious and bold. Fokine had told Karsavina that he wanted to see the beating of mighty wings in the role. Mason was a proud, soaring creature, with a huge jump and a powerful sense of magic. She created 'a being of thrilling force', wrote Clement Crisp; 'you can feel the air stir as the Firebird blazes through Kostchei's garden.'[21] That spring, the Company toured to Seoul and the United States – the first time the Company had visited America without a New York season. The new *Sleeping Beauty* was more warmly received abroad than in London, but *Mayerling* was severely criticised. Back in London, the Company celebrated de Valois's eightieth birthday with a performance of *The Sleeping Beauty*, before setting off for more performances in Athens.

At the end of the season, Dowell announced that he was joining American Ballet Theatre. In the autumn, Seymour accepted an invitation to direct the Munich ballet. Two more dancers left in 1978: Parkinson moved to ABT as ballet mistress; Jenner went to Australia. Sibley, whose recent career had been beset with injuries, retired altogether in May 1979. The Royal Ballet had started the decade with stars galore. Now it looked thin on top.

Though Morrice had no guest dancers, Robert Irving returned to conduct several performances in the 1978–79 season, including fine accounts of *Serenade* and *The Sleeping Beauty*. There were no new productions until well into the New Year. Morrice programmed revivals of *Beauty* and *Swan Lake*, and a number of Ashton ballets. As promised, the absence of guests led to a range of debuts, with young dancers moving into solo and principal roles. Mark Silver danced a promising Beliaev in *A Month in the Country*, and followed it with a confident Prince in *The Sleeping Beauty*. Rosalyn Whitten danced her first Aurora; Porter made an admired debut in *Swan Lake*. Just before Christmas, the Company revived *Birthday Offering*. Unusually, Morrice put on a second cast of this starry ballet, highlighting his rising soloists. Pippa Wylde was already grand, while Rosato showed her supple back in Elvin's variation. These were encouraging signs, but promoting youthful talent led to uneven casting in other ballets. In March 1979, Deirdre Eyden made her debut in *Symphonic Variations*, cast with older and more experienced performers. This is a ballet for three well-matched ballerinas: Eyden, making an admirable debut, was overshadowed. 'I do not remember a season in which I have been so bothered by differences of age and physique,' wrote Mary Clarke. 'I can't believe that all the mispairings were accidental and it is a dreadful comment on The Royal Ballet that they do not seem to be able, with their wealth of young talent, to come up with the right "mix" for *Symphonic Variations*.'[22] Morrice was eager to promote his young dancers; he needed to do more to support them. In the next decade, this lack of support would lead to far more pronounced problems.

La Fin du jour, MacMillan's latest ballet, had its premiere in March 1979. Set to Ravel's Piano Concerto in G, it was a fantasy about 1930s fashions – in clothes, sports, attitudes. The dancers – dressed by Ian Spurling in pastel sports clothes, golf suits for the men, swimming costumes for the women – started in mannequin poses. In the slow movement, Penney and Park pulled on goggles, turning their bathing caps into flying helmets. Teams of men lifted them through the air, turning them into aviatrixes and then, as Croce pointed out, into flying machines. The ballet ended with the cast in evening dress. On the last chord, Park shut the door at the back of the stage: the end of an era. *La Fin du jour* was elegant and sophisticated, danced with great freshness, and received very warmly by critics and audiences. The first performance was disrupted by a dispute with the stage staff; the other two ballets – MacMillan's *Diversions* and *Elite Syncopations* – were given in Spurling's creamy set for the new ballet. At the end of the programme, Princess Margaret presented MacMillan with the *Evening Standard* award. He was given an ovation, with more showers of flowers.

The next new production was an unexpected disappointment. Balanchine's *Liebeslieder Walzer*, danced to two sets of Brahms part-songs, was made for New York City Ballet in 1960. Four couples, in heeled shoes and evening dress, dance a series of waltzes. In the second episode, Balanchine takes the waltz from the ballroom to the ballet stage. The same dancers return, the women in tulle and pointe shoes, their dancing now heightened, the courtesy of the ballroom replaced by greater mystery. The ballet was loved in New York, and had been popular in London with Balanchine's own company in 1965. The Royal Ballet production was poorly dressed but strongly cast; Vergie Derman was gloriously elegant, Mason marvellously grand. Several critics hailed it as a masterpiece, though they complained about David Hays' flimsy designs. The ballet remained resolutely unpopular. An audience that had welcomed *Dances at a Gathering* walked out of *Liebeslieder Walzer*. 'In all of Covent Garden, seventeen of us truly loved it,' said Ross MacGibbon, one of the dancers of the cast. 'The first cast, the second cast, and Norman Morrice.'

The spring season was dominated by a revival of *Manon*. In June, the Company set out on an American tour, visiting Washington, Montreal, Vancouver, San Francisco, Los Angeles and Mexico City. Just before they left, on 23 May 1979, a gala was held to celebrate Margot Fonteyn's sixtieth birthday. She appeared in a new Ashton solo, *Salut d'amour à Margot Fonteyn*. Fonteyn, in heeled shoes and a chiffon dress designed by William Chappell, sat dreaming in a chair, then got up to dance. Most of the movements were for her arms and torso, still beautiful and beautifully expressive: echoes of the many roles Ashton had made for her. At the end, her choreographer came to escort her offstage. They exited doing the 'Fred step' – a step from one of Pavlova's ballets, which he had put into nearly all his own works as a good-luck charm. It brought the house down; after cheers and curtain calls, Fonteyn and Ashton danced it again.

The evening continued with *Symphonic Variations* and ended with *Façade*, with Fonteyn and the seventy-year-old Helpmann dancing the Tango. When they reached the point where he should turn her upside down, she gave him a dizzy look, wagged a finger, and they both swept happily on.

The Fonteyn gala was a moment of blissful nostalgia, one of the Company's family celebrations. As Fonteyn's long career came to a close, The Royal Ballet was looking for signs of renewal. The Company, almost fifty years old, was seeing signs of promise and of disquiet. The 1980s were not going to be easy.

ABOVE The new generation: Bryony Brind, Ravenna Tucker and Fiona
Chadwick as solo Shades in *La Bayadère*: © Zoë Dominic
PREVIOUS PAGE *Gloria.* Jennifer Penney and Julian Hosking in MacMillan's
First World War lament: © Dee Conway

At the start of the 1980s, reviews of The Royal Ballet take on a note of nervous optimism. There were fine performances in these years – promising debuts, impressive performances by individuals, strong revivals of single productions. Critics hailed them with relief, looking hopefully for signs of a more general return to form. These moments of excellence were no longer assumed to be characteristic. Something was slipping, and slipping badly.

This was to be the most difficult period in The Royal Ballet's history. As it reached its golden jubilee, the Company suffered a weakening of its technical foundations. Dancers who had emerged in the 1960s and 1970s remained strong, Collier pre-eminent among them; some of the younger generation kept a firm grip on their technique. Around them, standards slid. What changed? There are two films of The Royal Ballet in *Romeo and Juliet*, one made in 1966 with Nureyev and Fonteyn, the second made in 1984 with Eagling and Alessandra Ferri. Both give pictures of The Royal Ballet as a whole. The later film shows the dancers' collective involvement in the drama – and records, amongst other things, the superb Mercutio of Stephen Jefferies. Yet the Company's acting registers more strongly than the steps. In corps scenes, feet and turnout are slack; musical phrasing has been evened out by dancers who lack the speed and strength to vary their attack. The 1960s dancers, with their clear upper bodies and quick feet, look ready for *The Sleeping Beauty*. The mid-1980s dancers do not. The strengths and weaknesses of the later *Romeo* exemplify a loss of consistency across the Company, across the repertory. The sense of drama and commitment remained, but the dancers were working from a weakened technical base. Yet the Company staff included teachers who had been there since before the 1960s, who had overseen the glories of *Beauty* or *La Bayadère*. The obvious change was the appointment of Norman Morrice.

On paper, Morrice's policies were intelligent and interesting. In the eight years of his regime, he tried to encourage younger dancers, to respond to the boom in British modern dance, to bring distinguished painters to the Company and to encourage new choreography. He was loyal to his dancers and to his choreographers. Yet he found it hard to impose his policies, harder to bring them to a happy conclusion. The promotions of his second season had produced an effect of uneven casting; other plans failed to develop effectively. This was a deeply troubled time for the Company.

Morrice's third season opened with *Romeo and Juliet* in October 1979. Dowell, who was still to make occasional appearances with The Royal Ballet, returned to partner Park's Juliet. The following mixed bills were worrying. *Dances at a Gathering* was cancelled, replaced by the unpopular *Liebeslieder Walzer*. In the 1970s, Robbins had said that Royal performances of *Dances* should include at least two of the trio of Nureyev, Dowell, Wall. This could no longer be achieved, and the Company has not revived the ballet since. Other programmes showed the wealth of The Royal Ballet's repertory: *The Dream*, *Symphonic Variations*, a Diaghilev triple bill of *Les Sylphides*, *Les Biches* and *Les Noces*. Too many showed a disturbing decline in technical standards. Footwork, traditionally one of the Company's glories, was sloppy; there was far too much playing for laughs. *Les Noces*, always cherished at The Royal Ballet, survived, but the other ballets showed a loss of discipline and balance.

Swan Lake, which opened with Collier and Wall in December 1979, was the only new production of that autumn. Morrice's version was not *very* new. Before his death in 1978, Leslie Hurry had made a choice of sets and costumes from his various Royal Ballet productions. Hurry's view of the ballet was still atmospheric, but there was a faded, old-fashioned look to the production. Collier, who had danced her first *Swan Lake* in 1973, had grown into the role. A dancer of bright vitality, she had recently found new depth and authority as Odette–Odile. Wall, who brought out the humanity of princely roles, partnered her warmly. Other casting tended to be made in what Mary Clarke called The Royal Ballet's 'civil service mode', with roles given according to seniority.[1] Morrice made few textual changes, but brought back Ashton's fourth act. The corps had lost some of their poetry, but looked best in Ashton's choreography.

Massine had died in 1979, and the spring of 1980 brought a revival of his *Mam'zelle Angot*. As the heroine, Collier was crisp and lively, with Rosalyn Whitten delightfully bubbly in a later cast. As in 1947, critics were dubious, but it was done with gusto and proved popular with audiences. The Company danced with fervent conviction in MacMillan's *Gloria*. MacMillan's First World War lament was inspired by Vera Brittain's *Testament of Youth*, with Poulenc's exultant *Gloria* as an ironic counterpoint to the stage action, showing ghostly figures on the battlefield. A few critics worried about this use of Poulenc, but *Gloria* received overwhelmingly good reviews. Andy Klunder, a sculpture student at the Slade, designed a stark landscape and stylised costumes – torn battle-dress for the men, pale silvery make-up and ragged dresses for the women. Penney, Eagling and Julian Hosking were intertwined in one pas de trois; Eagling danced a fast, raging solo, pointing an accusing finger. MacMillan's choreography was dominated by winding, twisting movements, with complex lifts and portentous gestures. In the classics, Penney was exquisite but lacked a touch of authority. Here she was transformed: Deirdre McMahon was struck by 'that shimmering, mysterious quality that makes *Gloria* so unforgettable. As so often in Macmillan ballets, Penney dances at full stretch and the results are breathtaking'. That year, she won the *Evening Standard* award for her work in MacMillan roles.

Morrice had hoped to revive *Ondine* in May 1980, but Ashton was reluctant. Instead, three works were introduced, making an ill-assorted triple bill. In *Troy Game*, made by Robert North for London Contemporary Dance Theatre, the Company's men strutted through macho poses. MacMillan's compellingly sinister *My Brother, My Sisters* had been made for the Stuttgart Ballet in 1978. An isolated family of five sisters and one brother act out cruel, incestuous games, playing at violence and death. 'He did two different endings,' remembers Rosato, who danced one of the sisters. 'We tried them both, but we stuck with the one that leaves the element of doubt. There's the little sister, the one everyone was mean to. At the end, we put masks on, sneak up on her, steal her glasses. She dies at the end. But is she dead? In one of the endings, she came back to life and frightened us.' The ballet was set to two scores by Webern and Schoenberg, with claustrophobic designs by Sonnabend. Her set showed a brooding moorland, landscape and sky painted on the backdrop and on a series of scrims hanging over the dancers' heads. The women's short dresses, decorated with large, clumsy patterns, suggested children's frocks. As the oldest sister, Penney became mean and menacing, tormenting the vulnerable Collier. Wayne Eagling danced the brother. Birgit Keil and Richard Cragun, from the original Stuttgart cast, gave guest performances later in the run. The last new ballet came from David Bintley, only twenty-two years old, but foremost among the new choreographers encouraged by Peter Wright at the Sadler's Wells Royal Ballet. *Adieu*, set to Andrzej Panufnik's Violin Concerto, was a melancholic abstract ballet. Bintley's use of his dancers was fluent, if not very individual.

In July, Norman Morrice staged a new production of *Giselle*. As with *Swan Lake*, he looked to The Royal Ballet's past, sticking close to the 1960 text. As in 1946 and 1960, James Bailey was the designer. Together, these productions implied that the Company was fixed in the past. Worse, Bailey's revised designs were badly realised and disastrously fussy. In the first act, the peasant girls were cluttered up with bows, frills, bunched fabric and aprons, all in bright, poorly chosen fabrics. Porter made her debut on the first night, replacing an injured Merle Park, but could meet neither the technical nor the dramatic demands of the role. The corps, too, were off-form, though Jefferies's sharply characterised Hilarion was admired. Makarova and Dowell, who returned as guests that month, did manage to transcend this unhappy production. Makarova made her debut in *A Month in the Country* later that season, still adjusting to Ashton style but with a vivid, impulsive characterisation.

There were more guests that summer. Gelsey Kirkland danced her first, riveting Juliet. Kirkland, also with ABT, seemed ideally at home in Royal Ballet repertory, alert to nuances of drama and style. At the very starry Benevolent Fund Gala that summer, she was a wild, fey Titania in the *Dream* pas de deux, with Dowell. Baryshnikov appeared at the gala and in *Romeo*, and again in Ashton's new ballet. *Rhapsody*, made for the Queen Mother's eightieth birthday, was a virtuoso display piece, with virtuosity as its subject. The music was Rachmaninov's *Rhapsody on a Theme of Paganini*, based on a famous melody by the celebrated violinist. In his first, explosive solo, Baryshnikov even sketched a violin-playing gesture between the dazzling jumps and turns. Ashton's choreography detached Baryshnikov from the ensemble, and even from his ballerina, Lesley Collier. As they swept in, one solo after another, the two leads seem almost to drive each other from the stage; the way he searches for her among the corps has more effect than their duet together. *Rhapsody* is brilliant, musical and odd: exciting but irregular. Collier was bright, astonishingly fast: 'tiny steps seem to fly like sparks from her feet,' wrote Clement Crisp.[2] Baryshnikov and Collier were framed by a corps of twelve. One dance gave each of the six women a few solo steps, highlighting the Company's rising generation. These six were already attracting notice in solo variations: Bryony Brind, Angela Cox, Gillian Kingsley, Karen Paisey, Genesia Rosato and Gail Taphouse. William Chappell's designs drenched the ballet in gold dust: bracelets, jewelled chokers, and in Baryshnikov's hair. The ballet has been redesigned twice.

Rhapsody, with its fireworks and its sense of promise, heralded the start of the Company's golden jubilee year. The 1980–81 season was filled with galas, new works and historical revivals. *Rhapsody* opened the season in October, sharing a bill with *Enigma Variations* and *Gloria*. Without Baryshnikov, the six young women drew most attention. The first new work of the season came in November. Glen Tetley, who had been central to Morrice's reinvention of Rambert, was invited to make a new work for The Royal Ballet. In *Dances of Albion: Dark Night Glad Day*, he yoked together two substantial Britten scores, the *Sinfonia da Requiem* and the *Serenade for Tenor, Horn and Strings*. The dance was full of muscular grappling and unspecified woe, but was strongly danced by Collier, Whitten,

Jefferies and Eagling. The same night, The Royal Ballet gave its first performance of *Dark Elegies*, Tudor's setting of Mahler's *Kindertotenlieder*. Made for Rambert in 1937, the ballet shows the people of a village mourning the death of their children. The Royal Ballet dancers missed the weight of earlier Rambert stagings, but Sandra Conley showed a moving sense of grief.

In December, the twenty-year-old Fiona Chadwick made her debut in *The Firebird*, dancing with tremendous ease and authority. She was an intelligent, musical dancer, with large, expressive eyes and a strong stage presence. The details of the role registered powerfully: Chadwick's jump was high and bold, and she showed an exultant glee when she led Kostchei's minions in their dance. In January, *La Fille mal gardée* celebrated its twenty-first birthday. At the curtain calls, Ashton brought on Nerina, Grant and Holden. Leslie Edwards was there too, still dancing his original role, Farmer Thomas; John Lanchbery conducted the music he had arranged. In February, David Wall returned from injury in a performance of *Mayerling*, and was welcomed with a banner lowered from the gallery. These good impressions were unsettled by some dishevelled Ashton revivals. *Daphnis and Chloë* came back in an untidy state; *A Month in the Country* looked mannered. Several ballets were poorly staged, with awkward lighting and scene changes. Porter appeared frequently, in ballets that needed greater technical resources. She looked a little like Fonteyn, and gained and suffered in consequence: she was given Fonteyn's roles, whether they suited her or not.

In April, Helpmann's *Hamlet* returned to the repertory. Dowell, his huge eyes made up extravagantly in Helpmann fashion, stalked through the ballet. To general delight, Sibley came out of retirement to dance Ophelia. Dowell had coaxed her back for a gala in 1980, then pointed out that *Hamlet* has almost no dancing, so she could take it on without risk. This was the start of Sibley's comeback, reviving her partnership with Dowell. *Les Sylphides* was revived in the same programme. New designs, by the painter John Hubbard, had been promised; these were cancelled due to lack of production time. The old Benois set was poorly lit, and the dancers looked strained. A later Stravinsky bill also suffered from short rehearsal time. David Atherton, scheduled to conduct *The Firebird* and *Scènes de ballet* as well as *The Rite of Spring*, finally appeared only in the latter, with poor musical standards in the other ballets.

Bryony Brind's debut in *Swan Lake* was the excitement of the season. Brind was tall, long-limbed and thin, with quick feet – unusual in so tall a dancer – and a supple back. Her torso, and her high, soft extensions, suggested Kirov as much as Royal Ballet style: Brind was a new kind of dancer for the Company. 'Following NASA's example The Royal Ballet has launched its secret weapon and like the space shuttle the new vistas produce frissons of anticipation, and fear,' wrote Deirdre McMahon.[3] Yet Brind's Swan Queen had old Royal Ballet virtues. In the second act, she built the way Odette leaves and returns to the prince with cumulative force, a current of energy running through the whole dance. She had the technique for ballerina roles, grandeur and distinctive stage presence.

MacMillan's two-act *Isadora*, which had its premiere at the end of April 1981, was an ambitious mess. It followed the life of the pioneering modern dancer Isadora Duncan from her early career to her death in a bizarre car accident, taking in a long series of lovers and the deaths of her children by drowning. Richard Rodney Bennett's commissioned score had pastiche elements, suggesting the composers Isadora had used for her dances. Freeman's scenario was helplessly repetitive. MacMillan's Isadora kept going to railway stations, kept seeing coffins, kept dancing explicit, acrobatic pas de deux. In *Mayerling*, the tautly realised duets had driven Rudolf's story forward; in *Isadora*, the heroine was repeatedly splayed and grabbed, without revealing more of character or plot. Isadora's art was lost in so much groping. Her originality was suggested, negatively, in skits of other dance forms – ballet in decadence, music-hall flamenco and an unjust send-up of Loie Fuller, another important early modern dancer. Throughout the ballet, MacMillan avoided academic steps and pointe-work. As Director, he had made a range of ballets displaying his dancers' classical technique. In later ballets, starting with *Requiem*, he experimented with a winding, grappling language. As the Company's academic strength slipped, MacMillan stopped challenging it.

MacMillan had thought of an *Isadora* ballet in Berlin, and

returned to it with Seymour in mind. As Ashton's *Brahms Waltzes* had shown, Seymour's bold voluptuousness, her sense of gravity, were perfect for Isadora. When she left to direct the Munich company, MacMillan cast Park, a thinner, drier, lighter dancer. He also decided to split the role, sharing it between Park and the actress Mary Miller, who declaimed monologues drawn from Isadora's writings and speeches. Dance was overshadowed by Isadora's words and screams, but there was no real innovation in this mix of speech and movement. *Isadora* had its defenders; there was praise for episodes within the ballet, notably the grief-stricken duet for Park and Rencher (as her lover, Paris Singer), lamenting the death of Isadora's children.

On 5 May 1981, fifty years after the first full night of ballet at the Old Vic, The Royal Ballet danced *The Sleeping Beauty*. Since its premiere in 1977, de Valois had kept a close eye on her production, revising and polishing. In 1981, she overhauled it completely, with some new costumes and scene painting. Collier and Jefferies led the anniversary performance. In her curtain speech, de Valois announced that the Company had a young generation as strong as any in the Company's history. Over the next few performances, she cast them in the ballet's many soloist roles. The debuts included Brind's Lilac Fairy, Ravenna Tucker and Nicola Roberts as Prologue fairies, Alessandra Ferri as Red Riding Hood. Michael Batchelor, whose fluent line had been praised in *Hamlet*, was a noble Florestan. This display of talent lifted spirits which were raised further by the anniversary gala at the end of May. A four-hour celebration of Royal Ballet repertory, chosen by Michael Somes, it featured dances from the Covent Garden and touring companies, with children from the School in the maypole dance from *Fille*. Collier was outstanding in a solo from *The Prince of the Pagodas*; Sibley and Dowell danced the *Dream* pas de deux. The first half ended with Cinderella's departure for the ball; in the last of three performances, the coach brought on Ashton and Fonteyn. The evening ended with the whole company waltzing on stage – Markova with Morrice, MacMillan with Wells, de Valois with Wall – as glittering confetti rained on the lighted auditorium.

In July, the Company returned to New York for the first time in five years. The Company's loyal American public was eager to see it, but the visit proved disappointing. *Rhapsody* was welcomed, with an ovation for Ashton, and *Hamlet* was exuberantly performed. *Swan Lake* was the most successful of the classical ballets. But *Isadora* was savaged, and critics pointed out the slippage in technical standards. The 'corps was still a model of uniformity but no longer a model of strict discipline', wrote Croce. 'It wasn't the corps that had danced *La Bayadère* . . . the loss to a great company of its stylistic sense is a loss of – not identity, precisely, but something critical to it. The Royal, in the last ten years, has lost its superego.'[4] Few of the younger dancers were cast: a Brind Odette–Odile might have lifted the season. Many reviews were warmer than Croce's, but the Company came home bruised. In London, ballet regulars were dismayed by the programme of the next season, which opened with *Isadora*. Attendances were already down. Critics were infuriated by Morrice's vagueness. 'You can't feel much confidence in the strength of a Director who answers some specific questions with a charming smile and "We don't know",' snapped a *Dancing Times* editorial.[5]

There was little classical choreography in the first weeks of the 1981–82 season, which was dominated by *Isadora* – with Chadwick remarkable in the title role – *Dances of Albion* and *Hamlet*. A revival of *Serenade* underlined the need for work on classical technique. The balance changed in December, with new productions of Ashton's *Illuminations*, made for New York City Ballet in 1950, and the divertissement from Bournonville's *Napoli*. The Bournonville needed more precision, but – like the rest of this bill – it was remarkable for showing off the younger dancers. *Illuminations* was a strange, symbolic ballet. Choreographing Britten's setting of Rimbaud's poems, Ashton showed a poet torn between Sacred and Profane Love. There were references to Rimbaud's life – no onstage homosexuality, but the Poet was shot, as Rimbaud had been by his lover Verlaine. Sacred Love became a muse figure, lifted soaring overhead. After an explicitly sexual duet with Profane Love, who had one pointe shoe and one bare foot, the Poet wiped himself down with her scarf before visiting an onstage pissoir. Cecil Beaton's designs, always chichi, had dated badly: Pierrot costumes, pompoms, men with bare chests and ruffs. Robert

Irving conducted the first performance. Penney was light and elegant as Sacred Love. Rosato was an abandoned Profane Love, and Ashley Page showed a magnetic, animal quality as the Poet. Ashton, who had returned to rehearse the production, saw that Page's movements were restricted by the Beaton costume. He made him rehearse in 'a very thick motorbike jacket . . . He said, "You've got to dance and come out of that thing." It was exhausting . . . but the next night – the first performance – the difference was just amazing . . . I remember Fred coming back afterwards and saying, "I don't ever want to see you dance in another way, it has to be that way, you have to tear your guts."'[6]

On the same programme, *Afternoon of a Faun* was well revived, with very young dancers. Brind and Page danced the first night. Later pairings were Ravenna Tucker with Guy Niblett, David Peden and Alessandra Ferri, Nicola Roberts and Stephen Sherriff. In February 1982, Nureyev – now in decline as a dancer – returned to the Company, bringing the rights to *La Bayadère* with him. The Royal corps was no longer world-beating, but soloists blossomed under his coaching. Brind, Tucker and Chadwick were superb Shades, phrasing their variations with shining confidence and attack. Nureyev made headlines when he chose Brind to dance Nikiya at a later performance; television reporters rushed to interview her. She made a sensational debut, her movements soft and expansive, her line clear. Deirdre Eyden replaced Brind as a Shade, dancing with grandeur. Following Covent Garden tradition, Brind's debut was greeted with a shower of daffodils. At that performance, *La Bayadère* was followed by *The Two Pigeons* in which Wendy Ellis slipped, breaking both wrists. Collier, in the audience, hurried round and finished the performance, dancing without stage make-up and with particular spontaneity.

Michael Corder, a dancer with the Company, had made several ballets in workshops and for the touring company. In March 1982, he made *L'Invitation au voyage* for Covent Garden. It was a lyrical, atmospheric work, set to songs by Duparc, with shimmering *art nouveau* designs by Sonnabend. Sibley and Ferri danced leading roles, joined onstage by mezzo-soprano Diana Montague. In April, Sibley returned in *The Dream*, partnered by Dowell. Her Titania was a revelation: wild, regal and danced with inflamed sensuality. Even at this performance, however, there were some empty seats. Attendances were affected by the Falklands war, and by repetitive programming. *Manon*, which had been given many performances every year, had dropped in popularity. Morrice's loyalty kept the ballet alive when Covent Garden considered dropping it, but, after so many performances, overacting was creeping in. MacMillan's next ballet, the short-lived *Orpheus*, had its premiere in June. It was part of an all-Stravinsky bill, framed by *The Firebird* and *Les Noces*, arranged to celebrate the centenary of the composer's birth. Georgiadis designed a dramatic set, with golden ladders leading to the underworld. The Danish guest artist Peter Schaufuss danced Orpheus, partnering Penney's Eurydice in convoluted, acrobatic duets. The season ended in July, with a run of performances at the Big Top in Battersea. That month, Prince Charles opened the new extension at the Royal Opera House, including two large ballet studios.

The 1982–83 season opened with a revival of *Mayerling*, including Ferri's debut as Mary Vetsera. Ferri was small, bold and wide-eyed, a natural star. Her Mary was urgent and dangerous, with a pliant movement quality and a slow, proud walk. The performance confirmed her as MacMillan's next muse. But the Muses in *Apollo*, revived in November, were cause for concern: too much flirting for Balanchine's classicism. Rosato and Brind both made good Sirens in *Prodigal Son*. Nureyev danced with the Company again this season, and in December he took charge of a whole triple bill. He partnered Park and Sibley in dances from Bournonville's *Konservatoriet*, a new production that lacked freshness. His own new ballet *The Tempest*, set to Lanchbery's arrangement of Tchaikovsky, starred Dowell as the magician Prospero with Eagling as Ariel and Wall as Caliban. The production had bold designs by Georgiadis, but little solid choreography. *Raymonda* Act 3 showed the Company responding to Nureyev's coaching; there were cheers for the Raymondas of Park, Sibley and Chadwick, and for the soloists. To the delight of audiences, Sibley had recovered the strength for technically demanding ballets. On New Year's Day, she returned to *Cinderella*, dancing a full-length ballerina role with simplicity, grandeur and heart. Eyden was a magical Fairy Godmother.

Coleman's Ashton Sister was one of the delights of *Cinderella* in the 1980s: a sweet, short-sighted maiden aunt. He would take his curtain calls in character, vision so blurry that he bowed to the curtain instead of the audience.[7]

Valley of Shadows, staged in March 1983, was MacMillan at his most confrontational. The ballet was based on *The Garden of the Finzi-Continis*, Giorgio Bassani's novel about an Italian Jewish family in the 1930s. In the book and the later film, the threat of Nazism hangs over scenes in the garden. MacMillan put that implied threat on stage in several concentration-camp scenes. Inevitably, this was controversial; it was also poorly crafted. As the ballet cut between the idyllic garden and the camp – and between music by Tchaikovsky and Martinu, the same combination as *Anastasia* – effects were weakened by repetition. Characters were sent to their doom before they were fully established. Wall and Conley were powerful as parents of the younger characters; Ferri gave a supple, dramatic performance. Critics turned in relief to *Requiem*, the Fauré ballet MacMillan had made in Stuttgart, warmly admired in Germany and in Britain. Working with Cranko's company, MacMillan used the tangling lifts that Cranko had made famous: the leading woman is tugged and manipulated mid-air. Yolanda Sonnabend designed a spare set of gauzes. Most of the dancers wore body tights with vein-like patterns, with the leading woman dressed in white draperies. Marcia Haydée gave a guest performance in her created role, with Eagling as the Christ figure.

In April 1983, the Company returned to New York for a short, successful season, starting with the premiere of Ashton's *Varii capricci*. The music was by Walton, and the ballet had echoes of Ashton's first Walton ballet, *Façade*. Dowell was another gigolo figure, dancing with Sibley's woman of the world. David Hockney designed the sets, with a bright swimming pool. The extravagant costumes were by the fashion designer Ossie Clark. The New York audience, delighted to see Ashton reunited with Sibley and Dowell, was enthusiastic. *Mayerling* was well received, with Ferri acclaimed as Mary Vetsera. After New York, the Company went on to Japan, South Korea, China and Hong Kong. The Company's status as cultural ambassador remained important. The visit to Seoul was the major event of the Korean–British Centennial, the anniversary of the first treaty with Korea. This was the Company's first visit to China, where they were welcomed with excitement. Every day, at least fifty dance students would cram into the studio to watch the Company in class. The Chinese orchestra rehearsed eagerly, delighted to have the chance to play music which had been banned during the Cultural Revolution of the 1960s. The ballet itself had an overwhelming impact on its audience. 'The stage looked so magical,' remembered one woman. 'I almost collapsed with the beauty of it. We were like babies, the beauty of the dancing and the music was so fresh to our senses.'[8] One performance was televised, reaching an audience of a hundred million people. Just before the Company's return, Kenneth MacMillan was knighted. Back at Covent Garden, there was a short summer season, including a revival of *Isadora* and the British premiere of *Varii capricci*.

The 1983–84 season opened with a run of *Swan Lake*, including Jonathan Cope's unscheduled debut as Prince Siegfried. A tall, long-limbed dancer, Cope showed elegant line, a soaring jump and clean, long-breathed phrases. Dancing with Pippa Wylde's Odette, he was already tender and princely. He was to become one of The Royal Ballet's most prized partners. Later programmes raised more doubts about the Company's classical style. *Monotones*, once the quintessence of Royal Ballet classicism, looked strained, with stiff upper bodies and unstretched feet. Ravenna Tucker showed a true sense of continuity in line and phrasing, but her companions could not match her. *Apollo* and *Raymonda* showed a similar loss of classical purity. '*Raymonda* mounts to a splendid theatrical climax that rouses the audience,' wrote Mary Clarke. 'But it is as yet a kind of fake success. The dancing does not stand up to hard scrutiny.'[9] The critic John Percival complained of 'the customary miscasting (based on the assumption that anyone who has been named a principal dancer must be suited to principal roles)' adding, 'some dancers were doing markedly less well than they did in the same roles only last season.' That year, while still dancing, Merle Park took over as Principal of The Royal Ballet School, where she dropped the old de Valois syllabus, rooted in Cecchetti's teaching, and brought in Russian training, based on the Soviet school founded by Vaganova.

Students were still coached in The Royal Ballet's repertory, but this was a complete alteration of the Company's technical basis. Cecchetti's emphasis on quick feet and fluent upper-body movement had helped to define the Company's style. Some of Ashton's steps – notably the 'skating' chassé used in *Les Patineurs* – were no longer being taught.

That season, Morrice focused on new ballets. Since MacMillan, the Covent Garden company had developed no new choreographer from within its ranks. The touring company, after its first, extraordinary success as a nursery for choreographers, had grown into a larger classical troupe with less time for new productions. Under Peter Wright, it was again nurturing new choreography, with several promising ballets. In the 1983–84 season, Morrice commissioned six new British ballets, from choreographers in and outside the Company. He also introduced a change in design policy, encouraging choreographers to work with easel painters. On 7 December 1983, there were premieres of two new ballets, both well received. David Bintley's *Consort Lessons* was a confident suite of dances to Stravinsky's Concerto for Piano and Wind Instruments. Terry Bartlett's designs suggested an architectural drawing of a great hall. Bintley used a cast of senior and junior dancers, led by Ferri and Collier. Steps were intricate, sometimes fiddly; Bintley was praised for his varied academic vocabulary. Richard Alston, a modern dance choreographer with Rambert, made the serene *Midsummer*, to Tippett's Fantasia Concertante on a Theme of Corelli. The backcloth was a painting by John Hubbard in glowing colours. The choreography was limpidly classical. The opening solo for Ashley Page was 'a sane, flowing array of unbroken phrasing, a melody in movement', wrote Alastair Macaulay. Brind and Cope danced a warmly lyrical duet. Macaulay added that *Midsummer* was 'a pastoral idyll so calm that some people find it dull'.[10] *Midsummer* also reflected changes in dance outside The Royal Ballet. The modern-dance boom had reached Britain in the 1960s and 1970s; new companies and festivals were springing up, finding new popularity. Morrice, who had overseen Rambert's transition from a classical to a modern company, had links to this world; his interest in easel painters may have been inspired by Rambert's striking design successes.

Romeo and Juliet Alessandra Ferri as Juliet: © Leslie E. Spatt

Anastasia (1971) Act One, showing Barry Kay's birch forest set. In the last act, film clips were projected onto the panels of the vortex: The Donald Southern Collection at Royal Opera House Collections

Elite Syncopations (1974) Vergie Derman and Wayne Sleep: © Leslie E. Spatt

Cinderella Tetsuya Kumakawa: photograph © Bill Cooper

Ondine Publicity shot of Sarah Wildor: photo Steve Hanson

Scènes de ballet Errol Pickford and Viviana Durante in a revival of Ashton's 1948 ballet:
© Leslie E. Spatt
Winter Dreams Irek Mukhamedov and Darcey Bussell in the 'Farewell' pas de deux of
MacMillan's Chekhov ballet: © Leslie E. Spatt

MacMillan's *The Judas Tree* with Irek Mukhamedov, Mara Galeazzi and Edward Watson:
© Dee Conway
Ondine Miyako Yoshida: Johan Persson / ArenaPAL

Giselle Johan Kobborg and Alina Cojocaru in the first act of Peter Wright's 1985 production
photograph © Bill Cooper
Requiem Leanne Benjamin and Carlos Acosta: Johan Persson / ArenaPAL

Ashton's *Daphnis and Chloë* Federico Bonelli and Alina Cojocaru in the finale: © Dee Conway

Nijinska's *Les Noces* Zenaida Yanowsky as the Bride: photograph © Bill Cooper

La Sylphide Ivan Putrov, with Laura McCulloch and Yuhui Choe: Johan Persson / ArenaPAL

MacMillan's *Manon* Tamara Rojo as Manon, José Martín as Lescaut and Genesia Rosato as Madame: Johan Persson / ArenaPAL

In January 1984, the Paris Opéra stars Elisabeth Platel and Charles Jude gave guest performances in *La Bayadère*. Both were glamorous and authoritative. Sibley returned to the ballet later that season, dancing with magnificent grandeur and freedom. Brind, so impressive at her debut, was still an admired Nikiya, but had become tentative and genteel. From the start of her career, critics had urged the Company to nurture Brind, to give her support and coaching. The younger generation were being given roles, but little preparation for them. Some, like Chadwick, kept their technique and managed to develop. Others slipped back from the standard of their own debut performances, or burnt out altogether.

MacMillan continued to work in a grim vein. *Different Drummer* had its premiere in February 1984. This was a danced version of Buchner's play *Woyzeck*, whose soldier hero finally commits first murder and then suicide. MacMillan's production, to music by Webern and Schoenberg, was influenced by German expressionism, with distorted body language. David Drew's Captain and Jonathan Burrows's Doctor, Woyzeck's tormentors, were nightmarish grotesques. As Woyzeck, the inarticulate, humiliated hero, Wayne Eagling had convoluted steps, clinging close to the ground. As Woyzeck's unfaithful mistress, Ferri danced acrobatic duets but little solo work; the critic Stephanie Jordan worried that MacMillan was using her as 'the beautiful, Italian, passionate, just-do-anything-you-like-with-me sort of ballerina'.[11] Sonnabend's sets were abandoned late in the rehearsal period, and the ballet was performed on a blank set, with a few flats from another production framing the action. *Different Drummer*, with its deliberate exaggerations, was passionately performed. It was remarkably popular.

In April, The Royal Ballet staged *Return to the Strange Land*, its first work by the Czech choreographer Jiří Kylián. The 'strange land' is death or the unconscious, and the dancers, in drab leotards, wind themselves around each other in woeful attitudes to music by Janáček. The cast was led by Brind, Hosking and Ferri. It was followed by Derek Deane's new *Fleeting Figures*, a pure dance work set to Suk's Serenade for Strings. Deane had made several successful pas de deux for gala occasions, but did not look ready for a full-scale work. Maria Almeida, standing in for an injured Collier, had her first leading role.

There were three new Juliets that season. In April, Chadwick made her debut as Juliet, with yearning line, clean footwork and a vivid, headstrong characterisation. Ferri, a natural choice for Juliet, caused a sensation in the role that month, and was later filmed – although, after a series of impassioned roles, she was in danger of typecasting. Tucker, the third to make her debut, danced ardently, innocence and ecstasy in her beautifully stretched line and footwork. That summer, she made her debut as Aurora, dancing with radiant fullness of movement.

The summer season, which followed a visit to Manchester, was dogged by bad luck. Many of the dancers were ill, affected by the blood disease toxoplasmosis, possibly contracted in China. Morrice, too, was ill. Injury rates were high throughout the season, and the dancers worked to rule after a salary dispute. Performances were strangely inconsistent: the corps that was sloppy in *Les Biches* looked transformed in an all-Stravinsky programme that included *Scènes de ballet*. At a press conference, Morrice admitted that de Valois was giving what she called 'survival classes', an attempt to correct faults in younger dancers before they became habitual.[12] That summer, Somes left The Royal Ballet. Always irascible, he had become more so under Morrice's regime. The ballet staff had complained to the Chairman of the Board, but Somes did not leave until he had a violent row with MacMillan in the summer of 1984. MacMillan himself took a step back from The Royal Ballet, becoming Associate Director of Baryshnikov's American Ballet Theatre that year. Ferri soon followed him to ABT.

In summer 1984, the Company went ahead with two new works. Corder's *Party Game*, set to Stravinsky's Concerto in D for Strings, showed five young dancers, in modern dress, flirting and provoking each other. Brind was the mistress of ceremonies; the two men shared The Royal Ballet's first long male kiss. The ballet was dominated by its Patrick Caulfield setting: walls striped like Royal Opera House wallpaper, and a huge round pouffe that was rolled across the stage. *A Broken Set of Rules* was Ashley Page's first professional work. The music was by Michael Nyman, the bold architectural designs by Deanne Petherbridge. Page, like his collaborators, deliberately set up classical patterns and then broke them. Page was eagerly aware of the contemporary-dance boom, regularly seen at Rambert and Dance Umbrella performances. 'Page's vocabulary is rich,' wrote Stephanie Jordan, 'his rate of ideas authoritative and his rhythmic sense finely developed.'[13]

Though welcome, the new choreography did not sell particularly well. The names were not known, and with prices rising, audiences were playing safe. 'That was disappointing,' admitted Morrice, 'but we are jolly well going to go on with presenting new choreographers because that is the life-blood.'[14] None of the new works had many performances; they were a risk for the Company, too. In its early days, the Company could be flexible about programming, giving more performances of a popular new work or dropping unsuccessful ballets. By the 1980s, it had to fit its programmes around those of the opera; the repertory was decided, announced and put on sale far ahead. It made it harder to run new works in, to let them find their place in the repertory.

The 1984–85 season began on 18 October, with a gala celebrating Ashton's eightieth birthday. The evening began with an uneven *Birthday Offering*. A series of divertissements ended with Sibley and Dowell, bringing the house down in the *Thaïs* pas de deux, followed by *Acte de Présence*, a number Ashton had made for a gala at the Met the previous year. To music from *The Sleeping Beauty*, Fonteyn reclined on a sofa, to be kissed awake by Ashton. A week later, Wall made his formal farewell to the Company in a powerful performance of *Mayerling*. Dowell had returned to the Company, as a dancer but also as Morrice's assistant. He was being groomed to take over the Company.

The next new production came in November. Bintley's *Young Apollo* was set to Britten's score of the same name, with two extra movements commissioned from Gordon Crosse. The painter Victor Pasmore designed abstract backcloths, and dressed the dancers in simple white tunics. It was a ballet stuffed with influences. Britten had been inspired by the last lines of Keats's *Hyperion*, the god guided by the muse Mnemosyne; Bintley's female lead, danced by Brind, echoed some of the poses Keats described. The diffuse choreography, which quoted Balanchine's *Apollo*, could not sustain quite so many ideas. In December, the Company unveiled a new *Nutcracker*. Peter Wright's production was influenced by the musicologist Roland John Wiley, who had researched early records of Ivanov's first production. The aim was an authentic recreation – though Wright added some of his own choreography, including an enchanting mime scene for the Nutcracker. The divertissements were stodgy. Julia Trevelyan Oman designed a party scene full of warm period detail, followed by a pink-and-platinum Kingdom of Sweets. Magic scenes were sweepingly done. Collier and Dowell led the first performance; Tucker later made a sweet, clear debut as the Sugar Plum Fairy. Gennady Rozhdestvensky conducted an urgent account of the score, thrilling in Tchaikovsky's rhythms and sonorities.

The next new production, a revival of *Ballet Imperial*, was perhaps the greatest disgrace in Royal Ballet history. Balanchine had died in 1983; this revival, uncredited, was put together by company staff. No one took responsibility for the production, which was under-rehearsed and badly danced, a shocking revelation of the Company's technical weakness. The Royal Ballet dancers could not meet the demands of Balanchine's speedy, brilliant ballet. New York City Ballet had brought the ballet to London in 1983; British critics and audiences had clear memories of the quick bravura that the ballet required. Now they were confronted with a company mugging its way through the steps, trying to act their way through a ballet that lives in dancing alone. Only Chadwick, in the third cast, had the necessary stamina and elegance. The production was let down further by its designs. This revival had been announced as a return to Berman's ermine and tutus; instead, Christopher LeBrun provided a wispy backdrop of a French triumphal arch – hardly imperial St Petersburg – and costumes laden with eagles and orders, with feathered head-dresses for the women. Musical standards were also low. Critics responded with fury; Morrice's regime was under siege from this moment.

Still reeling from *Ballet Imperial*, the Company went straight into a second design scandal. Corder's *Number Three*, danced to Prokofiev's Third Piano Concerto, was overshadowed by a row with its designer, the abstract impressionist painter Helen Frankenthaler. She designed striking backdrops, one for each movement. Corder, in a note added to the programme, expressed 'enormous enthusiasm' for these, but 'expressed some doubt as to whether his ballet will be shown to better advantage in the costumes which Miss Frankenthaler has designed, or in simple white costumes'.[15] Frankenthaler was furious; Tooley had to return from America to referee. As a compromise, three performances were given in costume, two in white leotards. After all the shouting, Corder's ballet was admired as a fluent, slightly spiky setting of Prokofiev.

After these two disasters, the Company left Covent Garden for a European tour lasting two months. When they returned to Covent Garden, in June, critical tempers were softened by Baryshnikov and Sibley in *A Month in the Country*, a performance of star glamour and emotional depth. The Royal Ballet's annual press conference was held at the end of June. The Company's management was scared. Preparing for hostile questions, the Press Officer wrote a list of problems that might be raised. It ran to four pages of bullet points, ranging from coaching to design policy to changes at the School. At the conference itself, which was covered by television news, it was announced that Morrice would retire at the end of the 1985–86 season. Anthony Dowell, his successor, was made Assistant Director, with immediate effect. 'In lighter moments, I have said I could have a hat made with "HMS Titanic" on it,' Dowell said ruefully.[16] In practice, he took over earlier than expected. Morrice was ill for much of the following season; he and the dancer David Drew later set up a successful choreography class at The Royal Ballet School. Monica Mason, who had become MacMillan's répétiteur in 1980, agreed to act as Dowell's assistant.

There was still a Covent Garden summer season to finish, with two more productions. *Half the House*, by company dancer Jennifer Jackson, was danced to Bartok's Divertimento for Strings, with a theme taken from the poet Cavafy. The choreography was rather overwhelmed by music and ideas. Wayne Eagling's *Frankenstein, the Modern Prometheus* was a splashy spectacle, without much in the way of choreography. The music was by the film composer Vangelis, the designs by the Emmanuels, who had made the wedding dress of Diana, Princess of Wales. The work was full of special effects, including an onstage orchestra lifted on a rising platform. *Frankenstein* was popular with a summer audience, and loathed by most critics. 'It is time once again for us to arm ourselves with pitchforks and flaming brands and make for Schloss Covent Garden,' wrote Clement Crisp. 'Up there the Baron has created a new Monster, and for the sake of dance, art and our national ballet, it had better be stopped in its tracks . . .'[17]

The 1985–86 season started with a revival of *The Sleeping Beauty*. Dowell, now obviously in charge, had made various changes to the production, improving the pacing of the last two acts. Technical standards were still shaky, though. Elisabeth Platel returned as a guest Aurora, with high, undistorted extensions and clear style. Another guest, Fernando Bujones, danced the *Corsaire* pas de deux with Tucker. These appearances, like Baryshnikov's that summer, had been Dowell's doing. Most changes of policy were being made gradually: 'It's like a big ship, you can't change course like *that*,' he says now. 'You have to come round gradually. But I had grown up with guest artists, from the beginning of my time with the Company – the Erik Bruhns, the Arovas. I wanted to have an open door, something to inspire the Company and the public.' Dowell was not confrontational; he hated scenes. Given the responsibility of the Company, though, he had to become more forceful. In 1987, de Valois berated him over the lighting of his new *Swan Lake*. 'I rallied and shouted right back at her,' he said later, still slightly surprised.[18] Lighting, and more particularly design, were to be a controversial aspect of Dowell's regime: he was keen to give the classics a new look, to move away from the recycled 1940s productions of Morrice's Directorship.

The first new production came in November. *The Sons of Horus* was another mythological ballet by Bintley, to a score by Peter McGowan. Terry Bartlett designed wire headdresses, suggesting the animal heads of Egyptian gods. Theme aside, the ballet was a set of neoclassical variations. It was followed by Peter Wright's new production of *Giselle*, warmly welcomed as a replacement for Morrice's unhappy staging. Wright's approach to the ballet, inspired by memories of Ulanova in the Bolshoi staging, was essentially dramatic. John MacFarlane's designs bring the forest very close to the village, with well-stocked log piles beside the cottages. The Wilis wore draped skirts, not long tutus. It's a coherent view of the ballet, though its naturalism closes in on the dancing. Acting had always been important at The Royal Ballet. The 1980s classical productions, produced at a time of slipped technical standards, were dominated by drama. In the first season of this *Giselle*, corps dancing was still uneven. The first night was danced by Collier and Jefferies, with Eyden a fine Myrtha. Two nights later, Maria Almeida made her debut as Giselle, partnered by Dowell. Almeida, an elegant dancer with beautiful legs and feet, put the accent back on dancing. Her second act was luminous, with finely textured footwork.

Giselle was followed by Christmas runs of *The Nutcracker*, *Manon* and *Fille*. The Company was moving towards block runs: fewer programmes in repertory at once, more consecutive performances. 'We were aiming for that,' says Dowell now. 'It helped the Opera House, and we thought the long runs would give the dancers stability. But we found that it doesn't work: you need the variety.' *Fille* brought other worries. Fewer Ashton ballets were being programmed, and the Company looked uncomfortable in their founder choreographer's style. Spontaneity returned in a guest performance by Fernando Bujones, a clean, quick Colas. Jonathan Burrows, who had taught folk dancing at The Royal Ballet School, proved to be a handsome Widow Simone, with a soft heart and touch of flirtation. That April, Ashton made his last ballet for 'Fanfare for Elizabeth', the gala celebrating the Queen's sixtieth birthday. He used Elgar's *Nursery Suite* – music de Valois had choreographed in 1932 – and showed the Queen and her sister, Princess Margaret, playing as children.

In May 1986, MacMillan staged a revised version of *Le Baiser de la fée*, his first work for the Company for more than two years. He kept most of the choreography originally made for Seymour; those soft, melting steps turned out to be very demanding. The greatest changes came in the Fairy's role. MacMillan made a new, intricate solo for Chadwick, showing off her sense of anger and wilfulness. As the Bride, Almeida showed her cool grace and musical phrasing.

Cope gave a handsome, expansive performance as the young man. In 1960, Rowell's designs had been an important part of the ballet's impact. They were replaced by Martin Sutherland's blandly alpine sets and costumes. The ballet was part of an all-MacMillan programme, framed by *Concerto* and the third act of *Anastasia*. Returning to one of her first leading roles, Collier was an uncompromising Anastasia. Making her debut, Rosato had a bleak sense of loss. In March, Gelsey Kirkland returned to The Royal Ballet, dancing Juliet. Her dancing had lost some power, but she still made haunting dramatic effects.

In June, *The Dream* was revived with new designs. David Walker, who had designed the 1964 costumes, was now responsible for the whole ballet. There were no radical changes. Sibley and Dowell returned as Oberon and Titania, dancing with miraculous fluency and grandeur. They were followed by Paisey and Phillip Broomhead, both making their debuts, shaping steps cleanly and giving weight to the mime scenes. Michael Coleman was a sweetly bashful Bottom, with brilliant pointe-work. *Scènes de ballet* was strongly revived, with a superbly musical performance by Chadwick. In July, the Company set off to British Columbia for a week of sold-out performances at the Expo '86 World Festival. The new *Baiser de la fée* was particularly admired. While they were in Vancouver, the Company gave the world premiere of Bintley's new ballet. *Galanteries*, set to movements of a Mozart Divertimento and Serenade, was a light, understated suite of dances, inclined to daintiness. Jan Blake dressed the dancers in shades of slate and charcoal, with an abstract backdrop.

This had been a caretaker season for Dowell, overseeing the works that Morrice had programmed. With the next season, 1986–87, he set out his vision for the Company. An Ashton triple bill included the first performances of *Symphonic Variations* in five years, with Somes brought back to rehearse it. The autumn repertory included *Mayerling*, the de Valois *Beauty* and ballets by Robbins. Cynthia Harvey joined the Company from ABT, and Kirkland appeared as a guest star. Bintley moved from the Sadler's Wells Royal Ballet to Covent Garden, becoming Resident Choreographer. Isaiah Jackson was appointed Principal Conductor.

The season opened with *La Valse, Galanteries*, the Company's first staging of Robbins' *Opus 19: The Dreamer* and a revival of *The Concert*. The programme was cautiously welcomed. The effects of the slump would not vanish overnight; there was still a lack of strength in some of the dancing. *Opus 19: The Dreamer* was an odd setting of Prokofiev's First Violin Concerto, a man's vision of an elusive woman. The ballet was not liked, but Harvey's authority and clean technique made an immediate impression. *Symphonic Variations* was the biggest news of the season. Somes's revival was clear and decent, with some fine dancing from two casts. Yet the ballet had lost its old blitheness; it no longer looked like a signature work. *Mayerling* was strongly revived, with Derek Deane as Rudolf and Chadwick assertive as Mary Vetsera. Harvey, dancing a full British repertory, made a good debut as Larisch. Harvey also gave her first London Aurora, a clear and generous performance. Kirkland's guest appearance in the role was delicate, compelling, sometimes exaggerated. In the Rose Adagio, her leading prince was Donald MacLeary, officially retired but still, on occasion, a superb partner. He had been appointed Répétiteur to the Principal Artists in 1985, going on to coach Darcey Bussell throughout her career.

At Christmas, the Company staged *Beauty and the Beast*, Eagling's follow-up to *Frankenstein*. This time, critics and audiences were unanimous: despite striking designs by the illustrator Jan Pienkowski, the ballet was long and empty. The biggest drama came on opening night, when Dowell was injured and Cope stepped smoothly in.

In March 1987, Dowell unveiled his new *Swan Lake*. Rather than the traditional Sergueyev text, Dowell, advised by Roland John Wiley, worked from a new transcription of the Stepanov notation. Like the recent *Nutcracker*, this production aimed at authenticity. Up to a point: Dowell made no attempt to bring back the Second Cavalier (Benno), who until the late 1950s had done much of the partnering in Act 2. He wanted to keep Ashton's show-stopping Neapolitan dance, but Ashton refused, hurt that his other dances had been cut. Dowell and his designer, Sonnabend, added a further concept: not only would this *Swan Lake* go back to the 1895 production, it would be set *in* 1895, the time of Petipa, Ivanov and

Tchaikovsky. Court costumes had the historical detail of *Mayerling*. Sonnabend's designs were admired and disliked in equal measure. Sets were sumptuously grand, inspired by Fabergé eggs and decorated with filigree squiggles. The court ball became a Venetian carnival, dominated by tarnished mirrors. The swans now wore longer, softer tutus, with headdresses in silver wire rather than feathers. So much spectacle drew attention away from the ballet's lyric tragedy. Dowell's production, too, was busily naturalistic, especially in a first act filled with drunken cadets and dropped goblets. When the orchestra played the Swan theme for the first time, the prince was deep in conversation with his tutor. Following 1895 precedent, Bintley's new first-act waltz included a maypole. The fourth act, with Ivanov choreography, is Dowell's simplest and finest.

Harvey and Cope opened the production. Her dancing was clean and secure, steps freshly shaped. Cope was strong and elegant, ardent in acting and partnering. Bergsma was a magnificent Queen Mother, her mime grand and musically phrased, while Mason led the Czardas with panache and absolute authority. Dowell had acknowledged that the Company's dancing standards needed work; solo dances were uneven, but the corps were improving. The end of that season saw the retirement of Jill Gregory, Ballet Mistress since 1952. She was succeeded by Rosalind Eyre, who had joined The Royal Ballet in 1958. Dowell's *Swan Lake*, immediately popular, was scheduled in large blocks: eighteen consecutive performances. They sold out.

The Company followed *Swan Lake* with intensive foreign touring: Korea and Japan in April and May, followed by a return to Russia in June. This time they took no nineteenth-century classics, concentrating on dramatic ballets. In Moscow, they danced in the small, inadequate Operetta Theatre, with its dangerously uneven stage. The whole company was happier in Leningrad, dancing at the Kirov Theatre. The Company was well received. *Manon* and *The Dream* were liked, though Russian critics questioned the mime and dramatic pacing of both ballets. *Gloria* was admired without reservation. 'I have no words for this ballet,' said one Leningrad woman, 'only tears.'[19] The most eagerly awaited ballet was *A Month in the Country*, with its Russian theme. When the curtain went up, said Rencher, 'we were awash with applause.' Ulanova came to congratulate Sibley after her Moscow performance; the Kirov ballerina Kolpakova did the same for Marguerite Porter in Leningrad. In *Soviet Ballet*, the critic Nicolai Elyash wrote that 'the good feelings awakened in us long ago during the guest visit of 1961 grew into affectionate love'.[20]

Back in London, the Company spent a week at the Big Top in Battersea before returning to Covent Garden. During Paul Hamlyn week, when the charity funded special performances for audiences who had never been to Covent Garden, the Company gave its first performance of Ashley Page's *Pursuit*. Jack Smith designed a back-cloth of geometric shapes in bold colours, with more patterns on the dancers' tights. Page's choreography, set to the driving *Suns Dance* by Colin Matthews, was dry, quick and thrusting, with Almeida glamorous in the lead.

The 1987–88 season opened with still more *Swan Lake*s. Brind, replacing Harvey on the first night, had lost her former strength and grandeur. It was followed by an all-Stravinsky triple bill, marvellously conducted by Bernard Haitink, Music Director of the Royal Opera. Harvey and Almeida made their debuts in *The Firebird*: cleanly danced, but missing the power of the role. Chadwick had gone on growing through the difficult years, her dancing proud and scrupulous. She danced the lead in all three Stravinsky ballets: bold and musical as the Firebird, grand and simple as the ballerina in *Scènes de ballet*, powerful in *The Rite of Spring*. Collier, too, was outstanding in *Scènes de ballet*, with a musical sparkle to her dancing. That season, MacMillan cast a man, Simon Rice, as the Chosen Maiden (now called the Chosen One). Brind danced her first *Giselle* in December. She no longer looked like a classical dancer, but her mad scene was vividly wild, verging on hysteria.

That winter, Ashton returned to supervise a new production of *Cinderella*. As with *The Dream*, a Bardon–Walker production was revised by Walker only, the designs fussier and brighter. As always, Ashton urged his dancers to bend more, to co-ordinate head, shoulders, hands, eyes. It made this a more stylish revival, though technical foundations were still not secure. 'It certainly doesn't evoke the Ashton who is said, years ago, to have cried, "Give me footwork, give me footwork" at rehearsals,' wrote Alastair

Macaulay.²¹ There were no such doubts about Almeida, coached by Ashton for the gala opening. Her Cinderella had an expansive new radiance, a greater variety of expression. Her musical phrasing had gained in subtlety, and she projected boldly without loss of poise. She was partnered by Cope, who danced with smooth line and unforced power. Harvey was a musical Cinderella, and Collier showed new grandeur in the role.

Dowell was eager to bring in guest artists, and in January 1988 he made one of his most important invitations. Nureyev returned to dance *Giselle* with his Paris Opéra protégée, Sylvie Guillem. Guillem was an unorthodox ballerina: tall, long-limbed, with a glamorous stage presence and an effortless high extension that set a worldwide ballet fashion for 'six o'clock legs'. Throughout this romantic role, she included the high extensions. Dancing an unfamiliar production, she had an onstage fall early in the second act. It didn't matter: the Covent Garden audience was already entranced, applauding throughout the ballet and giving her a standing ovation at the end. She would soon be back.

Jennifer Penney retired in February, making her farewell in *Manon*. Paying tribute to her at the end of the season, Dowell recalled how she would repair and re-repair her shoes. Partnering her, he would look down her long legs and wrinkle his nose at the latest patch; once, on stage, he looked down to find she had written 'Hello Sailor' across her instep.²² A few days before, Sibley danced what proved to be *her* last Manon, though not yet her retirement. Both dancers were given long, loving ovations. There were few programmes at Covent Garden that spring. Dowell was still pursuing block runs: where Morrice had averaged eight full-length ballets and twenty-seven one-act works per season, the 1987–88 season had slipped down to five long and thirteen short ballets. The number of performances had also declined. While The Royal Ballet went through its doldrums, the Royal Opera had been booming. For the first time, opera was outselling ballet – and opera prices were higher. When Jeremy Isaacs succeeded Tooley as General Director, he cut the number of ballet performances, and of new productions, still further.

The next new productions came in March. *Bugaku*, a Japanese-style duet to music by Toshiro Mayuzumi, was an odd choice for the Company's next Balanchine ballet. Wayne Eagling and Bryony Brind danced the premiere. Bintley's new *Still Life at the Penguin Café* was set to percussive, lightly minimalist music by Simon Jeffes' Penguin Café Orchestra. Bintley arranged a series of dances for endangered species, arranged as if for a café cabaret. The dancers were dressed in clever animal costumes by Hayden Griffen: mask heads, whole-body costumes for the penguin waiters. Phillip Broomhead's Southern Cape Zebra had striped body-tights and a striped, stiffened mane, whisking brushes to suggest a tail. A group of women in animal-skull hats ignored his plight, and all the animals ended up in a cartoon ark. The dancing rather got lost under the costumes and the message, but Bintley's ballet was cuddly, piously conservationist and immediately popular.

Dowell, who had fond memories of *Ondine*, had been trying to persuade Ashton to agree to a revival of the ballet. (He would later encourage MacMillan to return to *The Prince of the Pagodas*, another ballet of the late 1950s.) Though Beriosova and Nerina had both given some performances of the ballet, it had been dropped when Fonteyn stopped dancing it. Ashton was tempted when Gelsey Kirkland, a dancer who had seemed ideally suited to Ashton roles, expressed an interest. Even then, Ashton remained cagey. 'He said, "Well, you can *announce* it,"' says Dowell, pulling a wry face at the memory, '"but I might change my mind once I've seen rehearsals."' The ballet was reconstructed by Christopher Newton, the Company's Ballet Master, working from film and from dancers' memories. Kirkland pulled out, but *Ondine* went ahead, with Almeida and then Harvey in the title role. Thirty years on, critics dealt with the ballet more kindly, praising the beguiling dances for Ondine.

On 6 June 1988, de Valois celebrated her ninetieth birthday with a gala in aid of The Royal Ballet School Appeal. The programme included a hornpipe danced by boys from the Lower School, Sibley and Dowell in the pas de deux from *The Dream*, Nureyev and Almeida in the last act of de Valois's own *Sleeping Beauty*. Nine days later, Dowell and Isaacs announced their plans for the next season. MacMillan would choreograph a new production of *The Prince of the Pagodas*. He had chosen the nineteen-year-old Darcey Bussell, from the corps of Sadler's Wells Royal Ballet (soon to be Birmingham Royal Ballet), to play the heroine. She would move to Covent Garden at the start of the next season. Christopher Newton became the Company's Artistic Co-ordinator, while Christopher Carr succeeded him as Ballet Master. Announcements made, the Company set off on a tour of Australia. In Brisbane, the last stop of the tour, MacMillan felt ill while visiting a friend, a doctor, who took him straight to hospital, where heart trouble was diagnosed. 'It was very serious and we were terrified he wouldn't pull through,' recalled Mason. 'I remember [his wife] Deborah saying to me, "this was very serious. We just don't know how long he can survive."' MacMillan recovered, and slowly returned to work on *The Prince of the Pagodas*. 'The Royal Ballet were very good,' he said, 'they gave me a whole year to do it in, because the doctor had said to me, "You should only be working an hour and a half a day."'[23]

That August, Ashton died at his home in Suffolk. In November, his memorial service was held at Westminster Abbey. The congregation was the Abbey's largest for thirty years; many people were moved into St Margaret's, the church next door. 'He was a very *human* human being,' Fonteyn said in a tribute read by Michael Somes, 'and for that, as much as for his extraordinary talents, he was beloved by all.'[24] In October, the 1988–89 season opened with Ashton's *Ondine*; the second programme included a revival of *Rhapsody*, well coached. Baryshnikov was still a near-impossible act to follow, but Errol Pickford was vigorous, Bruce Sansom highly finished. The young Viviana Durante, moving into leading roles, danced with musical wit, legs and feet clearly stretched. Here were hopes of recovery, yet there were still worries about the state of Ashton's legacy: the number of ballets in repertory, and the technique needed to dance them.

Bintley's new ballet, *The Trial of Prometheus*, was set to a commissioned score by Geoffrey Burgon. Stephen Jefferies was the hero, creating the first human beings. The Olympian gods mock his efforts – Bintley dropped hints that he had his critics in mind – but his created humans go forth and prosper. Terry Bartlett dressed the creatures as anatomical drawings, in body-tights decorated with bone and muscle – in general colour, rather like the tribe in MacMillan's *Rite of Spring*. Dancing together, they quoted Balanchine's *Apollo*. Bintley's classical dances were full of steps, but they remained dry, lacking rhythmic shape. *The Spirit of Fugue*, which had its premiere in November, had a similar lack of danced energy. Peter McGowan's new jazz score was modelled on Bach, Bartlett's set showed fretwork pillars marked with footprints, and the dancers included Bussell and Deborah Bull. Again, there were *Apollo* references – this time on the same bill as *Apollo* itself, with Guillem long-limbed and cool as Terpsichore.

Christmas was dominated by *Cinderella* and *Romeo*. Musical standards were rising, with performances conducted by Mark Ermler and Haitink. Makarova returned as Juliet, partnered by the ardently boyish Julio Bocca. In January, Durante danced an eager, rebellious Juliet, partnered by Sansom. She had a clear technique, with fluent line and crisp footwork. In March, she danced one of the two ballerina roles in Balanchine's *Capriccio for Piano and Orchestra* (better known as *Rubies*), made in 1967. Since Balanchine's death, a Trust had been set up to administer his ballets, and *Rubies* had been carefully taught. The thrust hips did not come naturally to Royal dancers, but the long-limbed Bussell, the second ballerina, did look at home in this choreography. André Levasseur's sets resembled slabs of strawberry pudding, and he dressed the dancers in unfortunate shades of pink. In February, the Company visited Bristol and Birmingham with a repertory of *Romeo* and *Ondine*. Durante, who had already danced *Swan Lake* at short notice, stepped in for Almeida in *Ondine*. Dowell, delighted, promoted her to Principal. She was twenty-one.

In February 1989, Sylvie Guillem left the Paris Opéra for The Royal Ballet. Questions were asked in the French parliament; *Le Monde* called Guillem's defection 'a national catastrophe'.[25] At Covent Garden, Guillem would be Principal Guest Artist. This was a new title; Nureyev and Makarova had danced regularly with the Company, but always as guest artists. Guillem had a firm contract that gave her control over her repertory. Dowell, who had grown up just as Nureyev galvanised the Company, may have hoped Guillem would have a similar effect. Not quite: despite the contract, Guillem never involved herself with the Company as her mentor had done. She did help to break the Fonteyn mould, however. Deborah Bull, who joined the Company in 1981, remembers girls longing for dark hair and oval faces; the overt promotion of the Fonteyn-ish Porter in Fonteyn roles had not been an accident. Guillem, on the other hand, was the tallest dancer to have performed most of her Royal Ballet repertory; other tall women, including Bussell, could now see themselves as Juliet, Manon, Natalia Petrovna. Aspects of Guillem's dancing were fiercely criticised in London: the sky-high legs, the frosty stardom. She drew headlines and excited audiences, and she had the tonic effect of putting other dancers on their mettle. At their first *Swan Lake* together, Cope showed a new burst of virtuosity in the third act. Over the next few seasons, Bussell and Guillem would make their debuts in the same ballets, often close together; press and fans made eager comparisons.

The Prince of the Pagodas, announced for May 1989, had been postponed as a result of MacMillan's illness. Dowell decided to replace it with Makarova's American Ballet Theatre staging of the full-length *Bayadère* – having been its first-cast Solor when he was with ABT. Lavish spectacle was clearly popular: the full-length *Le Corsaire* had been one of the hits of the Kirov Ballet's 1988 summer season. In the west, *La Bayadère* was known for the classical purity of the Kingdom of the Shades. In the complete ballet, that near-abstract classical showpiece was framed by several acts of orientalist hokum, filled with processions, bared midriffs and bravura dances. The Royal Ballet staging used Pier Luigi Samaritani's sets, full of perspective architecture and lushly painted jungles, with new costumes by Sonnabend.

La Bayadère was immediately popular as spectacle and star vehicle, but this was not natural territory for The Royal Ballet. The leading characters swear by sacred flames, threaten vengeance, declare that they have killed tigers in the hunt. It needs belief on a large scale, and at first the Company lacked conviction. Mime roles were typecast, and self-conscious. There were some splendid effects in Makarova's staging, like the weighted, predatory walk with which the heroine's rival Gamzatti comes to claim Solor after the Shades scene. But the new Shades act did not match memories of the last production. The corps was reduced from thirty-two to twenty-four, and the grandeur of Royal Ballet corps dancing had not returned. The ballet was carried by its central performances. On the first night, Guillem was Nikiya, stronger in the orientalist poses than the pure classical dancing. Chadwick gave an imperious account of Gamzatti, dance and acting boldly projected. Cope was a strong, noble Solor. The seventeen-year-old virtuoso Tetsuya Kumakawa, who had just won the Prix de Lausanne, soared and bounded as the Golden Idol – a career-defining performance. With *glasnost* in the Soviet Union, Russian dancers were beginning to make guest appearances in the West. In the first of a series of guest appearances, the Kirov ballerina Altynai Asylmuratova was an extraordinary Nikiya, partnered by Farouk Ruzimatov. In this cast, Guillem was a vehement, glamorous Gamzatti.

La Bayadère had another long run, with debuts from a range of dancers, followed by a revival of *The Sleeping Beauty* and a visit to Plymouth. Ashley Page's *Piano*, set to Beethoven's first piano concerto, had its premiere in July, during the Plymouth season. The painter Howard Hodgkin's backcloth showed huge, sweeping brushstrokes in blue and green. Dancers made exits and entrances down flanking staircases, but Page failed to get to grips with the ambitious music. By now, the Company was showing signs of recovery. New dancers were emerging, and were to develop more steadily, more securely than the blighted springtime generation of the 1980s. In 1989, dancing standards were still variable, but excitement and audiences were growing. The challenge was to pull the Company up further, to maintain the recovery in the changing climate of the 1990s.

NINE

Recovery and closure

1990–99

ABOVE William Forsythe's *Steptext*. Adam Cooper and Deborah Bull:
© Leslie E. Spatt
PREVIOUS PAGE Kenneth MacMillan rehearsing Darcey Bussell and
Jonathan Cope in *The Prince of the Pagodas*: © Anthony Crickmay

The Royal Ballet made a hopeful start to the 1990s. There were signs of renewal, an improvement in technique and in confidence. Work was still needed on the Company's style, but energy levels were rising. There was broader recognition, too: The Royal Ballet had stars who were known outside the specialist ballet audience. At the same time, the Company's circumstances were changing. At the start of the 1990s, The Royal Ballet had two choreographers on the staff, MacMillan and Bintley. By the end of the decade, for the first time in its history, it was without a resident choreographer. After the dance boom of the 1960s and 1970s, there was now a world shortage of choreographers. As Guillem's arrival suggests, ballet was also becoming more international. Dancers were no longer tied to their own company, their own school. Dowell brought in more guest artists; he also saw some of his own dancers leave in search of different opportunities.

The Company also faced a changing financial climate. In June 1988, Jeremy Isaacs, the new General Director of the Royal Opera House, announced that the Arts Council grant formed a shrinking proportion of the budget. Covent Garden had neither European levels of state funding nor American levels of sponsorship. The gap had to be filled, creating new pressure to play safe with more blockbusters, fewer mixed bills. Ticket prices rose sharply. In this decade, the Royal Opera House would be closed for redevelopment, promising better facilities but leaving the ballet and opera companies temporarily homeless. The closure period was to be extraordinarily tense; The Royal Ballet would be heavily affected by the management of Covent Garden itself.

The 1989–90 season opened at the end of September with another run of *La Bayadère*. Guillem and Cope returned on opening night, now with some sadness. Cope and Almeida, his wife, had announced that they would retire from dancing at the end of the season. Bussell danced Gamzatti: no match for Chadwick as an actress, and inclined to follow Guillem in high extensions, but already showing scale and abandon in her dancing. Worries about the Ashton repertory were heightened by an untidy revival of *A Wedding Bouquet*, overacted and underdanced, with Derek Jacobi an exaggerated narrator.

In December, days before MacMillan's sixtieth birthday, *The Prince of the Pagodas* had its premiere. This was an explicit change of direction for MacMillan. Throughout the 1980s, he had focused on expressionistic dance. Now, as the senior British choreographer, he returned to classicism, and to *The Sleeping Beauty*, dedicating the new ballet to Fonteyn. MacMillan's plan was to revise Cranko's original narrative, emphasising the characters' inner lives. Colin Thubron turned the Princess Rose's journey into a series of dreams. But her visions – violent encounters with the suitors she rejected in the first act – tell us little about her; the violence seemed out of place. The storyline remained chaotic, and oddly paced. The music, though marvellous, comes in very long stretches, prompting some dryly academic choreography. In the early 1970s, MacMillan had approached Britten, asking if he could cut some of the music. The composer, already very ill, had been reluctant; his estate now allowed few cuts to the score.

The second *Pagodas*, like the first, was flawed. Yet it showed MacMillan responding to his dancers, and most of all to Bussell, whom he had noticed when she was still at school. He showed off her expansive movements, her sweeping limbs and strong, flexible feet. Much of the footwork was intricate, but Bussell never looked rushed: she sailed through with innocent sweetness. Jonathan Cope, as the Salamander Prince, went from elegant lines to bold, wriggling lizard movements. Chadwick was splendidly charismatic as the wicked sister Epine, while Dowell was the white-faced old Emperor, given doddering but nippy footwork. Kumakawa danced the heroine's Fool, and there were solos for Princess Rose's suitors, the Kings of North, South, East and West. The corps dances were deliberately demanding, sometimes dryly so. Georgiadis's designs were grand and airy, with bronze banners and sliding pagodas. The court were Elizabethan, with ruffs and full-skirted costumes, shade-dyed to fade from black to red.

This *Prince of the Pagodas*, with all its faults, had full and enthusiastic houses. On 31 March 1990, with many people delayed by the 'poll tax' riots in central London, the auditorium was packed from the first interval on. During the ballet's first season, Guillem danced Princess Rose with aplomb. Not long afterwards, she and MacMillan fell out over her interpretation of *Manon*: their row was broadcast over the Covent Garden tannoy, with both shouting at the tops of their voices. 'In Paris, it's different,' says Dowell now. 'In The Royal Ballet, the creators are stars, you wouldn't dream of speaking to Ashton or MacMillan like that.' Guillem danced her first Ashton role, Cinderella, that Christmas. She was fluent and assured, but adjusted the choreography to include her high extensions. The sparkling small steps of the ballroom solo were suddenly enlarged, feet lifted to hip rather than calf height. By now, the ballet's Ugly Sisters were right over the top, comedy getting lost in exaggeration.

In January 1990, *Fille* was revived, now with the pas de six from Chaboukiani's *Laurentia* as a curtain-raiser. Chaboukiani's Soviet bravura didn't suit the Company, though Almeida danced her variation with aplomb. *Fille* itself was well revived. On the first night, Collier was a warm Lise, scintillatingly precise, while Jefferies danced with humour and generosity. Coleman, a sweet-tempered and inventive comedian, gave his last performance as the Widow Simone this season. With long runs, Dowell could give his young dancers plenty of debuts, and there were two new Colases this season. Errol Pickford showed an explosive flair in the bravura steps. Stuart Cassidy, a dancer of open, easy presence, danced and acted with affecting directness. *Fille* was followed by Bussell's first *Swan Lake* – tentative, but she danced with a fluid softness that was particularly affecting in the last act.

Asylmuratova, building a close relationship with the Royal, danced Odette–Odile and Giselle that season. There was a new Giselle from within the Company, too. Nicola Roberts, making her debut in April 1991, was deeply absorbed in the world of the ballet, affectingly spontaneous in her response to events and to everyone else on stage.

But there were disappointments this season as well. Performances were disrupted by injury and a shortage of rehearsal time. A proposed American tour fell through, a new William Forsythe ballet was cancelled due to the choreographer's heavy schedule, and David Bintley's next ballet was postponed until August. Instead, *A Month in the Country* was revived for Guillem. Her dancing was steely, unyielding, though her acting was intelligent and self-possessed. On the same programme, Bussell made her debut as the woman in *Song of the Earth*, dancing with new maturity.

Guillem's first Juliet came on May 1990. She dropped her sophistication for a performance of eager abandon, giving Juliet a youthful gaucheness in the early scenes. She danced with scrupulous care for the choreography, partnered tenderly by Cope. Two days later, they danced the roles again at a gala for Margot Fonteyn, with Nureyev as Mercutio. Now widowed and very ill, Fonteyn had little money for medical bills. John Tooley arranged a benefit for her, the proceeds to be paid into a trust which would support her during her lifetime and help young dancers, or older disabled ones, after her death. For one last time, Fonteyn appeared on stage at Covent Garden, acknowledging the love and admiration of the audience. She died in 1991.

In June, the Bolshoi star Irek Mukhamedov left his home company to become a full-time member of The Royal Ballet. At the age of thirty, he was eager for a wider repertory: 'I have danced *Spartacus* enough,' he said in a television interview.[1] He was a powerfully built dancer, blazingly charismatic, with dark eyes and a huge jump. Acting and dancing, he had the old-school Bolshoi virtues of breadth and intensity. In July, he and Bussell danced MacMillan's new 'Farewell' pas de deux at a gala for the Queen Mother's ninetieth birthday, planned as part of *Winter Dreams*, a new ballet based on Chekhov's *Three Sisters*. MacMillan showed off the full-scale dancing of his stars: Bussell's bounding jeté, Mukhamedov's scissoring jump and passionate, attentive partnering. As he caught hold of her, she stretched up and into a backbend, outburst and resignation in a single surge of movement. She was not a natural actress, but MacMillan built drama around the lavishness of her dancing.

This duet was performed again at the last bill of The Royal Ballet season. The programme was blighted by technical mishaps. For David Bintley's *The Planets*, Ralph Koltai had designed a set so elaborate that it needed a forty-minute interval to be taken down. Early in the first performance, the metallic rings of Koltai's Saturn got stuck. After a long, unscheduled wait, Isaacs came out to offer the audience free drinks. At this first, interrupted viewing, and again the following season, *The Planets* was fervently disliked. The dances were fussy, made more so by Sue Blane's costumes. In the *Venus* section, Brind had her last new role with The Royal Ballet. She was increasingly absent through ill health, and left the Company at the end of the 1990–91 season. The other new ballet was William Tuckett's *Enclosure*. Dana Fouras waited in suspense, surrounded by numbered doors, as other dancers clattered wooden chairs. Tuckett was to be the first of several choreographers thrown too quickly onto the Covent Garden stage.

It was a messy end to a season full of new beginnings. Guillem and Mukhamedov were important influences on the Company, while the youngest generation of dancers showed new confidence, a happy lack of inhibition. MacMillan had returned to the Company, finding new inspiration in Bussell and Mukhamedov. At the same time, programming remained stodgy, relying increasingly on a small number of full-length ballets. The start of the 1990–91 season was dominated by *The Prince of the Pagodas*, *La Bayadère* and *The Nutcracker*. Mukhamedov's first full role with The Royal Ballet was Solor in *La Bayadère*. He had the weight and authority for the ballet, acting on a grand scale. His dancing was below form, but gained power as the season continued. Collier was a tender Nikiya, with Deborah Bull an emphatic, imperious Gamzatti. Jefferies was deeply affecting as the High Brahmin: no camp, no exaggeration, but a man soberly in love with Nikiya.

In November, Balanchine's 1972 *Stravinsky Violin Concerto* was added to the repertory. It has bold steps, sharp rhythms and leading roles for two ballerinas, and it was scrupulously staged and danced. Bussell again showed a natural flair for Balanchine, while Durante and Cassidy were strong and clear. The rest of the programme sagged, however. Ashley Page's latest ballet, *Bloodlines*, had a complex set, a factory world with vein-like pipes, designed by Deanna Petherbridge. Bruce Gilbert's electronic score thumped rhythmically, but Page's choreography was emptily repetitive.

At Christmas, Christina Johnson and Ronald Perry, both from the Dance Theatre of Harlem, gave handsome guest performances in *The Nutcracker*. They were also involved with a new education scheme, 'A Chance to Dance'. In collaboration with the Dance Theatre of Harlem, The Royal Ballet's Education Department set out to encourage children from different ethnic backgrounds to try ballet. Just as more girls than boys try ballet classes, British ballet students were overwhelmingly white – and so was the Company. Constance Tomkinson, secretary to de Valois in the 1940s, remembered Madam's fury when the father of a South African dancer wrote to complain that another Company member, also South African, was 'tainted with coloured blood'. De Valois told him that she hired dancers for talent, not race, and that his daughter should feel 'privileged to work with a dancer of such promise'.[2] In America, however, the Company had played in segregated theatres, while Johaar Mosaval, a South African of Malaysian extraction, had been left behind when the touring company visited his home country in 1954 and 1960. Most of the Company's non-white dancers had been pale-skinned; none was of African descent. The 'Chance to Dance' scheme set out to redress the balance, with Johnson, Perry and other Harlem dancers invaluable as role models. Dancers and musicians visited schools, initially in Lambeth, Hammersmith and Fulham, with lecture demonstrations and auditions for after-school classes.

MacMillan's *Winter Dreams* had its premiere in February 1991, on a night of heavy snow. This version of Chekhov's *Three Sisters* focused on the married Masha's love for Vershinin, with one pas de deux for declaration and the other, already seen, for farewell. Peter Farmer designed a gauze backdrop of bare birches, behind which the family is dimly visible at dinner: a provincial town in a northern winter. The pianist Philip Gammon chose and played music by

Tchaikovsky, with Russian guitar music for character scenes. When Mukhamedov's Vershinin, a disruptive romantic presence, walked across the stage, flutters of interest or hope went through the rest of the cast. Durante was vivacious as the youngest sister, Irina, in dances with intricate footwork. Stephen Wicks and – replacing an injured Cassidy – Adam Cooper were her suitors. MacMillan made a superb role for Dowell, as Masha's husband Kulygin. He danced his jealousy in a constrained walking solo, broken up by jerks and twitches. The elegant Dowell was transformed, but his classical strength was still at the heart of his dancing, projecting those convulsive steps. His movements turned in on themselves, while an underlying grace beamed through: Kulygin's heart underneath his unhappy awkwardness.

Winter Dreams was uneven, and too long. MacMillan, who had not aimed to show the whole play, put far too much of it in: the many minor characters slowed the action. But the ballet was warmly welcomed. It shared a bill with a new production of MacMillan's *Danses concertantes*. In 1979, Georgiadis had redesigned the ballet for the touring company. Now MacMillan turned to Ian Spurling for completely new designs.His set and costumes suggested an art-deco swimming pool, with dancers in bathing costumes. It was bold and bright, but many missed the glowing colours of Georgiadis's first production. Durante, Sansom and Pickford led the ballet with sharp attack.

Durante and Sansom had danced *Manon* together in January 1991. They were well matched – both light, elegant dancers – and showed a new ardour in these roles. Durante made a mercurial Manon, flicking quick, flirtatious feet. The question of partnerships was much discussed that season. Bussell, scheduled to dance the ballet with Mukhamedov, proved to be too tall for him – and by now, a cast change involving both Bussell and Mukhamedov was front-page news in Britain. Mukhamedov was not a natural Des Grieux: the long phrases and flowing lines made for Dowell did not sit ideally on his bulkier frame. His line was precise rather than lyrical, but he danced boldly, eagerly, and built up a strong rapport with Durante, Bussell's replacement. This revival was full of starry debuts. Mukhamedov went on to dance Lescaut to Asylmuratova's radiant, capricious Manon. Guillem also made her debut, in time making Manon one of her signature roles. In these early perform-ances, she added writhing arms to the brothel dances, though her torso remained unbending. Guillem's sheer glamour suited the role: all eyes were on the heroine.

Agon was the next revival, with Bussell outstanding in the pas de deux, boldly unfurling long, beautiful limbs. She went on to dance this and other Balanchine works at New York City Ballet, and was acclaimed on the choreographer's home ground. *A Month in the Country* was danced on the same bill as *Agon*. As Natalia, Asylmuratova danced with magnificent scale and grandeur; Rosato made a moving debut in the role. This programme was impressive, but did not do particularly well at the box office. The more the Company concentrated on star casting and evening-length ballets, the harder it became to sell adventurous programmes, however well reviewed. Of all Ashton's short works, *Month* was revived most often, because it had a plum role for a dramatic ballerina. The Company's advertising had acquired a West End emphasis, promis-ing spectacular designs, wigs, sets. The next new ballet, Bintley's *Cyrano*, was lavishly dressed by Hayden Griffen, filled with props and hats. 'You do realise', a props maker told Bintley before the premiere, 'your confounded bakery scene needs more props than the whole of *Carmen*?'[3]

Bintley's ballet, danced to a very pedestrian score by Wilfred Josephs, was sunk by a poor choice of subject. Rostand's play is all about the power of language: the large-nosed hero wins Roxane's love by eloquence, by wit, by *words*. The contrast between the bril-liant, ugly Cyrano and the handsome, dumb Christian was lost in a ballet. Characters had to fall back on laborious mime, while Bintley showed scant invention in the few dance scenes. Jefferies, in his first big created role, did everything he could for the ballet.

The season ended with an impressive tribute to Nijinska, crisply conducted by Barry Wordsworth, the Company's new Music Director. *Les Biches* was played too much to the audience, but it was well rehearsed and clearly danced. Durante made a cool, pre-cise Garçonne, with elegant line. Bussell's Hostess had sharp footwork and bold rhythm, but she missed the character's sophistication. *Les Noces* was powerfully performed, and the bill was completed by a crisp revival of *Scènes de ballet* – a reminder that Ashton had brought Nijinska's ballets to the Company. Dowell invited Sibley, celebrated in this ballet, to coach his young dancers. The use of star coaches was one of the innovations of Dowell's regime. He brought many of his former colleagues back to work on revivals, a practice that has become standard at The Royal Ballet. Durante gave a stylish account of the ballerina role, while the corps, lovingly rehearsed, danced with authority.

That summer, the Company toured to America, welcomed back to the Met after an eight-year absence, opening with several casts in *Swan Lake*. In the *New York Post*, Clive Barnes called Dowell's production 'the best *Swan Lake* in captivity anywhere', although like other New York critics, he criticised Sonnabend's designs.[4] In fact, they had never looked better than on the wide stage of the Met, the overwhelming detail broadly spaced. Durante, on the first night, was below her usual form, but Sansom's elegance was praised; he went on from the American tour to a year's leave at San Francisco Ballet. Bussell was immediately adored, and Mukhamedov – known from his Bolshoi performances – was already a star. Both were cheered in *Winter Dreams*, though the ballet was criticised for its episodic structure. A few critics were charmed by *Still Life at the Penguin Café*; the rest, like their British colleagues, sternly disapproved. *The Prince of the Pagodas* was generally disliked, despite Bussell and the Britten score. There were questions about The Royal Ballet's classical style, but its high energy and focus were admired – 'a company renewed', wrote Anna Kisselgoff in the *New York Times*. This was a confident return to the scene of former triumphs.

Back in London, the start of the 1991–92 season was badly disrupted. The orchestra went on strike, preventing the first few performances, before the revival of *Afternoon of a Faun* had to be cancelled. Robbins, who refused to let his ballets be performed without his supervision, was too busy to cast and coach the production. The ballet was replaced by divertissements. Durante and Cassidy were fluent in the *Thaïs* pas de deux, while Guillem danced *La Luna*, a solo by Maurice Béjart, and Balanchine's *Tchaikovsky pas de deux*. At her own request, she danced with Adam Cooper, who had shown considerable stage presence in several solo roles. Like Cope, Cooper became a superlative partner, sure and attentive. Good partnering became a hallmark of Dowell's regime. That season, the tall Hungarian Zoltan Solymosi joined the Company to dance with Bussell: limited as an actor, but handsome support.

Balanchine's *Symphony in C* was taken into the repertory in November 1991. This tutu ballet, made for the Paris Opéra in 1947 under the name *Le Palais de Cristal*, brims over with glorious classical dancing. Each of the four movements has its own ballerina, supported by her court of cavalier, soloists and corps de ballet. The finale brings on the whole cast, a sunburst of energy. Balanchine's choreography, exhilarating and demanding, was a serious stretch for the Company. On the first night, Guillem danced the slow second movement, but lacked the movement texture and the smooth bourrées needed for the role. Chadwick was bright and musical in the third movement, with its suggestion of country dances. John Taras, staging the ballet, restored the role's tricky double sauts de basque for Chadwick, who had danced the step with aplomb in *Ballet Imperial*. Cassidy and Bull showed breadth and attack in the fourth movement. Later that season, Bussell gave a grand, soft account of the second, her feet beautifully flexible and strong.

Between the two Balanchines, there was a pair of new works. One was Tuckett's *Present Histories*, a slight work showing ambiguous relationships at a party. The other was an extract from Jonathan Burrows' *Stoics*, a deadpan comedy which had had its premiere at the tiny theatre The Place – and which, though praised, did look small on the Covent Garden stage. Burrows, who had formed his own company in 1988, left The Royal Ballet that season. He was not the only one: several dancer-choreographers left during the 1980s and 1990s. Some, like Burrows and Russell Maliphant, were eager to try different movement styles, but there was a shortage of opportunity at The Royal Ballet. As the touring company settled into its Birmingham home, it was no longer a choreographic nursery for the bigger Royal Ballet. Covent Garden was an intimidating stage for trainee choreographers, while the falling number of triple bills made it hard to make a habit of new work.

Before leaving, Burrows played a warm Widow Simone at the next revival of *Fille*. His Lise was Nina Ananiashvili – the first Russian to dance the role, but not at home in Ashton's choreography. She had already danced *The Prince of the Pagodas*, and would return to dance other ballets, including *Cinderella*, *The Firebird* and *Symphony in C*. With Collier, Mukhamedov, valiantly tackling British footwork, made an ebullient Colas. Now in her forties, Collier was 'going through that phase of a late flowering that can be so moving in a ballerina', wrote David Vaughan in 1994.[5] Mukhamedov's other regular partner was Durante, who danced her first *Giselle* in January 1992. She was a shy, vulnerable Giselle, very light in the dances of the second act. Mukhamedov brought a profound sense of romanticism to his role, of love and doom. The Royal Ballet had a fine team of character artists for *Giselle*. As Giselle's mother, Sandra Conley was loving and concerned, her mime scene urgent and musical. Rosato was a haughty Bathilde, imperious and spoilt, yet she could give the role different inflections. At one later performance, she smiled sadly when Giselle admitted she was in love. Unknowingly, both women were engaged to the same man, but Rosato's Bathilde had already seen through him.

Having failed to secure a new Forsythe ballet for Guillem, the Company staged *In the middle, somewhat elevated* in 1992. Forsythe, an American based in Germany, had made the ballet for the Paris Opéra in 1987, with Guillem in the leading role. To a pounding, slicing electronic soundtrack by Thom Willems, dancers in teal leotards dance wrenched classical steps, legs splayed and lines exaggerated. Forsythe presents his cast as athletes with moody catwalk attitudes, strolling on to dance, walking out on duets without acknowledging their partners. Guillem led The Royal Ballet staging, quick and lithe in her created role, partnered by Hilaire. Bussell, Bull, Michael Nunn and Peter Abegglen danced with breakneck daring. The Royal Ballet's staging of *In the middle* was Britain's first sight of Forsythe's new style, and opinion was violently divided. Many critics loathed it, but a new audience came to Covent Garden to see it, often skipping the other works on the programme. Those other ballets, that season, were by Ashton. *Monotones* still revealed a lack of security in classical dancing; the

Company's technique had improved, its energy and confidence rising sharply under Dowell, but it had not regained its Ashtonian identity.

The Judas Tree, which was to be MacMillan's last ballet, had its premiere in March 1992. The bold, strongly textured score was commissioned from Brian Elias. MacMillan had had trouble with new scores before – as with *Images of Love* in 1964, when he had been shocked by Tranchell's orchestration. This time, a recording was made of the music, and he choreographed to tape. The painter Jock McFadyen designed a building-site set, real scaffolding and burnt-out cars in front of a misty blue industrial landscape. The tower of Canary Wharf, light winking, set the ballet in present-day London. Mukhamedov, in jeans and cropped T-shirt, was the building-site Foreman, leading a gang of workmen. Durante made her entrance under a white sheet before taunting the Foreman and the other men, strutting and flaunting herself. She is gang-raped and killed. The Foreman hangs himself after betraying his gentle friend, danced by Michael Nunn. The Woman returns, wrapping the sheet around her, to mourn the bodies.

This was a brutal work, more brutal from the naturalism of its setting and movements. In 1960, an onstage rape had been a breakthrough for MacMillan. Since then, he had returned almost habitually to sexual violence, without always finding the same psychological insight. Many critics saw misogyny in the gang-rape of *The Judas Tree*. At the same time, the ballet was praised for the vigour of its choreography. There were no disagreements about the Company's performance, however. Mukhamedov, Durante and the Company's men danced with reckless commitment. Michael Nunn, one of the younger soloists, was outstanding as the Friend. When the ballet was revived the next year, Leanne Benjamin gave a pungent performance as the Woman. *The Judas Tree* was followed by a tour to Japan, and a summer season dominated by *Romeo and Juliet*. The 1992–93 season opened in October with Bussell in *Swan Lake*. The production had been slightly revised, and now included Ashton's Neapolitan pas de deux.

Congratulating Mukhamedov after *Winter Dreams*, MacMillan had exclaimed, 'And now for *Mayerling*!'[6] The ballet, out of repertory for six years, was carefully revived, with some revisions. On the first night, having gone backstage in the interval, MacMillan collapsed on his way back to his seat. He died during the third act. As his wife went to fetch their daughter, the news began to spread through the building, rumours reaching the dancers in the wings. At the end of the performance, Jeremy Isaacs made an impulsive decision. With the dancers visibly distressed, and Mukhamedov near tears, he announced MacMillan's death to the audience. Isaacs wrote later: 'It would be obscene, it seemed to me, to rejoice with Kenneth dead.'[7] The audience left the theatre shocked and in silence. MacMillan, who did not live to see the end of his ballet, saw enough to be proud of his cast. Mukhamedov was a wild, brooding Rudolf, with superb stamina in this long, difficult role. Durante's Mary was supple and abandoned. As Larisch, Collier showed a calculating streak, a sly delight in intrigue, with a sudden rush of horror when she saw Rudolf's misery.

With MacMillan's death, The Royal Ballet changed. He was the last choreographer to have a shaping influence on the Company, to define its identity and style. He had discovered and challenged generations of Royal Ballet dancers. He was not replaced as Principal Choreographer. Dowell continued to commission new ballets from Page and Bintley, but few of their works for the Company lasted beyond one or two seasons. Critics and balletomanes are always ready to look back to golden ages, but there was a real change towards the end of the twentieth century – not just at The Royal Ballet, but internationally. The century's early and middle years had been a period of extraordinary choreographic richness; the new generation could not match it. 'At the moment there are no giants, and they happen so rarely,' Monica Mason would say in 2005. 'We now have such an enormously full chest of treasure that you can happily dig into, but dancers need to have things made on them. So new choreography is absolutely crucial. But we must have choreographers who are going to understand The Royal Ballet and be able to serve a large company on a big stage in a big theatre.'[8] The Company joined the rest of the ballet world, looking for new work from a dwindling number of choreographers. Nor did 1990s conditions favour young dancemakers. Covent Garden, under financial pressure, cut back on the ballet company, sometimes asking Dowell to change programmes at the last minute. 'It put enormous strains on the Company,' he remembered. 'The rehearsal time got very tight, and we only just got things together . . . If the rep has been changed it's because of financial problems'.[9]

Dowell found it hard to fight against the combined weight of the Board, the Royal Opera and the General Director, all inclined to favour opera. 'People did say I should have been tougher,' Dowell said later. 'I don't go in and bang my fist on the table, but I do have a pragmatic streak. I knew it was about survival.' For the next five seasons, the Royal Opera would stage more than twice as many new productions as The Royal Ballet. In 1992–93, a revival of *The Prince of the Pagodas* was replaced by *The Sleeping Beauty*, 'in order to generate further much-needed income, and meet public demand'.[10] Jonathan Cope, who had returned to the Company, partnered Bussell in her first Aurora.

The next new production, loathed by most critics, was a guaranteed box-office smash. In 1971, Ashton had made the choreography for the film *The Tales of Beatrix Potter*. For Christmas 1992, Dowell transferred the dances to the stage, with dancers in detailed animal heads by Doboujinsky. Ashton's steps were inventive, with delicate footwork for the mice, but at seventy minutes this was a very long ballet. 'I did worry for the dancers, under the weight of the costumes,' remembers Dowell. 'In the film, they could rest between takes, but on stage they had to dance right through. When they took those heads off, they'd be *that* colour' – pointing at Covent Garden's crimson plush. That spring, Bintley resigned as Resident Choreographer, frustrated by a lack of commissions. *Tombeaux*, which had its premiere in February 1993, was perhaps Bintley's best work for the Company. It was set to Walton's Variations on a Theme by Hindemith, with echoes of Ashton's *Scènes de ballet*. The fashion designer Jasper Conran dressed the women in exquisite inky tutus, shade-dyed in black and indigo, the men in high-necked body tights. His set showed a deep blue forest, with a gateway in the shape of a lion's mouth. There was complex partnering for the leading couple, Durante swept upside-down over Sansom's head before flowing down his back.

Bintley's ballet was over-busy, but ended vividly: Durante spinning on a darkening stage, as Sansom ran in widening circles around her.

Like *La Bayadère*, the next new production came from American Ballet Theatre. Dowell, who had enjoyed dancing Baryshnikov's version of the Petipa ballet *Don Quixote*, restaged it for his home company in April 1993. Mark Thompson's new sets were strong and atmospheric: a sun-baked courtyard, a cave shadowed by stylised windmill sails. His costumes were no help to the dancing, with black clothes against black backdrops and comic windmill headdresses for the corps de ballet. The Company was not at home in the bravura oomph of the choreography; even Mukhamedov, splendid in the Bolshoi production, forced his effects. The mime scenes, which might have suited The Royal Ballet, had been cut almost to nothing. Later that month, *Ballet Imperial* was revived, with its Berman designs restored, to mark the tenth anniversary of Balanchine's death. Durante lacked authority in the ballerina role. Bussell had real glow in the Beryl Grey role, but some trouble with the speedy footwork.

After a tour to Paris, Turin and Istanbul, the Company returned to Covent Garden for a short summer season. *La Ronde*, which Tetley made for the National Ballet of Canada in 1987, was a version of Schnitzler's daisy-chain drama, set in fin-de-siècle Vienna. A Prostitute sees a Sailor, who goes on to meet a Parlourmaid, and so on back to the Prostitute. The play showed social class and the spread of syphilis; the ballet was just one grope after another. Chadwick's Actress and Page's Count managed to establish their characters, but it was an uphill struggle. The failure of *La Ronde* was more disturbing because this was not a new ballet: the Company bought it with eyes open. It was framed by Balanchine's *Prodigal Son*, Mukhamedov's eager Prodigal brought low by Rosato's Siren, and *Checkmate*. Bussell's Black Queen was strongly danced but lacked dramatic power.

With no Resident Choreographer, Dowell began a search for talent. The 1993–94 season opened with a bill of new productions, advertised as 'White Hot and Different'. 'De Valois and Ashton didn't have to deal with marketing,' says Dowell ruefully. 'When I saw that title, I knew we were handing ourselves to critics on a plate.' That slogan, wrote Clement Crisp, 'might better be applied to a shower of boiling lead'.[11] The first programme included two works by company dancers. Matthew Hart, whose lively *Street* had been a hit at Birmingham Royal Ballet the previous season, made *Fanfare* to a score by Brian Elias, with designs by Sonnabend. His fluent choreography was overwhelmed by these powerful collaborators. Tuckett's *If this is still a problem*, set to Ravel, showed Cope, Collier and William Trevitt in an ambiguous relationship, but did not gel. The third new production was Forsythe's *Herman Schmerman*, made for New York City Ballet in 1992. After a fast opening quintet, Guillem and Cooper danced a combative duet, full of yanked extensions. The fashion designer Versace dressed Guillem in a transparent top, her breasts visible, while Cooper changed into a yellow skirt halfway through. His stage presence now matched hers; they made it a lively struggle of wills. The evening ended with *Different Drummer*, with Mukhamedov a powerfully simple Woyzeck.

The season looked up with Sarah Wildor's debut as Juliet. Wildor, a delicate blonde, had stood out since her schooldays, dancing leading child roles in *The Nutcracker* and *Swan Lake*. Ashton had rehearsed her for his *Nursery Suite*. She had an expansive movement quality, expressive and immediate. As Juliet, she was open and spontaneous, caught up in the music and in each moment of the story. For Christmas, the Company settled down to *Beatrix Potter*, now given as a double bill with *Ballet Imperial*. Perhaps the management hoped that little girls would be enchanted by the tutus, but it made a long, poorly balanced programme. Bussell made an impressive debut in the ballerina role, dancing with grand speed and definition. *Mayerling*, revived after Christmas, had been due to open with Zoltan Solymosi. When he was injured, Cooper stepped in, giving a terrifying performance. By the last act, his Rudolf was visibly beyond help and beyond control, exhausted and driven. It was Cooper's second performance of the ballet. His first had been another last-minute substitution, taken with an aplomb that earned him the Company nickname 'Super Cooper'.

In February 1994, the Company set out on a new kind of

regional tour. Touring within Britain was still an Arts Council requirement, but it remained expensive and difficult. 'Dance Bites', another hopeful marketing title, was an attempt to solve several problems at once. The Company would send a group of dancers on tour, in productions that did not require much scenery. At the same time, new choreography could be tried in the smaller touring venues. The plan had echoes of the 1970s New Group, and it came up against the same problems. Regional audiences, who had fewer opportunities to see dance, tended to want traditional productions. Few of the new *Dance Bites* works had much substance, and fewer were designed to appeal to a general audience. It might have helped to include a classical set-piece in each programme: *Monotones*, given an uneven performance on the first tour, did not really qualify. Page's *Renard*, set to Stravinsky's score, was the most successful of the 1994 works. Trevitt was a lithe Fox, with Cooper as the Goat.

In April, the Company returned to America. Dowell's new production of *The Sleeping Beauty* had its premiere at the John F. Kennedy Center in Washington DC. President Clinton was in the audience for the gala opening. Dowell used a traditional Royal Ballet text: after Sergueyev, with MacMillan's Garland Dance and Ashton's Vision Solo. It was the designs that made this *Beauty* so controversial. Maria Bjornsen, a theatre designer whose past work included the musical *The Phantom of the Opera*, chose an exaggerated look for the ballet. Huge pillars, in tilted false perspective, loomed over the action. A view up into a cupola dominated the Prologue, seen through a vast oval frame, with a banqueting table jutting out into the dancing area. Colours were acid or icy; the last act was lurid bronze yellow. Throughout, scenery and costumes were at war with the choreography. As the Prologue fairies held their line of arabesques, poses and floor pattern stretching towards the infant Aurora, the slanting scenery dragged the eye in the wrong direction. Aurora made her first entrance down steep stairs within the oval frame – a gingerly beginning for a dance that is a burst of joy. At least one young Aurora was seen crossing herself before starting down those stairs. Bjornsen's designs were certainly theatrical, and this *Beauty* proved popular as spectacle, but it was spectacle at the expense of the ballet itself. People left the theatre remembering the sets and forgetting the dancing.

Bussell, the first-night Aurora, had the scale and the radiance to cut through the scenery. She danced with expansive lustre, sweetness of personality matched with grandeur. As the Lilac Fairy, Chadwick – herself a magically musical Aurora – glowed with confident goodness. Clinton, then embroiled in allegations of misconduct, came to meet the dancers after the gala. He 'could do with a Lilac Fairy' at the White House, he told Chadwick, 'to put everything right'. She grinned back at him: 'I'll come round any time, with my magic wand.'[12] After Washington, the Company went on to West Palm Beach, Orange County, Austin, Houston and New York. The tour was warmly reviewed, but dogged by injury and illness. Bussell, injured before the first night, had danced through on cortisone injections. By the time the Company reached New York, Bussell, Chadwick, Collier and Guillem were all off. Durante carried the season, dancing at least once in every ballet and ending with a last-night Aurora 'so glistening', wrote Clive Barnes, that 'it challenged history and memory both'.[13] Miyako Yoshida, on loan from Birmingham Royal Ballet, made her first appearances with the Company.

The Company returned to London for a busy summer season, featuring two Page ballets. The new *Fearful Symmetries* had its premiere in June 1994. It was danced to John Adams' fast, pulsing score of the same name, with quick, aggressive dances by Page. Antony McDonald's set had huge panels hanging over head, glowing different colours with changes of lighting. Mukhamedov partnered Ann de Vos and Dana Fouras in fast, aggressive duets; this was Page's most successful ballet since *A Broken Set of Rules*. It was followed by a revival of *Renard*, first seen in the Dance Bites tour. This season ended sadly. With the Royal Opera House under severe financial pressure, Dowell was encouraged to cut expensive older dancers. Fiona Chadwick was told that her contract would end the following season. Dancers and fans were angry about the treatment of Chadwick, hustled out after an impressive career with the Company. She gave her last Royal Ballet performance, as Juliet, on 20 April 1995.

The 1994–95 season opened with the new *Sleeping Beauty*, which was greeted with outrage by critics but sold very well. Bjornsen's designs aside, *Beauty* forced a look at the Company's classical standards. Dancing in this *Beauty* was neat and unified, with some fine individual performances, but the old grandeur of style had not been regained. This first London view of the production was disrupted by injury, which also affected a series of Ashton revivals. Ashton would have been ninety in 1994, and that year there were celebrations throughout the dance world. A conference was held at the Roehampton Institute, with generations of Royal Ballet dancers and staff involved. The year crystallised worries about Ashton's legacy. His work, once at the heart of The Royal Ballet's identity, had been allowed to slip from the repertory. The previous season, only *The Dream*, *A Month in the Country* and the controversial *Tales of Beatrix Potter* had been included. And although the Company's technique had improved, the changes that affected *The Sleeping Beauty* also affected the Ashton repertory. The Company now looked more at home with MacMillan or even Forsythe ballets than they did with their founder choreographer. During Ashton's lifetime, Dowell had worked hard to bring works back into repertory: starting his Directorship with *Symphonic Variations*, persuading Ashton to work on *Cinderella* and to agree to the revival of *Ondine*. There were more revivals in the 1994–95 season, without restoring the sense that Ashton was home ground for the company he had helped to create.

Dowell also decided to have some of the ballets redesigned, starting with *Daphnis and Chloë*. Martyn Bainbridge's first scene was framed by pale stone walls, marked with Greek letters, and naturalistic stage trees. The sea was visible through a screen of horizontal threads, suggesting a heat haze. Costumes were far from Ashton's idea that these events 'could happen today': men and women wore gauzy, crinkled tunics suggesting ancient Greece. This was Bainbridge's first work for ballet. Aspects of his designs were handsome, but the combination did not work well on stage: too much white and cream, too much decoration on the costumes, not enough colour in the joyful finale. Casting, that season, was affected by injury. The guest artist Trinidad Sevillano, who had worked with

Ashton at London Festival Ballet, replaced Sarah Wildor as Chloë. Cassidy was a handsome Daphnis, with Cooper fiercely charismatic as the rival shepherd Dorkon. Yet this revival had lost the ballet's sense of magic, of divinity, though Haitink conducted a magnificent account of Ravel's score. The new *Daphnis* shared a programme with *La Valse*, divertissements – with Collier, returning from injury, tenderly musical in the *Birthday Offering* pas de deux – and an unevenly cast *Symphonic Variations*, blighted by injury. The Ashton season had some successes. *The Dream* was lovingly restored, dances polished and any overacting removed. Peter Abegglen was an endearing Bottom, simple and spontaneous, though Kumakawa could not resist embellishing Puck's dances with yet more jumps and turns. In *Façade*, Stephen Jefferies was a gloriously funny Dago.

The 1994–95 season also featured a brave search for new choreography. Dowell had commissioned a new ballet from Michael Clark, the angelic, rebellious dancer who had left The Royal Ballet School for modern dance, shock headlines and stardom. Clark, who had suffered from heroin addiction, was known to be erratic; Dowell decided it was worth the risk. Clark's work on the new ballet was obsessive. 'I've never worked with anyone who could take an hour deciding which way the palm of the hand should face,' said Bull at the time. She felt they were 'getting somewhere really exciting', but the ballet was never finished.'[14] It was postponed, at Clark's request, and then dropped. The programme was hastily rejigged, with *Herman Schmerman* – now with guest artists Wendy Whelan and Albert Evans from New York City Ballet – and Page's *Fearful Symmetries*.

Spirits lifted with some ballerina performances. In December, Belinda Hatley danced her first Aurora, showing striking Royal Ballet virtues: harmonious line, musical phrasing and a warm response to other dancers on stage. The tall Zenaida Yanowsky made an elegant Lilac Fairy. Bussell, injured for most of this season, returned in *Swan Lake*, dancing with gorgeous scale and warmth, the Company around her rising to the occasion. That January's Dance Bites tour was notable for a revival of Balanchine's 1972 *Duo Concertant*. Two dancers stand listening to Stravinsky's duet for violin and piano, moving out to dance. Wildor, partnered by

Trevitt, caught that listening quality in the carriage of her head, in dancing that responded to the music's phrases and to its inner pulse – entrancing from the first rocking step.

In March, *Duo Concertant* was danced at Covent Garden as part of an all-Stravinsky bill. Page's new setting of the *Ebony Concerto*, played by the London Jazz Ensemble, was an aggressive quartet in his usual mode, danced by Bull, de Vos, Cooper and Kumakawa. *Petrushka* was revived for Mukhamedov, who was conscientious but miscast. Now in his middle thirties, he was still dancing classical roles, but as his virtuoso technique waned the management were considering character ballets for him. That season, there was a second scandal over new choreography. Clark's ballet had been dropped; now Forsythe, due to make a new work, pulled out. He told the Company, in a fax filled with theoretical-philosophical terms, that his priorities had changed. He now wished to work in collaboration with his own dancers: 'choreographically, I no longer exist . . .'[15] After much outcry, he gave the Company *Steptext*, danced to a sliced-up recording of the Bach *Chaconne*, with Bull alert and pugnacious in the leading role. Forsythe and his associates added *Firstext*, an introductory work that showed the choreographer at his most post-modernist. The house lights were switched on and off as the audience stumbled in; the words 'The Organisation of Culture' were projected on stage. Guillem and Cooper were already there, dancing in half-light that was dimmer than that in the auditorium.

Rhapsody, another redesigned Ashton ballet, was the last new work of the season. The set, by the painter Patrick Caulfield, had grand arcs of bright colour. The costumes were just as bold, marked with trefoils, spots and slashes of contrasting colour. The set, particularly, had its admirers, but it overpowered the dancing. Ashton's ballet was danced with more aggression and less musicality. In the Baryshnikov role, Kumakawa sailed over every technical hurdle, but turned steps into stunts, missing the wit and fantasy. In a second cast, Wildor showed beautiful upper-body detail in the ballerina role, but lacked strength in her legs and feet. Collier, now listed as a guest artist, danced her last *Giselle* on 29 July. It was a loving farewell, with – according to the stage doorman – more flowers than for Fonteyn's sixtieth birthday.

Following a tour to Korea, Japan and the United States, the 1995–96 season opened with *Swan Lake*. The injured Bussell was replaced by Yoshida, who had now transferred from Birmingham to Covent Garden. A tiny, precise dancer, Yoshida lacked scale, though her dancing was always crisply articulated. Bussell returned in time to dance a fine Terpsichore in *Apollo*, with Bull and Hatley as the other Muses. Cope gave a clean, powerful performance of the title role. Solymosi, also scheduled to dance it, had left The Royal Ballet after disagreements during rehearsals, causing a flutter of headlines.

In December, Twyla Tharp, the American modern-dance chore-ographer, came to Covent Garden to create a new ballet for the Company. She was known for fast, witty choreography, but *Mr Worldly Wise* – her only evening-length ballet to date – was an odd, expensive, disappointing allegory, danced to a compilation of Rossini numbers. In the title role, Mukhamedov was a wild roman-tic in an out-of-control world. He learned about grace and humility from his vision of Bussell's Mistress Truth-on-Toe, but was still chasing ideals as the ballet ended. Kumakawa was the hero's side-kick, Mr Bring-the-Bag. These characters were surrounded by surreal supporting characters, including monks and dancing vegeta-bles. Performances were fine, and David Roger's costumes were clever and lively, but the ballet was incoherent.

At Christmas, the Company danced *Beatrix Potter*, programmed with *Les Patineurs* or with *Peter and the Wolf*, which Matthew Hart had made for young Royal Ballet School students that summer. Hart's next work for the Company was the misguided *Dances with Death*, an AIDS ballet set to Britten's Violin Concerto. The ballet was a stylised drama, with healthy dancers in white body tights, the infected in red. The red Cooper embraced Cope, who then returned to his girlfriend Hatley. Both were claimed by Bussell's red-clad Death – a role that suggested the Black Queen from *Checkmate*. Though the dancers served him well, Hart could not measure up to the marvellous Britten score; critics wondered what kind of support the young choreographer had been given. Page's new ballet, . . . *Now Languorous, Now Wild*, was short and slight, a duet for Durante and Mukhamedov to Lizst. The evening ended with *The Invitation*, a fine revival coached by Seymour and Linden. As the girl and her cousin, Benjamin and Cassidy were heartfelt, if mature in physique. Mukhamedov and Rosato, the Husband and Wife, gave devastating performances.

The Royal Gala on 20 February 1996 was an anniversary performance of *The Sleeping Beauty*: fifty years since the reopening of the Royal Opera House. Twenty-eight of the 1946 dancers appeared onstage at the end – including Leslie Edwards, who had retired just three years before. When de Valois, now ninety-eight, came onstage to cut the cake, the Queen stood up in her box to applaud her. It was an occasion for nostalgia, but it prompted gloomy comparisons between *Beauty*s past and present. In March, there was a third Dance Bites tour. Christopher Wheeldon, a former Royal Ballet dancer who had moved to New York City Ballet in 1993, returned to make a lyrical ballet to Tchaikovsky's *Souvenir de Florence*. Four couples danced in a ballroom setting; the ballet was light, fluent and promising. Back at Covent Garden, Cooper was an intense, impassioned Poet in a revival of *Les Illuminations*. This all-Ashton bill included *Symphonic Variations*, still uneven, and *The Dream*, kept in much better shape.

MacMillan's *Anastasia* was the last new production of the season. Barry Kay's evocative designs had perished in storage; the new version was by Bob Crowley, who had worked with MacMillan on his last project, the National Theatre production of *Carousel*. The first act was now set on the Imperial yacht, the stage dominated by a funnel decorated with the Imperial eagle. Huge, slanting chandeliers hung over the ballroom scene. Crowley's work was handsome, but the Kay designs were still missed; quite apart from their beauty, they had helped to unite MacMillan's ballet. Durante was a fine Anastasia on the first night, with Cooper rough and tender as her peasant husband. That summer, Durante took a year off from the Company, trying acting before she returned in 1997. In June, the Company made a zigzagging but very successful tour, with dates in western Europe, Buenos Aires, Israel and Istanbul.

The new season, the last before the Royal Opera House closed for redevelopment, began in October 1996 with an all-Ravel programme. Rosato was sumptuous in *La Valse*, with *La Fin du jour* and *Daphnis and Chloë*. There was one new work, Wheeldon's

Pavane pour une infante défunte. Wheeldon's duet had a fashion-plate elegance: Bussell on pointe in a long satin skirt, in front of a giant, upside-down arum lily by Bob Crowley. As Bussell bourréed, Cope unwound the skirt, leaving her in soft trousers for the dance that followed. Wheeldon's steps were not particularly distinctive, but he presented his dancers with confidence and style. In *Daphnis*, Mukhamedov played the pirate chief with broad exuberance, with Wildor a musical Chloë. This programme was followed by *Romeo* and a revival of *The Prince of the Pagodas* – now slightly cut, but still too long. With Cope injured, Cassidy was a princely partner for Bussell, angry and tormented when transformed into a salamander.

The next new production came in November. Ashley Page's *Two-Part Invention* was a confused and unmanageable work. In the first section, danced to Robert Moran's *32 Cryptograms for Derek Jarman*, nine of the Company's youngest dancers crossed and recrossed the dimly lit stage, with a video-screen film of the same dancers. The second part, to Prokofiev's Fifth Piano Concerto, was a tutu ballet, with the men in dinner jackets. The younger dancers of the first part kept reappearing, like ghosts. In February, after a winter run of evening-length ballets, the Company staged Twyla Tharp's *Push Comes To Shove*. She had made the ballet for American Ballet Theatre, and for Baryshnikov, in 1976. To a vaudeville prologue by Joseph Lamb, and then a Haydn symphony, Tharp had translated Baryshnkov's classicism into American jazz. The steps had an improvisatory flair, with blindingly fast contrasts and shifts of rhythm. In The Royal Ballet revival, Kumakawa had the fireworks but not the rhythm: he belted through the ballet, a dazzle of technique without much expression. Wildor and Bussell were lively in the ballerina roles, and there was stylish solo dancing from Nunn and Bull.

In March, the Company set out on a Dance Bites tour. These were Adam Cooper's last performances as a member of The Royal Ballet. On leave from the Company, he had created the role of the Swan in Matthew Bourne's *Swan Lake*. It had made him a star. He had returned to The Royal Ballet, but wanted more chances to dance outside.

The Company returned to Covent Garden for a difficult summer season. *La Bayadère* gained in strength after a shaky first night. *Anastasia* was well rehearsed, with Gillian Revie impressive in the title role, but the ballet was beset with technical troubles, with the third-act film breaking down completely at one performance. *Apollo* had to be cancelled after a disagreement over casting with the Balanchine Trust. Having negotiated casting with the Trust, The Royal Ballet then switched dancers without consultation. The Trust, already doubtful, was also unhappy with the state of the revival, and withdrew The Royal Ballet's licence to perform *Apollo*. *The Judas Tree* was substituted at the last minute, making an oddly balanced programme. The same night, the Company gave the premiere of Tetley's *Amores*, another ballet full of athletic lifts and turns, with music by Michael Torke. The choreography had little substance, but the dancers did Tetley proud.

Despite the troubles of this season, the Company was rising to challenges, dancing with attention and attack. In May and June, The Royal Ballet toured to California and Japan, returning to Covent Garden for a last fortnight. The closing gala, the last performance before the builders started work on the theatre, was held on 14 July. It ended with Bussell as the Lilac Fairy from *The Sleeping Beauty*, dancing the old House to sleep.

With its home theatre closed, The Royal Ballet was in for a difficult two years. The Covent Garden management had hoped to move the ballet and opera companies into a single alternative theatre – a choice between the smaller Lyceum, usually given over to musicals, or a large, purpose-built temporary theatre by Tower Bridge. Both projects fell through, leaving the companies homeless. In the event, they played short seasons in a range of venues across London. The whole closure period was overshadowed by a sense of crisis at Covent Garden. In 1995, when the Royal Opera House received Lottery funding for the redevelopment, *The Sun* had attacked the grant as elitist, starting a sour debate about culture and funding. That winter, *The House*, a fly-on-the-wall television documentary, focused on backstage and management troubles. As Covent Garden prepared for rebuilding, its senior management went into meltdown. Isaacs had stood down in December 1996, to be replaced by Genista McIntosh – who left in May 1997. She was replaced by Mary Allen, formerly Secretary-General of the Arts Council. By now, a Parliamentary inquiry into the Royal Opera House had been set up, chaired by Gerald Kaufman. In November, the Culture Secretary Chris Smith suggested that English National Opera should move in with the Royal Opera and The Royal Ballet at the redeveloped Covent Garden. He commissioned a report on the 'The Future of Lyric Theatre in London' from Richard Eyre – which rejected his proposal outright, and urged that The Royal Ballet be given real parity with the opera company within Covent Garden. The goings-on at the Royal Opera House were repeatedly compared to a soap opera. Mary Allen, who left in March 1998, later compared her time as Chief Executive to 'living in a thriller . . . Listeners would move from a stance of interested sympathy to one of fascinated horror, sitting on the edge of their seats and saying, "Yes, and then what happened?"'[16]

These were Covent Garden troubles. The Royal Opera House was accused of mismanagement; The Royal Ballet itself came out of the closure period in good financial shape, without making a single person redundant. There had been considerable pressure to save money by cutting Company numbers, dropping as many as twenty dancers. 'If you reduce the Company, yes, you save money on salaries,' says Anthony Russell-Roberts – the Company's Administrative Director, and Ashton's nephew – 'but you shoot yourself in the foot, because you have no chance of earning big income. What we needed to do was to have some blockbusting seasons in London, with big, well-known ballets that would sell, therefore justifying keeping the Company together.' Dowell, Russell-Roberts, Mason and Artistic Administrator Jeanetta Laurence developed a populist schedule for large London venues. They took risks in staging these big ballets, saving money by cutting rehearsal time. 'There were accusations that we'd produced a bloody boring programme,' admits Russell-Roberts. 'My reply to that was that it was an essential programme for closure. We had a fig-leaf of artistic respectability each year, but the most important thing was achieved: we kept the Company together. And the Company understood that, they bought into it and stuck with us.'

This policy had teething troubles. The Royal Ballet opened the

1997–98 season at the Labatt's Apollo, a big converted cinema in Hammersmith, West London. It was an awkward theatre for dance, with poor sightlines. There were other troubles. Bussell, Mukhamedov and Bull were all injured. At one performance of *Giselle*, the dry ice in the second act settled rather than dispersing, forming an oily film on the stage. The Queen of the Wilis slipped, regained her balance, slipped again and fell. The performance had to be stopped while the floor was cleaned. This first blockbusting season was not a financial success; the Company and the Apollo lost money. The large theatre did not sell out, though houses improved when ticket prices were lowered. Yet The Royal Ballet played to 52,000 people in three weeks, reaching beyond the regular ballet audience. Performances were strong, with the whole Company rising to the challenge of the new conditions. Guillem and Cope opened the season with a dashing *Romeo and Juliet*, splendidly conducted by Victor Fedotov. Yoshida danced a striking Giselle, with an uncanny mad scene, the character's derangement expressed in her blank, unseeing stare and the fragile carriage of her head.

In November, the Company danced *The Sleeping Beauty* in Madrid. They were still in Spain when the Kaufman report, a spiteful document, was published, laying blame on Mary Allen and the Board. Mary Allen's resignation was refused, for the moment; the Board's was accepted. Meanwhile, The Royal Ballet returned to London, to a very successful Christmas season at the Royal Festival Hall. *The Tales of Beatrix Potter* was followed by *Cinderella*, with Guillem now a warmer heroine, taking rather more care with Ashton's choreography. The Festival Hall season was followed by another Dance Bites tour, which was on a larger scale this year. The programme included *Las Hermanas*, MacMillan's version of Lorca's play *The House of Bernarda Alba*. The ballet, created in Stuttgart in 1963, had been staged by the touring company in 1971. A domineering mother rules her five daughters; the eldest is engaged, but the family is torn apart when the youngest seduces the fiancé. Tuckett's new work was the lively *Puirt-a-beul*, a folk-inflected dance to Celtic mouth music. Wheeldon made *A Royal Ballet*, a neatly classical pas de quatre tied to Beethoven's variations on 'God Save The King'. As Clement Crisp complained, 'There may be a more intractable tune than our nation's anthem, but I do not know it.'[17]

In June, after a visit to Frankfurt, the Company celebrated the hundredth birthday of Ninette de Valois. They gave a week of performances at the Barbican Theatre, starting with a tribute evening. The Barbican, a fine stage for modern dance, was inconvenient for the ballet company. The stage is wide but shallow, with little space for an orchestra. The players were grouped on several levels, making it hard to balance the sound. The birthday evening opened with *The Rake's Progress*. Made for smaller stages, the ballet lost some of its effect at the Barbican. Cassidy, making his debut as the Rake, was still adjusting to the ballet. Wildor was a touching Betrayed Girl, but smaller roles were overacted. This opening ballet was followed by a series of dances taken from de Valois ballets. Her works provide few party pieces. Taken out of context, and performed without sufficient period style, many of the excerpts looked faded. Mukhamedov was a clawing Satan in the dance from *Job*; Bussell's Black Queen was blandly danced. *Every Goose Can*, the only item specifically made for a gala, was the most successful, danced with breezy assurance by Matthew Dibble. The evening ended with a weak *Birthday Offering*. At later performances, Page's new *Cheating, Lying, Stealing* replaced the excerpts. The music was by David Lang (who described it as 'ominous funk') and Michael Gordon, with the band Icebreaker playing live on stage. Mukhamedov and Durante grappled obsessively, watched by Trevitt and Mara Galeazzi.

The Barbican week had worried the Company's admirers: it looked out of touch with its past, unsure of its own identity. Things looked up later in the summer, with a season at the London Coliseum. The Company danced under the auspices of Victor Hochhauser, the impresario who had long presented the Bolshoi and Kirov companies in Britain. As with the Russian seasons, prices were high and repertory determinedly populist, but the Company was back at a theatre suitable for ballet, and houses were full and enthusiastic. *La Bayadère* lacked conviction, but Guillem, Cope and Mukhamedov danced a sensational *Manon*. Cope had long since become Guillem's favourite partner, building a particular rapport onstage.

The 1998–99 season was promising. Sadler's Wells, expanded and rebuilt with Lottery funding, was due to open that autumn. The Company would be returning to its old home, and to a more adventurous repertory. The Sadler's Wells programme was dominated by triple bills, by Ashton and by modern choreography. Things sounded good. By the time rehearsals started, though, another crisis had arisen. Covent Garden's debts remained unmanageable. The next opera season was called off altogether, the Royal Opera House would reopen with a reduced number of performances, salaries would be renegotiated. 'These discussions took place about The Royal Ballet without any involvement with The Royal Ballet,' says Russell-Roberts. 'We were aware that they were going on, but we weren't involved. It was announced to us, two days before the start of the season, that the Company had been saved.' The dancers were offered part-time contracts, thirty-six weeks a year. If they did not agree by 26 October, The Royal Ballet would be disbanded.

De Valois's breakthrough, achieved when her company first moved to Sadler's Wells, had been regular paid work for her dancers. She had built up a company by ensuring their livelihoods, giving them the opportunity to concentrate on classical ballet. Taking the Company part-time would reverse that achievement. How could company fitness, let alone style, be maintained in thirty-six weeks a year? And would the Company's leading dancers stay, when conditions were so much better elsewhere? Dowell and Russell-Roberts were ready to resign. 'We believed – and I know this to be the case – the dancers would rather have gone out of business than accept that,' says Russell-Roberts now. The Royal Ballet and its Governors went back to look at the Royal Charter, which guaranteed the Company's independent existence: if necessary, they could pull out of the Royal Opera House altogether, though this would leave them with uncertain funding and no home. The first result of the thirty-six-week offer came on 3 October, when Tetsuya Kumakawa left the Company, cancelling his scheduled Sadler's Wells performances.

The Company opened at Sadler's Wells on 20 October 1998, its future still undecided. Union representatives leafleted the audience; critics raged at the threat to the Company. The first week of performances was lively. MacMillan's *Concerto* was cleanly revived, followed by some of the Dance Bites works and *In the middle, somewhat elevated*. Carlos Acosta, a dazzling Cuban virtuoso, made his debut with the Company in *In the middle*. Trevitt covered for Kumakawa at a performance of *Mr Worldly Wise*. The programme on 26 October – an all-Ashton bill of *Les Patineurs, Enigma Variations* and *Birthday Offering* – started late. Contract negotiations were still going on. Resolution came, not through the Royal Opera House, but through private sponsorship. Russell-Roberts organised a consortium of donors who pledged enough money to keep the Company full-time for the next three years. The Royal Ballet had survived.

As the dancers relaxed, the season picked up. The performance on 26 October had been understandably tense. Though *Birthday Offering* had improved, with Yoshida quick and clear in the Fonteyn role, it was still shaky. The last programme brought *Sawdust and Tinsel*, an inconsequential new Page ballet, danced to Poulenc's Double Piano Concerto. The dancers were circus performers: a bearded lady, a lion tamer, an illusionist. The ballet's point remained unclear. The programme included *Las Hermanas* and *Raymonda*, splendidly led by Bussell, with Hatley outstanding among the soloists. The Wells season ended in November, with *Mr Worldly Wise* and – a Covent Garden tradition moved north to Islington – a shower of flowers from loyal fans. The Company went on to Belfast, where *Manon* was greeted with a standing ovation. Before the Company left Ireland, however, five resignations had been announced. Kumakawa, starting his own company in Japan, invited five of the Company's men to join him. William Trevitt, Michael Nunn, Stuart Cassidy, Gary Avis and Matthew Dibble would all be leaving The Royal Ballet.

Michael Kaiser, the new Executive Director of the Royal Opera House, had come to Belfast to see the Company. 'This is a terrific opportunity,' he told Dowell. 'Go out and hire the five best male dancers in the world.'[18] Over the 1990s, the Company had become more international, a smaller proportion of dancers coming from

The Royal Ballet School. Now that process was intensified. The Kirov's Igor Zelensky was already partnering Bussell. At Christmas, at the Royal Festival Hall, Acosta made a sunny debut in *Fille*, partnering Hatley's musical, mischievous Lise. Acosta's dancing was big, soft and perfectly finished, his stage presence easy and warm. Jonathan Howells was a marvellous Alain, serious and gently puzzled – 'a real *person*,' said David Vaughan, 'with a life of his own.'[19] Lanchbery returned to conduct, and the whole company was in happy form. Another new man arrived in March, in time for the next Dance Bites tour. Johan Kobborg, formerly of the Royal Danish Ballet, appeared in Michael Corder's *Masquerade*, a bright if not particularly individual setting of Stravinsky's *Pulcinella*. Kobborg had fast, clean Danish footwork, with brilliant beats and jumps, and he was a stylish partner for Durante. The regional tour was followed by an astutely timed tour to Japan and China. The tour came between British Prime Minister Tony Blair's visit to China and the Chinese President Jiang Zemin's trip to Britain; the ballet was back in its role of cultural ambassador. In Beijing, *Romeo and Juliet* was given a standing ovation.

Back in London, the summer season was held at Sadler's Wells. Once again, repertory was more varied. *Ondine* looked better at the Wells than it did at Covent Garden. Wildor was bewitching in the title role, fluid and wilful. Cooper, back as a guest artist, partnered ardently and put some life into the ballet's blank hero. The new work of the Wells season was *The Turn of the Screw*, Tuckett's version of the Henry James ghost story, with Mukhamedov as Quint and Sansom cross-dressing as the wraith Miss Jessel. The ballet was strongly performed by a cast that included Yanowsky, Mukhamedov and Monica Mason, but James's ambiguous plot did not translate into dance.

The rebuilt Royal Opera House was finished on time and on budget. At last, The Royal Ballet had enough rehearsal rooms at Covent Garden, including the huge Clore Studio, made possible by a donation from the Clore-Duffield Trust, chaired by Dame Vivien Duffield. There was also a new studio theatre, generously supported by the Linbury Trust, set up by Lord Sainsbury and his wife, the dancer Anya Linden. There was more space for audiences, too, with an end to the old upstairs-downstairs divisions – in the old house, as in so many West End theatres, there had been different entrances for the main auditorium and the cheaper gallery. Confronted with the work of architect Jeremy Dixon, a hostile press melted. Opera and ballet fans queued all night to buy tickets for the new season, and were welcomed by Bussell when the box office opened. The theatre opened in December, with several performances of a gala programme. After a concert performance by the Royal Opera, Nicola Tranah appeared as the Lilac Fairy, now waking the theatre. Dowell's gala was fast-paced, confident and filled with a sense of occasion. In twenty-five excerpts, the programme covered the Company's history since 1946. Bussell, in the Messel tutu, danced the Rose Adagio. There were glimpses of *Symphonic Variations*, *La Fille mal gardée*, *La Bayadère*, *Romeo and Juliet*, *Manon*, *Fearful Symmetries*. The evening ended with a grand défilé, set to the closing music from *The Firebird*. 'When I hear that music, I'm still moved to tears,' says Dowell now. The last dancers to appear were two young students from the School, representing the Company's future. A new era had begun.

TEN

Regeneration

2000–05

ABOVE Christopher Weeldon's *Tryst*, with Jonathan Cope and Darcey
Bussell: © Dee Conway
PREVIOUS PAGE Ashton's *Sylvia*. Marianela Nuñez and Rupert Pennefather
in the last act pas de deux, with Sarah Lamb and Deirdre Chapman as
attendants: © Bill Cooper

For The Royal Ballet, the last five years have been a time of extremes. The Company moved smoothly into a new century, plunged and made a spectacular recovery. Most of the crises of the 1990s had been imposed from outside: Dowell and his dancers struggled with troubles at Covent Garden. With the appointment of Ross Stretton as Director, there was a crisis within the ballet company, a loss of belief in its basic identity. Dowell stood down in 2001, after the most confident season of his Directorship. He had directed the Company for fifteen years, longer than anyone since de Valois. Stretton was to last a single season. His year in office was a time of internal crisis, with the Company taken against its traditions, away from the qualities that made it The Royal Ballet. When Monica Mason replaced him, she was an immediate steadying influence. The surprise was the nerve and conviction with which she took up the Directorship. She did not simply bring the Company back on track; she transformed it. By returning to the heritage Stretton had abandoned, Mason rejuvenated her Company.

For his last two seasons, Dowell was backed by a newly supportive Covent Garden management. The number of ballet performances, and productions, increased. It showed in newly varied repertory, though the first programme of the 1999–2000 season, billed as 'A Celebration of International Choreography', fell rather flat. Dowell's regime had been criticised for limited programming, for a failure to invite more choreographers from outside the Company. This bill began with a work by the British modern-dance choreographer Siobhan Davies, and ended with a new Page ballet. In between, there was a changing selection of recent works, performed by guest artists and dancers of The Royal Ballet. The selection changed from night to night, depending on guest stars, but was generally underpowered. Davies's ballet, *A Stranger's Taste*, was a size too small for the Covent Garden stage. The collage soundtrack, mixing seventeenth-century harpsichord and John Cage music for prepared piano, sounded scratchy and thin in the large theatre. Page's *Hidden Variables*, set to a score by Colin Matthews, was the Page mixture as before. Dancers strutted around Antony McDonald's moving set, but the ballet lacked coherent shape.

The reopened theatre had its teething troubles. Before closure, stage machinery had depended on First World War submarine engines and human muscle. The new, up-to-date machinery was temperamental. Dowell's opening gala had been given limited technical rehearsal. He had been terrified that something would stick, very publicly, before a television audience. In fact, the glitches did not show up until later in the season. Page's ballet was first delayed and then cancelled at one performance. On the first night of *The Nutcracker*, the Christmas tree refused to grow. Peter Wright had revised his production, bringing in several aspects of his recent version for Birmingham Royal Ballet. Drosselmeyer, extravagantly played by Dowell, became a magician figure with a glittering cloak. Wright's alterations were no improvement, but this remained a confident staging, given conviction by the whole company. Howells was a serious, romantic Nutcracker, and Bussell, partnered by the guest artist Roberto Bolle, was a gleaming Sugar Plum Fairy.

In January 2000, Dowell revived *Rituals*, out of repertory since 1977, as part of a MacMillan triple bill. The ballet's stylised image of Japanese culture was still remote, though Revie and Bull gave a sensitive account of the final childbirth section. *Coppélia*, surprisingly, had been out of the repertory even longer, since 1970. Though a new production had been suggested, the Company returned to de Valois's 1954 staging, with its Osbert Lancaster designs. Acosta was a good-humoured Franz, and Yoshida sparkled neatly, but the ballet had lost some of its exuberance.

The first excitements of the season came in March, with an all-Ashton triple bill. *Les Rendezvous*, like *Daphnis* and *Rhapsody*, suffered an unwelcome redesign. Anthony Ward's new scenery was violently bright, with stylised green trees and a lurid sun. The women wore dresses with huge polka-dots, the men striped blazers and straw hats over their tights. It was not elegant; the ballet's sense of fashion suffered. The dancing needed more flow, but the choreography remained crisp and lively. It was followed by *Symphonic Variations*, still showing touches of strain, and *Marguerite and Armand*. This caused a flutter: the ballet had been the exclusive property of Fonteyn and Nureyev. Now it was to be danced by Sylvie Guillem. That made it a different kind of vehicle: she danced it with several different Armands, starting with the vehement Nicholas Le Riche. It had become a star role, rather than a celebration of a partnership. Guillem's own acting was clearly projected, her dancing sinuous. She carried the ballet on star power, and kept it in repertory, but could not conceal its thinness.

There was more star-spotting later that month. Following a series of injuries, *Symphonic Variations* was recast several times. At last the Fonteyn role was given to Alina Cojocaru, an eighteen-year-old member of the corps de ballet. She learned the ballet in five days, and danced it serenely, with musical phrasing. Cojocaru, born in Bucharest and trained in Kiev, looked at home in this most British of ballets. It was a sign for the future: as The Royal Ballet became more international, it could still find dancers who could perform its native repertory – and the Canadian Jaimie Tapper and the Danish Kobborg were both praised in *Les Rendezvous*.

After *The Turn of the Screw*, Tuckett made another ballet with an intractable story in April. *The Crucible*, a loose adaptation of Arthur Miller's play about a New England witch-hunt, was luridly designed by the cartoonist Ralph Steadman. Costumes were garish, with the leaders of the Puritan community wearing crosses like antennae. The complex set kept changing, with lurking demon figures and forests of crosses. Tuckett's dance drama was flattened by all the carry-on. Mukhamedov danced John Proctor, with Yanowsky as his wife Elizabeth and Wildor as the accused girl Abigail. The music was a selection of pieces by Charles Ives. *The Crucible* appeared on a 'New World' bill, paired with Balanchine's *Serenade*, grandly led by Bussell, and *The Concert*, Guillem's nicely underplayed debut as a comedienne.

There was a Diaghilev celebration programme in May, with two new productions. Nijinsky's *L'Après-midi d'un faune* had caused a scandal in 1912. After watching a group of nymphs, a faun approaches one, who runs away, dropping her scarf. As the ballet ends, the faun lowers himself onto the scarf with a masturbatory gesture. A furious debate followed the Parisian first night, with the sculptor Rodin writing in Nijinsky's defence. His choreography was innovative, and strange: the dancers move in angular profile, like figures on an ancient frieze, and their steps are not linked to Debussy's sensuous score. This is the only Nijinsky ballet that can be said to have survived in performance, with several revivals from the 1930s on. The Royal Ballet version, by dance scholars Ann Hutchinson Guest and Claudia Jeschke, used material from Nijinsky's notation. Mukhamedov was now an unpersuasive faun. Acosta was warmer and softer, but not entirely at ease with the drama. Yanowsky, as the nymph, gave the strongest performance. She gives the faun a long look before running away, a powerful moment with Yanowsky's large eyes and steady gaze. Bakst's scenery looked magnificent: a wall of colour, a golden-green Arcadia. *Jeux*, another Nijinsky–Debussy ballet, was less convincing. Scholars Millicent Hodson and Kenneth Archer had pieced together a reconstruction from photographs and other contemporary records: a thin approximation.

The reopened opera house had a second auditorium, the Linbury Studio Theatre, allowing small-scale performances of new work. The first programme, in June 2000, included *Symbiont(s)*, a duet by modern dance choreographer Wayne McGregor. It showed off Bull and the red-haired, hyper-flexible Edward Watson. Wheeldon's new work was *There Where She Loves*, a series of duets to songs by Chopin and Weill. Cojocaru was light and quick in a springtime number; Bussell danced a breaking-up duet with Cope. Wheeldon's choreography was confident, but the relationships tended to the sentimental. Revised as *There Where She Loved*, the work was taken into repertory by San Francisco Ballet. There would now be regular evenings of new work at the Linbury, where Tuckett, who had had trouble on the main stage, developed several successful productions in this smaller space. With the official season over, the Company returned for more performances that summer, presented by Victor Hochhauser. Bussell had an unexpected hit in *The Concert*, dancing with wide-eyed innocence as comedy kept happening to her.

There was another new arrival in this summer season. Tamara Rojo, Spanish-born and trained, had danced an eye-catching Chosen Maiden in MacMillan's *Rite of Spring* with English National Ballet. Mason, who had coached her, was impressed. When Bussell was injured at the end of the summer season, Rojo stepped in to dance a boldly dramatic *Giselle*. The corps rose to the occasion, deeply involved in the onstage story. Rojo joined the Company at the start of the next season.

The 2000–1 season, Dowell's last as Director, was also his most relaxed. The ballet company had been given better support in the reopened Royal Opera House, with a more varied repertory. For this season, Michael Kaiser told Dowell to put on whatever he wanted – 'with one exception, my poor *Beauty*' – and it was a strong end to his regime. Strong, and with an element of nostalgia. Dowell's favourites were the ballets he had danced, not those he had commissioned.

The season opened in October with *Swan Lake*, and continued with a revival of *Shadowplay* – the Tudor ballet that had helped Dowell develop his stage persona. Acosta could not match Dowell's extraordinary fluidity, but his dancing was soft and focused. Watson was nervily intense in the second cast. It shared a bill with Michael Corder's new *Dance Variations*, set to a score by Richard Rodney Bennett, led by Bussell and Cope. Corder's choreography was polished but lacked individuality. It was dominated by Anthony Ward's set, a burst of abstract colour. *Ondine* was revived in November, led by Wildor's darting, musical mermaid. Rojo also danced the ballet, her first big British role with the Company. She was a guileless Ondine, with a childlike streak – genuinely indignant in the ship scene, as children are when falsely accused.

Tudor's *Lilac Garden*, which Dowell had danced in 1968, had never quite established itself in Royal Ballet repertory. Nevertheless, it was confidently revived in 2000. Guillem was the woman facing a loveless marriage, dancing with focus and some extravagance. Christopher Saunders, 'The Man She Must Marry', gave a performance of cold power, weighted and authoritative. Since the early 1980s, critics had complained about unbalanced mixed bills. This programme, of British ballets to French music, conducted by

Emmanuel Plasson, brought nothing but praise. *La Valse*, *Symphonic Variations* and 'white' *Monotones* looked more assured than they had in a long time, while *Gloria* was powerfully danced.

That Christmas, *The Nutcracker* brought several important debuts – Cojocaru as Clara and Ivan Putrov, another Kiev-trained dancer, as an elegant Nutcracker. In 2000, the young Putrov was still very slightly built, but showed clean line and a soft continuity of movement. The Argentinian Marianela Nuñez, who replaced the pregnant Darcey Bussell as the Sugar Plum Fairy, was another recent recruit. She had danced as a 'baby ballerina' in her teens, but was told she was too young to join The Royal Ballet at fifteen. She was offered a contract, on condition that she spent a year at the School before joining the corps de ballet. A dancer of strong technique, Nuñez also had an exuberant flow to her movements, bright and free.

The Nutcracker was followed by a happy run of *La Fille mal gardée*, and a revival of *Romeo and Juliet*, with newly revised designs by Georgiadis. The heavy permanent set of MacMillan's ballet was an obstacle to touring; the new version was lighter and more flexible, without doing much to change the essential look of the ballet. Georgiadis's Verona still had its look of marble, of solidity and shifting colour, but there were new frescos in Friar Lawrence's cell. More controversially, Juliet now had no real balcony, no balustrade to lean on or, as Seymour had done, to arch voluptuously over. Rojo, a dancer who took an essentially dramatic approach to her roles, made a strong debut in this *Romeo*. The same week, Cojocaru made an unscheduled debut, replacing the injured Leanne Benjamin. By now, both were being discussed as the Company's next-generation ballerinas. Both were also partnered by Kobborg, who had already established himself as one of the Company's leading men: quick and light, with cut-glass footwork, the celebrated beaten steps of the Danish school.

On 8 March 2001, Ninette de Valois died at the age of 102. She had been in frail health for some time, but had celebrated her centenary at White Lodge, The Royal Ballet Lower School. She had founded not one but three companies – the two branches of The Royal Ballet, plus the State Ballet Company of Turkey – and seen her models and methods taken up across the world. At Covent Garden, her death was marked by a minute's silence; at Birmingham Royal Ballet, by a minute's applause. Foremost among her qualities, Dowell remembered, was her practicality. There could be no question of stopping work to mourn her: 'Get on with it, dear,' she would have said.[1]

The next performance was the premiere of a new triple bill, including another new work by Page. Critics and audiences lost patience with *This House Will Burn*, a confused and long-winded ballet to a forty-minute score by Orlando Gough. The dancers, in Page's familiar gloomy lighting, twisted themselves into knots while suggesting vicious if ill-defined relationships. Kobborg smothered Galeazzi with a pillow; Watson appeared to die, then reappeared wearing a dress. Two children, students from the School, appeared on stage to watch some of the action. Stephen Chambers and Jon Morrell designed a pile-up of a set, several different rooms, with mirrors, gauzes and a kitchen sink.

Cojocaru's lightness, vulnerability and air of youth made her a natural Giselle. She made her debut in April 2001, to immediate excitement. She was lively in the first act, ready to tease Kobborg's Albrecht, sorrowful and tender in the second. Partnered by Kobborg, she danced with fluent delicacy throughout, footwork beautifully shaped. Later that month, the Company danced a superbly planned bill of Stravinsky ballets: *The Firebird*, *Agon* and *Les Noces*, cleanly rehearsed and strongly danced. Dowell's farewell season ended with a double bill of *The Dream*, slightly untidy, and *Song of the Earth*, with Rojo impressive as the Woman. There was also a final gala for Dowell, a lively series of divertissements. Sibley returned to dance *Soupirs*, the duet Ashton had made for them late in their careers. Wildor and Cooper danced *Varii capricci*, Kumakawa made a prodigal return. Rojo and Acosta danced an exuberant *Don Quixote* pas de deux, throwing off virtuoso steps with flirtatious ease. There was an appearance by comedians Dawn French and Jennifer Saunders, on whose television show Dowell had appeared with Bussell. The high gala prices for Dowell's farewell were criticised, but the performance raised £700,000 for The Royal Ballet School. Much of the gala programme was repeated during the Hochhauser summer season, before the Company toured to America.

Dowell's last season had been full of Royal Ballet history: his own links with Ashton, MacMillan, de Valois, Nijinska. The next season's repertory, already announced, showed a completely different tack. The Australian Ross Stretton had been a surprise appointment for The Royal Ballet. When Dowell announced his retirement, the dancers had held a sweepstake on the next Director. Thirty names had been put into a hat: Stretton's was not among them. (There was a blank – and therefore winning – ticket, which was drawn by Sylvie Guillem.) Stretton had danced with American Ballet Theatre, where he had become assistant artistic director before going on to direct the Australian Ballet. In London, he had the support of his interview panel. Michael Kaiser, who had been executive director at ABT before moving to the Royal Opera House, was keen to appoint Stretton. More generally, there was an urge for change at Covent Garden. Since MacMillan's death, the search for new work had been dispiriting. Dowell had concentrated on home-grown choreographers, rarely looking abroad. Kaiser had said, on arriving at Covent Garden, that The Royal Ballet needed more Nacho Duato; Stretton proclaimed his interest in choreographers like Duato, Kylián, Maurice Béjart and Mats Ek. These were established names in Europe, but few European choreographers had lasted long at The Royal Ballet. Robbins and Balanchine had stayed in repertory; the ballets by Petit or John Neumeier had not. Stretton was also appointed before the critical and audience success of Dowell's last season. During the 1990s, with dwindling performances, and an emphasis on evening-length works, the view had grown among the Covent Garden management that Ashton was dated, that MacMillan repertory should be limited to blockbusters like *Romeo and Juliet* and the increasingly popular *Manon*. Stretton's emphasis on European choreography over 'heritage works' – a term that implied the native repertory consisted of dusty museum pieces – was welcomed.

By the time Stretton got to Covent Garden, Michael Kaiser had left, returning to work in America. He was replaced by Tony Hall, the former head of BBC News. Disquiet began not long after Stretton arrived. As casting for next season began to be announced,

Sarah Wildor found that she had no leading performances. She offered her resignation, which Stretton accepted. The new director favoured Rojo and, especially, Cojocaru, both technically strong dancers who had emerged in the previous season. Wildor had technical flaws – her feet were not strong – but she was musical and expressive, generally seen as the Company's finest Ashton stylist. It was a shock to find that The Royal Ballet now had no place for her. It had no place for Mukhamedov, either. Now forty-one, no longer a virtuoso, he was swiftly dropped, given no opportunity to say farewell to his devoted London public. He organised his own charity gala at the Coliseum that September, a huge success.

Stretton had been hired as a new broom. He knew little of the native repertory, and had not been brought in to cherish the Ashton or MacMillan repertories. That season, there was just one MacMillan work, the ever-popular *Romeo and Juliet*, and two Ashtons, *A Month in the Country* and *Marguerite and Armand*, both now seen as Guillem vehicles. Nor was there much sign of the promised new choreography. Stretton's season was dominated by full-length blockbusters, with just ten programmes and no mixed bills until after Christmas. The Royal Ballet's grant had been increased when Covent Garden reopened, yet Stretton planned fewer performances of fewer ballets than ever before.

At first, Stretton had hoped to open with Cranko's *Onegin*, but the production was delayed. Instead, he chose *Don Quixote*, throwing out the Dowell–Baryshnikov production in favour of Nureyev's version for the Australian Ballet. On the first night, the ballet, and the Company, looked dispirited. Once again, *Don Quixote* was weighed down by designs, this time by dowdiness. Ann Fraser's sets were timid and drab, while Barry Kay's costumes were dully unflattering. Colours were flat, there was no hint of Spanish sunshine, and Charles Barker conducted a plodding account of Minkus's score. Rojo, who had danced the pas de deux from this ballet so exuberantly, looked dampened in this production. Kobborg, too, looked ill at ease. Critics were furious: 'a provincial-looking squib,' wrote Ismene Brown.[2] Later casts did their best to lift the ballet. Nuñez and Acosta were lively; Cojocaru sparkled with both Putrov and guest artist Angel Corella. It was still a dreary start to the new regime – the more so because the Company danced nothing else until December. Dowell had moved away from block bookings; Stretton brought them back.

Cranko's *Onegin*, which opened in time for Christmas, was more warmly received. The ballet is based loosely on Pushkin and Tchaikovsky, though the music, Tchaikovsky arranged by Kurt-Heinz Stolze, includes nothing from the opera *Eugene Onegin*. Cranko focuses almost exclusively on his four principals, Tatiana and her sister Olga, Olga's fiancé Lensky and his friend Onegin. Pushkin's most famous scene comes when the bookish Tatiana, infatuated with the brooding Onegin, writes him a love-letter. In the ballet, this becomes a pas de deux: she dances with an idealised Onegin who steps out of her mirror. Cranko also brings the women into the duel scene, with Tatiana and the frantic Olga hurling themselves at the men, trying to stop the fight caused by Onegin's flirtation with Olga. The ballet builds to a final duet between Onegin and the now married Tatiana, danced to music from the symphonic poem *Francesca da Rimini*.

Cranko's ballet, one of his most popular works, is choreographically thin. It needs the resources of a big company, but the corps, once on, have little to do. The big pas de deux are often strikingly unmusical; changes in the score catch the women slap in the middle of a complex lift. Yet there are effective theatrical moments, such as the mirror in the pas de deux, while the big roles offer juicy theatrical opportunities. The Royal Ballet responded eagerly to this new dramatic challenge, and audiences watched with enthusiasm. Cooper was a Byronic Onegin on opening night, though Rojo was more convincing as a woman of the world than as an ugly-duckling teenager. Cojocaru's Olga was ardent and enthusiastic, dancing with clean attack, while Ethan Stiefel, a guest from ABT, was a handsome, handsomely danced Lensky. Further casts followed.

Critical reaction, softened by *Onegin*, froze again in response to Stretton's first triple bill, sold under the name *Memories*. It was an evening of nostalgia and wafting chiffon, short on variety or solid choreography. In *Beyond Bach*, by the Australian Stephen Baynes, a woman in eighteenth-century dress led on dancers in tunics for a series of blandly classical dances. Tudor's *The Leaves are Fading*, made for ABT in 1975, started with Genesia Rosato reminiscing, looking back on a series of duets to Dvořák. Cojocaru and Kobborg were springy and blithe in the spring duet, with Rojo and Martin Harvey warm as an adult couple. Idealised remembered youth, with pretty steps, well-mannered flirting, a wistful sense of time passing. *The Leaves are Fading* is full of things that people do in ballets, rather than convincing an audience that this is what these dancers do in this ballet. The evening ended with *Marguerite and Armand*, which had welcome bite by comparison. In February 2002, Princess Margaret died. She had been President of The Royal Ballet for forty-six years, coming regularly at home and abroad. She was succeeded by the Prince of Wales, with Lady Sarah Chatto as Vice President.

The next triple bill came in March 2002, after a run of *La Bayadère*. Stretton revived *In the middle, somewhat elevated* and brought in *The Vertiginous Thrill of Exactitude*. This is Forsythe's look at classical ballet, five dancers stabbing their way through academic steps to the finale of Schubert's Ninth Symphony, the 'Great' C major. Steps, set brutally fast, follow a tick-tock rhythm, slamming jumps and pointe-work into place. Every move is distanced by irony; it's a clever-clever piece. Stretton had come in promising Nacho Duato: there were two Duato ballets on this bill. In *Remanso*, to piano music by Granados, three men partnered each other in pursuit of a rose. *Por Vos Muero*, which Stretton had introduced as 'an absolute masterpiece', was set to sixteenth-century Spanish music and whispered poetry. Courtly lovers swooned and gesticulated, gripped by unspecified emotion, while holding masks or swinging censers. These were weak ballets, giving no challenge to the dancers. After the marvellous demands of *The Firebird*, *Agon* and *Les Noces*, the dancers were left with waffling contemporary dance. The new ballets were not masterpieces. They were not even new. If Stretton had invited Ek, Duato or even Baynes to make new works for the Company, the dancers would have had the experience of working with choreographers. Instead, Stretton had filled the repertory with second-hand duds. The Company's prestige, and its box office, suffered.

Stretton's repertory had put great strain on the dancers. He programmed his few mixed bills very closely together, so that most of the new works were being rehearsed at the same time. Guillem refused to dance *Giselle* as well as the Mats Ek *Carmen*, ballets in completely different styles, but her younger colleagues went ahead with similar combinations of work. As the injury rate soared, the dancers' complaints became public. Perhaps, said Kobborg at an open rehearsal, 'The Royal Ballet needs to have more dancers or to do fewer ballets.'[3] Moreover, Stretton's casting was wildly uneven. He put Cojocaru on in most of the repertory, relentlessly promoting her as the Company's newest star: she was scheduled for more than fifty of the year's 157 performances. Several other principals were neglected – as Wildor would have been, had she stayed. Injuries to the Company's men led to a desperate shortage of partners, even with such guests as Stiefel and Corella making regular appearances. By now, Stretton's management style and his taste were under general attack. Revivals of *La Bayadère* and *Giselle* were well reviewed, but most of Stretton's own choices were neither popular nor critical successes.

The Ek *Carmen*, made in 1992 for the Cullberg Ballet, used Rodion Shchedrin's arrangement of Bizet, originally written for Maya Plisetskaya. Ek's version is long, cartoonish and wearisome. His choreography depends heavily on the deep plié in second position, matched with chattering gestures. Feet were flexed, characterisations heavily stylised. The story was half acted out, half sent up. Ek's Carmen struts, smokes a cigar, flaps her long, tinsel skirts. Seducing the hero José, she pulls a red scarf from inside his shirt. Confronted with the bullfighter Escamillo, she pulls another long scarf, this one pink, from his flies. José's mother, a character named M, worries earnestly at the edges of the story. Characters shrieked and cackled, or indulged in repetitive dances. Guillem ran rampant through the ballet, followed by Rojo. Cope was an elegant Escamillo, with guest artist Massimo Murru as the put-upon José. Yanowsky showed sculptural force as M. Between Guillem and Ek's theatricality, *Carmen* had some admirers.

Tryst, a new ballet by Christopher Wheeldon, former Royal Ballet dancer and now installed as resident choreographer at New York City Ballet, to a score by James MacMillan, had been planned before Stretton's arrival. The new Director had doubts about the idea, but was persuaded to go ahead with the commission. *Tryst*, which had its premiere in May 2002, proved to be the hit of the season. Wheeldon arranged his corps de ballet in blocks and lines, movement flowing across the square to MacMillan's shimmering strings and brass fanfares. Pulled up on pointe, the women ripple their torsos, or stand in profile like Egyptian wall paintings. Wheeldon showed Balanchine influences without losing his own voice. At the heart of the ballet, Cope and Bussell danced a long pas de deux, coming on stage in a weighted walk. Cope folded Bussell through different positions, limbs curling in and unfolding. She lay down like a sphinx, torso reared up, and was slowly lifted upright, still holding that position. Wheeldon set up different rhythms, letting them wash through his corps, but some of those patterns sank into repetition, losing scale and impact. *Tryst* was still The Royal Ballet's best new work in a long time. Throughout, the cast danced with attention, bodies fully stretched, movements cleanly articulated. They looked taut even when lying down. Jean-Marc Puissant's set, lit by Natasha Katz, framed the dancing in plain blocks and atmospheric shadows.

In June, the Company toured to Australia, returning in time for a gala for the Queen's Golden Jubilee. The Company had given two tremendously successful gala programmes in the new Covent Garden, the swift and comprehensive opening gala and Dowell's more leisurely, nostalgic farewell evening. For the Golden Jubilee, Stretton simply chose excerpts from ten ballets in current repertory, adding a section of *Birthday Offering*. There was scant acknowledgement of the Company's last fifty years: it was a grudging, untidy programme, poorly lit and under-rehearsed. The Company, and the Royal Opera House, were embarrassed by it.

By this point, Stretton's position was becoming untenable. The injury rate was still high: in the summer season, the scheduled principals appeared in two out of twenty-two shows. The dancers considered a vote of no confidence in their Director, then asked their Equity representatives to make complaints to Tony Hall. Casting decisions were given as a main concern. 'There is a complete lack of information,' said one dancer. 'We never know whether we will be involved in a production or when that will be.'[4] Rumours had begun to reach the press about inappropriate relationships between Stretton and younger dancers. There was also considerable unhappiness about Stretton's choice of repertory. The 2002–3 season would mark the tenth anniversary of MacMillan's death, yet Stretton's celebration season included just five of his ballets – four from mainstream repertory, plus *The Prince of the Pagodas*. Stretton had told MacMillan's widow that her husband deserved to be remembered for his greatest works, adding that the shorter ballets were chamber works, suitable only for specialist audiences in smaller theatres. Lady MacMillan told Tony Hall that she had lost confidence in Stretton, and was prepared to withdraw The Royal Ballet's right to perform his works. Threatened with the loss of the MacMillan repertory, and faced with complaints from all sides, the Board decided that Stretton must go. After meeting Colin Southgate, Chairman of the Board, Stretton simply left Covent Garden. He did not clear his desk; he did not say goodbye.

Ross Stretton died of melanoma in June 2005, having been ill for some time. Illness may have affected his career at Covent Garden. Brought in as a moderniser, trying to adjust to the individual politics of a new company, he had resisted offers of help. He had had some important successes. *Onegin* and *Carmen* were both popular, *Tryst* was impressive. Other decisions had been unhappy or misguided, and he had misread the character of the Company he was there to lead. His season as Director was a shock for The Royal Ballet, but one that had unexpected benefits. By the 1990s, the Company's unparalleled repertory was being eroded. Too many core works were slipping out of performance. Ashton was no longer central to the Company's identity. By throwing out The Royal Ballet's own repertory so decisively – and he programmed nothing by Balanchine, Nijinska, Fokine or Robbins – Stretton had reminded audiences and management how important it was. The Royal Ballet's values and inheritance began to be reassessed.

The other vital change happened unobtrusively. Monica Mason, who had stayed on as Assistant Director under Stretton, now took over as Acting Director of the Company. At first, Mason was seen as a caretaker, a safe pair of hands while a new Director could be found. Once in power, however, Mason proved to be The Royal Ballet's best Director in years. A warm, gracious woman, with an unmistakable sense of integrity, Mason had spent her whole career with the Company. She had had particular responsibility for the MacMillan repertory, and had also specialised in helping dancers return from injury. She was closely involved with The Royal Ballet School, but also ready to welcome outside dancers into the Company, replacing the men who had left with dancers from Italy, Russia and Georgia.

Mason's first decisions underlined her loyalty to the Company and to its dancers. She dropped two of Stretton's programmes, Angelin Preljocaj's *Le Parc* (made for the Paris Opéra in 1994) and *The Prince of the Pagodas*. They would be replaced by two mixed bills, one marking the tenth anniversary of Nureyev's death, the second a programme of short MacMillan works. Mason made an immediate impact on the Company, steadying its nerves, and on Royal Ballet audiences, too. At a performance soon afterwards, she came on stage to announce a cast change, and was welcomed with cheers.

The new season opened in October with a revival of *Tryst* and *Carmen* plus one new production, *Gong*. This ballet, made for American Ballet Theatre in 2001, was the Company's first work by the American modern-dance choreographer Mark Morris. It is set to Colin McPhee's shimmering *Tabuh-Tabuhan*, a tribute to the gamelan orchestras McPhee had heard in Bali. Isaac Mizrahi dressed the dancers in bright clothes, with flat tutus for the women and gold earrings for everybody. Morris matches the score with witty exotic poses, off-balance moves, intricate patterns. *Gong* is bright, musical, full of danced texture. It remained a lively ballet, danced boldly and well.

The season continued with a superb *Mayerling*, revived with the help of David Wall and Lynn Seymour. Kobborg and Cojocaru danced the first night with furious intensity. As Rudolf, Kobborg built momentum through the ballet, pushing the story onwards. His dancing was taut, with a sharp sense of stage space. In the opening ball, his solos cut diagonals through the drifting, waltzing corps de ballet, Rudolf moving against the tide of the court. Cojocaru, tiny and young, danced Mary Vetsera with a kind of headlong *naïveté*. There was a gauche hero-worship in her readiness to fit in with Rudolf's fantasies. Cojocaru did not romanticise the character, but she gave her surprising, delicate grace. At the next performance,

Cope was a highly strung Rudolf, long limbs ready to collapse in on himself. Rojo's Mary had a voluptuous force. As she aimed the gun at Rudolf, playing up to his obsessions, she stood with feet apart, legs braced; the lines of her body were full, blunt and bold. The ballet was well served by its large cast, with Yanowsky an outstanding Empress. After *Mayerling*, the Company revived *Swan Lake*. There were fine individual performances, but the production as a whole looked stodgy. There was work to be done on the Company's classical technique and style.

In January, The Royal Ballet staged Kylián's *Sinfonietta*, danced to Janácek's score. The ballet is full of loud statements of non-specific emotion, with the dancers soaring through Kylián's happy jumps and wistful brow-clutching. It shared a bill with *Winter Dreams* and the season's one Ashton work, *Scènes de ballet*. The ballet's speed and precision came as a shock to a new generation of dancers; at first they thought the finale had been taught at double-speed. Cojocaru made a nervy debut in the ballerina role, racing ahead of the beat. In later performances, she began to fill out the musical phrase, to weight the dancing with greater authority.

Spring was dominated by the new *Sleeping Beauty*. Stretton's announcement of this production had caused dismay. Dowell's exaggerated production needed replacing, but it had kept The Royal Ballet's Sergueyev text. Stretton, ignorant or careless of Royal Ballet tradition with the ballet, had asked the Kirov ballerina Natalia Makarova to stage the new production. Understandably, she had gone back to the Soviet text she had grown up with, changed in many important details. The Prologue fairies no longer had cavaliers; Ashton's dances were dropped; floor patterns were changed and flattened. The old Royal text of *The Sleeping Beauty*, the loveliest in the world, was thrown away. The new production had other blemishes. Makarova added a new Cupid figure, a small child weighed down by a curly wig, to introduce scenes. This was gratuitously cute, and it weakened the drama of the story. Instead of seeing Aurora and loving her, the prince was shot by Cupid's dart: he became a puppet. Throughout, dramatic impact was limited by the changed text. The dancers were encouraged to adopt a Kirov style, arching their backs, and to avoid all contrast in musical phrasing. It was as if this court, these fairies, thought it was bad manners to notice the difference between a 4/4 time and a waltz. Luisa Spinatelli's designs were pretty but bland. The first night was filled with technical glitches: sliding curtains that would not slide, a Panorama that stuck.

The Company danced this *Beauty* well, however. In a show of strength, Mason cast seven Auroras in the production's first week: Bussell, Cojocaru, Yoshida, Rojo, the guest artist Roberta Marquez, Nuñez and Tapper. On the first night, Bussell again danced through an injury. Nuñez replaced her in the coda, whizzing on with brilliant speed and attack. Cojocaru looked happiest in the production. With her Russian training, she elegantly fitted Makarova's Kirov-style production. Rojo managed to dance with old-style Royal Ballet shading, and to restore some drama to the story. Over the first week of this production, old Royal details started to creep back into the text, though it remained an alien *Beauty*.

The tribute to Nureyev was staged in April 2003: a revival of *Apollo*, a programme of divertissements associated with Nureyev and *Raymonda* Act 3. Carlos Acosta, neglected under Stretton's regime, was invited back for *Apollo*. Mason had acknowledged that Mukhamedov had been unkindly treated: he was invited back twice that summer. He made his first appearance in the Nureyev divertissements, dancing an unconvincing reconstruction of *Poème tragique*, Ashton's first solo for Nureyev. Kumakawa danced the solo from *Le Corsaire*, while Kobborg staged the duet from *La Sylphide* (a foretaste of his 2005 production for the Company). This section of the programme was oddly handled. Guillem, in tribute to her mentor, had suggested the use of film and photographs. She arranged a big screen behind the dancers, with huge images of Nureyev looming distractingly over them. From the stalls, it was hard to see the dancing at all. At the time, headlines were grabbed by the returning men and by the weirdness of the film clips. In retrospect, *Raymonda* was the most significant item on the programme. In solo roles, Laura Morera, Tapper and Nuñez showed a new glow and contrast in their dancing. It was the effect that Nureyev's coaching had always had on the Company. Ten years after his death, Mason had found ways to achieve the same effect.

The MacMillan triple bill, replacing *Pagodas*, opened at the end of April. *Danses concertantes* was buoyantly revived, now in its original Georgiadis designs, a glow of green and blue. Mukhamedov returned in *The Judas Tree*, and several casts made their debuts in *Gloria*. All three ballets were lovingly revived, but this bill, like the Nureyev programme, did not sell well. The box office was affected by both the Iraq war and the outbreak of SARS. Mason 'learnt quickly how hot a Director's seat can be'.[5] There was a new ballet at the end of the season, Bintley's *Les Saisons*, danced to Glazunov. The opening section, a series of winter solos, was the strongest. Bintley gave chances to established and promising young dancers: Tapper, Deirdre Chapman, Lauren Cuthbertson, Galeazzi and Nuñez, all dancing with verve and attack. Spring was a duet for Cojocaru – in danger of typecasting, with her air of youth – and Kobborg; the ballet tended to unravel as it proceeded. Charles Quiggin's flowery costumes were exaggerated, but Peter J. Davison's sets were simple and effective. That summer, the Company returned to Russia, taking *Swan Lake*, *Tryst* and a series of Ashton and MacMillan ballets to the Maryinsky and Bolshoi theatres.

The 2003–4 season, the first to be planned entirely by Mason, proved to be a carefully balanced programme, with major Ashton and MacMillan revivals, an emphasis on classicism and new work brought in from outside. Jeanetta Laurence, the Company's Artistic Administrator, was now appointed Assistant Director. The season opened quietly. *La Bayadère* was stodgily revived, though it brought several fine debuts: Nuñez as both Gamzatti and Nikiya, the nineteen-year-old Lauren Cuthbertson as Gamzatti and Thiago Soares, a versatile young Brazilian soloist, as Solor. The Company was still feeling the loss of Cooper, Kumakawa and the five men he had taken with him. Mason brought in dancers from outside the Company. The Italian Federico Bonelli and the Kirov dancer Viacheslav Samodurov joined the Spanish José Martín, the Bulgarian Valeri Hristov and the Georgian David Makhateli. Roberta Marquez, a familiar guest artist from the Company's two Makarova productions, became a principal at the start of the season. Other dancers, including Nuñez and Putrov, had received much of their training overseas, spending some time with The Royal

Ballet School before coming into the Company. Mason was very ready to look outside: The Royal Ballet had become a much more international company.

Wheeldon's *Polyphonia*, a setting of Ligeti piano music made for New York City Ballet in 2001, was staged at Covent Garden in November 2003. Its angular shapes and musical focus showed the influence of Balanchine, yet this was more than a dutiful imitation. When NYCB danced it, they showed characteristically American qualities: the scale of movement, the command of space. With the Royal Ballet staging, *Polyphonia* proved to be a transatlantic ballet, showing off the British company's lyricism. It starts with quick complications, four couples in purple leotards dancing overlapping motifs. They move on to languidly acrobatic pas de deux. For the number 'Arc-en-ciel', from Ligeti's *Etudes I*, Wheeldon literally set airborne arcs. The leading man lies down to partner his ballerina, Cope turning Benjamin – who had speeded up her return from maternity leave to dance the ballet – lazily through the air. In the second duet, Hristov and Deirdre Chapman waltzed across the stage, Chapman swept into a dip as the music quietened. But the waltz kept going, and Hristov rocked her in time while she was down there.

In December, *Polyphonia* was followed by a group of new works. Russell Maliphant's *Broken Fall*, staged at Covent Garden, was co-produced by The Royal Ballet with George Piper Dances, the Company set up by William Trevitt and Michael Nunn. They partnered Guillem in a series of death-defying lifts and falls, Guillem balanced on one man's shoulders, plunging almost to the ground before being caught. Yet the mood was even, unshowy. This production shared a bill with Morris's *Gong* and two more new works. Tuckett's *Proverb* was a slight duet for Yanowsky with Cooper, another returning prodigal. *Qualia*, by the modern-dance choreographer Wayne McGregor, was more ambitious. The electronic music was by Scanner, while Ravi Deeprees designed an elaborate video backdrop, with images of dancers repeated and reflected. McGregor yanked the flexible Watson into ever more extreme contortions. Corps work was ill-focused. Like the Dance Bites programmes, this was an evening of good intentions.

Christmas was dominated by a new production of Ashton's *Cinderella*, staged by Wendy Ellis Somes. It was meticulously revived, the dances crisp and clear, though Ellis Somes's production surrounded the dances with too much finicking detail. Cinderella's coach now appeared on stage in the ballroom scene, and her train had doubled in length: the glorious descent of the staircase was framed by footmen running around with stools or dealing with the extra fabric. Christine Haworth's costumes were fussy, with Season Fairies in over-decorated layers of frilled netting. Toer van Schayk's sets used acid 1940s colours and slightly forced perspective. Yet the ballet was brightly danced. On opening night, Cojocaru and Kobborg gave warm, clean performances, though both were still growing into their roles. A year later, both had developed in confidence, musical timing and sheer radiance, dancing the ballroom scene with dreamy tenderness. Sleep and Dowell made starry but exaggerated Stepsisters, with Soares a lively Helpmann Sister in another cast.

In January 2004, the Company staged an all-Balanchine programme of *Agon*, *The Prodigal Son* and *Symphony in C* in tribute to the choreographer's centenary. Guillem made a glamorous but unduly flirty Siren, dancing against the grain of this fierce parable. In the same role, Yanowsky danced with steely continuity of movement. The Siren's characteristic walk, hips thrusting forward, was blatant but deliberate: nothing exaggerated, everything designed. Stepping back from Putrov's Prodigal, she snatched herself away, with a threat of violence in her quickness. During the duet, Putrov kept his whole body focused on Yanowsky, twitching himself back in moments of guilty repulsion. Robbed and stripped, he pressed himself into the ground, shaky at the knees: not just naked but shamed and shivering cold.

As Putrov was showing new maturity, Cuthbertson grew up fast. A long-limbed dancer, with clean lines and springy strength to her feet and back, she had won the Young British Dancer of the Year while still at The Royal Ballet School. For *Symphony in C*, she replaced the pregnant Bussell in the second movement. On the first night, she was understandably tentative. At the next performance, twenty-four hours later, she had grown into her role. Her dancing was smoothly textured, with a simplicity of gesture and long, full phrasing. That April, she danced her first Juliet, rising to the role's drama as well as its steps. She was partnered by Watson, a popular soloist given his first three-act lead. He made a coltish Romeo, almost goofy with love, though he was pushed by the role's fast, demanding steps.

Mason and Deborah MacMillan had considered reviving (and revising) *Isadora*, inevitably a controversial project. The balance of danced and spoken drama proved intractable, and *Anastasia* was revived instead. Just before his death, MacMillan had considered expanding the role of Rasputin for Mukhamedov. The notator Monica Parker, who had worked closely with MacMillan from the 1960s until his death, now adjusted the ballet. Rasputin was brought forward, a brooding presence, with Mukhamedov fierce-eyed but contained. Benjamin was an emphatic Anastasia, with Yoshida unexpectedly slinky as Mathilde Kchessinskaya, the Tsar's favourite ballerina. The dramatic instinct of Royal Ballet dancers was underlined on the first night. That summer, Mukhamedov returned in *Mayerling* – less athletic than before, but compellingly dramatic. He received an ovation, with a deluge of flowers to rival that in Collier's last *Giselle*.

Daphnis and Chloë was the last new production of the season, part of an imaginative programme marking seventy-five years since the death of Diaghilev. Craxton's designs were restored, with the painter returning to brighten his own bold colours. Reviving this ballet, Mason brought back more than Craxton's sunbaked Greece. The sense of sacred landscape had returned. As the corps danced their simple chain dances, winding through Ravel's lush score, the stage glowed with belief. Federico Bonelli, who had joined the Company that season, was the first Daphnis of this revival. He was ideally cast: a dancer of soft, unforced lyricism, with a velvet flow of movement and an essential innocence onstage.

Daphnis was followed by three Diaghilev revivals. Several of the Company's men bounded through *Le Spectre de la rose*, with Acosta and Putrov outstanding. Yanowsky was a charismatic Nymph in *L'Après-midi d'un faune*. The programme ended with *Les Noces*. Nijinska's ballet had always been carefully kept at The

Royal Ballet, but this was an astounding revival. Footwork had a fierce precision, jumps explosive as well as buoyant. The ballet builds in intensity: throughout this run, the corps seemed to start where they had left off at the last performance, achieving an unstoppable force. Here, as in Daphnis, conviction came from careful coaching, and from rising technical standards. In two years, Mason had had a transforming effect on her company.

That change became clearer with the next season. 2004–2005 was Ashton year, the centenary of the founder choreographer's birth. Mason planned a lavish celebration, reviving ballets long out of repertory. This honoured Ashton, but it also tightened the Company's technique and style. 'The Makarova *Sleeping Beauty* was supposed to produce a unified style across the Company,' says Lesley Collier, now Répétiteur to The Royal Ballet. 'And it did – but that was just one production. Now we're working across a whole season, so we can really lay foundations.' This repertory was visibly good for the dancers, challenging and strengthening their technique. 'To their astonishment,' smiles Mason, 'ballets that were made in the 1950s were very complicated and *very* challenging. They realised that, fifty years ago, people were doing tricky things. And I think that's *healthy*. When the Dorabellas [in *Enigma Variations*] started, they asked, "How do I run and travel?" And you say, "Well, just run on pointe. Yes, go on, keep running!"'

The Ashton centenary started abroad, with a visit to New York. The Royal Ballet returned to the Met for the Lincoln Center's Ashton Celebration programme, a season including performances by Birmingham Royal Ballet, Kumakawa's K Ballet and the Joffrey Ballet of Chicago. The whole season was warmly received; Cojocaru and Kobborg were acclaimed in *Cinderella*, and a range of principals was admired in a series of short divertissements. Back in Europe, there was more Ashton at a Paris Opéra gala celebrating the hundredth anniversary of the Entente Cordiale between Britain and France. Dancers from both companies appeared together in a series of Ashton numbers.

The 2004–5 season opened in October, with a triple bill of MacMillan's *Requiem*, Ashton's *A Wedding Bouquet* and *Les*

Noces. *A Wedding Bouquet*, with its mix of dance and dottiness, non sequiturs and characterisation, had often been overacted. Here it was lightly and spontaneously danced. Kobborg made a superbly sleazy Bridegroom, sidling and insinuating his way through his tango solo. Rojo's Julia had an air of doglike devotion, while Yanowsky's tipsy Josephine seemed carried away with surprise at her own antics.

Sylvia was the biggest undertaking of the Ashton centenary, the recovery of a full-length ballet not performed for thirty-nine years. Christopher Newton pieced the ballet together, working from rehearsal film, from his own and other dancers' memories. The sumptuous Ironside settings were carefully restored, with additional designs by Peter Farmer to cover any gaps. The Delibes score was less tenderly handled, given an oompah emphasis by conductor Graham Bond. At later performances, Ben Pope, more responsive to Delibes's lilting accents, also revealed more substance in Ashton's choreography.

Sylvia, a lavish and popular production, was a tough challenge for the dancers, and for Sylvia most of all. This 'garland for Fonteyn' was planned for a ballerina who would take charge of it, who had the strength and variety for the ballet's seven contrasting solos. Sylvia must go from Amazon to lover via victim and pretend seductress; the three 2004 Sylvias all caught aspects of the role. Bussell, in her first full-length ballet after maternity leave, danced with expansive grace but variable focus, losing the attack needed to clinch a phrase, a dramatic insight. Nuñez, livelier if not always musical, paced the duet beautifully, drawing its gestures into expressive phrases. Yanowsky, bold and confident, showed greatest command of the ballet as a whole. Around these three, the Company showed rising technical standards. 'It's hard,' acknowledged Vanessa Palmer, preparing to dance a huntress. 'It's *really* hard. We were all thinking it would be like *Ondine* – wave a scarf around and look divine in a long wig and a push-up bra. But no, it's *hard*. There we all are, with our bows and arrows, doing five fouettés and a temps levé in the wrong direction . . .'

Another Ashton programme followed, with *Scènes de ballet* and *Daphnis* framing a series of divertissements. These included two numbers from *Devil's Holiday*, a ballet that Ashton himself never saw. Made in 1939 for the Ballet Russe de Monte Carlo, the ballet's London premiere was cancelled when war was declared. The ninety-year-old Frederic Franklin, who had danced in that first cast, reconstructed two dances. The man's solo is all unfurling lines, with swooning falls to his knees. In the duet, the lovers float and slide, bending to right and left. Laura Morera and Martin Harvey danced with soft spontaneity. This bill also included the Awakening pas de deux Ashton had made for *The Sleeping Beauty*, with Bussell and Cope regal and tender in the call and response of its mirrored steps. Rojo's account of Ashton's *Isadora* waltzes divided opinion. Many admired the drama of her slow-paced, emphatic dancing; others found it operatic and exaggerated. So many short works allowed Mason to show a range of principals and soloists. Bonelli partnered Sarah Lamb in a ravishing account of the *Thaïs* duet. Lamb, a principal with the Boston Ballet, joined the Royal as a First Soloist and quickly moved into leading roles. She and Bonelli flowed effortlessly through this perfumed duet, her bourrées dreamily smooth.

A new unity of company style became clear with *Swan Lake*, back after two years and improved almost beyond recognition. The corps of swans had developed a collective poetry. A current of energy flowed through their dances, held in the new pliancy of backs, the new clarity of footwork. The national dances, not traditionally a Royal Ballet strong point, now had exuberant attack. Howells and Morera danced a sensational Neapolitan. There was a new gloss on the whole ballet, with several principals rethinking their roles. Cojocaru, still more Swan Princess than Swan Queen, produced some creamily beautiful dancing, while Benjamin showed the duality of swan and woman throughout the ballet. The greatest change was in Yanowsky. It had always been hard to find partners for this long-limbed, grandly built dancer. Kenneth Greve, a guest artist from Denmark, is six feet four inches tall; with such strong support, Yanowsky was free to dance with fresh abandon, opening up her torso with powerful expressive effect.

La Fille mal gardée made a welcome return in January 2005, with

Nuñez making a buoyant debut as Lise. The Company's dancing was fresh and confident, with Tuckett now an appealing, sweet-tempered Widow Simone. Throughout the season, dancers had been improving, building strength from one production to another. Good performances became better. Rojo, already a fine Manon, found new wit and depth for the next revival. Her Manon was appallingly funny in the brothel scene: a kitten with grand designs. When her rich protector G.M. gave her a bracelet, she tilted her wrist to let the diamonds catch the light, careful to let her hand rest on his thigh; an instant later, she cast a glance over her shoulder, to keep Des Grieux in line. Rojo made a natural flirt, entirely sure of herself and right out of her depth – it simply didn't occur to this Manon that she might be heading for disaster.

This happy season had its dramas, and its disappointments. A new Wheeldon ballet had been scheduled for March 2005, but had to be cancelled when the choreographer fell ill with a viral infection. The new work was replaced by Wheeldon's *Pavane*, elegantly danced but now looking very thin, and Balanchine's *Duo Concertant*, sweetly danced by Cojocaru and Kobborg, with musicians Peter Manning and Philip Gammon. In 2005, Gammon celebrated forty years as a pianist with The Royal Ballet: he had worked closely with Ashton and MacMillan, played for classes and rehearsals, played on stage in 'one of Ian Spurling's zany costumes' for *Elite Syncopations*. In one Los Angeles performance, he had played an ancient piano for *A Month in the Country*, only to find the middle D-flat key snapping off in his hand. He had to improvise his way through the rest of the ballet – which concludes in a minor key, making it difficult to manage without the missing note.[6]

Sharing a programme with *Duo Concertant*, *Rhapsody* was revived with new designs by Jessica Curtis. Her backdrop, a beautifully painted cloudy sky, suggested a non-specific location: it gave the ballet too much and too little context. The costumes were washed-out pastels and, as so often at Covent Garden, lighting was murky. Even so, the ballet outshone its settings. Benjamin, having a superb season, danced the ballerina role with unexpected flair and speed. One solo is full of stops, snapping from flat-out speed to held positions. Benjamin's stops were so sharp that they seemed almost to knock her off balance, propelling her joyfully into the rest of the dance. Acosta, a virtuoso dancer, lacked the wit for Baryshnikov's role. After a tentative debut, Putrov grew into the role, with arrow-sharp line and mercurial shifts of direction.

Mason turned to Christopher Bruce for the other new work of this season. Bruce, modern-dance choreographer and former director of Rambert Dance Company, had the experience to cope with Covent Garden's demanding stage, but *Three Songs – Two Voices* was a vague piece of nostalgia, a jigging evocation of Woodstock set to Nigel Kennedy's arrangement of Jimi Hendrix. The search for new choreography remains painfully difficult.

The 2004–5 season ended with revivals of *Les Biches* and *Symphonic Variations*, two of the Company's most elusive classics, and with Bussell's debut in *A Month in the Country*. Her dancing was glorious, torso curving through each change of direction, footwork blithely expressive. Bussell has grown as an actress, showing new dramatic involvement in *Manon* and in *Cinderella*, where she is less a waif than a lonely, capable girl. Her first Natalia Petrovna, still tentative, was best in snatched reactions. She was partnered by Rupert Pennefather, a tall young dancer with a strong technique. Dancing Beliaev's wistful solo to Polish themes, he looked caught up in the dance, as if these steps were his train of thought.

If *A Month in the Country* was promising, the rest of the bill felt like a homecoming. After a whole season of Ashtonian bending and quick footwork, the corps were fast and stylish in *Les Biches*. Making her debut as the Hostess, Deirdre Chapman was crisp and knowing, giving jazzy emphasis to the rhythms of the Rag Mazurka. There was still inhibition at the start of *Symphonic Variations*, but it vanished when Cojocaru and Bonelli began their duet, the ballet floating into radiance. Morera, Hatley, Kobborg and Steven McRae – just out of The Royal Ballet School, stepping into a virtuoso role with simple ease – danced their roles with assurance and love. Audiences did not want to let this *Symphonic Variations* go: throughout the run, they demanded more curtain calls after the lights went up, cheering the return of one of the Company's defining works.

*

When I started work on this book, I knew it would have a happy ending. Things had looked up with Stretton's departure: the Company steadied itself and regained its confidence. The surprise has been just how happy an ending this is. Heading for its seventy-fifth anniversary, the Company looks stronger under Mason's leadership than at any time since the 1970s. The Company itself has changed. Royal Ballet School dancers like Pennefather or Cuthbertson have been joined by dancers from all over the world. Nevertheless, Mason – whose Directorship has now been extended until 2010 – has restored the sense of shared style. In this recovered company, you can see qualities learned in one production and carried into the next. The whores in *Manon* show footwork, and musical timing, that promise well for the anniversary production of *The Sleeping Beauty*. After two controversial *Beauty*s, Mason plans to return to the old Royal Ballet text, with many of its Ashton additions, and to an updated form of the Messel designs. The production is scheduled for 15 May 2006, seventy-five years after the Company's first performance at Sadler's Wells. Preparing for its birthday, The Royal Ballet has reason to celebrate.

Chronology

Events and company premieres. Ballets made for the company in **bold**.
All premieres for the main company unless otherwise stated.

1928	13 December	**Les Petits riens** danced as curtain-raiser to *Hansel and Gretel*, Old Vic Theatre (choreography by Ninette de Valois)
1929	9 May	**The Picnic** (de Valois)
	19 December	**Hommage aux belles viennoises** (de Valois)
1930	18 December	**Suite of Dances** (de Valois)
1931	6 January	Sadler's Wells Theatre opens
	5 May	First full evening of ballet at the Old Vic: *Danse sacrée et danse profane*, **The Jackdaw and the Pigeons**, *Scène de ballet* from *Faust, Cephalus and Procris* (all choreography by de Valois)
	15 May	First evening of ballet at Sadler's Wells
	22 September	**Regatta** (Frederick Ashton)
		Job (de Valois)
	23 November	*Fête polonaise* (de Valois)
	16 December	**The Jew in the Bush** (de Valois)
1932	30 January	**Narcissus and Echo** (de Valois)
		Rout (de Valois)
	4 March	*Le Spectre de la rose* (Michel Fokine)
		Italian Suite (de Valois)
	8 March	*Les Sylphides* (Fokine)
	11 March	*The Enchanted Grove* (Rupert Doone)
	19 March	**Nursery Suite** (de Valois)
	24 September	To Copenhagen for first overseas performances
	5 October	*Le Lac des cygnes*, Act 2 (Lev Ivanov)
	11 October	**Douanes** (de Valois)
	17 October	*The Lord of Burleigh* (Ashton)
	1 November	*The Origin of Design* (de Valois)
	15 November	*The Scorpions of Ysit* (de Valois)
1933	17 January	*Pomona* (Ashton)
	7 February	**The Birthday of Oberon** (de Valois)
	21 March	*Coppélia* Acts 1 and 2 (Ivanov)
	26 September	**The Wise and Foolish Virgins** (de Valois)
		Blue Bird pas de deux from *The Sleeping Princess* (Marius Petipa)

	24 October	*Carnaval* (Fokine)
	30 October	*La Création du monde* (de Valois)
	5 December	**Les Rendezvous** (Ashton)
1934	1 January	*Giselle* (after Jean Coralli and Jules Perrot)
	30 January	*Casse-Noisette* (Ivanov)
	3 April	**The Haunted Ballroom** (de Valois)
	9 October	**The Jar** (de Valois)
	20 November	*Le Lac des cygnes* (Petipa and Ivanov)
	19 December	**Uncle Remus** (Sara Patrick)
1935	26 March	*Rio Grande* (Ashton)
	20 May	**The Rake's Progress** (de Valois)
	June	Start of first regional tour by the Vic-Wells Ballet. Alicia Markova gives her last performance as a member of the Company in September. Frederick Ashton becomes the Company's resident choreographer.
	8 October	*Façade* (Ashton)
	26 November	**Le Baiser de la fée** (Ashton)
1936	10 January	**The Gods go a'Begging** (de Valois)
	11 February	**Apparitions** (Ashton)
	17 April	**Barabau** (de Valois)
	13 October	**Prometheus** (de Valois)
	10 November	**Nocturne** (Ashton)
1937	16 February	**Les Patineurs** (Ashton)
	27 April	**A Wedding Bouquet** (Ashton)
	15 June	**Checkmate** (de Valois)
1938	27 January	**Horoscope** (Ashton)
	7 April	**Le Roi nu** (de Valois)
	10 May	**The Judgement of Paris** (Ashton)
	10 November	**Harlequin in the Street** (Ashton)
1939	2 February	*The Sleeping Princess*
	27 April	**Cupid and Psyche** (Ashton)
	3 September	Britain declares war on Germany
1940	23 January	**Dante Sonata** (Ashton)
	15 April	*Coppélia* (Petipa/Cechetti), new production of Acts 1–3
	24 April	**The Wise Virgins** (Ashton)
	6 May	Start of propaganda tour of Holland. Germany invades Holland on 10 May 1940
	4 July	**The Prospect Before Us** (de Valois)
1941	27 January	**The Wanderer** (Ashton)
	28 May	**Orpheus and Eurydice** (de Valois)
1942	14 January	**Comus** (Robert Helpmann)
	19 May	*Hamlet* (Helpmann)
	24 November	**The Birds** (Helpmann)
1943	6 April	**The Quest** (Ashton)

	25 October	*Promenade* (de Valois)
1944	20 June	*Le Festin de l'araignée* (Andrée Howard)
	26 October	*Miracle in the Gorbals* (Helpmann)
1945	8 May	Victory in Europe declared
	17 October	It was announced a smaller, second company would be established and remain at Sadler's Wells Theatre. Initially called the Sadler's Wells Opera Ballet.
1946	20 February	Sadler's Wells Ballet reopen the Royal Opera House, Covent Garden, with a new production of *The Sleeping Beauty* (Petipa)
	8 April	First performance by Sadler's Wells Theatre Ballet, at Sadler's Wells
	10 April	*Adam Zero* (Robert Helpmann)
	24 April	*Symphonic Variations* (Ashton)
	12 June	*Giselle* (new production)
	12 November	*Les Sirènes* (Ashton)
1947		From 1947 the Sadler's Wells Opera Ballet was known as Sadler's Wells Theatre Ballet.
	6 February	*The Three-Cornered Hat* (Léonide Massine)
	27 February	*La Boutique fantasque* (Massine)
	25 March	*La Fête étrange* (Howard) for Sadler's Wells Theatre Ballet (the touring company) Covent Garden production 11 December 1958.
	19 May	*Adieu* (John Cranko) for Sadler's Wells Theatre Ballet
	26 November	*Mam'zelle Angot* (Massine)
1948	11 February	*Scènes de ballet* (Ashton)
	6 April	*Children's Corner* (Cranko) for Sadler's Wells Theatre Ballet
	25 June	*The Clock Symphony* (Massine)
	25 November	*Don Juan* (Ashton)
	23 December	*Cinderella* (Ashton)
1949	18 July	*Sea Change* (Cranko) for Sadler's Wells Theatre Ballet
	9 October	First visit to North America, opening at the Metropolitan Opera House, New York with *The Sleeping Beauty*
	20 December	*Beauty and the Beast* (Cranko) for Sadler's Wells Theatre Ballet
1950	20 February	*Don Quixote* (de Valois)
	5 April	*Ballet Imperial* (George Balanchine) Theatre Ballet Covent Garden production 22 September 1959
	5 May	*Ballabile* (Roland Petit)
	14 September	*Trumpet Concerto* (Balanchine) for Sadler's Wells Theatre Ballet
	19 December	*Pastorale* (Cranko) for Sadler's Wells Theatre Ballet

1951	13 March	*Pineapple Poll* (Cranko) for Sadler's Wells Theatre Ballet
	5 April	*Daphnis and Chloë* (Ashton)
	8 May	*Harlequin in April* (Cranko) made for Sadler's Wells Theatre Ballet. Covent Garden production 5 March 1959
	9 July	*Tiresias* (Ashton)
	12 December	*Donald of the Burthens* (Massine)
1952	4 March	*A Mirror for Witches* (Howard)
	4 April	*Bonne-Bouche* (Cranko)
	21 April	*Reflection* (Cranko) for Sadler's Wells Theatre Ballet
	3 September	*Sylvia* (Ashton)
	19 September	*Ile des Sirènes* (Alfred Rodrigues) for Sadler's Wells Theatre Ballet
	18 December	*Le Lac des cygnes*, new production
1953	3 March	*The Shadow* (Cranko)
	9 April	*Veneziana* (Howard)
	2 June	*Homage to The Queen* (Ashton)
	5 June	*Blood Wedding* (Rodrigues) for Sadler's Wells Theatre Ballet
1954	25 February	*The Lady and the Fool* (Cranko) made for Sadler's Wells Theatre Ballet. Covent Garden production 9 June 1955
	2 March	*Coppélia*, new production
	24 May	*Café des Sports* (Rodrigues) for Sadler's Wells Theatre Ballet
	23 August	*The Firebird* (Fokine)
1955	6 January	*Rinaldo and Armida* (Ashton) *Variations on a Theme of Purcell* (Ashton)
	18 January	*Danses concertantes* (Kenneth MacMillan) made for Sadler's Wells Theatre Ballet. Covent Garden production 13 March 1959
	1 April	*Madame Chrysanthème* (Ashton)
	26 May	*House of Birds* (MacMillan) for Sadler's Wells Theatre Ballet
	13 October	*Saudades* (Rodrigues) for Sadler's Wells Theatre Ballet
1956	15 February	*La Péri* (Ashton)
	1 March	*Noctambules* (MacMillan)
	5 May	Twenty-fifth birthday performance, including premiere of *Birthday Offering* (Ashton)
	29 May	*Somnambulism* (MacMillan) for Sadler's Wells Theatre Ballet
	7 June	*Solitaire* (MacMillan) made for Sadler's Wells Theatre Ballet. Covent Garden production 17 September 1957.

	27 August	*The Miraculous Mandarin* (Rodrigues)
	31 October	Royal Charter granted. Sadler's Wells Ballet renamed The Royal Ballet. Public announcement of the Charter and name change on 16 January 1957
1957	1 January	*The Prince of the Pagodas* (Cranko)
	18 March	The Sadler's Wells Theatre Ballet changed to The Royal Ballet (Touring Section) and was usually referred to as the Touring Company
	26 March	*Petrushka* (Fokine)
	26 December	*A Blue Rose* (Peter Wright) for The Royal Ballet (Touring Section)
		The Angels (Cranko) for The Royal Ballet (Touring Section)
1958	2 January	*The Burrow* (MacMillan) for The Royal Ballet (Touring Section)
	20 August	*Agon* (MacMillan)
	2 September	*La belle Dame sans merci* (Andrée Howard)
	27 October	*Ondine* (Ashton)
1959	10 March	*La Valse* (Ashton)
	19 October	*Antigone* (Cranko)
	10 December	*Sweeney Todd* (Cranko) for The Royal Ballet (Touring Section)
1960	28 January	*La Fille mal gardée* (Ashton)
	12 April	*Le Baiser de la fée* (MacMillan)
	30 September	*Giselle*, new production
	10 November	*The Invitation* (MacMillan) made for The Royal Ballet (Touring Section)
		Covent Garden production 13 December 1962
1961	14 February	*The Two Pigeons* (Ashton) made for The Royal Ballet (Touring Section)
		Covent Garden production 16 October 1962
	15 June	The Royal Ballet makes its first visit to Russia, opening in Leningrad with *Ondine*
	16 June	Rudolf Nureyev defects from the Soviet Union
	15 September	*Diversions* (MacMillan)
		Jabez and the Devil (Alfred Rodrigues)
	12 December	*Perséphone* (Ashton)
1962	21 February	Rudolf Nureyev dances *Giselle* with Margot Fonteyn, starting a legendary partnership and a long association with the Royal Ballet
	3 May	*Napoli* divertissement and flower festival at Genzano pas de deux (Bournonville)
		The Rite of Spring (MacMillan)
	11 July	*The Good-Humoured Ladies* (Massine)
1963	15 February	*Symphony* (MacMillan)

	12 March	*Night Tryst* (Alan Carter)
		Marguerite and Armand (Ashton)
	26 March	*Elektra* (Helpmann)
		Ninette de Valois retires as Director of The Royal Ballet at the end of the 1962–63 season, succeeded by Frederick Ashton.
	27 November	*La Bayadère*, 'The Kingdom of the Shades' (Petipa)
	12 December	*Swan Lake*, new production
1964	12 February	*La Création du Monde* (MacMillan) for The Royal Ballet (Touring Section)
	2 April	*The Dream* (Ashton)
		Images of Love (MacMillan)
	7 May	*Serenade* (George Balanchine)
	10 July	*Raymonda* (Pepita) for The Royal Ballet (Touring Section)
	2 December	*Les Biches* (Bronislava Nijinska)
1965	9 February	*Romeo and Juliet* (MacMillan)
	24 March	*Monotones* (Ashton)
		Polovtsian Dances from *Prince Igor* (Fokine)
1966	10 February	*Brandenburg Nos 2 and 4* (Cranko)
	18 February	*Card Game* (Cranko)
	23 March	*Les Noces* (Nijinska)
	25 April	*Monotones* 1 and 2 (Ashton)
	7 May	*Raymonda* Act 3 (Petipa) for The Royal Ballet (Touring Section).
		Covent Garden production 27 March 1969
	19 May	*Song of the Earth* (MacMillan)
	15 November	*Apollo* (Balanchine)
1967	25 January	*Shadowplay* (Antony Tudor)
	23 February	*Paradise Lost* (Roland Petit)
	26 May	*Concerto* (MacMillan) for The Royal Ballet Touring Company.
		Covent Garden production 17 November 1970
	18 December	*Sylvia* (one-act version)
1968	9 January	*Jazz Calendar* (Ashton)
	29 February	*The Nutcracker* (new production)
	25 October	*Enigma Variations* (Ashton)
	12 November	*Lilac Garden* (Tudor)
	17 December	*The Sleeping Beauty*, new production
1969	21 February	*Olympiad* (MacMillan)
	26 March	*Pélléas and Mélisande* (Petit)
1970		The Royal Ballet (Touring Section), the Touring Company, became The Royal Ballet New Group.
	9 February	*Lament of the Waves* (Ashton)
	2 March	*The Ropes of Time* (Rudi van Dantzig)

Frederick Ashton retires as Director of the Royal
Ballet at the end of the 1969–70 season, succeeded
by Kenneth MacMillan. The Royal Ballet reorganised
as one company, with a touring section called the New
Group.

	19 October	*Dances at a Gathering* (Jerome Robbins)
	9 November	**Field Figures** (Glen Tetley) for Royal Ballet New Group
		Covent Garden production 16 November 1971
	27 November	**Checkpoint** (MacMillan) for Royal Ballet New Group
1971	17 February	*Swan Lake*, revised production
	11 March	*Giselle*, revised production
	22 July	**Anastasia** (MacMillan)
	14 December	*Afternoon of a Faun* (Robbins)
1972	19 January	**Triad** (MacMillan)
	15 February	*Poème de l'extase* (Cranko)
	19 May	**Ballade** (MacMillan) for Royal Ballet New Group
	26 July	**Laborintus** (Glen Tetley)
	12 October	**The Poltroon** (MacMillan) for Royal Ballet New Group
	15 November	*Requiem Canticles* (Robbins)
		The Walk to the Paradise Garden (Ashton)
1973	25 January	*The Four Temperaments* (Balanchine)
		Prodigal Son (Balanchine)
		Agon (Balanchine)
	15 March	*The Sleeping Beauty*, new production
	19 July	*The Seven Deadly Sins* (MacMillan)
	10 October	*In the Night* (Robbins)
1974	7 March	**Manon** (MacMillan)
	7 October	**Elite Syncopations** (MacMillan)
1975	31 January	**Four Schumann Pieces** (Hans van Manen)
	4 March	*The Concert* (Robbins)
	5 March	**The Four Seasons** (MacMillan)
	April–May	The Royal Ballet's first tour to Korea and Japan
	11 December	**Rituals** (MacMillan)
1976	7 February	*Twilight* (van Manen)
	12 February	**A Month in the Country** (Ashton)
	28 September	The Royal Ballet New Group became The Sadler's Wells Royal Ballet with headquarters at The Sadler's Wells Theatre.
	18 November	**Voluntaries** (Tetley)
	23 November	*Adagio Hammerklavier* (van Manen)
1977	16 February	*The Taming of the Shrew* (Cranko)
	31 March	*The Fourth Symphony* (John Neumeier)
		Kenneth MacMillan retires as Director of the Royal

		Ballet at the end of the 1976–77 season, succeeded by Norman Morrice.
	14 October	*The Sleeping Beauty*, new production
1978	14 February	**Mayerling** (MacMillan)
	16 March	**The Outsider** (David Bintley) for Sadler's Wells Royal Ballet
	12 May	**6.6.78** (MacMillan) for Sadler's Wells Royal Ballet
1979	15 March	*La Fin du jour* (MacMillan)
	19 April	*Liebeslieder Walzer* (Balanchine)
	24 August	**Playground** (MacMillan) for Sadler's Wells Royal Ballet
	5 December	*Swan Lake*, new production
1980	13 March	**Gloria** (MacMillan)
	29 April	*Troy Game* (Robert North)
		My Brother, My Sisters (MacMillan)
		Adieu (Bintley)
	3 July	*Giselle*, new production
	4 August	**Rhapsody** (Ashton)
	27 November	**Dances of Albion: Dark Night Glad Day** (Tetley)
		Dark Elegies (Tudor)
1981	30 April	**Isadora** (MacMillan)
	5 May	Golden Jubilee performance of *The Sleeping Beauty*, followed by a Fiftieth Anniversary gala programme on 29 and 30 May 1981
	3 December	*Illuminations* (Ashton)
1982	2 March	**Quartet** (second movement) (MacMillan) for Sadler's Wells Royal Ballet
	16 March	**L'Invitation au voyage** (Michael Corder)
	7 April	**Quartet** (complete) (MacMillan) for Sadler's Wells Royal Ballet
	11 June	**Orpheus** (MacMillan)
	2 December	*Konservatoriet* (August Bournonville)
		The Tempest (Nureyev)
1983	3 March	**Valley of Shadows** (MacMillan)
		Requiem (MacMillan)
	19 April	**Varii capricci** (Ashton)
	May	Company's first visit to China
	7 December	**Consort Lessons** (Bintley)
		Midsummer (Richard Alston)
1984	24 February	**Different Drummer** (MacMillan)
	11 April	*Return to the Strange Land* (Jirí Kylián)
		Fleeting Figures (Derek Deane)
	24 July	**Party Game** (Corder)
	2 August	**A Broken Set of Rules** (Ashley Page)
	17 November	**Young Apollo** (Bintley)

	20 December	*The Nutcracker*, new production
1985	9 March	**Number Three** (Corder)
	25 July	**Half the House** (Jennifer Jackson)
	26 July	**Frankenstein, the Modern Prometheus** (Wayne Eagling)
	30 October	**The Sons of Horus** (Bintley)
	28 November	*Giselle*, new production
1986	8 May	*Le Baiser de la fée* (MacMillan) second production

Norman Morrice retires as Director of The Royal
Ballet at the end of the 1986–87 season, succeeded by
Anthony Dowell.

	12 July	**Galanteries** (Bintley)
	8 October	*Opus 19: The Dreamer* (Robbins)
	2 December	**Beauty and the Beast** (Eagling)
1987	12 March	*Swan Lake*, new production
	22 July	**Pursuit** (Page)
	16 December	*Cinderella*, new production
1988	9 March	*Bugaku* (Balanchine)
		Still Life at the Penguin Café (Bintley)
	20 October	**The Trial of Prometheus** (Bintley)
	22 November	**The Spirit of Fugue** (Bintley)
1989	14 March	*Rubies*, also called *Capriccio for Piano and Orchestra* (Balanchine)
	18 May	*La Bayadère* (Petipa) three acts, new production
	11 July	**Piano** (Page)
	6 October	*Other Dances* (Robbins)
	7 December	**The Prince of the Pagodas** (MacMillan)
1990	1 August	**The Planets** (Bintley)
		Enclosure (Tuckett)
		Farewell pas de deux (MacMillan)
	September	The Sadler's Wells Royal Ballet name changed to Birmingham Royal Ballet with the Company moved headquarters to the Birmingham Hippodrome.
	29 November	*Stravinsky Violin Concerto* (Balanchine)
		Bloodlines (Page)
1991	7 February	*Danses concertantes,* new production
		Winter Dreams (MacMillan)
	1 May	**Cyrano** (Bintley)
	20 November	**Present Histories** (Tuckett)
		Stoics Quartet (Jonathan Burrows)
		Symphony in C (Balanchine)
1992	13 February	*In the middle, somewhat elevated* (William Forsythe)
	19 March	**The Judas Tree** (MacMillan)
	29 October	Kenneth MacMillan dies backstage during a performance of *Mayerling*
	4 December	*The Tales of Beatrix Potter* (Ashton)

1993	11 February	*Tombeaux* (Bintley)
	12 May	*Don Quixote* (Petipa)
	4 June	*La Ronde* (Tetley)
	23 October	*Fanfare* (Matthew Hart)
		If this is still a problem (Tuckett)
		Hermann Schermann (Forsythe)
1994	18 June	*Fearful Symmetries* (Page)
1995	24 January	*Duo Concertant* (Balanchine) on Dance Bites tour. First performed at Covent Garden on 30 March 1995.
	30 March	*Ebony Concerto* (Page)
	27 April	*Firstext/Steptext* (Forsythe)
		Rhapsody, new production
	15 July	*Peter and the Wolf* (Hart)
	9 December	*Mr Worldly Wise* (Twyla Tharp)
1996	7 February	*Dances with Death* (Hart)
	18 October	*Pavane pour une infante défunte* (Christopher Wheeldon)
	26 November	*Two-Part Invention* (Page)
1997	13 February	*Push Comes to Shove* (Tharp)
	3 March	*Room of Cooks* (Page) made for Dance Bites tour
	30 April	*Amores* (Tetley)
	14 July 1997	Farewell Gala. Royal Opera House closes for redevelopment
1998	17 January	*Cheating, Lying, Stealing* (Page)
	23 February	*A Royal Ballet* (Wheeldon) made for Dance Bites tour
		Puirt-a-beul (Tuckett) made for Dance Bites tour
	4 November	*Sawdust and Tinsel* (Page)
1999	3 March	*Towards Poetry* (Mark Baldwin) made for Dance Bites tour
	26 July	*The Turn of the Screw* (Tuckett)
	1 December	Reopening of the Royal Opera House
	8 December	*A Stranger's Taste* (Siobhan Davies)
		Hidden Variables (Page)
2000	29 February	*Les Rendezvous,* new production
	6 May	*L'Après-midi d'un faune* (Vaslav Nijinsky)
		Jeux (after Nijinsky)
	6 June	*Symbiont(s)* (Wayne McGregor)
	28 October	*Dance Variations* (Corder)
2001	7 March	*This House Will Burn* (Page)
	8 March	Death of Ninette de Valois, aged 102
		Anthony Dowell retires as Director of The Royal Ballet at the end of the 2000–1 season, succeeded by Ross Stretton
	23 October	*Don Quixote,* new production
	22 November	*Onegin* (Cranko)

2002	26 January	*Beyond Bach* (Stephen Baynes)
		The Leaves are Fading (Tudor)
	4 March	*Por vos Muero* (Nacho Duato)
		Remanso (Duato)
		The Vertiginous Thrill of Exactitude (Forsythe)
	18 May	**Tryst** (Wheeldon)
		Ross Stretton retires as Director of the Royal Ballet in August 2002, succeeded by Monica Mason.
	22 October	*Gong* (Mark Morris)
		Carmen (Mats Ek)
2003	13 January	*Sinfonietta* (Kylián)
	29 April	*Danses concertantes*, new production
	21 May	**Les Saisons** (Bintley)
	13 November	*Devil's Holiday* (Ashton)
	15 November	*Polyphonia* (Wheeldon)
	3 December	**Proverb** (Tuckett)
		Broken Fall (Russell Maliphant)
		Qualia (McGregor)
2004	4 November	*Sylvia*, new production
2005	12 May	**Three Songs, Two Voices** (Christopher Bruce)

Notes

CHAPTER ONE PREPARATION

1 Quoted in Mary Clarke, *The Sadler's Wells Ballet*, A & C Black, 1955, p. 4
2 Alastair Macaulay conversation.
3 Ninette de Valois, *Step by Step*, W. H. Allen, 1977, p. 195
4 'Dame Ninette de Valois' obituary evening, BBC Radio 3, March 2001
5 'Dame Ninette de Valois', Radio 3
6 *The Sadler's Wells Ballet*, p. 5
7 Julie Kavanagh, *Secret Muses*, Faber and Faber, 1996, p. 2
8 *Come Dance with Me*, The Lilliput Press, 1992, p. 10
9 Ninette de Valois, *Step by Step*, W. H. Allen, 1977, pp. 1, 3
10 *Come Dance with Me*, p. 37
11 *Come Dance with Me*, p. 33
12 Ninette de Valois, 'Lydia Lopokova and English ballet', in *Lydia Lopokova*, London, Weidenfeld and Nicolson, 1983, p. 106
13 *Covent Garden Book* No. 1, 1946–47, p. 63
14 *Step by Step*, p. 126
15 Margot Fonteyn, *Autobiography*, W. H. Allen, 1975, p. 48
16 Ninette de Valois, *Invitation To the Ballet*, John Lane/The Bodley Head, 1937, p. 58
17 Kathrine Sorley Walker, p. 149
18 Beth Genné, *The Making of a Choreographer: Ninette de Valois and Bar aux Folies-Bergère*, Studies in Dance History 12, 1996, p. 26
19 Beth Genné p. 34
20 'Dame Ninette de Valois', Radio 3
21 *The Sadler's Wells Ballet*, p. 38
22 Haskell, *The National Ballet*, A & C Black, 1943, p. 20; *The Sadler's Wells Ballet*, p. 6
23 *The Sadler's Wells Ballet*, p. 45
24 *Invitation to the Ballet*, pp. 75, 86
25 Laurence Olivier in Harcourt Williams, ed., *Vic-Wells: The Work of Lilian Baylis*, Cobden Sanderson, 1938, p. 28
26 Richard Findlater, *Lilian Baylis: The Lady of the Old Vic*, Allen Lane, 1975, p. 135
27 *Come Dance With Me*, pp. 79–80
28 Findlater, p. 205
29 Findlater, p. 206
30 Findlater, p. 206

31 *Come Dance With Me*, p. 80
32 *Come Dance With Me*, p. 82
33 David Vaughan, *Frederick Ashton and his Ballets*, second edition, Dance Books, 1999, p. 134
34 Letter to Mary Clarke, 25 January 2004
35 Fonteyn, p. 60
36 Richard Shead, *Constant Lambert*, Simon Publications, 1973, p. 86
37 Haskell, *The National Ballet*, p. 21; de Valois, 'Lydia Lopokova and English Ballet', p. 109
38 Haskell, *Balletomania: An Updated Version of the Ballet Classic*, Penguin, 1977, p. 168
39 Letter to Mary Clarke, 6 October 1993
40 Richard Shead, Simon Publications, 1973, p. 97
41 *The National Ballet*, p. 17
42 Zoë Dominic and John Selwyn Gilbert, *Frederick Ashton: a Choreographer and his Ballets*, George G. Harrap, 1971, p. 76
43 Beth Genné, p. 13
44 Fonteyn, p. 51
45 Annabel Farjeon, 'Choreographers: Dancing for de Valois and Ashton', in the *Routledge Dance Studies Reader*, ed. Alexandra Carter, Routledge, 1998, p. 25
46 MacMillan interviews, produced by Lynne Wake, ROH Collections
47 Frederick Ashton, interview with Alastair Macaulay, London, June 1984
48 *The Fonteyn Phenomenon*, conference papers, forthcoming. My thanks to Alastair Macaulay, who allowed me to consult this material.
49 Dominic and Gilbert, p. 76
50 Keith Money, *The Art of Margot Fonteyn*, second edition, Dance Books, 1975, unpaginated
51 *Come Dance With Me*, p. 118.
52 Interview with Michael White, *About the House*, February 2005, p. 25
53 *Step by Step*, p. 55
54 Kirstein, quoted *Ballet*, November 1951, p. 12
55 *The Sadler's Wells Ballet*, p. 14
56 ROH Collections
57 *The Sadler's Wells Ballet*, p. 54
58 *The Sadler's Wells Ballet*, p. 52

CHAPTER TWO BUILDING BRITISH BALLET

1 Beth Genné, 'Creating a Canon, Creating the "Classics" in Twentieth-Century British Ballet', *Dance Research* 8: 2, Winter 2000, pp. 132–62
2 P. W. Manchester and Iris Morley, *The Rose and the Star*, Victor Gollancz Ltd, 1949, p. 57
3 Evelyn Williams, quoted in *The Sadler's Wells Ballet*, p. 41
4 Kate Neatby, *Ninette de Valois and the Vic-Wells Ballet*, London, British-Continental Press, 1936, p. 8

5 Findlater, p. 251
6 'The Vic-Wells Ballet' in *Vic-Wells: The Work of Lilian Baylis*, p. 95
7 *Vic-Wells: A Ballet Progress*, London, Victor Gollancz Ltd, 1947, p. 11
8 *The Sadler's Wells Ballet*, pp. 69–70.
9 *The Sadler's Wells Ballet*, p. 72
10 Beth Genné, p. 61
11 Kathrine Sorley Walker, *Ninette de Valois: Idealist without Illusions*, Dance Books, 1998, p. 115
12 Sorley Walker, p. 115
13 'The Vic-Wells Ballet', p. 96
14 *Markova Remembers*, Hamish Hamilton, 1986, p. 44
15 *Markova Remembers*, p. 44
16 *Vic-Wells: A Ballet Progress*, p. 13
17 *Markova Remembers*, p. 45
18 *The Sadler's Wells Ballet*, p. 81
19 David Vaughan, p. 70
20 Findlater, p. 262
21 Shead, p. 98
22 'Lydia Lopokova and English Ballet', p. 113
23 *Markova Remembers*, pp. 45-46
24 Barbara Newman, *Striking a Balance: Dancers Talk About Dancing*, London, Elm Tree Books, 1982, p. 17
25 'Creating a Canon, Creating the "Classics"', p. 140
26 *Come Dance With Me*, pp. 111–12
27 Fonteyn, p. 76
28 Fonteyn, p. 48.
29 *Vic-Wells: The Work of Lilian Baylis*, p. 100
30 Interview in television documentary *Tales of Helpmann*, directed by Don Featherstone, 1990
31 *Step by Step*, p. 65
32 *The Art of Margot Fonteyn*
33 *Gala Performance*, ed. Haskell et al., Collins, 1955, p. 43
34 David Vaughan, pp. 93–95
35 *Vic-Wells: A Ballet Progress*, p. 18
36 *Markova Remembers*, p. 47
37 *Come Dance With Me*, p. 65
38 *Invitation to the Ballet*, pp. 244–45
39 *Markova Remembers*, p. 45
40 Jasper Howlett, *Talking of Ballet*, Philip Allan & Co, undated, p. 50
41 Keith Money, *Fonteyn: the Making of a Legend*, London: William Collins Sons & Co Ltd, 1973, p. 27
42 *The Fonteyn Phenomenon*
43 Fonteyn, p. 42
44 Fonteyn, p. 54
45 *The Sadler's Wells Ballet*, p. 105n.

46 Sorley Walker, p. 185
47 Monica Mason interview. The exact wording varies from one Ballad Singer to another.
48 *Vic-Wells: A Ballet Progress*, p. 26
49 Elizabeth Salter, *Helpmann: The Authorised Biography of Sir Robert Helpmann, CBE*, Angus and Robertson, 1978, p. 64
50 Dominic and Gilbert, p. 223
51 Elizabeth Frank, *Margot Fonteyn*, Chatto & Windus, 1958, p. 29
52 Sorley Walker, p. 137
53 Clive Barnes, 'Frederick Ashton and his Ballets', *Dance Perspectives* 9, Winter 1961, p. 18
54 *Dancing Times*, October 2002, p. 67
55 Findlater, p. 255
56 *Vic-Wells: A Ballet Progress*, p. 26
57 *Gala Performance*, p. 40
58 *The Sadler's Wells Ballet*, p. 113
59 *The Art of Margot Fonteyn*
60 *Vic-Wells: A Ballet Progress*, p. 31
61 Fonteyn, p. 60
62 David Vaughan, p. 136
63 *The Sadler's Wells Ballet*, p. 126
64 Dominic and Gilbert, p. 55
65 Quoted in Alastair Macaulay, 'Dancing on Dry Ice', *Dancing Times*, February 1997, p. 415
66 *The Sadler's Wells Ballet*, p. 130
67 Barbara Newman, *Striking a Balance: Dancers Talk about Dancing*, London, Elm Tree Books/Hamish Hamilton, 1982, p. 91
68 Alastair Macaulay, 'Pamela May', *Dancing Times*, May 1997, p. 699
69 In conversation with Alastair Macaulay, 1997
70 Quoted Alastair Macaulay, 'Further Notes on Dance Classicism', *Dance Theatre Journal*, Spring 1997, vol. 13, no. 3, p. 28
71 *The Sadler's Wells Ballet*, pp. 137–38
72 Alastair Macaulay, 'Pamela May', *Dancing Times* May 1997, p. 701
73 Fonteyn, p. 77
74 Alastair Macaulay, 'The Sleeping Beauty – The British Connection', *Dancing Times*, September 2000, p. 1053
75 Cyril W. Beaumont, *The Sadler's Wells Ballet*, C. W. Beaumont, 1946, p. 78
76 Keith Money, *Fonteyn: The Making of a Legend*, p. 72
77 *Vic-Wells: A Ballet Progress*, pp. 87–88
78 *Gala Performance*, p. 73

CHAPTER THREE BALLET UNDER THE BOMBS

 1 *The Fonteyn Phenomenon*
 2 *Secret Muses*, p. 256

3 David Vaughan, *Frederick Ashton and his Ballets*, second edition, Dance Books, 1999, p. 179

4 Bradley diaries, 25 January 1940.

5 Fonteyn, p. 85

6 *Come Dance With Me*, p. 128

7 Johanna Beek, 'A Dramatic Episode', *Covent Garden Book*, no.1, p. 15

8 Meredith Daneman, *Margot Fonteyn*, Viking, 2004, p. 150

9 *The Sadler's Wells Ballet*, p. 171

10 Tyrone Guthrie, *A Life in the Theatre*, Hamish Hamilton, 1961, p. 199

11 Tyrone Guthrie, *A Life in the Theatre*, Hamish Hamilton, 1961, pp. 194–95

12 Beryl de Zoete, 'English Ballet in Wartime', in *The Thunder and the Freshness*, London, Neville Spearman Ltd, 1963, p. 61

13 Vaughan, p. 194

14 *Step by Step*, p. 52. De Valois mistakenly dates the return of the orchestra to 1942.

15 De Zoete, 'Frederick Ashton: Background of a Choreographer', 1942 essay reprinted in *The Thunder and the Freshness*, p. 42

16 Fonteyn, *Autobiography*, p. 87

17 ROH Collections

18 Agatha Christie, *They Came To Baghdad*, London, Collins 1951, pp. 120–21

19 Television documentary *Tales of Helpmann*, dir. Don Featherstone

20 *Balletomania, An Updated Version of the Ballet Classic*, p. 184

21 *Come Dance With Me*, p. 108

22 Daneman, p. 157

23 Anne Heaton, in Lynne Wake MacMillan interviews, ROH Collections

24 *The Sadler's Wells Ballet*, p. 187

25 *The Sadler's Wells Ballet*, p. 187

26 Royal Ballet press release announcing May's death, 8 June 2005

27 Sorley Walker, p. 241

28 *Come Dance With Me*, p. 166

29 *Secret Muses*, p. 308

30 Sarah Woodcock, *The Sadler's Wells Royal Ballet, now the Birmingham Royal Ballet*, Sinclair-Stevenson, 1991, p. 5

31 'The Vic-Wells Ballet', p. 98

CHAPTER FOUR COVENT GARDEN, AND THE WORLD

1 Beryl Grey interview

2 'Trooping the Colors at Covent Garden', in *Going to the Dance*, Alfred A. Knopf, 1982, p. 221

3 *Come Dance With Me*, p. 168

4 *The Sadler's Wells Ballet*, p. 203

5 *Time and Tide*, 2 March 1946

6 Alastair Macaulay, *Margot Fonteyn*, Sutton Publishing, 1998, p. 43

7 Pamela May interview

8 Pamela May in conversation with Alastair Macaulay, 1996–99
9 Fonteyn, *Autobiography*, p. 85
10 Shead, p. 148
11 Andrew Motion, *The Lamberts: George, Constant and Kit*, Chatto and Windus, 1986, p. 238
12 Undated letter to Frederick Ashton, ROH Collections
13 *Ballet Annual* 2, 1948, p. 17
14 Sorley Walker, p. 116
15 Edwin Denby, 'New York City's Ballet', in *Dance Writings*, Dance Books, 1986, p. 428
16 *Striking a Balance*, p. 99
17 David Vaughan, p. 229
18 Edwin Denby, 'Ashton's *Cinderella*', in *Dance Writings*, pp. 359–60
19 *Come Dance With Me*, p. 203
20 Daneman, p. 230
21 Motion, p. 247
22 *The Sadler's Wells Ballet*, p. 240
23 Pamela May, dictated to Gail Monahan
24 *The Sadler's Wells Ballet*, p. 241
25 *Dance News*, 15: 5, November 1949
26 Sorley Walker, p. 55
27 Doris Hering in *Margot Fonteyn Tribute*, New York Public Library for the Performing Arts, 16 May 1991
28 Quoted in London *News Chronicle*, 11 October 1949
29 Undated cutting
30 'Trooping the Colors at Covent Garden', p. 227

CHAPTER FIVE INTERNATIONAL COMPANY

1 Fonteyn, p. 48
2 Franklin White and Bryan Ashbridge, *Sadler's Wells Ballet Goes Abroad*, Faber and Faber, undated, p. 3
3 Confusion was so general that even the correction was mistaken: the coming-of-age is often described as the company's *twentieth* birthday. It was the nineteenth.
4 *The Sadler's Wells Ballet*, p. 253
5 White and Ashbridge, p. 23
6 Daneman, p. 261
7 'Dame Ninette de Valois' obituary evening, BBC Radio 3, March 2001
8 Vaughan, p. 246
9 'The Royal Ballet in New York', in *Afterimages*, Adam and Charles Black, 1978, p. 378
10 Vaughan, p. 249
11 Motion, p. 253
12 Letter from Alex Martin, ROH Collections .
13 *The Adventures of a Ballet Critic*, p. 215

14 *The Sadler's Wells Ballet*, p. 265

15 *Come Dance With Me*, p. 118

16 *Step by Step*, p. 57

17 *Secret Muses*, p. 403

18 *Time* magazine. 14 November 1949, p. 31

19 Alastair Macaulay conversations

20 *Ballet Annual* 8, 1954, pp. 26–27

21 Simon Fleet (ed.), *Sophie Fedorovitch: Tributes and Attributes*, privately printed, 1955, p. 22

22 Minutes 22 May 1946, item 3

23 Letter from de Valois to Lord Waverley, 20 February 1953, Pritchard collection

24 Minutes CGC/60/3, item 3 (b)

25 Norman Lebrecht, *Covent Garden: The Untold Story*, Pocket Books, 2000, p. 179

26 Keith Money, *Fonteyn, the Making of a Legend*, Collins, 1973, p. 145

27 *Ballet Annual* 8, 1954, p. 42

28 Vaughan, p. 271

29 23 September 1953, quoted Clement Crisp, ed., *Ballerina: Portraits and Impressions of Nadia Nerina*, Weidenfeld & Nicolson, undated, unpaginated

30 *The Fonteyn Phenomenon*, forthcoming

31 Fonteyn, p. 153

32 Crisp, ed., *Ballerina*, unpaginated.

33 Alexander Bland, *The Royal Ballet: The First Fifty Years*, p. 219, Doubleday & Company, Inc., 1981

34 Sarah C. Woodcock, p. 107

35 David Gillard, *Beryl Grey*, W. H. Allen, 1977, p. 93

36 Edward Thorpe, *Kenneth MacMillan: The Man and the Ballets*, Hamish Hamilton, 1985, p. 31

37 Sarah Woodcock, 'MacMillan and design', *Revealing MacMillan: A conference marking the 10th anniversary of the death of Sir Kenneth MacMillan*, Royal Academy of Dance, 2004, p. 103

38 Vaughan, p. 283

39 *Ballet Annual* 11, 1957, p. 31

40 *Secret Muses*, p. 446

41 *Secret Muses*, p. 422

42 *Ballet Annual* 11, 1957, p. 40

43 Alexander Bland, p. 116

44 Fonteyn, p. 166

45 Alexander Bland, p. 118

46 'The Royal Charter: A Memorandum', *Step by Step*, p. 78

47 Cranko quoted in John Percival, *Theatre in My Blood: A Biography of John Cranko*, The Herbert Press, 1983, p. 114

48 *Observer*, 6 January 1957, in *Observer of the Dance 1958–1982*, Dance

Books, 1985, p. 14
49 Daneman, p. 334
50 Lynne Wyke interviews, ROH Collections
51 *The Times*, September–October 1960, reprinted *Dance Writings*, p. 402
52 ROH Collections
53 Lynn Seymour in Lynne Wake interviews, ROH Collections
54 Barbara Newman, *Antoinette Sibley: Reflections of a Ballerina*, Century Hutchinson, 1986, p. 86
55 Keith Money, *Margot Assoluta*, Fair Prospect Imprint, New Zealand, 2000, p. 145

CHAPTER SIX BEAUTIFUL PEOPLE
1 Clive Barnes, 'Frederick Ashton and his Ballets', *Dance Perspectives* 9, Winter 1961, p. 20
2 *The Times*, September–October 1960, reprinted *Dance Writings*, p. 403
3 Woodcock, 'Macmillan and design', *Revealing MacMillan*, p. 105
4 'The Royal Ballet in the USA', *Ballet Annual* 16, 1962, p. 50
5 Anya Linden, MacMillan interviews, Lynne Wake, ROH Collections
6 Lynn Seymour, MacMillan interviews, Lynne Wake, ROH Collections
7 Woodcock, p. 136
8 Ninette de Valois, *Step by Step*, W. H. Allen, 1977, p. 61
9 *Secret Muses*, p. 456
10 Crisp, ed., *Ballerina*, unpaginated
11 Margot Fonteyn, *Autobiography*, W. H. Allen, 1975, p. 209
12 Crisp, ed. *Ballerina*
13 *Step by Step*, p. 104
14 Quoted in Barbara Newman, *Antoinette Sibley: Reflections of a Ballerina*, Century Hutchinson, 1986, p. 156
15 Julie Kavanagh, *Secret Muses: The Life of Frederick Ashton*, Faber and Faber, 1996, p. 479
16 Vaughan, p. 313
17 Monica Mason, interview on *Night Waves*, BBC Radio, 4 December 2003
18 Minutes CGC (1959) 9, 27 October 1959, item 5 (d)
19 Vaughan, p. 335.
20 Board minutes CGC (63) 1, item 5(d)
21 Lynn Seymour, *Lynn: An Autobiography*, Granada Publishing Ltd., 1984, p. 145
22 Bland, p. 140
23 Monica Mason, quoted in Sarah Woodcock, 'More than Just Fonteyn's Partner', *Dancing Times*, November 2004
24 Antony Dowson, quoted in 'More than Just Fonteyn's Partner'
25 Quoted in Nicholas Dromgoole, *Sibley and Dowell*, Collins 1976, p. 106
26 Ninette de Valois, quoted in 'More than Just Fonteyn's Partner'
27 Edwin Denby, 'The Toumanova Problem', in *Dance Writings*, Dance Books, 1986, p. 308

28 'You are my son.' Vaughan, p. 344.
29 BBC Ashton programme.
30 TV documentary *Out of Line*, produced by Derek Bailey, BBC, 1990
31 Ballet Sub-Committee Minutes, meeting 7, 22 September 1964, item 2
32 Lynne Wake, MacMillan interviews, ROH Collections
33 *The Sunday Times*, 6 March 1966, reprinted in *Buckle at the Ballet*, Selected Criticism by Richard Buckle, Dance Books, 1980, p. 153.
34 Newman, *Antoinette Sibley*, p. 132
35 Vaughan, p. 350
36 'At the Supermarket', *New Yorker*, July 17 1989, p. 86
37 Interview in *Out of Line*
38 Nancy Goldner, in *The Stravinsky Festival of the New York City Ballet*, Eakins, New York, 1973, pp. 27–28
39 *Sunday Times*, 20 November 1966, reprinted in *Buckle at the Ballet*, p. 205
40 'How to Be Very, Very Popular', *New Yorker*, 11 November 1974, reprinted in *Afterimages*, A & C Black, 1978, p. 86
41 *Secret Muses*, p. 499
42 *Ballet Review*, vol. 2, no. 6, pp. 32–45
43 Newman, *Antoinette Sibley*, p. 149
44 *Ballet Review*, vol. 2, no. 6, pp. 32–45
45 Statement from the Royal Opera House, *The Dancing Times*, February 1970, p. 236
46 Vaughan, p. 366
47 Vaughan, p. 371

CHAPTER SEVEN A NEW ERA

1 Peter Wright, 'MacMillan and the Royal Ballet', in *Revealing MacMillan*, Royal Academy of Dance conference papers, p. 12
2 Vaughan, p. 370
3 Minutes, Ballet Sub-Committee 70/1, 13 April 1970, item 2 (b)
4 Deanne Bergsma, in Newman, *Striking a Balance*, pp. 289–90
5 'Royal Jitters', *New Yorker*, 27 May 1974, reprinted in *Afterimages*, pp. 65–66
6 *Sunday Times*, 26 March 1972, reprinted in *Buckle at the Ballet*, p. 267
7 *The Fonteyn Phenomenon*, forthcoming.
8 *Sibley and Dowell*, p. 215
9 Alastair Macaulay, 'Kenneth MacMillan', *Times Literary Supplement*, June 2003
10 Lebrecht, p. 307
11 Natalia Makarova, *A Dance Autobiography*, A & C Black, 1980, p. 149
12 *Striking a Balance*, pp. 373–74
13 *Dancing Times*, April 1974, reprinted in *The Nature of Ballet*, Pitman Publishing, 1976, p. 116

14 The Royal Line', *The New Yorker*, 17 May 1976, in *Afterimages*, p. 219
15 Letter from Robert Armstrong to Claus Moser, Chairman of the Board, 30 March 1976, with Board Minutes, ROH Collection
16 Interview, Deborah MacMillan
17 Bland, p. 195
18 Diane Solway, *Nureyev: His Life*, Weidenfeld & Nicholson, 1998, p. 426
19 Writing as James Kennedy in *Guardian*, quoted in *Dancing Times*, June 1981
20 Croce, in the New Yorker, 10 July 1978, reprinted in *Going to the Dance*, pp. 105–6.
21 *Financial Times*, 7 April 1978
22 Mary Clarke, *Dancing Times*, May 1979

CHAPTER EIGHT CHANGE OF DIRECTION

1 *Guardian*, 7 December 1979
2 *Financial Times*, 7 August 1980
3 *What's On*, 18 April 1981
4 'The Royal at Fifty', *New Yorker*, 10 August 1981, pp. 399–400
5 Mary Clarke, 'Hope and Pray', *Dancing Times*, September 1981, p. 822
6 Panel discussion in Stephanie Jordan and Andrée Grau, ed., *Following Sir Fred's Steps: Ashton's Legacy*, Dance Books, 1996, pp. 191–92
7 Alastair Macaulay, *Dancing Times*, February 1983
8 Judith Mackrell, *Guardian*, 8 May 1999
9 *Guardian*, 18 November 1983
10 *Guardian*, 31 December 1983
11 *New Statesman*, 2 March 1984
12 Transcript of Ballet press conference, 21 June 1984, ROH Collections
13 *New Statesman*, 9 August 1984
14 Transcript of Ballet press conference, 26 November 1984, ROH Collections
15 *Dancing Times*, May 1985, p. 677
16 Transcript, press conference, 24 June 1985
17 *Financial Times*, 29 July 1985
18 Lebrecht, p. 348
19 Tamara Finch, 'Royal Ballet in Russia', *Dancing Times*, August 1987, p. 959
20 Tony Devereux, 'What Does Russia Think of the Royal Ballet?', *Dancing Times*, p. 442
21 'At the Ball: The New Production of Ashton's *Cinderella*', *Dancing Times*, February 1988, p. 432
22 Jeremy Isaacs, *Never Mind the Moon*, Bantam Press, 1999, p. 85
23 TV documentary *Out of Line*, produced by Derek Bailey, BBC, 1990
24 ROH Collections
25 Solway, p. 496

CHAPTER NINE RECOVERY AND CLOSURE

1 *Omnibus*, produced by Julia Matheson and Jill Evans, BBC, 1991
2 Constance Tomkinson, *Dancing Attendance*, Michael Joseph, 1965, p. 79
3 *Daily Telegraph*, 2 May 1995
4 Quoted Jack Anderson, 'New York Newsletter', *Dancing Times*, September 1991, pp. 1113–14
5 'Celebrating Ashton,' *DanceView*, Spring 1995
6 'Royal Ballet Revivals', *Dancing Times*, December 1992
7 Isaacs, p. 136
8 Sarah Crompton, 'The Woman who Rescued the Royal', *Daily Telegraph*, 10 September 2005
9 Lebrecht, p. 394
10 *Dancing Times*, November 1992, p. 148
11 *Dancing Times*, December 1993, p. 263
12 Darcey Bussell with Judith Mackrell, *Life in Dance*, Arrow Books, 1998, p. 202
13 *Dance Magazine*, November 1994
14 *Guardian*, 21 November 1994
15 *Guardian*, 30 March 1995
16 Mary Allen, *A House Divided: The Diary of a Chief Executive of the Royal Opera House*, Simon & Schuster, 1998, p. 14
17 *Dancing Times*, September 1998, p. 1104
18. Lebrecht, p. 459
19 *Dancing Times*, February 1999, p. 397

CHAPTER TEN REGENERATION

1 Jann Parry, *Observer*, 11 March 2001
2 *Daily Telegraph*, 25 October 2001
3 Ismene Brown, *Daily Telegraph*, 22 March 2002
4 *Independent*, 9 August 2002
5 Ballet Association interview, http://www.ballet.co.uk/magazines/yr_04/jan04/interview_monica_mason .htm
6 Noel Goodwin, 'Forty Years On', *Dancing Times*, July 2004, p. 23

Index

Figures in italics indicate captions.